F W LANDEEN
12 - 1963

D1017561

The
JOEY ADAMS
Joke Dictionary

BOOKS BY JOEY ADAMS

THE
JOEY
ADAMS
JOKE
DICTIONARY

by JOEY ADAMS

THE CITADEL PRESS / NEW YORK

SECOND PRINTING, FEBRUARY, 1962

Copyright © 1961 by Joey Adams. All rights reserved. Published by the Citadel Press, 222 Park Avenue South, New York 3, N. Y. Manufactured in the United States of America.

Library of Congress Catalog Card No.: 61–18494

CONTENTS

FOREWORD

Anybody can be funny if he has the tools. Any comic worth his weight in laughs must be prepared for battle. Jokes are a comedian's stock in trade. And that's the reason for this dictionary—to stock you up with enough jokes so you can trade laughs with the best of us.

Anybody who wants to make funny for the people, be he doctor, lawyer, or professional comic, must have a joke file ready for any emergency—like in case he should bump into an audience or a roomful of hecklers or a traveling salesman.

The standard dictionary defines a joke as: Something said or done to excite laughter or amusement . . . a thing or person laughed at rather than taken seriously. But I wouldn't give a Funk or a Wagnall for all the jokes in the world if you don't stick 'em in the right place. To paraphrase old Willy Shakespeare, "The joke's the thing"—but only if it's in the right place at the right time.

This dictionary has gags on any subject from the astronauts to the zoo and jokes from any type of comic from Berle to Berman. If you want to say, "A funny thing happened to me on the way to the office . . . ," look under A for Automobile, T for Traffic, or O for office, and you're bound to find something appropriate. If you're going to Dallas and you want to do a joke about it, look under T for Texas or M for Money. If you're lookin' to rap your Mother-in-Law, look under M for Mother-in-Law. If you're lookin' to praise your Mother-in-Law, look under P for Psychiatrist.

If you're a comedic kleptomaniac and admire the work of a certain comic, we have that too. From the old school we go from

9

Amsterdam (Morey) to Youngman (Henny) and in the New school we have anyone from Berman (Shelley) to Winters (Jonathan). But you'll find that most of the comics didn't go to school.

Every major comedian is known for his own special "shtick" and, bearing this in mind, you'll find this dictionary even more valuable. For instance, if you're looking for Negro jokes, you can look under N for Negro or G for Gregory (Dick). Or if you're looking for jokes about the suburbs, look under S for Suburbs or K for King (Allan).

There are jokes here for every occasion, laugh-lines for every emergency. If you're making a speech at a drug convention, you can find Doctor jokes, Sick jokes, Pill jokes, and Accident jokes. If you want to impress the guys at your office, there are jokes in every category from Booze to Broads to Boozed-up Broads. If you want to be the clown prince of your country club, we list all sports from Golf to Swimming to Fishing to Lying.

Anybody can use this book. All you have to know is the alphabet. If you get in the habit of consulting this dictionary any time you're going to make a speech, or go to a party, or write to a friend, or con your boss, or sell the buyer, or weasel your wife, you'll not only have the funniest bone in town but you'll get to know the alphabet better. Take a tip from me . . . I've been doing this for years and one thing about me—I may not be the greatest comedian but I sure know how to spel goode.

So if you're on the dais at a political rally, look under P for Politics, R for Republicans, D for Democrats—or C for Crooks. You'll find jokes that'll make you the life of the party. There are Boy Scout jokes and Martian jokes. There are Sex jokes and Russian jokes. We got Kid jokes and Animal jokes. We got jokes about every business and every holiday. We got Train jokes, Plane jokes, Boat jokes and Travel jokes. We give you jokes on Wholesale, Retail or a Fire Sale and witticisms by anyone from Hope to Huxley.

Laughter is a vaccine for the ills of the world. A dose of joy is a spiritual cure. So use this dictionary to choose a joke instead of a sword. Say something funny instead of something nasty. Throw a punch line instead of a punch. Laugh and the world laughs with you . . . especially if it's a good joke.

JOEY ADAMS

The
JOEY ADAMS
Joke Dictionary

A

ABBREVIATIONS (see also Grammar, School, Words)

"You should have written S.W.A.K.—Sealed With a Kiss—on the back of the envelope. You did seal it with a kiss, didn't you?"

"No—with a little mucilage."

He went to college and received an M.A. and a B.A. but his P.A. still supports him.

"This is the year 1961 A.D."
"A.D.?"
"Yeah, All Day."

ABSENT-MINDED (see also College, Zoology)

"What's that string tied to your finger for?"
"To remind me to mail a letter."
"Did you mail it?"
"I forgot to write it."

I used to be very absent-minded. So I hit on an idea where I could cure myself. One night, before I went to bed, I took a piece of paper and pencil and I wrote, "Coat in the closet . . . hat on the rack . . . Tie in the bureau . . . pants on the chair and shoes and stockings on the floor." And then I went to sleep.

The next morning when I got up, I checked each item on the paper and sure enough there was everything just where I put it. My shoes and sox on the floor, pants on chair, tie on bureau, hat on rack, coat in the closet. Then I looked in the bed and whatta ya think? I'm not there.

A man in a restaurant absent-mindedly started off with someone else's umbrella, and when the owner, a matronly lady, jumped up to make a scene, apologized profusely and returned it. Later that day he stopped at a repair shop to pick up three umbrellas he had left there. Walking out of the store with his three umbrellas, he ran smack into the lady from the restaurant. She eyed him coldly, and sneered, "I see you've done pretty good for yourself today."

MAN ON THE STREET: Why did you put your hand in my pocket?
PICKPOCKET: Beg your pardon, sir, I am so absent-minded. I used to have a pair of pants just like those you are wearing.

ACCIDENTS (see also Automobiles, Transportation, Death, Traffic)

13

"Ma'am, your husband has just been run over by a steam roller!"

"I'm in the tub. Slip him under the door."

The foreman of the lumber camp put a new workman on the circular saw. As he turned away, he heard the man say, "Ouch."

"What happened?"

"Dunno," replied the man. "I just stuck out my hand like this, and—well, I'll be damned. There goes another one!"

The policeman rang the doorbell, not knowing quite how he was going to break the news. The door opened and she stood there gazing anxiously into the law-enforcement officer's eyes.

"I'm sorry to tell you this Mrs. Murphy," he said, "but your husband's new watch is all broken."

"All broken?" she exclaimed. "How did it happen?"

"A piano fell on him."

"My uncle died in the spring and fall."

"How could he die in the spring and in the fall?"

"Warden pulled the spring, and he died in the fall."

"How come the right side of your car is painted yellow and the left side is painted red?"

"I know it doesn't look good, but in case of an accident, you should hear the witnesses contradict each other."

I guess the reason there are less train accidents than auto accidents is because you never hear about the engineer driving with his arm around the fireman.

ACTORS (see also Agent, Television, Theater, Radio, Hollywood, Movies, Motion Pictures, Films)

You hear about the nearsighted Hollywood actor? He bought the Pacific Ocean thinking it was a swimming pool.

For years the no-talent actor was trying to get into a Broadway play, and got to be a pest. Finally a kind-hearted producer told him, "Look, I'll give you a one-line part in my next play, but promise me you won't hang around. I don't want you to hang around the theater. Don't come to rehearsal, just come here the night of the play."

Thrilled, the actor went home and rehearsed his part over and over again. In his sleep, he was saying, "Hark, I hear the cannons roar." Finally, the night of the show he went to the theater and, with great anticipation, got ready to go on. Finally, the stage manager pushed him on stage. He stood out there and suddenly there was a cannon's shot. The actor turned and said, "What the hell was that?"

There was the actor who was so vain that when he opened his refrigerator and the little light went on—he took a bow.

At a Hollywood dinner a star actor was given a long, drawn-out introduction, telling how great he was. When the actor came out, he said, "After that introduction, I can hardly wait to hear what I have to say."

An unemployed actor applied for a Santa Claus job at a large midtown department store. He told the interviewer that he had experience working two winters in the largest department store in Brooklyn. The interviewer said, "Well, that would be fine for an off-Broadway store, but we want Broadway experience."

ADOLESCENTS (see also children, Kids, Baby, Dating, Offspring, Youth)

MOTHER: Now, Willie, I want you to go in and kiss the new nurse.
WILLIE: Yes, and get my face slapped like Papa did?

TEACHER: Forgotten your pen? What would you call a soldier who went to battle without a gun?
PUPIL: I would call him a general.

"There, there, little boy, don't cry. I know how it is."
"Yeah? How the hell is it?"

PLUMBER: I've come to fix the old tub in the kitchen.
YOUNG SON: Mama, here's the doctor to see the cook.

ANNIE: Come in and see our baby.
TEACHER: Thank you, but I will wait until your mother is better.
ANNIE: You needn't be afraid. It's not catching, teacher.

DOG CATCHER: Do your dogs have licenses?
SMALL BOY: Yes, sir, they're just covered with them.

ANXIOUS MOTHER: But sir, do you think my boy is trying?
MASTER: Yes, madam, your son is the most trying boy in school.

TEACHER: Johnny, would you like to go to Heaven?
JOHNNY: Yes, but mother told me to come home right after school.

"My, Grandpa, what a lot of whiskers! Can you spit through them all?"

"Yes, Sonny, I can."

"Well, you'd better do it now, cause they're on fire from your pipe."

"Why don't ya treat your Pa with more respect?"

"I'm disappointed in him. Ma tells me the stork brung me."

ALICE (age seven): Auntie, were you ever in a predicament?

MAIDEN AUNT: No, dearie, but Heaven knows, I've tried.

"Did God make you, Daddy?"

"Certainly, sonny."

"Did He make me, too?"

"Of course. Why?"

"Well, He's doing better right along, isn't He?"

FOND MOTHER: Quiet, dear, the sandman is coming.

MODERN CHILD: Okay, Mom, a dollar and I won't tell Pop.

ADVERTISEMENTS (see also Newspapers)

"Didn't you advertise for a wife the other day?"

"Yes, and I got hundreds of replies and they all said the same thing."

"What was that?"

"You can have mine."

Advertising certainly brings results. Why, yesterday I advertised for a night watchman and just last night I was robbed.

Samson had the right idea about advertising. He took two columns and brought down the house.

The owner of a fish store advertised, "We sell anything that swims." A man came in the next day and demanded Esther Williams.

An advertisement appeared in the paper: Wanted—Young man with ambition. Must like to travel. Chance for rapid advancement. Write to Cape Canaveral.

ADVICE (see also Fathers, Lawyers, Kids, Youth)

A woman phoned the Legal Aid Society for some advice. "I want to know if I can get a divorce because of my husband's flat feet," she asked.

"Hmm," answered the lawyer cautiously, "I don't think so, unless you can prove his feet are in the wrong flat."

17

The only thing to do with good advice is to pass it on.

It is never of any use to oneself.

—Oscar Wilde

An out-of-towner asked a native New Yorker's advice, "How can I get to Carnegie Hall?" The New Yorker replied, "Practice."

AGE (see also Kids, Women, Ancestry)

A trim-looking octogenarian was asked how he maintained his slim figure. "I get my exercise," he boasted, "acting as a pallbearer for all my friends who exercise."

"How long have you known her?"

"Why, I've known her ever since we were the same age."

An elderly couple appeared before the judge in a divorce court.

The judge said to the woman, "How old are you?"

"Eighty-six," replied the woman.

"And you, sir?"

"Ninety-two years old," replied the husband.

The judge said, "How long have you been married?"

"Sixty years," said the husband.

"Sixty years married and now you want a divorce?" the judge exclaimed.

The wife turned to him and said, "Look judge, enough is enough."

Her family didn't approve of her marrying me. Mostly because of the difference in our ages. She was nineteen and I was poor.

A lonely man was lamenting to his bartender, "It's terrible growing old alone."

"But you have your wife," said the bartender.

"My wife hasn't celebrated a birthday in eight years."

"I hope I look as good as you do when I'm your age."

"You did."

Even though Mr. Goldberg was sixty-five, he still loved to chase after young girls. A neighbor brought this to Mrs. Goldberg's attention and asked her what she was doing about it. "Who cares? Let him chase girls," she said. "Dogs chase cars, but when they catch them, they can't drive."

AGENTS (see also Actors, Television, Theater, Radio, Hollywood, Movies, Motion Pictures, Films)

An agent submitted the name of his singer-client to Dick Rodgers for a role in the film version of *Sound of Music*. Dick Rodgers heard the client's name and told the agent she wouldn't do. "We saw her for *Me and Juliet*," he said. "The girl we're looking for must be five foot one. Your client is at least five foot eight."

The agent sat back, smiled, and said, "But have you seen her lately?"

An agent was discussing an act with a stubborn club owner. "I got an act," said the agent, "who'd be great in your club. He specializes in putting his right arm into a lion's mouth."

"That sounds interesting," said the owner. "What's he call himself?"

"Lefty," said the agent.

Two actors were discussing their agent. One said, "He's so mean, if you kicked him in his heart you'd break your toe."

An act walked into the office of an agent who booked the jobs in the classy country clubs of Scarsdale.

Guy took his suitcase, opened it, and fifty mice in Tuxedos jumped out and set up their instruments on top of the suitcase.

Guy snapped his fingers, and the little mice played music that sounded like the New York Philharmonic. He snapped his fingers again, and the little mice played a great Lawrence Welk arrangement. Snapped again, and the mice played better than Stan Kenton's jazz band. Then the mice all went back in the trunk.

Guy said to agent, "Well?" Agent said, "I'll see." Guy said, "Whatta ya mean; what's the matter with this act?" Agent said, "Well, they play all right but the drummer looks too Jewish."

An agent watched an act where a guy was shot out of a cannon 100 feet in the air, and as he came down, he played a violin solo in midair. When he finished, the agent turned to his friend and said, "Well, he's no Heifetz."

AIR FORCE (see also Army, Astronauts, Airplanes)

My brother was in the Air Force. He brought down five planes. All his own.

An Air Force Major was just promoted to Colonel and got a new office. The first day an airman knocked on the door to speak to him. The Colonel, wanting to impress quickly, picked up his phone and said:

"Yes, General, I thank you, sir, Yes, I'll see you soon." Then hanging up the phone, he said,

"And what can I do for you airman?"

The airman said, "I came to install your phone, sir."

The pilot was limping home after a mission, with his plane pretty banged up. He reported to the air tower, said both his engines were gone, and his one wing was falling off. He ended by saying, "Await further orders." The conning tower voice came back and said, "Repeat after me. . . . 'Our Father who art in Heaven. . . .'"

AIRPLANES (see also Air Force, Astronauts, Jets)

The passengers seated in the plane in flight heard this over the intercom system. "Sit back and relax. This plane is entirely automatic. Automatic pilot, automatic food servers, and automatic landing devices. You are perfectly safe. Enjoy your ride. Nothing can go wrong . . . nothing can go wrong . . . nothing can go wrong . . . nothing can go wrong. . . ."

During my plane trip, we lost one engine and everyone got excited and scared. The man next to me said, "Everybody's panicking. Quick, do something religious." So I took up a collection.

PILOT, TALKING TO PASSENGERS: Sit back and enjoy the trip.

You will know immediately if anything goes wrong. Our co-pilot will become hysterical.

The passenger list on one flight across the Atlantic included people of many different nationalities. During the course of flight, a storm blew up and forced the pilot to lighten the weight of the plane. He asked for volunteers to bail out.

A Frenchman arose and yelled, *"Vive la France,"* and jumped out the door. Then an Englishman got up and yelled, "Long live the Queen," and leaped out. Finally, a Texan arose and shouted, "Remember the Alamo," and pushed a Mexican out the door.

Before her first plane ride a little old lady was told that chewing gum would keep her ears from popping during the flight. After finally landing, she turned to her seat companion and said, "The chewing gum worked fine, but how do I get it out of my ear?"

YOUNG LADY PARACHUTIST to traveling companion making a jump: This is frightfully slow. Isn't there some way of speeding things up?

SWEET YOUNG THING: It must be wonderful to be a parachute jumper. I suppose you've had some terrible experiences.

PARACHUTIST: Yes, Miss, terrible. Why, once I came down where there was a sign KEEP OFF THE GRASS.

A government inspector visiting an air field inquired about a former student of the corps who had been transferred.

"Why did he go in the air service?" he asked.

"He was no earthly good," replied a ground crew member.

ALCOHOL (see also Drink, Drinkers, Drunks, Booze, Saloons, Liquor)

CUSTOMER: I'll take a Doctor Jekyll and Mr. Hyde cocktail.
BARTENDER: A Doctor Jekyll and Mr. Hyde cocktail?
CUSTOMER: Yeah, one drink and you're another man.

(Knock on door) "Are you Mrs. Schmitz?"

"Yes, I am."

"Are you sure you're Mrs. Schmitz?"

"Surely, I'm sure I'm Mrs. Schmitz?"

"Well, come down and pick out Mr. Schmitz. The rest of us want to go home."

He was so drunk that when he came out of the hotel and saw a man with gold braid and medals on his chest, he said, "Will you call me a cab?"

The man was offended and he said, "How dare you insult me? I'm no doorman—I'm an Admiral in the Navy."

"All right," corrected the drunk, "call me a boat, I'm in a hurry."

"How did you get arrested?" asked a man who had come to bail a pal out of jail.

"Well, my friend told me when I got home late to take off my clothes and shoes and sneak up the stairs quietly."

"Well, how could you get arrested doing that?"

"When I got upstairs I found it was the elevated station."

DRUNK: Has Mike been here?
MAN: Oh, yes, he was here about an hour ago.
DRUNK: Was I with him?

He was so drunk, he spent all night throwing pennies in the sewer and looking up at the clock on the City Hall to see how much he weighed.

SHE: Why is it that you're much more affectionate after a few drinks?
HE: All I can get to drink is rubbing alcohol.

"Your uncle is always drunk. I'd think he'd get run over crossing the streets."

"He'll never get run over. He always carries a box marked DYNAMITE and no one ever hits him."

They are hard drinkers. In fact, they had their water cut off on Monday and didn't discover it until the following Saturday.

"Have a Scotch and soda."
"No."
"Why not?"
"I've never had a drop of liquor in my life."
"Try this and see how it tastes."
"Hey, you bum. This is rye."

"I fell downstairs with two pints of rye."
"Did you spill any?"
"No, I kept my mouth closed."

"I wish I had my wife back."
"Where is she?"
"I sold her for a bottle of whiskey."
"So you found out that you really love her?"
"No, I'm thirsty again."

"I found a ten dollar bill today."
"I knew that."
"How?"
"I smelled it on your breath."

ALPHABET (see also Grammar, School)

"What letter in the alphabet is drunk?"
"I'll bite. Which one is it?"
"The wobble-you!"

"Now, Billy, what letter in the alphabet comes before 'J'?"
"I dunno."
"What have I on both sides of my nose?"
"Freckles."

"I'll bet you don't know the alphabet."
"B — L — X — U — Y."
"Where did you ever learn an alphabet like that?"
"When I was having my eyes tested."

AMBITION (see also Success, Famous, Recognition, Opportunity)

Smith, who was out of work, met Jones on the street.
JONES: I heard you refused a job as president of the Apex Company!
SMITH: Yeah, there was no chance for advancement!

"How old are you?" asked the office manager of an applicant for a job.

"Twenty-seven," answered the young man.

"Well, what do you expect to be in three years?"

"Thirty," the young man replied without hesitation.

SON: Dad what was your ambition when you were a kid?

FATHER: To wear long pants. And I've got my wish. If there's anybody in this country that wears his pants longer than I do, I'd like to see him.

Two college presidents were discussing what they'd like to do when they retired.

1ST PRESIDENT: I'd like to be superintendent of an orphan asylum, so I'd never get any letters from parents.

2ND PRESIDENT: Well, I've a much better ambition. I want to be warden of a penitentiary. The alumni never come back to visit.

AMOROUS (see also Love, Lover, Osculating, Kiss, Romance, Necking)

Have you heard of the fellow who was disappointed in love three times? One girl refused to marry him, and the other two accepted.

"Darling, how can I ever leave you?"

"By bus, taxi, street car or subway."

"I'm afraid of love, Señor."

"Then you'd better stay away from me, Señorita, I'd scare you to death."

"There's a light burning in my eyes."

"A light burning?"

"Yes."

"Who pays the bills?"

MAN: I love you.

GIRL: Hold me in your arms. Not so tight. I haven't eaten in three days.

MAN: Then put your arms around me. I ate yesterday.

"Did you have a reputation for being a great lover?"

"Man, every time I kissed a girl in the cornfield, the corn started popping."

"Show me one lovesick man and I'll show you fifty lovesick women."

"Say, how long is that offer good?"

AMSTERDAM, MOREY

A chestnut is a guy who's crazy about chests.

"Honey, wake up, there are burglars in the kitchen! I think

they're eating the biscuits I baked this morning!"

"What do we care, as long as they don't die in the house!"

She said, "Kiss me, Kiss me."
He said, "What, are you crazy? I'm a married man. I shouldn't even be doing this . . ."

I was a Boy Scout till I was sixteen . . . Then I became a Girl Scout.

Nothing is all wrong. Even a clock that stops is right twice a day.

People who live in glass houses might as well answer the doorbell.

Pet lovers, save money—feed peanuts to your cats. Instead of milk, they'll drink water.

You wanna lose ten pounds of ugly fat? Cut off your head.

Guy went in a drugstore and said, "Gimme some roach powder."
Clerk said, "Should I wrap it up?"
Guy said, "No, I'll send the roaches down here to eat it."

ANALYSIS (see also Psychiatrist, Insane Asylum)

I realized after four years and $10,000 worth of analysis that if I'd had the $10,000 in the first place, I wouldn't have needed the analysis.

ANCESTRY (see also Age)

OLD FRIEND: I understand you have been having your family tree looked up.
MR. NEWLYRICH: Yes, and it cost me five thousand dollars.
OLD FRIEND: Quite expensive, wasn't it?
MR. NEWLYRICH: Yes, but it cost only two thousand to have it looked up. The other three thousand was what I paid to have it hushed up.

We all spring from animals, but some of us didn't spring far.

A kind old lady stopped to speak to a park caretaker who was jabbing scraps of paper with a stick.
OLD LADY: Don't you find that work very tiring?
CARETAKER: Not so very, Mum, You see, I was born to it— my father used to harpoon whales.

MARY: My whole family follows the sea. My brother is an officer on a ship.

LOUISE: Really? What is his capacity?

MARY: About four or five quarts.

HOSTESS: How far back do you trace your ancestors?

BORED GUEST: Well, I had an old uncle who was traced way out to San Francisco before they got him.

ANIMALS (see also Birds, Chickens, Cows, Dogs, Elephants, Horses, Insects, Zebra, Zoo, Zoology)

"That's a beautiful stuffed lion you've got there. Where did you get him?"

"In Africa, when I was on a hunting expedition with my uncle."

"What's he stuffed with?"

"My uncle."

"How do porcupines make love?"

"Very carefully."

The mother scolded her son for pulling the cat's tail. The young boy replied, "I'm not pulling the cat's tail. I'm standing on it, and he's doing the pulling."

I wouldn't say it rained hard, but some nut at the zoo was loading the animals onto an ark.

How to tell the difference between a male and female worm: The female doesn't signal when she turns.

A skunk family was cornered by a pack of wolves. The mama skunk said to her babies, "Let us spray."

A woman called the vet to administer to her sick cat. The animal doctor examined the cat and told the woman the cat was expecting.

"That's impossible," said the woman. "She hasn't been near a male cat."

Just then a big tom cat walked into the room. "How about him?" asked the doctor.

"Don't be silly," said the woman. "That's her brother."

ANTIQUES, (see also House, Suburbs)

When the wife came home with her arms loaded with antiques, the husband commented, "I'm amazed to see all the things you would rather have than money."

APARTMENTS (see also Rooms, Hotels, House, Neighbors)

She asked me for the rent three times last week. If she asks me again, I'm going to move.

I have a swell room with northern exposure. No roof.

She's so flatheaded when she wants to ask me for rent she just sticks her head under the door.

"Of course, Van Buren is a nice place and my aunt's boarding house is okay for those who like to rough it. She has a roller towel there, and for ten years she's used the same towel."

"Why, that towel's had a longer run than *Uncle Tom's Cabin.*"

My landlord bought his niece a doll house and it has two mortgages on it.

"Why don't you take that complaint to the landlord?"

"That landlord of ours? Why, if we told him the roof leaked, he'd charge us extra for shower baths."

"That landlady's having plenty of trouble between her husband and the furnace."

"What do you mean?"

"Every time she watches one— the other goes out!"

ARABIA (see also Egypt)

In Arabia, I understand that a girl is proposed to by at least a dozen men who get down on their knees all at one time. Then she chooses one and the rest stay on their knees and wind up the occasion with the damndest crap game you ever saw.

ARITHMETIC (see also School)

"Here are four apples. Now tell me: How would you divide the four apples among five children?"

"I'd make applesauce."

"One time I won a prize in arithmetic. The teacher asked us what was 2×20 and I said 34."

"You know that was wrong— 2×20 is 40."

"I was closer to it than anyone in the class."

"Take thirteen from twenty. What's the difference?"

"That's what I say—what's the difference?"

"Johnny, if your father earned forty dollars a week and gave your mother half, what would she have?"

"Heart failure."

"Put two and two together and the result is always what?"

"Bridge."

"Mum, do you know how to get the cubic contents of a barrel?"

"No, ask your father."

"If you had five apples and now you only have two apples, what would I have taken?"

"An awful chance of getting your eye blacked."

"Find the greatest common denominator."

"Great heavens—is that thing lost again?"

ARMY (see also Air Force, Harvey Stone, War)

The troop train was passing through the private's home town. He hadn't seen his wife in six months and the train was making a fifteen-minute stop. He figured he'd run home and say hello. He did, and returned to the train just in time.

A buddy saw that he was dripping wet and asked, "What happened?"

"My wife was in the tub," he replied.

When I was in the army my outfit was so chicken the chaplain went AWOL.

The army now has a reserve plan which is referred to as the Army Installment Plan. Six months down and you pay for the rest of your life.

A private was rushing into the Army PX when he bumped into the Colonel and almost knocked him down.

"Ooops," said the private and went on in.

The Colonel stopped him and said, "Hold it soldier, don't you see these two eagles on my shoulder?"

"No," said the private, "and you wouldn't either if you laid off that PX beer."

SHE: What's your rank?
HE: Pfc.
SHE: What's that?
HE: Praying for civilian.

SOLDIER: Do you know that ugly sap of an officer standing over there? He's the meanest egg I have ever seen.
GIRL: Do you know who I am? I am that officer's daughter.
SOLDIER: Do you know who I am?
GIRL: No.
SOLDIER: Thank God.

Two soldiers went out one night and got well tanked-up on the far-famed Blacksburg corn. About two hours later, the following conversation ensued:

"Has the moon come up yet?"

"Naw, but it feels like it's on its way."

COMMANDER: Now suppose you are on your post one dark night. Suddenly a person appears from behind and wraps two strong arms around you so that you can't use your rifle. What will you call then?

SOLDIER: Let's go, Honey.

1ST SOLDIER: I've been a soldier in every part of the world and have never received a scratch.

2ND SOLDIER: What is this power you have over women?

Mose and Sam digging a trench in France. A shell flies over and bursts. Then others.

Between the fifth and sixth Mose asks: "Don't you think it's about time we done got religion?"

"You suttinly is a shiftless boy, Mose. I done got religion when dat fust shell bust."

CADET: Look me over, little girl. I'm a big West Pointer.

GIRL: I don't care if you're an Irish Setter.

"Fix bayonets," commanded the lieutenant.

The Company fixed bayonets, with the exception of Private McBride, who regarded his bayonet and then the lieutenant with surprise.

"Why sir," said McBride, "My bayonet isn't broken."

ART (see also Museum)

An art collector spotted an ad in the paper for a Van Gogh for $250. Although he was positive it was a misprint, he rushed over to the address listed in the ad. "It's no mistake," said the lady who had placed the ad. "It's a genuine Van Gogh." The collector quickly made out a check and bought the painting. "I don't get it, lady," he questioned after the sale. "You could get at least a hundred times as much for this picture."

"Well," explained the woman, "my husband died two weeks ago and stipulated in his will that the picture was to be sold and the money given to his secretary. And I," she added triumphantly, "am the executrix of his will!"

"She's as pretty as a picture."

"She is?"

"Yeah, she's always got the same expression."

ART CRITIC: Are you doing anything in the nude now?

ARTIST: Only bathing, sir.

As the artist heard his wife coming up the stairs he quickly said to his model, "Quick, take your clothes off."

ART: A collaboration between God and the artists, and the less the artist does, the better.

A woman in Greenwich Village looked at a sidewalk painter's wild modern painting and said, "It's frightful." The artist said, "I only paint what I see." The woman replied, "You shouldn't paint when you're in that condition."

There's an artist who paints a picture in five days and thinks nothing of it, and neither does anyone else.

Most famous artists die in poverty and the rest live in it.

ARTIST: Shall I paint you in a fur coat?
MODEL: No, that's okay, just wear your smock.

MAN: Do you think you can paint a good picture of my wife?
ARTIST: Sure, you'll jump every time you look at it.

"Honey, I just bought a Rembrandt!!"
"Oh, you know I don't like sports cars."

CRITIC: How do you get such a modernistic, wild effect?
ARTIST: I use a model with hiccups.

ASNAS, MAX (see also Restaurant)

The Lox and Bagel Confucius said of wealth—"I was born poor, and I will die poor. But in between, I'd like to be rich."

Comedian Alan Gale was once about to leave Max's Stage Delicatessen to visit his niece. Max said, "Listen, let me get you some cookies to take her." Gale said, "Forget it Max, she's only three months old." Max said, "So are the cookies!"

Max said of diets—"The best exercise to lose weight is to shake your head back and forth 'NO.' "

Max Asnas now has a record out with monologues. The record doesn't come with a record jacket—it comes in a brown paper bag.

Max once said of an oft-fighting show business couple— "They're proving that two can live as bitter as one."

Max swears that when the toaster at the Stage Delicatessen broke they were making toasted bagels by painting them with Man-Tan.

Someone once accused Max of hiring midget waiters so his sandwiches would look bigger.

ASTRONAUTS (see also Air Force, Airplanes, Space)

Our astronauts have the latest equipment. Inside the space capsule, they have oxygen masks, pressurized space suit, automatic control, safety ejector, and, in front of the seat, a little paper bag.

One astronaut's space suit costs 30,000 dollars. And it only comes with one pair of pants.

Big deal! Our astronaut went into space and back in fifteen minutes. I'd like to see him go crosstown in that time.

Many of our astronauts are so handsome, they've been offered Hollywood movie contracts— with Twenty-fifth Century Fox.

When our first astronaut returned safely from his trip, the other astronauts asked him if he could give them any advice. He said, "The whole secret is— don't look down."

The American space plan is to send three astronauts to the moon in the first rocket. Then in the second rocket, they'll send up Bob Hope to entertain them.

The American space plan is a little slowed down. We plan to send up three astronauts in one rocket, and there's still a little disagreement on who should sit by the window.

We'll never have women astronauts. They would never all agree to wear the same style suit.

ATHLETES (see also Sports, Baseball, Football, Basketball, Swimming)

"Did you have many athletes in your college?"
"Oh no—we wouldn't have any athletes around our college."
"Why not?"
"Well, haven't you heard about their feet?"

"Did you ever notice during the Gay Nineties there were very few girl athletes in those days? I wonder why?"
"Because they were all bustle-bound."

"What race did you run in?"
"The human race. Ha-ha—I got you then."
"What are you laughing at? You weren't in it."

ATTORNEY (see also Lawyers, Judges)

"Law offices of Cohen, Coldfarb, Cohen and O'Kavity."

"How did O'Kavity get in there?"
"He put up the money."

"I chased an ambulance three miles."
"Did you catch it?"
"Yes, and there was already a lawyer in it."

LAWYER: You have only six dollars? Then your relatives must come across.
DEFENDANT: Not a chance. They want to see me hung, so that they can divide the six dollars.

They're telling of a shyster lawyer around town who has chased so many ambulances that it has affected his speech. If you listen closely, you'll notice that he speaks with a slight accident. . . .

"Here, you in the overalls, how much are you paid to stand up there and tell lies?" asked the attorney.
"Less than you are, or you'd be in overalls, too."

"Where were you on the afternoon of the 16th?"
"With a couple of my friends."
"Thieves, probably."
"Yessir — lawyers, both of them."

(He'll hear from my attorney —as soon as my attorney gets out of law school.)

Strangest question I was ever asked: "Am I legally married if the shotgun wasn't loaded?"

"I wish you had an alibi."
"So do I. Then I wouldn't need you."

"Are you severely injured?"
"Can't tell until I see my lawyer."

She knows a lawyer in Hollywood who has been without a client for so long he divorced his wife just so he would have a case.

AUSTRALIA

Australians have a tendency to turn the *a*'s into i's. An American was in an Australian hospital as a result of an automobile accident. When he regained consciousness, he asked the nurse: "Was I brought here to die?" and the nurse said, "No, you were brought here yester-die."

AUTOMOBILES (see also Cars, Transportation, Traffic, Driving, Sports Cars)

The best way to stop that noise in your car is to let her drive.

Burns and Allen were driving one night when they ran out of gas. Poor George had to hike ten miles with a heavy can to the nearest garage. "Don't forget to look for a station that gives green stamps," said Gracie.

A woman driver wouldn't have as much trouble squeezing into a parking space if she would imagine it was a girdle or a pair of shoes.

The traffic was so terrible the cars were bumper to bumper. Some were even closer than that. What traffic! One guy bought a car from a used car lot, and after two hours, he had to sell it back to the dealer—he couldn't get it out on the highway.

A friend of mine who was out driving that day was hit by another automobile. He wound up with eight holes in his hood and it wasn't a Buick. The top was down, and it wasn't a convertible! My friend looked like he had just finished ten rounds with Ray Robinson. From out of nowhere, a lawyer came. "Look here, man, I can get you some damages!"

The fellow said, "Nothing doing. I've got plenty of damages already. What I need are some repairs!"

He had to push his automobile two miles to a garage. And the way those garages take advantage of you! They made him push it back again two miles so they could send out a tow car for it!

One last word of advice: If you're out driving, just make sure you have a car.

❖❖

B

BABIES (see also Adolescents, Children, Kids, Offspring)

The tourist said, "Any big men been born around here?" The native replied, "No, best we can do is babies. Different in the city, I suppose."

The proud father stood over his baby and said, "I'm going to give you things I never had . . . girls."

The first lesson that a baby learns at his mother's knees is to be very careful of her stockings.

I know a baby that sucks thumbs—other people's thumbs.

Babies haven't any hair;
Old men's heads are just as bare;
Between the cradle and the grave
Lies a haircut and a shave.
—SAMUEL HOFFENSTEIN

BACHELORS (see also Dating, Flirtation)

Steve Masters, of the Masters Discount House, parsed the word "bachelor" for me. A bachelor is a guy who wants to have a girl in his arms without having her on his hands.

A bachelor is a man who never makes the same mistake once.

The employer explained why he'd hire a married man instead of a bachelor: "The married men don't get so upset if I yell at them."

The bachelor: A fellow who comes to work every morning from a different direction.

"Gee, Harry's been lucky in love."
"You mean he always gets his woman?'"
"No, he's still a bachelor."

A bachelor is a guy who thinks before he acts and then doesn't act.

Bachelors like girls who avoid being called flirts by giving in easily.

A bitter bachelor once said: "I wish Adam had died with all his ribs in his body."

Bachelor's theme song: I plucked a lemon in the garden of love.

BALDNESS (see also Hair, Barbers)

A baldheaded man is one who came out on top and still lost.

What a woman said about a baldheaded man: "I love to run my fingers through his hair because I can make better time on the open road."

FATHER: No, you can't wear your hair like Elvis Presley.
SON: But Dad, you wear yours like Yul Brynner.

The suspicious wife went over her husband's suit for traces of red or blonde hair, but found none. Finally, she said to her husband, "Aha, so you're going out with baldheaded women!"

"My hair's falling out. What can I get to keep it in?"
"A paper bag."

He isn't bald; he just has a tall face.

BANDS (see also Orchestra, Music, Musicians, Instruments)

"I have twenty men in my band.
"You ought to go to Canada, the police wouldn't follow you there."
"I didn't do anything."
"You must have done something, or all those men wouldn't be following you."

"Isn't he rather young to be leading an orchestra?"
"Not the way he leads it."

"What are you going to play next, Maestro?"
"I like it when you call me Maestro—it gives me that international flavor."
"Garlic will do the same."

"I can't find my baton."
"Can't you lead without it?"
"It isn't that—I've got something in my tooth."

"That's a hot band you have there."
"They're going to be much cooler this summer. I'm adding three wind instruments."

"I had an orchestra."
"What was it composed of?"

"A violin, an accordion—"
"And a tin cup?"

"He knows everything about music."
"Oh, not everything."
"What is there about music that he doesn't know?"
"That I just dropped his violin down the elevator shaft."

"You are three bars ahead of the rest of us."
"Yes. But didn't I tell you that I could play to beat the band?"

"Say, let me have $5.00."
"What for?"
"For $5 I could get a band that is better than this."
"What would you do with the change?"

"What do you think my orchestra is?"
"Oh, so you're wondering, too."

"How much does he get for playing the fiddle?"
"Seven hundred and fifty dollars a week."
"What? For running a horse's tail over a cat's gut and making it screech?"

"I want it played the way I told you. Forget the way it was written. All I can say is that you're a lousy musician."

"Listen, if I was a musician I'd be sitting in the band playing the clarinet instead of leading the band."

"Anyone want any brains? You want some brains?"
"No, I don't need any brains."
"Oh, I forgot; you're an orchestra leader."

"What's wrong with that arrangement?"
"You wrote in a part for a shoe horn."
"That was to give the music a little soul."
"That's good. Soul music from a heel."

"His cousin has one of the biggest orchestra leaders in New York after him."
"Who's he playing with now?"
"The leader's wife."

They were a three-piece band. They only knew three pieces.

The piano player wasn't part of the regular band, but he had the car.

He was the leader of the band. He always finished four bars ahead of everyone else.

The band leader wrote a symphony for twenty-six bass drums

and a saxophone. He called it *Holiday for Strings*.

Introduction: You've heard of the sweetest band this side of heaven. Well this is what was on the other side.

The drummer has three sets of drums—one to play on, one to practice on, and one to eat off.

This band has played many a champagne hour—without instruments.

The new pupil listened to the band for a few minutes. Then the teacher asked, "Where is the trumpet section?" The pupil pointed to the oboe section. In disgust, she turned to the conductor and said, "This guy doesn't know his brass from his oboe."

BANKS (see also Loans, Money, Cash, Credit, Checks)

A woman went into the bank and noticed there was a new face behind the window. "Has the cashier gone away to take a rest?" she inquired. "No," replied the new man, "he's gone away to avoid it."

"This is to inform you that this is the last time we will spend four cents to let you know you have two cents!"

MAN: Can you direct me to the Fifth National Bank?
KID: Sure, if you give me a dollar I will!
MAN: A dollar! Don't you think that's too much money?
KID: No, sir! Not for a bank director!

A man asked for a $100,000 loan from the bank. The bank president remarked that it was a lot of money and asked the man for a statement. "Yes," said the man, "I'm optimistic."

A bank is a place where you keep the government's money until the tax man asks for it.

A bank robber opened the safe with his toes just so he could drive the fingerprinting experts crazy.

The captured bank robber was told that the bank's hidden camera had taken pictures of him, and it was this that led to his capture. The bank robber replied, "Gee, do you think I could have some wallet-size for my wife?"

BANQUETS (see also Speakers, Speech, Dais)

After Fred Allen had paralyzed a banquet audience, Adlai Stevenson, who was scheduled to follow him, weakly stood up and said, "Gentlemen, I was in the lobby before, talking to Mr. Allen and he confessed to me that he didn't have a speech for tonight's occasion. I graciously gave him my speech. So you have just heard it."

BARBERS (see also Hair, Baldness)

A customer just back from London said to his barber, "Over there, I was able to get a haircut for only 65¢." The barber replied, "Yeah, but look at the fare."

A Times Square barber advertises: SIX BARBERS—CONTINUOUS DISCUSSION.

After a haircut, when the barber says, "Is that the way you want it, sir?" drive him crazy and say, "Not quite, a little longer in back."

CUSTOMER: Are you the barber who cut my hair last time?
BARBER: I don't think so. I've been here only six months.

CUSTOMER: Why did you drop that hot towel on my face?

BARBER: You didn't think I was going to burn my fingers!

BARRY, DAVE

My wife never stops for a red light when she's driving. She says, "You see one or two, you've seen them all."

Did you hear about the whale who fell in love with a submarine? The whale followed the submarine all around the ocean, and every time the submarine shot off a torpedo, the whale gave out cigars.

I was driving along and I saw this sign that said "Motel" and under it it said "TV." I stopped at the place, got a room, and found out there was no TV set. I told the manager, "There's a sign outside that says TV." The manager said, "Yeah! Tourists Velcome."

My wife discovered a new way to hold the bills down. She switched to a heavier paperweight.

I used to do the voice of the lion for MGM Pictures. I got five thousand dollars and some stomach relief.

BARTENDERS (see also Alcohol, Drink, Drinkers, Drunks, Booze, Saloon)

A man walked into a bar, had a beer, and left fifty cents on the counter, which the bartender put in his pocket. The owner saw what happened and said, "What do you think you're doing?" The bartender calmly replied, "How do you like that, a guy comes in, has a beer, doesn't pay the check, and leaves me a fifty-cent tip."

A drunk ran into a bar and asked the bartender how high a penguin was. The bartender told him about waist high. The drunk asked if there were any penguins that were taller, and the bartender told him there weren't. The drunk then said, "Oh, my gosh, then I just ran down two nuns."

The bartender redecorated his bar. He put new drunks around it.

SON: Daddy, what is the person called who brings you in contact with the spirit world?
DAD: A bartender, my boy.

A man came into a bar, drank half his beer, and threw the rest of it over the bartender. He then apologized profusely and explained it was a nervous compulsion. The bartender suggested he see a psychiatrist. Six months later the man returned to the same bar and did the exact same thing. This time the bartender was indignant. "I thought you went to see a psychiatrist," he said. "I did," the man said. "Well," said the bartender, "it certainly didn't do much good." "Oh, yes," the man said, "I'm not embarrassed about it anymore."

BASEBALL (see also Sports)

Watching baseball games on TV is very educational. It used to take me ten minutes to shave. Now I can do it between innings.

It's been very hectic having Marilyn Monroe coming to the games at Yankee Stadium. Every time she sits in the stands, the seventh inning stretch lasts three hours.

A couple of Yogi Berra's waggish teammates on the New York Yankee Ball Club swear that one night the stocky catcher was horrified to see a baby toppling off the roof of a cottage across the way from him. He dashed over and made a miraculous catch—but then force of habit proved too much for him. He straightened up and threw the baby to second base.

The conceited new rookie was pitching his first game. He walked the first five men he faced and the manager took him out of the game. The rookie slammed his glove on the ground as he walked off and yelled, "Damn it, the jerk takes me out when I have a no-hitter going."

Mickey Mantle, the great Yankee star, was walking in civilian clothes outside the Stadium and was obviously favoring his bad leg. A woman passing by asked a friend, "What's wrong with him?" "He got hurt playing baseball." "Won't they ever grow up?" the woman replied.

SHE: Oh, look, we have a man on every base.
HE: That's nothing, so has the other side.

The radio announcer was transmitting a play-by-play account of the World Series game. At an exciting moment he yelled out: "He swang at it!"
Seventeen sets in Boston burned out.

BASKETBALL (see also Sports)

After a recent college scandal, the coach asked his star basketball player why he looked so sad. The player replied, "It's because my father is always writing me for money."

The coach walked into the dressing room between halves to bawl out his highly-touted college team. He looked at them and said, "You guys are playing like a bunch of amateurs."

The basketball star was in danger of flunking out of school. A special test was given him orally by the Dean as a last attempt to pass. His coach accompanied him to the test to help.
The Dean asked, "How much is eight times seven?"
"Fifty," replied the star.
"Wrong," said the Dean. "I can't pass you."
"Aw, Dean," said the Coach, "C'mon, he only missed it by two."

BEACH (see also Swimming)

Someone once described Coney Island as a place where the beer cans come to spawn.

Two bopsters got lost on the Sahara Desert, and, after three hours walking, one turned to the other and said, "Man, what a beach!"

If you ever get hungry on the beach, you can always eat the "sand-wich-is" there.

An old fellow was told by the doctor to bathe his feet in salt water and they would feel better. So next day, the guy went down to the beach and filled his pail with water from the ocean. A lifeguard, wanting to have some fun, said to him, "That pail of water will cost you 25 cents." The guy gladly paid. Couple of days later, he came back when it was low tide. He looked at the lifeguard and said, "My, you're doing a great business today."

Two guys were sitting on the beach and one said to the other, "Do you like bathing beauties?"
The other guy said, "I don't know, I never bathed any."

BEATNIK

Definition of a beatnik: A man on the bottom looking down.

He: What's a beatnik?
She: A tired Santa Claus.

A beatnik home is one in which, no matter what time of day it is, you can always use the shower.

Two beatniks were walking down a street, and a man in front of them fell into a manhole. The man looked up and said, "Hey, fellow, give me a hand."
So, the two beatniks applauded.

BE-BOP (see also Bopsters)

Definition of a hipster: A musician who knows where the melody is buried.

BEGGARS (see also Tramps, Money)

LADY TO BEGGAR: Aren't you ashamed of yourself to stand here begging on the street?
BEGGAR: What do you want, lady, I should open an office?
LADY: You're not ashamed to ask for a penny? You have two good arms!
BEGGAR: For your lousy penny, I should cut off an arm?

BERLE, MILTON

Now take my wife—please.

I just flew in from Florida—and my arms are tired.

I just got back from Lindy's. I always go over there for a cup of coffee and an overcoat.

What is this, an audience or an oil painting?

I'm your MC. MC—that's mental case.

Guy called up his doctor and said, "My kid just swallowed a pen. What should I do?"

Doc said, "Use a pencil."

I know there's an audience out there; I hear you breathing.

My girl was so skinny she swallowed an olive and four men left town.

I had a hotel room that was so small, the mice ran around hunchback.

I'm so nervous, I keep coffee awake.

I know a three-fingered pickpocket. He steals bowling balls.

What is this, an audience or a jury?

I was an old newspaper man, but I found out there's no money in old newspapers.

I was so drunk last night I picked up a snake and hit a stick.

I never file my nails—I just cut them off and throw them away.

I call my kid Webster. Words can't describe him.

BERMAN, SHELLEY

Phone conversation of the world's greatest theatrical agent:
"Hello, Eleanor? . . . . did you

put my call through to Africa yet? . . . Fine, I'll take it here . . . How are you Al, kiddo, kiddo? This is Artie. Yeah, fine. Fine, I'm glad to hear it. Tell me, how is Mrs. Schweitzer? Good. Good.

Listen Dockie—I got some very good news for you, Dockie boy. Your American tour is all set—you're all booked up. You open in Chicago at the Chez Paree . . . yeah, the Chez in Chi. Listen, Al baby, I had to do a little maneuvering. I'm afraid they wouldn't take you as a straight organ player, so what I did, see—I sold you as a combination organist-comedian see, so I tell you what to do—you dress up your act with a little patter—you know a few of those funny little anecdotes you pick up around the leper colonies. . . . Okay, Al . . . fine, baby, give my regards to the Missus, fine, goodbye. . . .

Eleanor you got Picasso . . . where on six, okay, I got it. Hello Pablo baby, how are you fine— yeah it's all set; she wants you to start painting on Thursday. Yeah, this Thursday . . . right . . . and remember, Pab baby, go over it once more . . . yeah she wants the kitchen in green and the bathroom in baby blue—fine, Pab . . . okay, bye."

BETTING (see also Gambling, Las Vegas)

"I'm positively through with gambling forever."

"Forever? I don't believe it."

"Is that so? I'll bet you five dollars I'll quit."

"Let's go and play some poker."

"No, thank you. I don't play the game."

"I was under the impression you played poker."

"I was under that impression myself—once!"

"You don't even know where you are! I'll wager you twenty dollars you're not even here and I'll prove it."

"All right, go ahead."

"You're not in St. Louis?"

"No, I'm not in St. Louis."

"And you're not in Chicago?"

"No, I'm not in Chicago."

"Well, if you're not in St. Louis or Chicago, you must be some place else, and if you're some place else you can't be here." (Other guy snatches money)

"I didn't lose—give me back my money."

"Whadda-yuh mean?"

"You took the money right out of my hand."

"I did not."

"You did."

"Listen, you said I wasn't here—I was someplace else. And if I was someplace else I couldn't be here. And if I couldn't be here, how could I take your twenty dollars?"

BIG GAME (see also Hunting)

"Once I shot a buck."

"You did?"

"Yeah, then I shot two bucks, then I shot three bucks and then I shot five bucks."

"Then what happened?"

"Somebody hollered 'cheese it the cops'—and I dropped the dice and ran."

"Son, do you like steeple chasing?"

"I don't know . . . I never chased any."

"How do you know you hit that duck?"

"I shot him in the foot and in the head at the same time."

"How could you possibly hit him in the foot and head at the same time?"

"He was scratching his head."

"While we were hunting a big animal passed by me."

"Reindeer?"

"No, it just poured, darling."

"I shot this tiger in India. It was a case of me or the tiger."

"Well, the tiger certainly makes the better rug."

"If an elephant charges you, let him have both barrels at once."

"And the gun, too, so far as I'm concerned."

"While we were hunting, I could have shot a bear."

"Why didn't you?"

"I didn't like the look on his face—he wouldn't have made a good rug."

"I shaved every morning."

"You mean to tell me you shaved while you were hunting?"

"Yeah, I had a lot of close shaves."

"I went hunting—and shot a raccoon."

"Was it a big one?"

"Was it a big one? I found two college boys in it."

"Say, boy, did you see a fox run by here?"

"Yes, sir."

"How long ago?"

"It'll be a year next Christmas."

"Why was he arrested?"

"For shooting quail."

"Doesn't he know quail isn't in season?"

"Well, when it is in season, the quail aren't around, and there are lots of them when it isn't the season. If the quail don't obey the rule, he won't either."

BIRDS (see also Animals)

Two penguins from the South Pole were madly in love with each other, and they had planned to get married, but somehow they got separated. Finally, at Christmas time, one penguin received a telegram from the other that read: MERRY XMAS, I AM WITH BYRD.

Here's a shaggy bird story. As you know, lovebirds are so devoted that if one dies, legend says, the other dies of a broken heart shortly afterwards. Confronted with such a tragic situation, an ingenious pet owner stuck a mirror inside the cage of the surviving lovebird. The lonesome bird, seeing his image, emitted a joyous chirp, snuggled contentedly against the mirror, and lived happily for many years. Then, one day a careless clerk upset the cage, dropped it to the marble floor, and caused the lovebird to die—of a broken mirror.

BIRTHDAYS (see also Age, Kids)

My wife wanted some pearls for her birthday so I gave her an oyster and a rabbit's foot.

There's the story about the fellow who each day walked to work and passed a window where he saw a lady hitting a boy over the head with a loaf of bread. The fellow decided it was none of his business and walked on. He saw this same thing happen every morning for five months—each day, the lady hitting the boy with a loaf of bread. Then, one morning he saw the woman toss an entire chocolate cake into the boy's face. Astounded, he peered into the open window and asked why. "Oh," the lady said, "it's his birthday."

BISHOP, JOEY

Dean Martin and Frank Sinatra will now tell you about some of the good work the Mafia does.

Dennis the Menace has a great TV show but a terrible barber.

Art Linkletter has interviewed so many children he can't talk to you unless he bends down.

How do you do, William Bendix! Don't act up or I won't buy your washing machine.

When I performed in Washington for the President, I didn't stay at the White House. My mother wasn't too crazy about the neighborhood.

The traffic was so heavy yesterday I drove fifteen miles in neutral.

American TV shows are very big in Europe. Lloyd Bridges is a national hero in Venice.

My family was so poor we couldn't give my sister a sweet sixteen party till she was twenty-eight.

I don't want to be a star overnight. I got a lot of things to do tomorrow.

BOB AND RAY (Bob Elliott and Ray Goulding)

Kids, send in for your do-it-yourself hydrogen bomb kit. Be the first on your block to rule the world.

They're going fast, folks, so send in soon for your "get rich quick" burglary kit.

Buy Bob and Ray coffee. It's packed in a vacuum as clean as you'll find in your own vacuum cleaner.

We're now offering a special April sale on used Christmas cards.

And now to our on-the-spot reporter, Wally Ballu, and his wife Hulla. . . .

And now it's time for *Our Gal Saturday* who asks the question, "can a girl from a small mining town out west find love and happiness in a small mining town out east?"

And now our story asks the question, "can a nice run-of-the-mill girl find happiness running a mill?"

There's been a crisis here at CBS. They had an emergency case in Studio 25 when young Dr. Malone dropped his pince-nez during a delicate operation. They tried to reach Doctor Stanton but he was on a house call.

BOOKS AND AUTHORS (see also Novels)

All the historical books which contain no lies are extremely tedious. (Anatole France.)

If you want to get rich from writing, write the sort of thing that's read by persons who move their lips when they're reading to themselves. (Don Marquis.)

When I want to read a book, I write one. (Disraeli.)

HE: I'm reading a sad book.
FRIEND: What book?
HE: *Lady Chatterley's Lover*.
FRIEND: That's not a sad book.
HE: It is—at my age.

A goat in Hollywood was wandering around a movie lot when he came across some reels of film. He ate heartily and was walking away when another goat asked him how he like eating the film. "Oh, I liked the book better," he replied.

A publisher received an unsolicited manuscript entitled, How to Make Your Own Mink Coat. Opening line in the book was: "First catch sixty-two minks. . . ."

BOOZE (see also, Alcohol, Bartenders, Drink, Drinkers, Drunk, Saloon, Liquor)

"I went to a dozen different bars this afternoon, but I couldn't get what I wanted."
"That's funny. What did you want?"
"Credit."

"Take a drink of this."
"Yes . . ."
"Pour that back into the lamp."

He was a drinking man. He took his likker where he found it and they usually found him where he took his likker.

He dropped a little of that stuff in the goldfish bowl, the fish drank some of it, hopped out of the bowl and chased the cat down the street.

Week-end liquor—you drink it on Monday and the week ends right there.

The only new fiction he reads is the liquor labels.

Leave the gin on the table. I may think of something I wanna forget.

"King Alcohol reigns over you."
"Well, darling, into each life some reign must fall."

"Have a drink of elephant whiskey?"
"What's that."
"Take one drink and you throw your trunk out the window."

"Here's a message from the people upstairs."
"Put it under the door."
"I can't. I might spill it."

"What're ya drinkin'?"
"Northwest Mounted."
"What do you mean?"
"It always gets its man."

"Have you a bottle opener in the house?"
"No, he's away at college."

"Lips that touch liquor shall never touch mine."
"Your lips?"
"My liquor."

Drank so much beer that when he ate a pretzel you could hear it splash.

People who carry glass bottles shouldn't sit on stone benches.

The girl who drinks like a fish shouldn't be surprised if her head swims.

BOPSTERS (see also Beatniks, Be Bop)

Two bopsters were attending a concert when a fire broke out. All the musicians cleared the stage, and the audience began heading for the exits. "Come on, man, let's beat it," said one. "You go ahead, man," replied the pal. "I want to dig this crazy finale."

Two bopsters visited the Swiss Alps. A skier whizzed down the chute, then up into the sky. "We're in luck, man," grooved one bopster. "Somebody here sells our brand of cigarettes."

BOSS (see also Employment, Executive, Business)

Two men were discussing their employers. "My boss," said one, "is a no-good cheap skate. He should only drop dead." "My boss," smiled the second, "is different. You just can't help liking him, 'cause if you don't he fires you."

The new maid was the slowest thing on two feet. It took her at least three times as long as anyone else to do something. One day, the boss of the house reached her boiling point. "You're worse than a snail," she screamed. "Tell me, Alice, is there anything you can do fast?" Alice thought for a moment and then replied, "Get tired."

BOXING (see also Sports, Fight)

BOXER: Have I done him any damage?
DISGUSTED SECOND: No, but keep swinging. The draft might give him a cold.

"What are you putting in your glove?"
"My good luck piece—my horseshoe."

"Don't be frightened—I'll not hit you with both hands."
"You won't?"
"No, I'll only hit you with one

hand. I'll need the other to hold you up."

BRIDES (see also Bridegrooms, Wedding, Newlyweds)

A young bride complained to a grocer about the flour she bought being tough. "Tough?" the grocer said in surprise. "Yes, tough," she replied. "I made biscuits with it, and my husband couldn't eat them."

BRIDEGROOMS (see also Brides, Weddings, Newlyweds)

The bridegroom tried to fool everybody in the hotel lobby by letting his bride carry the luggage.

USHER: Are you a friend of the groom?
LADY: Indeed no! I'm the bride's mother.

The groom didn't get his pants back in time for the wedding, so he sued the tailor for promise of breeches.

BROKE (see also Money, Cash, Checks, Budget, Banks, Cheap)

"We went to dinner to discuss the budget."

"Well?"
"We figured everything up—and when we deducted the cost of the dinner we found we were eighty cents in debt."

"This is no time to pick on me."
"No? Why not?"
"I just lost my bankroll."
"Well, three dollars is three dollars."

"If you're broke, why don't you hock your overcoat?"
"I did."
"What did you get for it?"
"My spring coat."

He's got nothing—and very little of that.

"What happened to the money? I want the truth."
"You do?"
"Yes."
"Then you don't want my story?"

"Go on, what's the matter with you?" protested Al, "I've got all the money I'll need for the rest of my life—providing I drop dead on the spot."

I'm financially embarrassed. I'm eight dollars short of having twenty cents.

"Whatever became of that friend of yours that used to have money to burn?"

"He's sifting ashes."

I'm so flat they could play me on the victrola.

BUDGET (see also Money, Cash, Checks, Banks, Broke)

Asked the meaning of the word "budget," one little boy replied, "It's a family quarrel."

BUSINESS (see also Wholesale, Retail, Boss, Employment, Wearing Apparel, Shoe Business, Clothing Business)

ONE BUSINESSMAN TO ANOTHER: We're a non-profit organization. We didn't mean to be, but we are.

A minister consoled a member of his congregation, "And remember, there'll be no buying or selling in heaven." The businessman replied, "That is not where business has gone."

A guy walks into a garment store and says, "Hey, Harry, I was sorry to hear about your fire." Harry quickly replies, "Shhh, the fire's not till tomorrow."

BUTCHER

A woman walked into a butcher shop and told the owner, "That chicken I bought from you yesterday had no wishbone." The butcher answered, "Madam, our chickens are so contented that they have nothing to wish for."

BUTCHER SHOP

"How much do you pay?"
"Three dollars a week—but what can you do to make yourself useful around a butcher shop?"
"Anything."
"Well, be specific. Can you dress a chicken?"
"Not on three dollars a week."

CUSTOMER: Look here, butcher, you are giving me a big piece of bone. With meat as high as it is I don't want all that bone.
BUTCHER: I'm not giving it to you, mister, you're paying for it.

"Hello! This is Mrs. Jones. Will you send some nice cutlets right away?"
"I'm sorry but we haven't any cutlets."
"Well, then, a couple of nice, lean pork chops."
"We haven't any pork chops either, Mrs. Jones."
"Oh, how provoking! Then a

small sirloin steak will have to do."

"We haven't any steak."

"For heaven's sake! Aren't you Smith, the butcher?"

"No, I'm Smith, the florist."

"Oh! Well, send me a dozen white lilies. My husband must be starved to death by now."

❖❖

C

CAMPUS (see also College, University, School)

"So you managed to escape from college?"

"Yeah, I'm a fugitive from a brain gang."

"Would you like to buy a magazine?"

"What's the idea?"

"I'm working my brother's way through college."

"He wants to be a college man, so he put hair tonic on his slicker, trying to make a raccoon coat out of it."

"When you were in college what did you go in for?"

"Because it was raining."

"I'll let you know I got a letter at college."

"I know—a letter from the Dean saying you'd better settle down and study or they'd kick you out."

"Well, I see you went to a fraternity."

"Oh, no. I just sat on a stove by mistake."

"I'm taking three courses in college: French, Spanish and Algebra."

"Let me hear you say 'Good Evening' in Algebra."

"What is your son taking in college?"

"Oh, he's taking all I've got."

"I'm going to enter the diplomatic service."

"Domestic or foreign?"

"Neither. I'm going to be president of a university."

"Are you a college man?"

"No—a horse stepped on my hat."

CANADA

Up in Canada they have an organization called the Royal Canadian Mounted Police. They have the reputation of always getting their man. We got the same thing here in this country. We call it Selective Service.

It gets so cold in the northern Canadian woods the women wear mink girdles.

CANNIBAL

Let's tell about this cannibal. He was dressed up in European fashion, sent to college, and grew up to maturity in the ways of civilization. Then came his first trip on a luxury liner. Now, the former cannibal went for his first sitting in the first-class dining salon. In most decorous fashion, the steward asked him: "Would you like to see the menu?" "No," sez he, "I'd like to see the passenger list."

CARS (see also Autos, Transportation, Traffic, Accident, Pedestrians)

In Warsaw, two strangers were standing admiring a brand-new shiny automobile. One said enthusiastically, "A handsome machine, isn't it? Just another triumphant exhibit of Soviet ingenuity and initiative." The other man said, "But that's an American car. Can't you tell one when you see one? Didn't you know that?" The other man replied, "Yes, I knew it, but I didn't know you!"

LITTLE WILLIE: Mama, what becomes of an automobile when it gets too old to run any more?
MOTHER: Why, somebody sells it to your father for a used car— as good as new.

PHI BETA: You know, the manufacturers say it takes three thousand bolts and nuts to hold an automobile together.
PHI GAM: Well, it only takes one nut to scatter it all over the country!

"Well, your car surely does run smoothly," gushed the high school girl on her first date.
"Wait a minute—I haven't started the engine yet," said her escort.

GRACIE: My uncle just had his car overhauled and it cost him $50.
BOB: Fifty dollars for overhauling a car?
GRACIE: Yes, he was driving on the highway and a policeman overhauled him.

CARTER, JACK

Hi Fi is very old. God built the first speaker system from one of Adam's ribs.

God made Man before Woman, because he didn't want any advice on how to make Man.

Adam and Eve used to talk:
ADAM: Ugh.
EVE: Ugh.
ADAM: Ugh.
EVE: Ugh.
ADAM: Ugh.
EVE: Ugh, Ugh.
Even then, Woman had the last word.

And the cavemen came, and they hit girls over the heads with clubs and carried them off. You could always tell the prettiest girl in the tribe—the one with the split lip, broken nose, black eyes. . . .

And the cavemen had no money. They used to use fish as money. And when they made a phone call, they'd drop the fish in the slot. That's why even today you hear operators say (hold nose), "Your number, please."

But Conrad Hilton is redoing the Leaning Tower of Pisa as a hotel. He's calling it the "Tilton Hilton."

CASH (see also Money, Loans, Banks, Checks, Broke, Budget, Cheap)

"I don't like the cashier you hired. He limps and stutters."
"What of it?"
"Why did you hire him?"
"So he'll be easy to identify if he runs away."

If you think money doesn't talk then just try to telephone without a dime.

"I'll give you a hundred dollars to do my worrying for me."
"Great. When do I get paid?"
"That's your first worry."

We all wish that the men who owe us money had memories like the men we owe money.

When a man shows a big wallet, a girl with ideas will always show a little purse in her lips.

"Will you please explain to me the difference between shillings and pence?"
"You can walk down the street without shillings."

"How many cigars do you you smoke a day?"
"About ten."
"What do they cost?"
"Twenty cents apiece."
"My, that's two dollars a day.

How long have you been smoking?"

"Thirty years."

"Two dollars a day for thirty years is a lot of money."

"Yes, it is."

"Do you see that office building on the corner?"

"Yes."

"If you had never smoked in your life you might own that fine building."

"Do you smoke?"

"No, never did."

"Do you own that building?"

"No."

"Well, I do."

The money is in the care of our treasurer and we'll have it as soon as the G Men can lay their hands on him.

"Excuse me, sir; but you gave me a counterfeit bill."

"Keep it for your honesty."

"He found a ten dollar bill."

"I suppose he fainted on the spot."

"Yes, on the ten spot."

"Don't take any wooden money."

"I like wooden money."

"You like wooden money?"

"Yes, I'm starting a shavings account."

"Money talks."

"Yes, but all some of us can hear is the echo."

The partners agreed that whichever died first was to have $5000 put in his coffin by the other. Epstein died and Cohen put in a check.

"He has the first dollar he ever made."

"He must be very thrifty."

"No, he just started working yesterday."

CHEAP (see also Cash, Money, Loans, Banks, Budget, Broke, Checks)

A surly old miser became extremely ill and, in panic, sent for his priest. "If I leave $10,000 to the Church," he asked the man of God, "will my salvation be assured?" "I wouldn't say for certain," replied the clergyman, "but it's well worth trying."

He's so cheap that the only time he'll pick up a check is when it's made out to him.

CHECKS (see also Cash, Money, Loan, Banks, Broke, Cheap, Budget)

Man receives check, puts it in pocket, jumps out of hotel window and bounces for three days.

He wrote so many rubber checks he kept a vulcanizer in his pocket.

The check that used to come back "No Funds," now comes back marked "No Bank."

She has to work so hard for her money—Imagine—having to drive all the way downtown to pick up her alimony check!!

"Will you take my check?"
"Yes, I *would,* but you can't fool the government."

DINER: I'll write you a check for the $100.
MANAGER: No, thanks.
DINER: Why not? I have money to burn.
MANAGER: I hate the smell of burning rubber.

We know that your check is good, but we don't trust the banks.

"I'll send you my check for the first of the month."
"Could you give me a rough idea of what month?"

"Make the check out for $1000."
"Why $1000."
"If it's going to be bad, make it big and bad."

CHICKENS (see also Animals, Farm)

FIRST NEIGHBOR: What were all your chickens doing out in front of your house?
SECOND NEIGHBOR: They heard some men were going to lay a sidewalk and they wanted to see how it was done.

"Doesn't your dinner please you, sir?" inquired the waiter of the guest who sat staring disconsolately at his plate.
"Well," replied the guest, "you're correct about one thing. That is a spring chicken all right. I just bit into one of the springs."

PHILOSOPHICAL: It's a funny thing about chickens.
STOOGE: What's funny?
PHILOSOPHICAL: You know a chicken is the only animal you can eat before it's born.

The manager of a grocery store in boosting his wares told a customer:
"These are the best eggs we've had for years."
"Well, bring me some you haven't had so long," she told him.

OLD HEN: Let me give you a piece of good advice.
YOUNG HEN: What is it?
OLD HEN: An egg a day keeps the ax away.

FIRST FARMER: I crossed my hens with parrots to save time.

SECOND FARMER: Why did you do that?

FIRST FARMER: I used to waste a lot of time hunting for eggs. Now the hen comes up to me and says, "I just laid an egg— go get it."

CHILDREN (see also, Baby, Adolescent, Kids, Offspring, Youth)

I was a boy ever since I was six years old, and before that I was five.

Today, kids don't have to learn only the ABC's . . . they have to learn the NBC's and the CBS's. . . .

My parents almost lost me last year, but they didn't take me far enough out into the woods.

I knew a little kid who was so tough that at eight he ran away with the circus, and at nine, he brought it back.

I once got a dog for my kid. It was the best trade I ever made.

CHINA

An American standing at a bar in Hong Kong got into a conversation with the Chinese standing next to him. When the American asked what he did, the Chinese said, "Oh, I was a Chinese airman; I fight in Korea." The American asked him his name and he said, "My name is Chow Mein, I was a Kamikaze flier." The American said, "Who are you kidding, Chow Mein? I was a flier, too, and I happen to know if you were a Kamikaze flier you wouldn't be here right now. That was a suicide squad!" The Chinaman grinned and said, "Oh, me Chicken Chow Mein."

A tourist in China watched as three prominent Chinese were being buried. As the first casket was lowered, several Chinese women came forward, placing chickens, rice, bread, and wine on the coffin. "What's that for?" asked the visitor. "That is our custom," answered one of the mourners, "so that the body of the dead man will not go hungry." The same procedure was followed when the second casket was lowered. When the third was lowered, only a single cup of rice was placed on it. "Say," muttered the stranger, "how come they put so little food on that coffin?" The Chinese shrugged. "That was Sing Lee. He was on a diet."

When a Jewish kid gets Bar-Mitzvahed in China, he says, "Today, I am a man-darin."

In China, it's custom for a man never to take a girl out until he marries her. In this country, he never takes her out afterwards.

CHIVALRY (see also Marriage)

"I noticed you got up and gave that lady your seat in the tram the other day," said one neighbor to another as they met on the corner.

"Since childhood I have respected a woman with a strap in her hand," was the reply.

BOB: I saw a fellow strike a girl today.
DICK: You didn't let him get away with it, did you?
BOB: I went up to him and said, "Only a coward would hit a woman—why don't you hit a man?"
DICK: Then what happened?
BOB: That's all I remember.

"See that girl over there?"
"Yeah."
"She's fresh from the country and it's up to us to show her the difference between right and wrong."
"Okay, pal. You teach her what's right."

CHORUS GIRL (see also Girls, Proposals)

A chorus girl may not understand politics, but she sure can put a motion before the house.

CHRISTMAS (see also Xmas, Yuletide)

JANICE: What did you get in your stocking for Christmas?
JANET: Nothing but a runner.
JANICE: Well, what did you expect—a pole vaulter?

JAKE: What does it mean—"Yuletide Greetings?"
SAM: Lend me $5—you'll tide me over for a few days.

At Christmas time, every girl wants her past forgotten and her present remembered.

Two friends were walking along the snowspread streets on Christmas Eve, and noted to their companion the holly wreaths in the windows, the vari-colored lights on the trees, and the mistletoe over the threshold of their friend, Jones.

"Jones certainly does this Christmas spirit thing up brown. Observe that none of the sanctioned touches are lacking at his establishment. And see—there they are carrying in the Yule log."

"Say," ejaculated one, "that ain't no Yule log—that's Jones."

CHURCH (see also Religion)

Coming out of church, Mrs. Peterson asked her husband, "Do you think that Johnson girl is tinting her hair?" "I didn't even see her," admitted Mr. Peterson.

"And that dress Mrs. Hansen was wearing," continued Mrs. Peterson. "Really, don't tell me you think that's the proper costume for a mother of two."

"I'm afraid I didn't notice that either," said Mr. Peterson.

"Oh, for heaven's sake," snapped Mrs. Peterson. "A lot of good it does you to go to church."

A wealthy jazz musician decided to go to church one Sunday. After services, he approached the preacher with much enthusiasm. "Reverend," he said, "that was a swinging sermon, man. I flipped my lid—that was the grooviest."

"I'm happy you liked it," said the Reverend, "but I wish you wouldn't use those terms in expressing yourself."

"I'm like sorry, man, Reverend, but I dug that sermon so much," said the cat. "In fact, it sent me so much I flipped a C-note in the collection pot."

The Reverend replied, "Crazy, man, crazy."

"I hear you went to the ball game last Sunday instead of to church."

"That's a lie, and I've got a fish to prove it."

A small town is where people go to church on Sunday to see who didn't.

Sign on a Church in Portland, Oregon: COME THIS SUNDAY, AVOID THE EASTER RUSH.

CINEMA

The movie extra was fast becoming a problem to the director. He refused again and again to jump from the cliff into the water. Screamed the extra: "No, I won't do it. Why, there's only two feet of water at the bottom of that cliff."

"Of course," heckled the director. "Do you think I want you to drown?"

DIRECTOR: You have never been kissed before.
ACTRESS: What am I, a character actress?"

"The lion will pursue you for a hundred yards—no farther. Do you understand?"

"I understand—but does the lion?"

"Here is where you jump off the cliff.

"Yeah, but suppose I get injured or killed?"

"Oh, that's all right. It's the last scene of the picture."

"Every day at the studio I rub elbows with some of the biggest stars."
"You mean when you're serving the soup?"

CLEANLINESS (see also Health)

The family doctor was checking with the mother of four small children, one of whom he was treating for a cold.
"Have you taken every precaution to prevent spread of contagion in your family?" he asked.
"Absolutely, Doctor," replied the mother earnestly. "We've even bought a sanitary cup and we all drink from it."

JOE: I'm going home—I expect a phone call.
JACK: From whom?
JOE: I don't know.
JACK: Then how do you know the phone will ring?
JOE: I'm going to take a bath.
JACK: That's right—the phone generally rings when I take a bath.
JOE: Yeah, but sometimes I have to take two or three baths to make it ring.

CLERKS (see also Stores, Business, Department Store)

GIRL: (in Book Store) Do you keep *The Divine Woman?*
CLERK: Not on my salary!

YOUNG MAN: I want to buy a diamond ring.
SALESMAN: Yes, sir; how would you like to buy one of our combination sets. Three pieces —engagement, wedding, and teething.

CLERK: Why, madam, these are the finest eggs we've had for months.
CUSTOMER: Never mind, I don't want any eggs you've had for months.

SALESMAN: Of course, madam, we stand behind each bed we sell.
NEWLYWED: Hm—thank you. Could you show me something else?

"Are you a clock watcher?" asked the businessman of the haggard graduate who had just applied for a job.
"No," replied the average (but honest) student, "I'm a bell listener."

CUSTOMER: I'd like some rat poison.
CLERK: Will you take it with you?
CUSTOMER: No, I'll send the rats over after it.

CLOTHING (see also Clothing Business, Wearing Apparel)

Jack Spitzer, the Albany Ford dealer, drove home with this: "A few weeks ago I went out on a hunting trip with a friend of mine in the clothing business. We were walking through the woods when all of a sudden a huge bear came out from behind a tree and leaped at me. I screamed, 'Help me, is that a bear?' My friend said, 'How should I know? Do I deal in furs?'"

I got a friend who has so many suits, he keeps one aside, just for the moths.

His suit was so shiny, if it ever tore, he'd have seven years bad luck.

I happen to have a suit for every day in the year, and this is it.

He had a suit on that was made in London, and he looked like he swam back in it.

When he bought the suit, it looked like a page out of *Esquire*. Now it looks like it was condensed for *Readers' Digest*.

They gave away a penknife with every suit they sold. In case you got caught in the rain, you could slash your way out.

He had on a dinner jacket with dinner still on it.

He got a very expensive suit for a ridiculous figure. His!

COHEN, MYRON

A bunch of nudists were walking down Fifth Avenue, and in the middle of them was a lone nudist with a long beard that stretched to the ground. A passerby asked one of the nudists why the man had such a long beard, and the nudist replied, "Well, someone has to go for coffee."

A big business tycoon died and went to his eternal resting place. When he arrived in the other world, he was greeted by a salesman who used to visit him on earth. The salesman greeted him with a big hello. "Max, old boy, I'm here for the appointment." "What appointment?" asked the businessman. "Don't you remember?" asked the salesman. "Every time I used to try to see you at your office, you'd tell me you'd see me here."

A frightened little man boarded a plane and took his seat right next to a big, burly Texan. The little man was so scared of flying that he threw up all over the Texan sitting next to him. Luckily, the

Texan was asleep when it happened, but now the little man was more frightened than ever as to what the Texan might do to him when he woke. Finally, the Texan did wake up, and quickly, the little man said to him, "Feeling better now?"

A mother was telling a friend about her three sons.

"Sammy is a doctor; Benny is a lawyer." Her friend said, "I'll bet you're proud of them." "And Joe is a silk manufacturer," the mother continued. Her friend looked at her, "A silk manufacturer?" "Yeah," the mother said, "and you know what? He supports Sammy and Benny."

COLD (see also Health, Hypochondriac)

It was so cold in Florida they were selling frozen orange juice right off the trees.

It was so cold that the farmers had to milk their cows with ice picks.

COLLEGE (see also Campus, University)

It took her four years to get a sheepskin—and one day to get a mink.

"My cousin is in medical school."

"What's he studying?"

"Nothing. They're studying him."

My sister worked her way through college as a chambermaid and graduated magna cum laundry.

You can lead a girl to Vassar but you can't make her think.

I knew it was an Ivy League College. It had button-down windows.

My nephew sent me a note from college. "Dear Uncle . . . I'm doing well in everything except school."

INTERVIEWER: Tell me, Professor, you've taught for ten years at Yale, fifteen years at Oxford, nine years at the Sorbonne . . . tell me, what has been your biggest problem?
PROFESSOR: Spitballs.

1ST STUDENT: Congratulations! I hear you won a scholarship to Harvard Medical School.
2ND STUDENT: Yes—but they don't want me while I'm alive.

SON: My professor said that with a mind like mine I should study law.

FATHER: That's wonderful, son, I'm proud of you.
SON: He said I had a criminal mind.

COLLEGE APPLICANT: What courses do you have here?
INTERVIEWER: Quantitative Chemistry, Philosophy, Contemporary Anthropology, Abnormal Psychology. . . .
COLLEGE APPLICANT: Now wait a minute. I don't know how to read yet.
INTERVIEWER: Oh, another football player.

GIRL: Are you a freshman?
BOY: That's up to you.

An American reporter interviewed an Eton schoolmaster:
REPORTER: Do you allow your boys to smoke?
SCHOOLMASTER: I'm afraid not.
REPORTER: Can they drink?
SCHOOLMASTER: Good gracious, no.
REPORTER: What about dates?
SCHOOLMASTER: Oh, that's quite all right as long as they don't eat too many.

COMEDIAN

People say I have a wonderful delivery. Ten days for shirts and two weeks for sheets.

The last time he played a night club he was such a hit, the manager jacked up the price of sandwiches to twenty cents apiece.

When I was at the Palace, I drew a line two blocks long . . . but they made me erase it.

His jokes are original. But the people who originated them died years ago.

I wouldn't say his jokes are bad, but after every show he gives his writers a loyalty test.

He's a great comic; he just signed a contract with Warner Brothers. Now he's waiting for them to sign it.

COMMUNIST (see also Russia)

A visitor to Hungary asked one of the natives, "How many people would you estimate are against the Communist regime here?" and the native said, "Six." The visitor said, "Only six? Are you sure, only six?" The native replied, "Yes, six—you, I, he, she, we, and they."

COMPOSER (see also Music, Musicians, Instruments)

"Curse you, once more you are off your Beethoven."

"And again, my dear Gershitz, you have flown off your Handel."

"It seems to me the composer was under the influence of Gershwin when he wrote this number."
"No, it was cognac; I saw the empty bottle."

He may not be able to carry a tune, but he sure can lift them.

"He composes music in bed."
"What kind of music could that be?"
"Sheet music."

"Victor Herbert wrote *Mlle. Modiste.*"
"Did she answer him?"

"What did you ever write?"
"I wrote the score of the Army-Navy game."
"What was it?"
"Three to nothing."

"Everything he writes is no good."
"I know; I tried to cash his check."

To write a song hit you just take something composed by one of the old masters and decompose it.

"I have a wonderful ear. I can pick up anything that's musical."
"Let's see you pick up the piano."

Two song writers were told by a producer to write a song in the Stephen Foster style. They did so. And when they turned in the song, the producer said: "It's so much on the style of Stephen Foster that I'm afraid to use it. He might sue us."

"Let's do a little operetta of mine. I call it *The Chocolate Soldier!*"
"Straus wrote *The Chocolate Soldier.*"
"Then we'll make mine vanilla."

He writes songs with two guys who write the words and music.

Just placed a song with the Exclusive Music Co.—it's so exclusive that they're not even giving it out.

CONDUCT (see also School, Kids)

MOTHER: Where do bad little girls go?
GIRL: Most everywhere.

FATHER: D in work, D in effort, D in conduct. That settles it, Wilbur. From now on, you and I are through.
SON: Stop kiddin' yourself, Pop. Just remember that I'm still an exemption on your income tax return.

JANE: So you never let a man kiss you good night?"

LOUISE: No, by the time he leaves me it's always morning.

PATIENT: I've been misbehaving and my conscience is troubling me.

PSYCHIATRIST: I see, and since I'm a psychiatrist you want something to strengthen your will power?

PATIENT: No, something to weaken my conscience.

She bawled me out for eating with my fingers. But I've always said if food wasn't clean enough to pick up with your fingers, it wasn't fit to eat.

COOKING (see also Food, Meal)

I got a wife that dresses to kill and cooks the same way.

She runs the only kitchen in the world where flies come to commit suicide.

My wife offered me some biscuits and said, "Take your pick." She should have said, "Take your saw."

She was a peculiar sort of a woman. She would let her son sit on a cake while it was still baking, because she loved to watch her son rising in the yeast.

Then there was the woman who boiled her eggs for a half hour waiting for them to get soft. She was told to boil them for three minutes if she wanted them soft. So she boiled her potatoes for only three minutes, and she couldn't understand how they got hard so fast.

She got along fine in her cooking school until one day she finally burned something . . . her cooking school!

CONVICTS (see also Law, Jail)

As he was strapping the convict in the electric chair, the warden asked, "Have you any final wish?" "Yes," answered the book-of-etiquette victim with a sly glance at the prison matron, "allow me to give my seat to a lady."

A convict, telling how he got into jail, said, "I had the car so long that I completely forgot I had stolen it when I reported it stolen."

COPS (see also Police, Crooks)

That town had some of the best cops money could buy.

He was a great cop. He kept his ear to the ground and picked up all the dirt.

He was a great cop. Always assigned to headquarters. Cause he had a head as big as a quarter.

"Calling car 66."
"But we are car 99."
"No, you're car 66."
"How do you like that, we've been riding upside down!!!"

The cop requested duty on a motorcycle so that if there was any trouble he could make a quick getaway.

On a policeman's examination one question was, "What would you do to disperse a crowd quickly and quietly?" The answer: "I'd pass the hat."

COP: Pardon me Miss, but swimming is not allowed in this lake.
GIRL: Why didn't you tell me that before I undressed?
COP: Because there ain't no law against undressing.

Commenting on the recent police corruption in Chicago, Mort Sahl said, "It's the only place where a kid can play cops and robbers by himself."

COUNTERFEITERS (see also Police)

Number 32146, whom we'll call Blinky for short, was only recently taken from the mental ward of a prison and assigned a regular cell.

It all dates back to the reason for his incarceration. Blinky was known as the Grandpa Moses of counterfeiters. He was so meticulous copying a bill it took the eagle eye of a trained professional to detect his funny money from the real McCoy.

For many months, Blinky worked on what he thought was a foolproof set of engravings for a $10 bill. His chore completed, he wrinkled his work of art, compared it with the original through a powerful magnifying glass, and decided to test-pass it before going into volume production.

Within two hours Blinky was arrested. "I defy you," he raged at the Treasury agent, placing both the original and the spurious bill side by side, "to tell me the difference between these two ten-spots."

"There is no difference, Blinky," the T-man agreed, "and that's the trouble. Seems you only made one mistake. You copied your counterfeit from a counterfeit!"

This counterfeiter was going out of the business. So, in a last big fling, he made a $15 bill. He went into a candy store, bought a couple of 50-cent stogies, and handed over the bill. The clerk looked at it for a moment, went into the back of his establishment, came out, and gave him two $7 bills in change.

COURAGE (see also Army, War)

SUE: Last week when that bear got out you ran away and left me, and once you told me you would face death for me.
DICK: Yes, I would—but that bear wasn't dead.

"My uncle has twelve medals—he won them during the war."
"He must have been a great sharpshooter."
"No—a great crapshooter."

"I've told thousands of women where to get off."
"You must be a lady killer."
"No, I run an elevator in a department store."

COURTSHIP (see also Elopement, Dating, Amorous, Love, Lover, Osculating, Kiss, Romance)

JOHN: They say that kisses are the language of love.
PRISCILLA: Well, speak for yourself, John.

She could have married anyone she pleased. She just didn't please anyone.

ANN: We could never be happy, Dan. You know I always want my own way in everything.
DAN: But after we're married you can still want your own way in everything.

HE: (sneaking up behind She and covering She's eyes) I'm going to kiss you if you don't know who it is!!!
SHE: Abraham Lincoln?? George Washington?? Albert Schweitzer??

MEL: If you refuse to marry me, I'll hurl myself off that 200 foot cliff.
NEL: Ah, that's just a bluff.

FATHER: My boy, I never kissed a girl until I met your mother. Will you be able to say that to your son?
SON: Yes, but not with such a straight face.

COWARD

MANLY: Put up your hand and fight like a man.
WEAKLY: I'd rather put up my ears and run like a rabbit.

WILL: Why are your hands shaking?

BILL: I don't know, I guess they're just glad to see each other.

SHE: Don't be a coward, act like a man.

HE: How do you like that? My life is in danger and you want me to do imitations.

SHE: You shouldn't be afraid of him. He's an ignorant savage and you're an educated, intelligent man.

HE: What do you expect me to do; beat him to death with my diploma?

Once there was a very brave lion tamer who was not afraid of the most vicious lions in the menagerie. But he had a wife who did not like him to stay out late, and one night he did stay out late. When he realized it was midnight, he was panic-stricken. He didn't dare go home, but if he went to a hotel, his wife might find him. So he went to the menagerie, crawled into the lion's cage, and went to sleep with his head resting on the largest lion.

The next morning his wife began to hunt for him, and she looked all over town. Finally she came to the menagerie and saw her husband in the lion's cage. A look of contempt came over her face, and she snarled: "You coward!"

COWBOY (see also Horse, Horseback Riding, Western)

He walked in with a gun on each hip, and she walked in with a hip on each gun.

There they stood, the Bicarbonate Brothers: Wild Bill Hiccup and Hopalong Acidity.

When I was out West I punched cattle for six months. Then the cattle started punching back.

They were digging and digging until they found their bonanza. Then they split it up and today they have the biggest bonanza split out West.

He rode a horse like he was part of the animal. I hate to tell you which part.

Definition: Cowboy: A boy whose mother was a cow!

Out West you ride a horse and everything in front of you is purple and gold . . . and everything in back of you is black and blue.

COWS (see also Animals, Farm, Farmers)

"What is cowhide chiefly used for?"
"To keep the cow together."

CUSTOMER: Is this milk fresh?
FARMER: Fresh? Three hours ago it was grass.

SUE: My uncle can't decide whether to get a new cow or a bicycle for his farm.
JOHN: He'd certainly look silly riding around on a cow.
SUE: Yes, but he would look a lot sillier milking a bicycle.

"Why is this milk so blue?"
"Because it comes from discontented cows."

"Name five things that contain milk."
"That's easy. Ice cream, butter, cheese and two cows."

CREDIT (see also Creditors)

A disgruntled would-be joiner wrote a long and sordid letter to the Diners' Club claiming he couldn't understand why he was not acceptable. At the end he explained that he would like to get an answer and asked that it be addressed to the hotel on the letterhead. "This hotel," he said, "is one of my better creditors."

The funniest story going around Madrid, Spain, at the moment, happened the other evening at one of the best night clubs there. It seems that a certain newspaperman was attracted to a certain dancer at this club and asked if he might take her to another cabaret. The headwaiter said that such a thing could be arranged if the newspaperman was willing to pay for her time.

At the moment the scribe didn't have sufficient pesetas and asked if he could cash a Travelers' check. The headwaiter said no, but if the chap had a Diners' Club card he would charge off the date as dessert. And the deal was actually made!

BILL: Do you live within your income?
WILL: Heavens no!! It's all I can do to live within my credit!

The beggar stood at the street corner and asked a passing gentleman for money.
"Not now," said the gentleman, "but I'll give you something on my way back."
"Nope, that won't do," said the beggar. "Why you'd be surprised how much money I've lost giving credit that way."

CUSTOMER: I warn you, I won't be able to pay for this suit for six months.
TAILOR: Oh that's all right, sir.
CUSTOMER: Thank you. When will it be ready?
TAILOR: In six months, sir.

CREDIT MANAGER: Are you going to pay us something on that account?

CUSTOMER: I can't just now.

CREDIT MANAGER: If you don't, I'll tell all your other creditors that you paid us in full.

DEFINITION: Creditor: A man who has a better memory than a debtor.

CREDITORS (see also credit)

I met a fellow in Hawaii who told me he went there for respiratory trouble. He said back home his creditors wouldn't let him breathe easy.

CROOKS (see also Cops, Police, Thieves, Jail)

I always wondered what happens if a midget commits murder and is sentenced to the electric chair. What do they do . . . give him the electric high chair??

MAN: Pardon me. Miss, did you see a policeman around here?

YOUNG LADY: No!

MAN: Well, then hand over your dough and be damn quick about it!

ROBBER: O.K. Stick 'em down.

ROBBED: You mean stick 'em up.

ROBBER: Don't confuse me, it's my first job.

FINGERS: What ever happened to Knuckles, he used to be in slot machines?

ELBOWS: Oh, he went into bigger business.

FINGERS: What's he in now?

ELBOWS: Concrete.

He got caught stealing in the corset department and got sent up for a two-way stretch.

POLICE CHIEF: How did you learn so much about crime?

CRIMINAL: I started in a small way. Picking midgets' pockets.

CHIEF: How could you stoop so low?

Things are so tough in Chicago, I knew a gangster who had to let two cops go.

D

DAD (see also Fathers, Parents and Children)

PA: The man who marries my daughter will need a lot of money.
HIM: I'm just the man, then.

FATHER: You're getting too old to play with the boys.
DAUGHTER (innocently): I don't have to any more, father.

FATHER (to daughter's boy friend): Remember, young man, the lights are put out in this house at eleven o'clock.
BOY FRIEND: That's O.K. by me, sir.

FATHER: My son, I am a self-made man.
SON: Pop, there's one thing I like about you. You always take the blame for everything.

"Who says that all men are born free?" wailed the young father as he received the doctor's bill.

"Mary, is that young man there yet?"
"No, father, but he's getting there."

DAIS (see also Banquet, Speech, Speaker, Orators)

To many speakers a speech seems to be something that makes you feel numb on one end and dumb on the other.

A proverb for all banquet speakers—"The mind cannot accept what the seat cannot endure."

Winston Churchill offers this advice to speakers on a dais: "Say what you have to say and the first time you come to a sentence with a grammatical ending, sit down!"

Judge Jacob Braude said, "All work and no plagiarism usually makes a mighty dull speech."

George Jessel, toastmaster at so many banquets he's thinking of calling his autobiography *Dais Without End,* has the motto, "If you haven't struck oil in your first three minutes, stop boring!"

Lord Macaulay was being honored in London for fifty years of distinguished service to the crown. He began his speech of acknowledgment with these sad words: "Gentlemen, I understand that man inherited three basic vices: I must report to you that I quit one, and one quit me—but I still smoke."

At the Waldorf they had six daises, seating one hundred and forty prominent people at the General Omar Bradley tribute dinner. A very modest fellow sitting at NBC prez Bob Kintner's table squinted at the six daises and said, "And on the seventh dais they rested."

DANCING

HE: Dancers run in my family.
SHE: Too bad they don't dance.

After spending a romanceless weekend at a fancy resort, Sidney finally met a girl at the Sunday night dance. As he swung her around the dance floor in a swift rumba, he whispered in her ear, "Listen, baby, I have only one night left here."
She whispered back, "I'm dancing as fast as I can."

I used to dance with Arthur Murray, but I found out I liked girls better.

A drunken couple arm in arm in a bar walked over to the cigarette machine. He put a quarter in, pushed *Lucky Strike,* and grabbed her and started to jitterbug. She stopped and said, "Stop, silly—this is a rumba."

A neighbor of mine and his wife took up mamboing very seriously, but I saw them the other night on the dance floor. While the wife was doing the mambo he was doing the samba. I asked him how come and he said he was trying to quit by tapering off. . . .

DATING (see also Elopement, Love, Osculating, Kiss, Romance, Amorous, Necking)

CHARLES: Hello, darling, would you like to have dinner with me tonight?
CURRENT GIRL FRIEND: Oh, I'd be delighted, dear!
CHARLES: Okay. Tell your mother I'll be over at six o'clock and please not to have hash.

TED: The ex-debutante had a dance last night.
NED: What's an ex-debutante?
TED: A girl that came out last year and wishes she were back in this year.

SUITOR (to little brother): Here, take this quarter and go to see a show.
KID: No, I'll give you fifty cents to let me stay and watch.

"Resist the temptation," advised the moralist.

"I would," sighed the girl, "but it may never come again."

DEATH (see also Funerals, Dying, Undertaker)

"You know, in Egypt they have a peculiar superstition. They're afraid of burying people alive, so when a man dies they bury him for sixty days and then dig him up, place him on a cold slab, and have twenty beautiful girls dance around him for two hours."

"What good does that do?"

"Well if he doesn't get up—he's sure to be dead."

"Well," said the dying business man, "you better put in a clause about my employees. To each man who has worked for me twenty years I give and bequeath $50,000.00

"But," said the lawyer, "you haven't been in business twenty years."

"I know it, man, but it's good advertising."

"There goes the funeral of a great polo player."

"Yes, he rides just like he was part of the hearse."

DEFINITIONS

Alarm Clock: A small device used to wake up people who have no children.

Bigamist: A man who leads two wives.

Coward: One who in a perilous emergency thinks with his legs.

Diamond: A chunk of coal that made good under pressure.

Education: Something a boy spends years getting so he can work for a man who has no education at all.

Flirtation: Wishful winking.

Genius: The talent of a man who is dead.

Hollywood: Where you put on a sport jacket and take off your brain.

I.O.U.: A paper wait.

Janitor: A floor flusher.

Kleptomaniac: One who helps himself because he can't help himself.

Lonely person: A guy who can't admit that he finds himself poor company.

Marriage: A kind of friendship that is recognized by the police.

Nudists: Folks who grin and bare it.

Overeating: The destiny that shapes our ends.

Philosophy: Unintelligible answers to insoluble problems.

Religion: Insurance in this world against a fire in the next.

Spinster: A woman who is unhappily unmarried.

Television: Chewing gum for the eyes.

Undertaker: The last guy to let you down.

Vocabulary: Something a man can use to describe a shapely girl without using his hands.

Writers: Writers are born, not paid.

Yawn: A silence with an exclamation mark.

Zoo: A place where animals look at silly people.

DEMOCRATS (see also Politics, Republicans)

DEMOCRAT: The mayor stole the last election.
REPUBLICAN: No, he didn't.
DEMOCRAT: He did, too.
REPUBLICAN: No, he paid spot cash for it.

Mike met his friend Joe, who was sporting three hats, one on top of another.

"What's the idea?" demanded Mike.

"I've decided to become a Democrat," replied Joe.

"What are you wearing three hats for?"

"A Democrat has one hat to cover his head, another he tosses in the ring, and one hat he talks through."

"How did the audience receive your campaign speech when you told them you had never bought a vote?" the campaign chairman asked the Democratic candidate for governor.

"A few cheered, but the majority seemed to lose interest," he replied.

For twenty years two senators, one a Democrat and the other a Republican, quarreled every day. Finally a third party intervened. "Boys, this must stop," he said. "Let's have a drink together and make peace." The senators agreed, and when the drinks were served the friend cried, "Now make a toast to each other."

Raising his glass, the Democrat said, "Here's wishing for you what you're wishing me."

"Oh, now you're starting in again," yelled the Republican.

The continual row between Democratic Presidents and Republican Congressmen over the budget reminded one Senator of an Arkansas moonshiner who had been convicted a number of times. When he was again brought into court by the "revenoors," the judge told the culprit sternly: "Before passing sentence, I want to tell you that you and your sons have given this court more trouble than anyone else in the whole state of Arkansas. Have you anything to say?" The old fellow thought a moment, and then said, "Well, Judge, I jest want to say that we haven't given you any more trouble than you've given us."

Senator Barry Goldwater, speaking about the Democrats, said that they didn't know how to give a proper dinner. He said that a proper dinner usually could be gotten from an Arizona Republican, and that it consisted of a steak, a bottle of whiskey, and a hound dog. When a somewhat insulted Democrat asked him what the hound dog had to do with the dinner, the Senator replied, "Oh, he eats the steak."

DENTIST (see also Doctor, Teeth)

I recently heard of a dentist who had a television set installed in his operating room to distract his patients' attention. This led to some complications. For instance, one day a young boy called and said, "Mother says put her down for *The Price is Right* on Tuesday, and me for *Captain Kangaroo* on Wednesday."

Son: Why is it that dentists call their offices dental parlors?
Father: Because they are drawing rooms, son.

First Cannibal: Have you seen the dentist lately?
Second Cannibal: Yes, he filled my teeth at dinnertime.

The dentists' favorite marching song, so I understand, is *The Yanks are Coming*.

Tom: I'd like to go to a woman dentist.
Dick: Why do you want to go to a woman dentist?
Tom: Because it would be a pleasure to have a woman say "Open your mouth" instead of "Shut up."

A gangster went into a dentist's office and said to the dentist, "Pull my tooth."

The dentist asked, "Which tooth is it?"

And the gangster replied, "Find it yourself—I'm no stoolpigeon."

MAN: Hey, that wasn't the tooth I wanted pulled!
DENTIST: Calm yourself, I'm coming to it!

BUSINESSMAN: Only yesterday I lit my cigar with a twenty dollar bill.
HIS FRIEND: How extravagant!
BUSINESSMAN: It was a bill from my dentist, and I wasn't going to pay it anyway.

A Tulsa, Oklahoma oilman gushed into his dentist for an examination. The dentist dove into the oillionaire's mouth and said, "Perfect, man, perfect! You don't need a thing." "Well, drill anyway, Doc," the patient drawled, "I feel lucky this morning."

The dentist examined the nervous lady and finally said, "It looks like I'll have to pull your tooth." The woman squealed, "I'd rather have a baby." The doctor countered, "Make up your mind, lady, before I adjust the chair."

DEPARTMENT STORE (see also Clerks, Business)

"I'd like to see something in silk stockings."
"You men are all alike."

"Is the color fast?"
"Why don't you chase it and see?"

"When your father sent you for samples of cloth didn't he say what color and material he wanted?"
"I don't think it matters. He wants them for pen wipers."

I have a brother who works in a department store. Yesterday he came home and said he was fired. He made a mistake and took a sign off a blouse counter and put it on the bathtub display. The sign read: "How would you like to see your best girl in one of these for a dollar ninety-nine?"

DIET (see also Health)

Americans have more food to eat than people of any other nation on earth and more diets to keep us from eating it.

I just quit my onion diet. I lost ten pounds and twelve friends.

This is the prayer of a small girl: "Please, Lord, can't you put the vitamins in pie and cake instead of cod-liver oil and spinach?"

DISTANCE

YACHTSMAN: We're ten miles from land.
HIS GUEST: What direction?
YACHTSMAN: Straight down.

Two city dwellers moved to a home in the wide open spaces. Some time later they invited their first guests from the city.

A guest asked, "Why, you said it was only a hop, skip and a jump here. It's at least two miles from the station."

His host answered, "Sure, at the station you hop in a cab, skip a couple of miles and jump out here."

DIVORCE (see also Marriage)

HUSBAND: I want a divorce. My wife called me a lousy lover . . .
JUDGE: You want a divorce because your wife called you a lousy lover???
HUSBAND: No. I want a divorce because she knows the difference.

With the divorce I got custody of the kids and she got custody of the money.

The judge asked the young woman why she wanted a divorce.
"Our marriage was fine until the patter of feet around the house."

"Oh," the judge said, "Boy or girl?"
"Neither," she said, "It was the blonde next door."

For the woman that has everything—a divorce.

The only grounds you need for divorce is marriage.

DOCTOR (see also Dentist, Health, Physician, Hospital, Nurse)

The doctor rushed out of his study and instructed his wife, "Get me my bag at once!" "What's the matter?" she asked. "Some fellow just phoned and said he couldn't live without me." The wife thought a few seconds, then, "Just a moment," she said gently, "I think that call was for me."

Back home in East Texas, Old Man Jones confessed his troubles to the local doctor. "It's sort of ticklish to talk about, Doc," he apologized. "But I need some vitamins or something on account of when it comes to making love, I ain't got as much pep as I used to have." "Well, that's natural," the Doc consoled, "how old are you?" "Well, let's see. I'm a year older'n my wife and she's eighty-one. Guess I'm about eighty-two years of age." "And when did you first notice this lack of pep on your part?" "Well, the first time was last night. That wasn't so bad, but be-dogged if we didn't notice it again this morning."

The woman ear and throat specialist was all in a tizzy. Seems she wanted to paint the throat of a very chic patient—the trouble was she couldn't decide on a color!

DOCTOR: The check you gave me came back.
PATIENT: So did my arthritis.

DOCTOR: All right, now what seems to be the matter with you????
PATIENT: You studied for ten years. . . . you tell me. . . .

1ST DOCTOR: So this patient comes running into my office and immediately starts undressing. . . .
2ND DOCTOR: What's so unusual about that?
1ST DOCTOR: The nurse . . .?????

PATIENT: I sure hope I'm sick. . . .
DOCTOR: What kind of an attitude is that?
PATIENT: Well I'd hate to feel like this if I'm well. . . .

DOCTOR TO NEW MOTHER: Now don't worry about the baby . . .

just remember to keep one end full and the other end dry . . .

Never argue with a doctor. He has inside information.

The army doctor said to the young draftee, "I want a urine specimen."
"Sure," he said.
"All right," the doctor said, "Fill that bottle over there."
"From here??!!"

DOCTOR: You're in good health Mr. Johnson, you'll live to be 80."
PATIENT: Doc, I am 80.
DOCTOR: See, what did I tell you.

DOGS (see also Animals, Cats, Dog Racing)

"I bought a dog for five dollars and I sold him. How much did I lose?"
"You bought a dog for five dollars and you sold him and you want to know how much you lost? Well, what did you sell him for?"
"For chewing up the furniture."

The dogs in Siberia are the fastest in the world. That's because the trees are so far apart.

"My home town is so small our fire department consists of a horse cart and four dogs."

"What do the dogs do, haul the cart?"

"No, they find the hydrant."

Three dogs—An English bull, a French poodle and a Russian wolfhound—were talking. The English bull and the French poodle agreed that they loved their respective countries and were content to stay there. The Russian wolfhound said, "I have the best of everything to eat and drink in Russia, but I sure would like to go to America." "How come," the other two dogs asked. "Well," said the wolfhound, "I'd like to bark once in a while."

A very rich lady had a dog who had his own little doghouse complete with little furniture. A neighbor was looking at it one day and asked, "How does he keep it so clean?"

The owner said haughtily, "Oh he has a French poodle come in once a week."

A famous dog trainer gave a party in honor of his talented Alsatian. As part of the entertainment, the hound lumbered over to the baby grand, climbed on the stool and proceeded to play a Bach sonata. Halfway through, one of the guests spoke too loudly and the animal growled and chased the heckler into a neutral corner. "Don't worry," the dog's trainer shouted, "his Bach is worse than his bite."

DOG RACING (see also Dogs, Gambling)

"I went to the dog races last night and I bet on a dog called Wise Guy."

"How did you make out?"

"He lost. He went all right up to the middle of the race, then he stopped and turned right back to where he started from."

"What happened to him?"

"He found out the rabbit he was chasing was a dummy."

"I've got a new dog—a dachshund—I entered him in the races last Saturday."

"How did he make out?"

"It was a circular track and he overtook himself."

DRESS (see also Wearing Apparel)

WIFE: Does she dress like a lady?

HUSBAND: I don't know—I never saw her dress.

MARY: That dress is too tight for you. It's skin tight.

RUTH: It's tighter than my skin.

MARY: How could anything be tighter than your skin?

RUTH: I can sit down in my skin, but I'll be darned if I can sit down in this dress.

FIRST DRUNK: Look at that sign.
SECOND DRUNK: Whazzit shay?
FIRST DRUNK: Shays "Ladies Ready-to-Wear Clothes."
SECOND DRUNK: Well, ish damn' near time, ain't it?

BOSS: What's the matter with your suit? It's getting threadbare.
OFFICE BOY: Threadbare? Why, the last time I took it into town to get it cleaned, they sent it back on a spool.

A woman may put on a golf suit and not play golf—she may put on a bathing suit and never go near the water—but when she put on a wedding gown, she means business.

That fur coat is so cheap the moths hired doubles to eat it up.

Two college roommates met on campus.
"Say," asked the first, "what's the idea of wearing my raincoat?"
"Well, you wouldn't want your new suit to get wet, would you?" was the prompt reply.

SHE: Do you believe that tight clothes stop circulation?
HE: Certainly not. The tighter a woman's clothing the more she's in circulation.

The sports fan was describing his date of the previous evening.
"She wore one of those baseball dresses," he explained.
"What's that?" his friend inquired.
"A baseball dress? It had a diamond back, a grandstand view in front, and it showed a lot of beautiful curves."

GEORGE: Will you give me the address of your tailor?
FRED: Yes, if you won't give him mine.

TILLIE: You certainly look cute in that gown.
MILLIE: Oh, this? I wear it to teas.
TILLIE: To tease whom?

DRINK (see also Alcohol, Drinkers, Drunks, Booze)

Now that Alaska and Hawaii are states, the most popular American drink will probably be pineapple juice with ice in it.

DRINKERS (see also Drink, Alcohol, Drunks, Booze)

A heavy drinker was regaling his friends with his early life and the hard times he had. "Things were so bad," he recalled, "that sometimes I had to live for days on nothing but food and water."

A husband returned home late one night in a rather inebriated state and handed the wife his pay envelope. She opened it, looked inside and shouted, "This is only half of your salary. Where's the rest of it?" "I bought something for the house," he explained. "Oh, how nice," smiled the spouse. "What'd you buy?" To which her husband replied, "A round of drinks."

Lovable clown Joe E. Lewis has been warned many times about his drinking. "Don't worry about a thing," is Joe's answer, "I'm responsible for a new surgical technique. After my last operation, instead of stitches they used corks."

DRIVERS (see also Cars, Autos, Traffic, Transportation, Pedestrian)

OFFICER: Miss, you were doing sixty miles an hour!
SWEET YOUNG THING: Oh, isn't that splendid! I only learned to drive yesterday.

Boggs was halted by a traffic officer who demanded:
"What's the idea going seventy-five miles an hour in a twenty-five-mile zone?"
"I wasn't going seventy-five miles an hour," protested Boggs. "I wasn't going sixty, I wasn't going fifty. I wasn't even going forty —I wasn't . . ."
"Hey, look out!" yelled the officer. "In a minute you'll be backing into something."

A man was driving an auto with his wife in the back seat and stalled his car on a railroad track with the train coming. His wife screamed, "Go on! Go on!" Her husband said, "You've been driving all day from the back seat. I've got my end across, see what you can do with your end."

The new owner of a used car was driving his purchase home. He was rapidly questioning the wisdom of his bargain when an officer roared at him, "Hey! You're blocking up traffic. Can't you go any faster?"
"Yes, but I don't want to leave the car," was the disgusted reply.

Brought before a magistrate for speeding, the struggling young lawyer was asked to explain his haste.
"What is your alibi for speeding fifty miles an hour?" asked the judge.
"Well, your Honor, I had just heard, your Honor, that the ladies

of my wife's church were giving a rummage sale and I was hurrying home to save my other pair of pants."

Three men were repairing telephone poles. A woman passed by in her car, and when she saw the men climbing the telephone poles, she said, "Look at those darn fools—you'd think I had never driven a car before."

"I got rid of that rear noise in my car," stated the motorist.
"How did you do it?"
"I made her sit up front with me."

DRUGGIST

CUSTOMER: You made a mistake in that prescription I gave my mother-in-law. Instead of quinine you used strychnine.
DRUGGIST: You don't say? Then you owe me twenty cents more.

CUSTOMER: I can't sleep at night —the least little sound disturbs me. I'm a victim of insomnia. Even a cat on our back fence distresses me beyond words.
DRUGGIST: This powder will be effective.
CUSTOMER: When do I take it?
DRUGGIST: You don't. Give it to the cat in milk.

"A mustard plaster."
"We're out of mustard, how about mayonnaise?"

DRUNKS (see also Drinker, Drink, Alcohol, Booze, Liquor)

There are plenty of good cures for hangovers. One is to stay hungover. Eddie Condon's recipe starts like this: TAKE THE JUICE OF ONE QUART OF WHISKEY . . .

As the Poet Laureate of the drunks once said, "Each man kills the thing he loves." And with that, he opened up a fifth of rye.

A boozer wove into a bar and ordered a Scotch. After one drink he took his pants off. The bartender wanted to know what was going on or coming off. "I always take my pants off when I drink," hicc'd the man. "It's comfortable. Try it." So the bartender took his pants off and he agreed that it was comfortable. A few of the other drinkers saw and decided to go along. They took their pants off.

Pretty soon all twenty-three customers in the joint and the bartender were standing around and drinking—just wearing their shorts. A Joe E. Lewis protégé, who had been trying to outdo the master at all the neighborhood bars, staggered in, took a bead on on them and muttered, "What are you guys going to do if you get rejected?"

Joe E., by the way, was the boy who went to the store and asked the grocer for a fifth of milk. But now he says he's planning to give up drinking. "I'm beginning to see the handwriting on the floor."

A man was shocked when, inside a bar, he spotted his friend who had been a member of Alcoholics Anonymous for two years. "Sam, how come?" he asked. "It's nothing," came the reply, "I'm just tapering on."

A motorist was speeding down a country road when his car suddenly veered sharply, hit a soft shoulder, rolled over four times and wound up in the middle of a cornfield. A farmer, hoeing nearby, rushed over and saw the driver slowly crawl out. "That was a mighty bad spill you had there," the farmer remarked, "have you been drinking?" "You darn fool," the driver screamed at him, "of course I've been drinking. What do you think I am, a stunt driver?"

There's the high class drunk who says "Farmer, farmer," instead of "Hic, hic."

My uncle's boss told him whenever he got drunk he'd have to report to him the next day and tell him about it. One day my uncle staggered into the boss' office and announced he was drunk the night before.

"Why," said the boss, "you're drunk now."

"I know," said my uncle, "but I'm gonna report that tomorrow."

DYING (see also Death, Funeral, Undertaker)

As he lay on his deathbed he spoke, "Sara, I want you should know before I die that Ginsburg the tailor owes me $200, and Max the butcher owes me $50, and Lapidus next door owes me $300." His wife turned to the children and said, "What a wonderful man your fadder is . . . even when he's dying he's got the brains to realize who owes him money." The old man continued . . . "and Sara I want you to also know that I owe the landlord a hundred dollars" . . . to which his wife cried, "Ho ho, now he's getting delirious . . ."

As the elderly wife lay at death's door she said to her husband, "Max, do me one last request. Let my mother ride with you in the funeral car."

Angrily the husband replied,

"She should only drop dead and she can ride with you."

"Please," the wife pleaded, "grant me this one last request."

"All right," said the husband, "but I'm telling you—it's going to spoil my whole day."

An actor rushed hurriedly into an agent's office and told the secretary, "listen I must see him, it's a matter of life and death." "Why, what happened?" asked the secretary. "I'm dying to see him," was the reply.

Death is nature's way of telling you to slow down.

❖❖

E

EARS

The doctors operated on a friend of mine for a constant ringing in his ears before they found out he was a bellhop.

"You took the words right out of my ears," said the little boy to his mother.

"No, that's not right. It's you who took the words right out of my mouth."

"But I heard it before I said it."

EASTER

"By the way, where did you get that nice Easter tie?"

"What makes you think it's an Easter tie?"

"It's got egg on it."

"I'm going to buy a peacock."
"Why?"
"So I can have colored Easter eggs without coloring them. The peacock will lay colored eggs."

ECONOMY (see also Money)

They were trying to decide who was the stingiest man in town when someone told about Jones.

"One day Jones was walking down the street and he found a package of cough drops. That night he made his wife sleep out in the cold to catch a cold."

He's so stingy he heats the knives so his wife won't use too much butter.

SUE: Are you saving any money since you started your budget system?

HELEN: Sure. By the time we have balanced it up every evening, it's too late to go anywhere.

EFFICIENCY EXPERT . (see also Business)

An efficiency expert died and was being carried to his grave by six pallbearers. As they approached their destination the lid popped open and the efficiency expert sat up and shouted, "If you'd put this thing on wheels, you could lay off four men."

EGOTISM

An egotist is one who, reading a book and not understanding something in it, decides it is a misprint.

The inebriated young actor lurched into the lobby of a large hotel far from Hollywood. He looked into a mirror and smiled with pleasure, shouting, "Look! They've got a picture of me here, too!"

JUDGE: Who do you think is the best movie actor?
ACTOR: Myself.
JUDGE: Don't you think that is a bit egotistical?

ACTOR: Perhaps, your Honor, but you must remember that I'm under oath.

EGYPT

This is a shaggy camel story: When the party got to Egypt midway on their world cruise, naturally the first wonder they decided to visit was the pyramids. Approaching a drive-it-yourself camel dealer, the tourists inquired how much it would cost to rent a camel. "That depends," the camel man said. "Do you want one lump or two?"

ELEPHANTS (see also Animals)

Two elephants were talking. "I don't care what people say," said one of them, "I can't remember a thing."

Guy went to his psychiatrist and said, "Look, just answer me two questions."
Doctor said, "Certainly."
Guy said, "One—can I possibly be in love with an elephant?"
Doctor said, "Of course not. Now what's the other question?"
Guy said, "Where can I sell a rather large engagement ring?"

ELOPEMENT (see also Amorous, Engagement, Proposals)

LOVE (eloping with loved one, to taxi driver): How much is the fare?

DRIVER: That's all right, sir. The lady's father settled all that.

(Eloping bride receives wire from parent)—DO NOT COME HOME AND ALL WILL BE FORGIVEN.

EMPLOYMENT (see also Boss, Business, Executive)

My maid's idea of work is to sweep the room with a glance.

FIRST HOBO: I hate holidays.
SECOND HOBO: Me, too. Makes you feel so common, when nobody ain't workin'!

The kid was playing hooky from school. The father told the kid to go out and get a job. The problem child decided to be a bookmaker in his neighborhood. Instead of money, he dealt in pebbles.

One day another kid who was gambling with him came around with a big rock. "I better not take his bet," said the young bookmaker, "he must know something!"

The maid had been happily employed with the same family for ten years. One day the maid an-

nounced she was quitting because she was pregnant.

The mistress said, "Rather than lose you, we'll adopt the child."

A year later the maid again found herself "that way" and told her mistress, who again adopted the baby rather than lose her.

This happened a third time. Help was hard to get, so the mistress again volunteered to adopt the child. And the maid said, "Oh, no, not me—I won't work for a family that has three children."

ENGAGEMENT (see also Courtship, Elopement)

MARTHA: You know, you've been engaged to her a long time. Why don't you marry her?
BOBBY: I've been thinking about it—but where would I spend my evenings if I did?

ED: So you broke your engagement to Evelyn. Why was that?
TED: Well, I was only doing to the engagement what it did to me.

RUSS: Are you engaged to marry Bob?
NETTIE: Yes, I've promised to marry him as soon as he has made his fortune.
RUSS: That isn't an engagement —that's an option.

DICK: I hear you're engaged. Who's the lucky woman?
JOHN: Her mother.

ENGLAND

There's a university in England so conservative that it refuses to teach liberal arts courses.

A member of the faculty of a London medical college was chosen to be a honorary physician to the Queen. Proud of his appointment he wrote a note on the blackboard in his classroom: BEGINNING NEXT MONTH, it said, I WILL BE HONORARY PHYSICIAN TO QUEEN ELIZABETH. The next day when the professor returned to his classroom, he found the following line written below his notice: GOD SAVE THE QUEEN.

A visitor from London, startled at dead of night by a terrifying hoot, asked his host, "What's that?" "It's an owl," he was told. "I know," smiled the Britisher, "but who's 'owling?"

A couple of G.I.'s in Piccadilly were hoisting their third pint of bitters at a neighborhood pub when one nudged the other, saying, "Max, I think that high-classh, tony-lookin' gent hanging onto the barshtool there ish the Archbishop of Canterbury."

"You're shtupid drunk," hicc'd the other, "What's the Archbishop of Canterbury gonna be doing here in a creepy bar guzzling beer?" "I'm drunk? I'm drunk?" yelled the first. "That'sh what I shaid. You're drunk." "Anyway, I say he's the Archbishop of Canterbury." "You're crazy."

Two pints of bitters later, Max reeled off his chair and teetered toward the high-class tony-lookin' gent to see if he really was the Archbishop of Canterbury. When he asked the question, the man cursed him, his ancestors, his children, smacked him in the teeth, stepped on him, kicked him, told him to mind his own business and stalked out angrily. "Too bad," said Max, "now we'll never know."

After being injured in a cricket match (which wasn't cricket—it was crooked) the English sportsman went to a doctor who put three stitches in his wound. "That'll be five pounds," the M.D. told him. "Five pounds?" howled the injured one, "for three stitches?" "That's right," smiled the doctor. "Boy," said the patient, "am I happy you're not my tailor."

After spending a year at Oxford, the son of an old English nobleman returned home for his summer vacation. "And now that you've spent a year at the University, what did you find the hardest thing to deal with?" the old man asked. His son answered, "An old deck of cards."

A brilliant but homely English diplomat, sure he would land a position at the British Embassy in Washington, was heartbroken when he was nixed at zero hour. "I say, sir, but why was I turned down?" he asked his superior. "There's no doubt, Chauncey old man, that you're a whiz at foreign affairs," he was told, "but we cahn't possibly send anyone to Washington who doesn't look good before a TV camera."

A snobbish young Britisher who was so British he could barely talk a-tall visited Washington's home in Mount Vernon. He was promenading through the gardens when he spotted a hedge that looked like one he had back home in Stratfordshire on the Hertfordshire. "Ah, my good chap," he told the caretaker, "you see that hedge? George got that from jolly old England." "I don't doubt it," smiled the gardener. "As you probably know, he got this whole blooming country from England."

An American boasted to an Englishman about the speed of American trains. "In America," he bragged, "our trains are so fast that telegraph poles look like a continuous fence." "Ha," snuffed the Britisher, "that's nothing. I was on such a fast train in England last week that I passed a field of turnips, a field of carrots, one of cabbage and then a pond. . . . and we were going so fast that I thought it was broth.

BRITISH GUIDE: (showing place of interest): It was in this room that Lord Wellington received his first commission.
AMERICAN TOURIST: How much was it?

A man toddled into a London antique shop and offered for sale a piece of silk he claimed to be part of Sir Walter Raleigh's garment. The proprietor called his assistant, "Oh, Newton!" and Newt shuffled forward, affixed his eyeglass, studied the silk and wheezed, "It's Sir Walter's all right, but we have two yards of the same thing in our storeroom."

Next day the man returned with a piece of the original ark, and again the owner called, "Oh Newton!" and again Newt came forward, affixed his eyeglass, examined it and said, "It's from the ark but we have the rest of it in our storeroom."

The following week the same man returned. He told the owner he had one of Nero's eyes and said, "And don't send for Newt. I have the other one in my pocket."

ETIQUETTE (see also Manners)

There is no man so bad that a woman cannot make him worse.

A bird in the hand is bad table manners.

Is my face clean enough to eat with? Yes, but you'd better use your hands.

Social tact is making your company feel at home, even though they wish they were.

He's just bashful. Why don't you give him a little encouragement? Encouragement? He needs a cheering section.

He died an unhappy death. He was afraid his last breath would be a hiccough, and he wouldn't be able to say, "Excuse me."

"Do you know what to do with crumbs at the table?"
"Sure, let them stay there."

What is the first thing you do when you get up from the table? I put on my shoes.

He eats with his fingers and talks with his fork.

"You know, I think there's something wrong with my boss' eyes."
"How's that?"

"When I went into his office this morning he asked me three times where my hat was—and it was on my head all the time."

"Stop! Act like a gentleman."
"Sorry, but I don't do imitations."

"This man is following me around and he's been doing that for fifteen minutes. Tell him to stop."
"Don't be silly. That's the butler and he's trying to serve you cocktails."

"When I sneeze I put my hand in front of my mouth."
"Really, Phil? Why do you do that?"
"To catch my teeth!"

Another thing, the next time you butter your bread—when you've finished buttering it, don't fold it and then eat it.

He embarrassed us—he drank his soup and six couples got up and danced.

"When you yawn you put your hand to your mouth."
"What? And get bitten?"

EXAGGERATION

"Those Kansas cyclones must be terrible."

"G'wan, down in Florida the wind was so strong it blew out the fuses."

Two men met at a race track and started a conversation.
"I've got a horse that's faster than any automobile."
"Faster than any automobile? Who was he sired by?"
"What do you mean?"
"What was his father's name?"
"I told you he was fast. Why, he is so fast, he ran away before he found out what his father's name was."

He's the fastest person imaginable. He can ring the front doorbell, go to the back door and run through to the front of the house in time to let himself in.

EXAMINATIONS (see also College, School)

When better exams are made —they won't be passed.

"Whatcha been doing?"
"Taking part in a guessing contest."
"But I thought you had an exam in math."
"I did."

PROFESSOR: Why the quotation marks all over this paper?
STUDENT: Courtesy to the man on my right, professor.

"Did you pass your finals?"
"And how."
"Were they easy?"
"Dunno . . . ask Jim."

"I would have passed my examination but for one thing."
"What was that?"
"The little boy that always sits back of me was sick."

EXECUTIVE (see also Boss)

A good executive is a man who believes in sharing the credit with the man who did the work.

An executive came home one night and slumped unhappily into his favorite chair. Noticing his state, his wife asked what was wrong. "Well," he moaned, "you know those aptitude tests I'm giving over at the office? I took one today and it sure is a good thing I own the company."

EXERCISE (see also Diet, Health, Figure)

MIKE: What made you join the police force?
IKE: My doctor told me I should get more exercise.
MIKE: What has getting more exercise got to do with being a policeman?
IKE: Why should I walk on my

own time when I can be a policeman and get paid for it?"

DOT: Jim's father is an efficiency expert.
DASH: How's that?
DOT: He walks in his sleep so he can get his rest and exercise at the same time.

OUTDOOR MAN: What do you do for exercise?
BOOKWORM: Oh, I let my flesh creep.

EXPENSIVE (see also Money)

When the waiter brought the bill, the diner complained, "What's this five dollars for?" The waiter answered patiently, "A chopped liver sandwich." The diner screamed, "Whose liver was it—Rockefeller's?"

EXPLANATION

Myron Cohen says this drunk was walking along Fifth Avenue at 4 A.M. in a state of panic. A cop approached him and growled, "Do you have an explanation?" The poor soul answered, "If I had an explanation, I would be home with my wife."

EYES

PATIENT: Doctor, will I be able to read after I get my glasses?
DOCTOR: Indeed, you will.
PATIENT: Well, that'll be great. I never could read before.

The proofreader told his friend that when he went home in the dark he would open his newspaper.
"It's pitch dark and you sit down to read the paper?"
"That's right."
"Don't tell me you read in the dark."
"It rests my eyes."
"How can you see the print?"
"I can't. That's how it rests my eyes."

"What's the idea of that cross-eyed man for a store detective?"
"Well, look at him! Can you tell who he is watching?"

LOIS: I had trouble with my eyes —I saw spots in front of my eyes.
ANN: Do your glasses help?
LOIS: Yes.—Now I can see the spots much better.

F

FACE

Two beautifully groomed women entered a restaurant and passed the table where two men were seated.

FIRST MAN: Those girls look exactly alike. Are they twins?

SECOND MAN: Oh, no. They merely went to the same plastic surgeon.

The heavily jeweled dowager was consulting a specialist.

"What will the operation of lifting my face cost, doctor?" she asked.

"Five thousand dollars, madame."

"That's robbery," she protested. "Isn't there something less expensive I could try?"

"You might try wearing a veil," he answered.

FAMILY (See also Parents and Children, Dad, Father, Relations)

Due to the tax advantages of a partnership, Crosby has his family set up as a partnership. When the Internal Revenue office questioned Kathy Grant if she was actively engaged in the partnership she said, "of course. . . . I'm producing new partners."

In my family my mother got up at five o'clock every morning. . . . no matter what time it was.

TEACHER: How do you like your new home, Johnny?

JOHNNY: Great. It's so big all of us have our own rooms, except for Mom . . . She's still in with Dad.

My mother had some women's ailment and so she went to see her nephew, who was a gynecologist. After the examination was over she looked him straight in the eye and said, "Tell me, does your mother know how you make a living?"

FAMOUS

"Do you know who Patrick Henry was and what he did?"

"Sure. He's the fellow that started the gimmies."

"The gimmies?"

"Yeah—he said: 'Gimme liberty or gimme death.'"

"Why have people given up all other creeds and followed Mahatma Gandhi?"
"I guess because they would like to start life with a new sheet."

PAUL REVERE: (Shouting at window) Husband at home?
LADY: Yes.
PAUL REVERE: Tell him the British are coming. (Shouting at another window) Husband at home?
LADY: No.
PAUL REVERE: To hell with the British.

"He doesn't even know when George Washington was born. Washington was born in Virginia in 1732."
"I saw that in a book, but I thought it was the phone number."

FARM (see also Farmer)

1ST MAN: What do you know about farming?
2ND MAN: I come from a long line of men who spent their lives on farms.
1ST MAN: Oh, farmers.
2ND MAN: No, travelling salesmen.

GUY TRAPPED IN FIELD WITH BULL: Hey, is this bull safe?
FARMER: He's a darn sight safer'n you are.

1ST MAN: Crossing a cow with a mule? What do you expect to get?
2ND MAN: Milk with a kick in it.

1ST MAN: He told me to feed sheep ironized yeast.
2ND MAN: Why?
1ST MAN: So we can get steel wool from sheep. Yesterday we scraped off two pounds of Brillo.

1ST MAN: My father was a gentleman farmer. Every time he milked a cow he tipped his hat.
2ND MAN: Why did he tip his hat?
1ST MAN: He didn't have any pail.

FARMER: On my cattle ranch I got 5000 head of cows and one bull.
CITY MAN: You must be an independent man.
FARMER: Not half as independent as that bull.

FARMER: On a typical day I have to get up at six in the morning, then I work for five hours, then I take out a few minutes for lunch, then I work another five hours . . .
CITY MAN: With all that work, what do you grow?
FARMER: Tired.

FARMER: I redecorated the hen house and the chickens love it.

CITY MAN: What did you put in it?
FARMER: Roosters.

FARMER (see also Farm)

You gave me the wrong steer, said the milkmaid, as she came away with an empty pail.

Maw and Pa had an awful time getting married. Maw wouldn't marry Pa when he was drunk and Pa wouldn't marry Maw when he was sober.

"That's the last straw," said the farmer, "And there wasn't a dad-gummed needle in the haystack."

"Lived here all your life?"
"Don't know. Haven't died yet."

"What's your mother so upset about?"
"Oh, the cat went and littered up the place."

"He was tramped to death, by sheep."
"Sort of dyed-in-the-wool, eh?"

"Where does this land lead to?"
"Well it's led half of the young folks around these parts into trouble."

"Sammy, do you know what a gentleman farmer is?"

"Yes, Ma'am. It's a man who loves cows but doesn't know how to milk them."

FAT PEOPLE (also see Diet)

KEN: Davis certainly married a big woman, didn't he?
DAVE: Yes, but you ought to see the one he got away from.

He was describing his father to a friend.
"He is so fat in shorts he looks like a chiffonier," he said.
"How is that?" asked his friend.
"A big thing with drawers," answered the boy.

Two traveling acquaintances met after some years.
FIRST TRAVELER: I lost one hundred and seventy pounds since I last saw you.
SECOND TRAVELER: How so?
FIRST TRAVELER: My husband left me.

FATHERS (see also Dad, Family, Parents and Children)

"Why were you kissing my daughter last night in that dark corner?"
"Now that I've seen her in the daylight I sort of wonder myself."

"What do you think of them?" (Proud father of triplets).

"I'd keep that one." (Pointing to middle one).

A SMALL BOY: Dad give me a dime.

FATHER: Not today, sonny, not today.

SMALL BOY: Dad, if you'll give me the dime I'll tell you what the iceman said to Mama this morning.

FATHER: Here, son, quick, what did he say?

SMALL BOY: He said, "Lady, how much ice do you want this morning."

Nurse to expectant father:
"Just because you've been kept waiting so long doesn't necessarily mean the baby will be a girl."

FATHER: (At hospital looking through glass at newly arrived babies) Kitchy kitchy koo. Look she smiled . . . isn't she adorable.

FRIEND: But your kid didn't smile.

FATHER: I was talking about the nurse.

FATHER TO HIS YOUNG SON: How dare you disobey your mother! Do you think you're better than I am?

FEET

"I have a terrible corn on the bottom of my foot," said Jack.

"That's a fine place to have it. Nobody can step on it but you," replied Pat.

"Does he really have big feet?"
"Well, all I know is that when we were on the train together, he needed a shine, and the porter shined one of his shoes and a suitcase."

A pretty girl who was continually being kissed on the forehead must have invented high heels.

FIBBING (see also Lying, Lies, Liar)

"I used to hold him on my knee when he was a baby."
"But he's much older than you are."
"So all right—he used to hold me on his knee."

He calls himself a duke. The closest he ever came to royalty is when he was stung by a Queen Bee.

"If you tell lies you won't be like George Washington."
"Don't you tell lies?"
"No."
"You're like George Washington then?"
"Yes."
"Everyone tells lies. Mommy, and Uncle Louie and everyone."
"Well?"

"It's going to be awfully lonesome in heaven."

"What do you mean?"

"Just you and George Washington."

The best thing about telling the truth is that you don't have to remember what you said.

"Can you tell by your husband's face if he's lying?"

"Yes, if his lips are moving, he is."

FIGHTERS

The fighter was getting the beating of his life. Both eyes were cut and bleeding and his nose was broken. His ribs were the color of ketchup as he returned to his corner at the end of the fifth round. His manager consoled him as he applied medication to his busted face and body. "You're going great on the radio, the announcer is a friend of mine."

The fighter had been taking a beating for eight rounds. When he came back to his corner his second cautioned, "As it stands now, you gotta knock that guy out to get a draw."

PROUD PUGILIST: "The last guy I fought is still in the hospital."

"Yeah? What happened?"

"He broke his hand when he knocked me out."

That bum was knocked out so many times, he sells advertising space on the soles of his shoes.

FIGHTS

I had a terrible fight with my wife. I said, "You know, you're going to drive me to my grave." In two minutes she had the car in front of the house.

FIGURE (see also Diet)

In the twenty years we've been married not only has my wife kept her figure . . . she's doubled it.

WOMAN: You've just got to help me reduce. My husband just gave me a present and I can't get into it.

VIC TANNY: Don't worry, madame, in two weeks you'll be able to get into that dress.

WOMAN: What dress? It's a Volkswagen.

"She's built like the State of Indiana."

"What do you mean?"

"She's got a big South Bend."

She has an Atomic Bomb figure . . . lots of fallout.

"I've been making a survey of girls' figures in New York and comparing them to girls' figures in California."

"Well, what did you decide?"

"To keep studying."

She has a Supreme Court figure . . . no appeal.

Some women are terrible at counting calories . . . and they have figures to prove it.

FILMS

"I saw your new picture."

"Oh did you? I haven't seen it yet—today."

"Oh, yes, my father likes you in pictures. He sat close to the screen."

"He must like it."

"You know that scene where you dance with the leading lady?"

"Yes."

"He got up and cut in four times."

We're making a western picture. This is a western that'll make all the other westerns look like easterns.

"He liked the polka dot suit you wore in that picture."

"I didn't wear any polka dot suit."

"Not at first, but he was sitting in the first row with a plug of tobacco in his mouth."

This picture was photographed in a cemetery so it would have a plot.

The fellow is on the way to marry a movie actress and is delayed enroute. He wires her: DELAYED ENROUTE. DON'T MARRY ANYONE UNTIL I ARRIVE.

Because of the great number of foreign actors and actresses in Hollywood, someone placed this sign on the studio gate: ENGLISH SPOKEN HERE.

A male movie star, always thinking of his public, had an X-ray photo of his teeth retouched before showing it to the dentist.

Things are so quiet in Hollywood now that you can hear an executive dropped.

Describing the preview of a supposedly humorous picture: Everybody has a good time except the audience.

The movie extra went to the doctor who gave him five pills and told him to take one after every meal. That was a week ago and the extra has four pills left.

FIRES

FIRST FROM LEFT: There was a fire in the dressing room of the star backstage. The firemen were there six hours.

SECOND FROM LEFT: Six hours to put out a fire in a dressing room?

FIRST FROM LEFT: Oh, no—it took them one hour to put out the fire, but it took five hours to put out the firemen.

A new office boy was being shown his duties by the head clerk.

OFFICE BOY: What are those buckets for on the shelf in the back room?

CLERK: Can't you read? It says on them "For Fire Only."

OFFICE BOY: Then why do they put water in them?

CHORUS GIRL: Do you know you'd make a wonderful fireman?

PLAYBOY: How's that?

CHORUS GIRL: You'd never take your eyes off the hose.

FISHING

Two fishermen were trying to convince some friends of their luck. "I went fishing the other day," lied one, "and caught one of these big fish—let me see, what is it you call them?" he asked, turning to his fibbing partner. "Oh yes, you mean—whale," assisted the second fisherman. "No, not that," protested the first, "That couldn't have been it; I was using whale for bait!"

"And the fish we finally caught," said the second fisherman, "was too small to bother with, so we got a couple of men to help us throw it back into the water."

1ST MAN: Catch any fish in this stream?

2ND MAN: Nope.

1ST MAN: Then why do you fish here?

2ND MAN: Just for the halibut.

Lox—that's a herring with high blood pressure.

1ST WOMAN: You know, every time my husband goes fishing he comes back with something.

2ND WOMAN: Yeah, but who can eat sunburn and poison ivy?

1ST MAN: The big sardines in the ocean eat the little sardines.

2ND MAN: Really? How do they get them out of the can?

1ST MAN: A big crab bit off one of my toes.

2ND MAN: Really, which one?

1ST MAN: How do I know? All them crabs look alike.

My sister caught a fish . . . he's now my brother-in-law.

He tried to cross electric eel with jelly fish to see if he could get currant jelly.

FLIRTATION (also see Kiss, Love)

SHE: Spent the vacation up in the mountains.
HE: Really. Did you have a guide?
SHE: Well, only my conscience.

PRETTY SHOPGIRL: Could I interest you in a bathing costume, sir?
MR. GAY: You certainly could, baby, but my wife is over there at the glove counter.

SHE: Is it true that John stops and parks on the dark roads?
HER: No, he does the parking, I do the stopping.

HE: Why did you jump out of the car last night and start running home?
SHE: I was being chaste.

HE: Shall we waltz?
SHE: It's all the same to me.
HE: Yes, I've noticed that.

"And I," said Coed Kitty, "wear black garters in memory of those who have passed beyond."

HE: I love you more than I can say.
SHE: Yes, yes, go on.
HE: But I can't without your permission.

The little girl who used to want an all-day sucker, now just wants one for the evening.

"I'm a somnambulist."
"That's all right; I'll go to my church after we're married and you can go to yours."

"How old are you, Mary?"
"Fifteen."
"A girl of your age should tell her mother everything."
"I know it. But mother is so innocent, really, I haven't got the heart."

FLOWERS

1ST MAN: My girl friend always wears an intoxicating floral scent.
2ND MAN: Yeah, I've noticed— four roses.

MAN TO SHOPKEEPER: I want you to pick out a bouquet of flowers for my girl friend.
SHOPKEEPER: Long stems?
MAN: Yes, and she has beautiful hair, too.

1ST MAN: She bent over to cut some flowers.

2ND MAN: Early Spring bloomers, I guess?

1ST MAN: No, she wears the same kind all year round.

1ST MAN: These roses are $12.00 a dozen. I raised them myself.

2ND MAN: You raised them yourself?

1ST MAN: Yes, yesterday they were $10.00 a dozen.

QUESTION TO PONDER: What do you send to a sick florist?

FOG (see also England)

The fog is so thick in England, the farmers have to milk the cows by radar.

It's so foggy in San Francisco that on a clear day you can see the fog.

1ST MAN: She's the most beautiful woman in the world and yet I've never been able to really see her.

2ND MAN: Why not?

1ST MAN: Every time I look at her my glasses fog up.

It's so foggy in England, I was ten years old before I met my mother. And ten years later I found out she was my father wearing a kilt.

FOOD (see also Cooking, Meal Diets)

A couple of hoboes came to a backdoor and asked the lady of the house for some food. She said to them, "See that big rug hanging out there on the line? Well, beat the dirt out of that rug, and I'll give you both a nice lunch." They each got a large bat and started beating the rug. A short time later, the lady glanced out of the window and was surprised to see one of the bums jumping in the air, doing somersaults and back flips. She went out and said to the other man, "I didn't know your partner was an acrobat." He replied, "Neither did I, till I hit him in the shins with this bat!"

DINER: You call this creamed lobster your special? I can find neither cream nor lobster in it.

WAITER: Yes, sir. That's what makes it special.

When he heard that a rival restaurant had burned down, a restaurant owner said, "I'm sorry to hear about it, but it's the first time the food's hot in his place."

A hungry Irishman went into a restaurant on Friday and asked the waiter, "Have you any lobster?"

"No."

"Have you any shrimp?"

"No."

"All right," said the Irishman, "then bring me a steak smothered with onions. The Lord knows I asked for fish."

An old "sourdough" was lost in the Alaskan wilderness. He hadn't eaten in several days, and in a last desperate effort to stave off starvation, he killed his faithful dog, Rover, cooked him, and ate him. As he ate the meat off each bone, he piled the bones into a neat pile. Suddenly he gazed at the bones, and tears came to his eyes as he said to himself, "Gee, Rover would have loved those bones."

Metrecal, the new diet food just won the no belly (Nobel) prize.

"With Metrecal you now can drink your meals."

"Big deal. Dean Martin has been drinking his meals for years!"

FATHER: What have you learned to cook at cooking school?
DAUGHTER: We haven't gotten as far as cooking yet, we're only up to thawing.

I don't mind my wife serving TV dinners, but now she's starting to serve re-runs.

Joe E. Lewis has a new drink, Metrecal and gin: "I still see pink elephants but they're thinner."

FOOTBALL (see also Sports)

"Are those fifty-cent seats far from the scene of action?" asked a customer at the box office.

"No, not very far," answered the agent, "and besides, they're right across the street from a radio store that will broadcast the game."

HE: How did the college get such a bad name?
SHE: More men reported for football than were enrolled in school.

GRACE: The Sing Sing football team wants to play the West Point team.
GEORGE: I wonder why Sing Sing wants to play the Army.
GRACE: They probably want to prove the pen is mightier than the sword.

FOREIGN LANGUAGES

"Can you read Chinese?"

"Only when it's printed in English."

"Mr. Twirp, what do you know about French syntax?"

"Gosh, I didn't know they had to pay for their fun."

Sign seen in store window: ENGLISH SPOKEN — AMERICAN UNDERSTOOD.

FORTUNATE

If you did bring home the bacon it would be your luck to bring it home on Friday and wait till Saturday to eat it.

"Friday is very unlucky."
"What makes you think that?"
"Well, Washington, Napoleon, and Lincoln were all born on Friday and look at them all now —all dead."

He had tough luck. He had a check for ten dollars and the only person who could cash it was a fellow to whom he owed nine dollars.

Three on a match is bad, especially if it's a matrimonial match.

"You know, Gene, I've got a lucky charm that keeps me from going broke."
"Nonsense, I don't believe in lucky charms."
"I know what I know! With my charm I'll always have money in my pocket."

"What is this charm?"
"A hundred dollar gold piece!"

An engineer friend of mine, when taking his shower, slipped on the soap. Then he tore his shirt while he was putting it on. On the way out of the house he fell down the stairs.

He finally got out on his run, and as he was traveling sixty miles per hour, he looked ahead, and there he saw another train coming towards him at the same speed on the same track. He turned to the fireman and said, "Joe, have you ever had one of those days when everything went dead wrong?"

Take a chance, only fifty cents . . . The fellow wins . . . He offers the salesman either $1000 a year for life or $10,000 in cash . . . The fellow takes the cash . . . You'd better give me the ten thousand in cash. With your luck I wouldn't live another six months.

FOSTER, PHIL

I feel that certain jokes have been around long enough and used long enough, so I figure we form a joke "Hall of Fame." All the old jokes will be retired— given a number—and laid to rest in the "Hall of Fame," never to be used again.

Here are my contributions of jokes that are up for the "Hall of Fame:"

"Do you know how to drive a baby buggy?"
"No."
"Tickle its feet."

Guy walks in drugstore, says to clerk, "Make me a malted."
Clerk says, "Poof, you're a malted."

RESTAURANT OWNER: Do you like the food?
PATRON: I could get more nourishment biting my lip.

Inflation is really here. I gave my kid a nickel and he thought it was a medal.

Now that the war is over you can get parts for your head.

"Were you born in Brooklyn?"
"Yes."
"What part?"
"All of me."

"Did you get a haircut?"
"No I got all of them cut."

My uncle slept in the chandelier. He was a light sleeper.

FRANCE (also see French)

An American and French bride were discussing love. "A Frenchman is very subtle when it comes to love," the French girl explained. "He begins by kissing the fingertips, then he kisses the shoulder, then the back of the neck . . ." "Boy," the little American bride interrupted, "by that time an American husband is back from his honeymoon!"

In France, the postman isn't the only working person who who has to walk the streets to pick up the male.

Modern French Westerns are so adult that instead of having a bartender, the local saloon has a maître d'.

The proud old Frenchman put on the uniform and all the medals he had worn during his glory days in the First World War. He looked into the mirror and remembered how it had been. He noticed his five-year-old grandson staring at the medals. "What's the matter, lad?" he asked. "Oh nothing, Grandpa, but I was wondering why you're wearing your money outside your coat?"

During the German occupation of France a peasant who worked

for the underground was captured. Now and then he received a letter from his wife, who complained she was having a difficult time with their farm. She had plenty of seed potatoes but she couldn't plow the fields by herself. He wrote back, "It is all for the best, ma chère. Leave the fields unplowed. That's where the guns are."

Four days later, two truckloads of Gestapo men descended on the farm and dug up all the acreage. Frantically, the wife wrote to her husband telling him what had happened and asked him what to do.

He wrote back a brief note: "Now plant the potatoes."

A Brooklynite, touring Gay Paree, stopped a Frenchman and asked, "Where's the place the most of the Americans stay?" The Frenchman replied, "The first ten rows of the Folies Bergère."

My friend laughed when I spoke to the waiter in French but the laugh was on him. I told the waiter to give him the check.

A French husband raced into a psychiatrist's office and shouted, "Doc, you've got to help me. My wife thinks she's Brigitte Bardot." The headshrinker thought for a moment and then told the fellow,

"If you bring her in for treatments, I'm sure I can help her." "That's wonderful, Doc," the man smiled, "but make sure your office is heated, because my wife always goes around in the nude and I wouldn't want her to catch a cold."

The scene is a Paris street corner. A shady-looking character approaches a New York tourist and after glancing in all directions to see that he's safe, nudges the tourist and the following gab follows: "Americain?" . . . "Yeah." . . . "Tourist?" . . . "Yeah." . . . "Want whoopie?" . . . "Naaah." . . . "Postcards?" . . . "Naaah." . . . "Strip-tease night club?" . . . "Naaah." . . . "Strip-tease without night club?" . . . "Naaah." . . . "Model posing for artist?" . . . "Naaah." . . . "Artist posing for model?" . . . "Naaah." . . . "Kosher delicatessen?" . . . "Ah ha, now you're talking."

Two Parisians, François and Louis, got into an argument about a lady, and before you knew it one word led to another and thousands more followed, so they finally agreed to settle the matter by a pistol duel in the park. At seven on the appointed morning, François was on hand with his pistol and his second and his physician, but no Louis. A few minutes later a messenger arrived with a note from Louis which read: *Dear François, if I happen to be late, don't wait for me. Go ahead and shoot.*

From France comes the story of twin brothers in a historic French family. One was raised to become a soldier, the other a priest. But, as brothers sometimes do, they disliked each other intensely and had been away from each other for many, many years. One day they finally came face to face in the Eastern Station of Paris. By now the older brother had become a marshal of France and the younger brother a cardinal.

As the prince of the Church saw his brother on the platform, a mischievous smile appeared on his lips and walking over to the soldier he said, "Pardon me, Station Master, but when is the next train for Metz?" The marshal blinked for a moment, then saluted smartly and said, "Sorry, I really don't know, madame."

Things must be getting tough in France. I just got a post card from Paris and there was writing on it.

In France, the men like to stay out until the *"Oui"* hours of the morning.

FREAKS

"I'm going to join a circus."
"What are you going to do in a circus?"
"I'm going to be a midget."
"You're too big for a midget."
"That's the idea. I'll be the biggest midget in the world."

FAT LADY: The human skeleton won't eat anything but olives.
LION TAMER: He won't eat anything but olives?
FAT LADY: No. Tonight he ate so many olives for dinner that he looked like a string of beads.

"My brother won his fight last night," exulted Frank.
"Why, I didn't know he was such a good fighter," replied Sam.
"He isn't such a good fighter— but he had a lot of pictures tattooed on his chest and his opponent got so interested in the pictures he forgot to fight."

FRENCH (also see France)

1ST GIRL: So in Paris I met this masseur . . .
2ND GIRL: Not masseur, but monsieur. A masseur is a guy who rubs you, pinches you, squeezes you and massages you all over.
1ST GIRL: Like I said . . . I met this masseur.

I took my wife to the Folies Bergère. That's like taking a meatball to a twelve course dinner.

1ST GIRL: The French are so gallant . . . they always kiss a lady's hand.

2ND GIRL: They've got the right idea but their aim's a little off.

Overheard as Brigitte Bardot attended a movie premiere:

1ST WOMAN: She's beautiful. I wonder who made her dress.

2ND WOMAN: Probably the police.

FRESH PEOPLE

She had been conspicuously absent from the dance floor and her fiancé went out to find her. As they returned he said: "I saw that stranger kissing you."

"Yes," she answered.

"Where is the guy? I'll teach him a thing or two," he raged.

"Ah darling, I don't think you could," she sighed.

GERTIE: That fresh taxicab driver offered me a quarter for a kiss.

FRIEND: What are you looking in your pocketbook for?

GERTIE: Gee! I thought I'd lost the quarter.

A woman came up to a policeman on his beat and said: Oh,

officer! There's a man following me and I think he must be drunk.

The officer scrutinized the woman and answered, "Yes, he must be!"

"Who was that guy that kissed you today on the street?"

"I don't know, but he evidently knew me pretty well."

FRIENDS

Did you know that Marilyn Monroe and Jayne Mansfield are great friends? As a matter of fact, you might call them bosom pals.

1ST MAN: What do you mean—you were pen pals?

2ND MAN: We were at Alcatraz together.

I never realized what wonderful friends I had until I sailed for Europe. Then three of my buddies came to see me off. They brought candy, cigars and liquor. And when the boat left the pier there they were . . . eating, smoking and drinking.

When a fella needs a friend he often makes a mistake and gets a wife.

FUNERALS (see also Death, Dying, Undertaker)

A group of townspeople were seated in a local barbershop attempting to eulogize a citizen who had just died. For years the fellow had been the most hated man in town and no one could think of anything good to say about him. Eventually, after more than an hour of silence, the barber spoke up. "You know," he said, "I must admit he wasn't a hard man to shave."

A New York newspaper, in an article on air-raid procedures, stated, FUNERAL COACHES ALSO MUST PARK, BUT THE OCCUPANTS MAY REMAIN IN THEM.

A New Hampshire farmer had been urged to attend the funeral of his neighbor's third wife. "But I'm not going," he announced to his own spouse. "Goodness sakes, why not?" she asked. "Well, Mary, I'm beginning to feel kind of awkward about goin' so often without anything of the sort to ask him back to."

ITALIAN: Hey, whatsa a polar bear do?
FRIEND: What's a polar bear do? Why he sits on a cake of ice and wears a white fur coat. . . .
ITALIAN: Thena I ain't going toa doa it.
FRIEND: Do what?
ITALIAN: One ofa my paisans die and hisa wife wanna I should be a polar bear at his funeral.

Sign in front of a cemetery entrance: "Due to a strike, grave-digging will be done by a skeleton crew."

1ST MAN: What an expensive funeral. It must have cost his family a fortune.
2ND MAN: No he died on the Pay-as-You-Go-Plan.

FINNEGAN: And at my funeral I want you to pour a bottle of Irish whiskey over me grave.
MCBRIDE: Sure bucko . . . but would you mind if I passed it through me kidneys first?

WOMAN (to cemetery director): I can't find my husband's grave.
DIRECTOR: His name please . . .
WOMAN: Nick Knack . . .
DIRECTOR: Hmmm, we have no Nick Knack . . . but we have a Joan Knack.
WOMAN: That's him . . . everything's in my name.

A man went to Florida for his health but after two weeks he died and his body was shipped back home for the funeral. Two friends now look at him as he lies in his casket.
1ST FRIEND: Doesn't he look wonderful?
2ND FRIEND: Yeh, I think those two weeks in Florida did him a world of good.

FUR

This customer came into my show room and said he wanted something in a mink—my model.

Cross mink with kangaroo to get fur coats with pockets in them.

1ST GIRL: That's a gorgeous fur coat you're wearing. What did you do for it?
2ND GIRL: Just shortened the sleeves.

She says that coat is dyed mink. From the looks of it, it must have died a horrible death.

1ST GIRL: How did *she* get a mink coat?
2ND GIRL: The same way the minks get them.

The only way you can get a mink nowadays is to be like a fox and play cat and mouse with a wolf.

"I just gave my wife a chin-chinchilla coat."
"Chin-chinchilla coat? Why the double chin?"
"She eats too much."

1ST WOMAN: That's a beautiful mink you're wearing.
2ND WOMAN: Oh, it's just a little conversation piece I picked up.

—My husband never stops talking about it.

FUR COATS

Public Notice: WILL THE MAN WHO FOUND A FUR COAT HERE IN THE STUDIO LAST WEEK PLEASE RETURN THE BLONDE THAT WAS IN IT.

It seems there's a New York furrier who has been trying to get a longer-lasting, cheaper fur by mating a mink with a chimpanzee, but it doesn't work.—The sleeves are too long.

FURNITURE (see also Homes, House)

Sign above an antique shop. "Old furniture and junk bought. Genuine antiques sold."

All my furniture goes back to Louis the 14th . . . that is unless we pay Louis before the 14th.

I've got a sunken living room. —The plumbing leaks.

Is this French Provincial 1809? No, it's Sears Roebuck $148.

CUSTOMER: I'm looking for an unusual chair.
SALESMAN: Would you like to see Chippendale?

CUSTOMER: No. I saw those guys in vaudeville.

Is this Early American? No it's late depression.

"What happened to your Morris chair?
"Morris took it back."

This is period furniture. They let us keep it for a period; then they take it back.

"This bear skin rug cost me $2,000."
"From the looks of it I don't know who got skinned the most, you or the bear."

"What happened to your kidney table?"
"Oh it's floating around somewhere."

This is a genuine horsehair mattress. Every time you sit on it, it whinnies.

❖❖

G

GAMBLING (See also Betting, Las Vegas, Money, Racetrack)

One horseplayer to another horseplayer: You said he was a great horse and he sure is. It took eleven other horses to beat him.

As your plane approaches Las Vegas the stewardess says: "We are now approaching Las Vegas. Please fasten your money belts."

The trouble with hitting the jackpot on a slot machine is that it takes so long to put the money back in the machine.

"He's a poor loser."

"Did you ever hear of a rich one?"

"He died during a card game."
"What did he die of?"
"Five aces."

I wouldn't say the roulette wheel was crooked, but how come the table says Tilt?

One gambling hotel in Las Vegas will send a table and dealer to your room. "That's what we call room service here," the manager bragged.

It's still tougher to make a six with two threes than a Gabor with two Zsas.

Nevada is famous for its gambling. This is one place where money isn't everything—if you stay there long enough, it's nothing.

I bet on this horse yesterday and he went off at 10 to 1 . . . and came in at a quarter to four.

Never shoot craps with ladies. They get sore when you make passes at them.

1st Man: Did you bet on the fight last night?
2nd Man: Oh yes, with me $5000 is like nothing.
1st Man: How much did you bet?
2nd Man: Nothing.

GAMES (see also Sports)

We had a big party and all the folks at the party played a game I invented. It's called "Christmas Tree."
I never heard of the game. What is it like?
Everyone stands in the corner and tries to get lit up.

"By the way—you saw our bridge game last night. How would you have played that last hand of mine?" asked the dub.

"Under an assumed name," was the expert's reply.

"Hullo! City Bridge Department?"
"Yes. What can we do for you?"
"How many points do you get for a little slam?"

GARDENS (see also Homes)

Carl: What's that you have in your buttonhole?
Earl: Why, that's a chrysanthemum.
Carl: It looks like a rose to me.
Earl: Nope, you're wrong, its a chrysanthemum.
Carl: Spell it.
Earl: K-r-i-s . . . by golly, that is a rose!

"Now, this plant," explained the horticulturist patiently, "belongs to the begonia family."
"Ah, yes," chirped the sweet old lady, "and you're looking after it for them while they're away on a holiday?"

"I wonder," pondered the small boy, "why they always have such beautiful illustrations in seed catalogues."
"To show people what the seeds they planted would look like if they had ever come up," answered his disillusioned parent.

GEOGRAPHY

"Where are the Andes?"
"I don't know; if you'd put things where they belong, you'd be able to find 'em."

"Tommy, tell me where Mexico is."
"It's on page ten of the joggerfy."

"Where is the capital of the United States?"
"All over the world."

"You don't even know the shape of the earth."
"I do, it's square."
"No, it's round."
"Well, my brother says he's traveled to the four corners of the earth.'"

"Can you tell me how California is bounded?"
"It's bounded on the west by movie stars; on the bottom by oil; on the north by sun; on the top by sundown; on the south by Tia Juana and on the east by Maine."

GERMANY

Two Germans were talking. One said, "Do you know, if Hitler had lived he would have been seventy?" And the other German said, "Too bad, too bad." The first one asked, "What d'ya mean, too bad? That he's dead?" And the second German said, "Oh, no, that he was born!"

A German and Russian were on a river in Germany. The German was fishing on the American side and was catching fish right and left, one after the other, but the Russian on the Russian Zone side wasn't having any luck at all. He yelled to the German, "How do you manage to catch so many fish?" and the answer came back, "Over here the fish aren't afraid to open their mouths."

They tell the story in Berlin about an argument between an American officer and a Russian officer over what constituted democracy and in which country the real democracy was truly practiced. The American said, "Why, back home a fellow living out in the midwestern part of the country can hop a train, be in Washington in a couple of days, walk down Pennsylvania Avenue, make arrangements to get into the White House and walk into the President's office and say, 'Mr. President Kennedy, you're a stupid man.' He can do that and he wouldn't even be arrested."
The Russian officer said, "That's exactly the kind of democracy we have in Russia. A peasant from any small village

could start out for Stalingrad, get there in a couple of months—maybe—spend another few months getting to Moscow, go to the Kremlin, walk in, knock on Krushchev's door and say, 'Comrade Krushchev, President Kennedy's a stupid man'—and believe it or not, the peasant would not even be arrested."

Too bad Hitler isn't alive today —just look at all those houses in Germany that need painting.

GIFTS (see also Presents)

Why spend $10 on a bottle of toilet water? . . . Use my toilet and take all you want for nothing.

I wanted to get him a gift he'd really enjoy . . . but had trouble wrapping a saloon.

1ST MAN: I've got a complimentary ticket to *Camelot* and it's yours for the asking.
2ND MAN: Really?
1ST MAN: Yeah, I'm only asking $50.

1ST MAN: I think I'll buy him a present. What would a ten-year-old boy like?
2ND MAN: How about a nine-year-old girl?

WIFE: What do you want for Christmas?

HUSBAND: I'm tired of shaving with straight razors. How about one of those new Remingtons?
WIFE: Don't be silly. Whoever heard of putting your face in a typewriter?

HUSBAND: What would you like for our anniversary, dear?
WIFE: An alligator bag.
HUSBAND: Whoever heard of carrying around an alligator?

1ST MAN: You gave your girl cough drops? What kind of gift was that? You should have given her flowers.
2ND MAN: She had a cold. She wasn't dead.

1ST MAN: I got my wife a lady's wrist watch.
2ND MAN: Did she like it?
1ST MAN: Yes, but the lady came and took it back.

1ST WOMAN: I'm going to get my husband a jacket for his birthday.
2ND WOMAN: Smoking?
1ST WOMAN: No.
2ND WOMAN: Riding?
1ST WOMAN: No.
2ND WOMAN: What kind?
1ST WOMAN: Straight.

1ST WOMAN: Every Christmas my hubby gives me a V-neck sweater and I give him a V-neck sweater. We put on our sweaters . . .

2ND WOMAN: Then what?
1ST WOMAN: V neck.

HUSBAND: How would you like a 212-piece after-dinner set for our anniversary?
WIFE: I'd love it.
HUSBAND: Fine, I'll get you a box of toothpicks.

I went Christmas shopping for my wife. I'd like to get something for her but no one wants to make me an offer.

GIRLS (see also Women, Marriage)

I took her home in a cab last night and she was so beautiful I could hardly keep my eyes on the meter.

She's a cross between Queen of Sheba and Camille. Sort of Shlemille.

She had a head like a doorknob. Any man could turn it.

I don't know much about girls . . . only what I pick up.

I was out with a printer's daughter last night, but I wasn't her type.

My girl's like a band. She steps out fit as a fiddle and comes home tight as a drum.

1ST MAN: My girl is the home-loving kind.
2ND MAN: She is?
1ST MAN: Sure, when I'm not around, she's home loving another man.

She's a home-loving girl, but she does some loving in a car, too.

She not only has the seal of his approval but the mink, also.

She's been asked to marry many times . . . by her father and mother.

1ST MAN: I had a date with a girl from Palm Springs once. A window dresser.
2ND MAN: A window dresser?
1ST MAN: Yes, she never pulled the shade down.

She was a breathtaking girl. Every few hours she stopped talking and took a breath.

My girl is so dumb she thinks mechanized infantry is a new way of having a baby.

GOBEL, GEORGE

Our program tonight is being sent to our fighting men in Murphy's Bar.

For my birthday my wife sent me forty cuff links. Trouble is I have no shirts with French cuffs. So I had to have my wrists pierced.

I was on a tough horse, boy. I got up on him and all of a sudden he kicked so hard that he caught his own hoof in one of the stirrups. I said, "Horse, if you're getting on I'm getting off."

A lot of people ask me why I keep my left hand in one spot on this guitar, when other guitar players move it all around. Well, you see they're looking for a chord. I found it.

I had to take my kid to a psychiatrist who said he was a neurotic. I mean paranoic I mean . . . Well, he steals!

Had a terrible thing happen in the garden. I found a bachelor button in my black-eyed Susan's bed.

I had this idea to make the Great Wall of China into a handball court.

I make all the big decisions in my family and my wife make the small ones. She decides where we go out, whether to buy a car, etc. and I make the big ones—like whether to admit Red China.

GOLF (see also Sports)

A minister's assistant was watching while a member of the congregation was beating the minister at golf. He walked over to the fellow and whispered in his ear, "Remember the cloth, sir." "Cloth?" answered the congregant. "This is golf, not billiards."

Last Sunday while I was playing golf a man hit me with a golf ball. I said, "That will cost you five dollars."
The man said, "Well, I yelled 'Fore'!"
And I said, "I'll take four instead."

"What can I do to prevent me from topping all my drives?"
"Turn the ball upside down."

"When you were playing golf, did you ever shoot a birdie?"
"No, but I once shot at a duck."

"You made a pretty drive this afternoon."
"Which one do you mean?"
"The one where you hit the ball."

"So the judge fined you fifty dollars for hitting your wife with a club?"
"Oh, it wasn't so much for hitting her as it was for using the wrong club."

There are two times to address a golf ball, before and after swinging.

"Do you think it's a sin for me to play golf on Sunday?"
"The way you play golf—it's a crime to play any day."

"Murphy got rich quick, didn't he?"
"He got rich so quick that he can't swing a golf club without spitting on his hands."

"Say, caddy, why do you keep looking at your watch?"
"It isn't a watch, sir, it's a compass."

"There's a new dictionary of golfing terms just out."
"Well, if it's complete it will be banned."

"You think so much of your old golf game that you don't even remember when we were married."
"Of course, I do, my dear; it was the day I sank that thirty-foot putt."

He never swears when he makes a bum golf shot, but wherever he spits, the grass never grows again.

"Why on earth didn't you watch where the ball was going?"

"Because I didn't think it was going anywhere, sir."

"Well, caddie, how do you like my game?"
"I suppose it's all right, but I still prefer golf."

"A terrible course, caddie, a terrible course."
"Sorry sir, but this isn't the course, we left that an hour ago."

"Charlie plays a fair game of golf, doesn't he?"
"Yes—if you watch him."

A guy went into a sporting goods store to get some golf balls.
"Shall I wrap them up?" asked the clerk.
"No," said Lew, "tee them off. I'll drive them home."

GOSSIP (see also Wife)

1ST GOSSIP: Why did they separate?
2ND GOSSIP: Nobody knows.
1ST GOSSIP: Oh, how terrible.

If you tell a man anything, it goes in one ear and out the other. And if you tell a woman anything, it goes in both ears and out of her mouth.

She was debating on the best means of dropping her current flame.

"Are you worried because you think he'll tell lies about you?" asked her friend.

"I don't mind the lies, but if he ever tells the truth, I'll break his neck," she answered.

GOULD, SID

Good evening, ladies and gentlemen—do I have time to do more?

I almost didn't get here tonight. I just got out of a sick bed. My girl friend has the flu.

They threw a great party for me my first night in town. . . . What a party. . . . Case comes up Friday.

My friend only lived ten miles from my hotel—by phone.

But what a party he threw— whisky flowed like glue.

My friend had quite a house . . . twenty-three rooms . . . all rented.

What a house! I've heard of sunken living rooms, but thirty feet?

I tried a new brand of whisky. It's called "Old Factory Whistle." One blast, and you're through for the day.

Actually, I do a lot of work on television. As a matter of fact, before I left New York I fixed two sets.

I was at this restaurant and what dishes they served! No food —just dishes.

GRAMMAR (see also School)

"Lay down pup—lay down. Good doggie—lay down, I say."
"You'll have to say 'Lie down' —that's a Boston terrier."

"Did you study your history?"
"Naw, I ain't had no time for nothin' but my English."

"Name a collective noun."
"Ash can."

"William, construct a sentence using the word 'archaic.' "
"We can't have archaic and eat it, too."

All right, now we'll make up sentences using the word "beans."
1ST: My father grows beans.
2ND: My mother cooks beans.
3RD: We are all human beans.

"Correct this sentence: It was me that spilt the ink."
"It wasn't me that spilt the ink."

"Do you come from Boston?"

"Certainly not! I'm talking this way because I cut my mouth on a bottle."

Mason-Dixon line is the division between "you all" and "youse guys."

GREGORY, DICK

The Negro must come out in favor of national defense, because what's the use of sitting in the front of a bus that's exploding.

I was so excited when I came north and sat in the front of the bus that I missed my stop.

I waited five days at a white lunch counter but when they finally served me, they didn't have what I wanted anyway.

I've been using *Man-Tan.* That's instant *Mau-Mau.*

In the Congo they call Mort Sahl the white me.

Pay attention and heed my words because the way things are going in Africa—who knows? Someday you may be working for me.

I never worry and fret about getting a sunburn.

The new nuclear submarine we have now is the best. It stays under water for two years and only comes up to the surface so the crew can re-enlist.

Nothing is free today. Even if you join the Ku Klux Klan you have to pay for your own sheet.

GRIDIRON (see also Football, Sports)

He played halfback on the team and way back on his studies.

"What is a pigskin used for?"
"To hold the pig together."

"How is it you haven't gone in for football?"
"If those men want to wallow in the mud, let them clean themselves up."
"What has mud got to do with football?"
"They wanted to put me on the scrub team."

"Have you ever had any football experience?"
"Well, not exactly, although I was hit by a truck and two sedans this summer."

"Your brother enjoys playing football?"
"No, but he wants seats to the games after he graduates."

"Why did they stop that man when he was running with the ball?"

"You know, the object of the game is to make a goal. He was on the other side."

"I don't see why they have to knock him down to tell him about it. Everyone makes mistakes."

My nephew has given up his job in a watermelon store and gone on the college team. Every time he passes on the football, he sits down and plugs it to see if it's ripe.

"My brother made a ninety-eight yard run in the big game."

"He did? That's great!"

"Yeah, but he didn't catch the man ahead of him."

Football Coach (to Players): And remember that football develops individuality, initiative, and leadership. Now, get in there and do exactly as I tell you.

GROCERY STORES (see also Clerks)

"Would you like some wax beans, ma'am?"

"Go away with your lousy imitations. I want real ones."

"Is that the head cheese over there?"

"No, ma'am, the boss ain't in."

"Sufferin' snakes! You sold the wrong eggs to that last woman."

"How so?"

"You sold her some of the lot we dated September tenth and it's only September 1st now."

"How much are your peaches?"

"Penny each, lady."

"I'll have one, please."

"Givin' a party, lady?"

"We have some very nice alligator pears this morning."

"How silly—why, we don't even keep goldfish, mister."

"I want to buy some lard."

"Pail?"

"I didn't know it came in two shades."

GUIDE (see also Hunting)

"This, ladies and gentlemen, is the largest waterfall in the Alps. May I ask the ladies to cease from talking for a little while so that we may hear the roar of the waters."

GUNS (see also Hunting, Big Game)

"My father always carries a young horse pistol with him."

"A young horse pistol?"
"Yeah—a Colt."

"Now, take this rifle and find out how to use it."
"Tell me one thing. Is it true that the harder I pull the trigger the farther the bullet will go?"

"Wake up, John, wake up! There's a burglar in the house."
"Well, I've no revolver. You go and look daggers at him."

SMALL SON: Mother went down to buy a revolver.
VISITOR: Did your father tell her what kind to get?
SMALL BOY: No, he doesn't even know she's going to shoot him.

FIRST CONVICT: He pointed his gun at me.
SECOND CONVICT: Did he shoot?
FIRST CONVICT: He couldn't. I had my finger over the hole.

❖❖

H

HABITS

The young wife was heartbroken.
"What's the matter?" asked a friend.
"Oh, my husband is so absentminded. After breakfast he left a tip on the table and when I handed him his hat, he handed me another tip."
"Well, that's nothing to worry about. It's just force of habit."
"That's what worries me. He kissed me when I gave him his coat."

1ST MAN: I'm a man of regular habits.

2ND MAN: Then how come you were seen sitting in the park at 3 A.M. with a girl?
1ST MAN: That's one of my regular habits.

1ST WOMAN: How did you break your husband of that habit of staying out all night?
2ND WOMAN: When he came in late one night, I called out: "Is that you, Ralph?" His name is John.

HACKETT, BUDDY

Boy, that President Kennedy is great. And under all that hair there is a hat.

You, of course, can never bribe a cop. But sometimes you get a state cop with a rented suit.

I remember I was driving and I hit a motorcycle cop. He walked over to me with a big grin on his face ear to ear.—He had the handle bars stuck in his mouth.

I married a very young wife. She was seventeen. I tell you the truth, I didn't know whether to take her on a honeymoon or send her to camp.

Beautiful girl walked into a Chinese restaurant and sat down. The waiter was quite taken by her and after taking her order walked back into the kitchen and said to the chef—"Boy, there's a girl out there built like the Brick Wall of China."

All my wife wants from my life is to take out the garbage. When I'm away on a trip she mails me the garbage.

HAIR (see also Barber, Baldness)

"I have a date with my sweetheart and she doesn't know I wear a wig."
"For heaven's sake—keep it under your hat."

"Had a tough time raising this mustache."

"Well, crops are bad everywhere this year."

After my uncle shaved yesterday he used flour instead of talcum powder.
Why did he do that?
I don't know, but when he gets hot now, he breaks out in biscuits.

RALPH: He spilled rum on his whiskers and in lighting his cigarette his whiskers caught on fire.
DICK: What did he do then?
RALPH: Oh, he just fiddled with his whiskers while rum burned.

I met a scientist in Borneo who's working on a hair formula. He has no formula for growing more curls but they have a way of shrinking your head to fit the hair you've got.

1ST MAN: I bought a new hair tonic that was guaranteed to grow hair on a billiard ball.
2ND MAN: Did it work?
1ST MAN: Yeah, but it sure slowed up the game.

KID: Grandpa, did you once have hair like snow???
GRANDPA: I sure did.
KID: Well, who shovelled it off?

WIFE: Do you like my hair in an upsweep?
HUSBAND: No . . . where did you sweep it up from????

CUSTOMER TO BARBER: What do you have for gray hair?
BARBER: The greatest of respect.

WIFE: Darling, come over here and let me run my fingers through your hair.
HUSBAND: Certainly, honey. My, but you're affectionate today . . .
WIFE: It isn't that. I just washed my hands and I can't find the towel.

SHE: Blonde hair runs in my family.
HE: Don't look now, but your blonde hair's running.

SHE: I'm blonde on my mother's side and blonde on my father's side.
HE: You're also blonde on the peroxide.

SHE: Will you love me when my hair has turned to silver?
HE: Why not? I loved you through five other shades.

HATS (see also Clothing)

That hat looks like a pushcart that made good.

SHE: And this hat won't ever go out of style.
HE: Yeah it'll look just as silly ten years from now.

1ST MAN: When a woman's down in the dumps . . . she buys a new hat.
2ND MAN: So that's where they get them.

WOMAN: That's the hat I want . . . the one with the lettuce top the carrot sides and the cherry trimmings.
SALESMAN: Shall I wrap it for you?
WOMAN: No, I'll eat it here.

1ST MAN: Why do you let your wife wear such silly hats?
2ND MAN: Well she wears the plants in our family.

SALESWOMEN: And this hat is very practical. When you're not wearing it you can always use it to dust the house.

HAWAII (see also Beach)

In Hawaii they have the same weather all year round. Then how do they start their conversations?

In Hawaii they're certainly farm-minded. The dancers are always rotating their crops.

I followed two gals around for a week in Honolulu, with a lawn mower.

HEALTH (see also Doctors, Physicians, Hypochondriacs, Illness)

"Early to bed, early to rise makes a man healthy, wealthy, and wise."
"Oh yeah. . . . did you ever see a milkman?"

"She went to Arizona for asthma. . . ."
"What's the matter. . . . she couldn't get it here?"

"How do you stay so healthy?"
"I eat plenty of vitamins, proteins, and carbohydrates."
"What? No food at all . . . ?"

"Charlie just had an operation."
"How does he feel?"
"Not so good. . . . the doctors removed his money."

"I feel so healthy that when I get up in the morning I jump out of bed and start doing exercise."
"Frisky!"
"Thank you . . . with a little soda on the side. . . ."

HEAVENS (also see Church)

St. Peter was interviewing a pretty girl at the Pearly Gates. "While you were on earth," he asked, "did you indulge in necking, petting, smoking, dancing—"
"Never! Never!" she roared emphatically. "Then why haven't you reported sooner?" asked St. Peter. "You've been dead a long time."

HECKLERS (see also Comedians, Insults)

Call out the narcotics squad—165 lbs. of dope just walked into the room.

You're nobody's fool, but see if you can get somebody to adopt you.

Why don't you blow your brains out? You've got nothing to lose.

If they ever put a price on your head . . . take it.

I must say you have a ready wit; let me know when it's ready.

He says he's a self-made man and I think it's nice of him to take the blame.

He's called a big thinker . . . by people who lisp.

When he was born, his father came into the room and gave him a funny look. Do you know—he's still got it.

If I've said anything to insult you, you may rest assured I tried my best.

He loves Nature . . . in spite of what she did to him.

What did you do . . . get up on the wrong side of the floor this morning?

You have a nice voice . . . you ought to cultivate it . . . and then plant potatoes in it.

HENPECKED (see also Wife, Marriage)

He's so henpecked that the only time he opens his mouth is to asks his wife where the mop is.

You can always tell a henpecked husband in a brawl. He's the one who holds his wife's coat.

HEREDITY

FIRST CLUB MAN: Do you believe in heredity?
SECOND CLUB MAN: Absolutely —that's how I got all my money.

"She loves to dance—dancing is in her blood."
"She must have poor circula-tion—it hasn't got down to her feet yet."

Real Estater Lou Sacher socked me with this fact: Parenthood is hereditary. If your parents didn't have children, chances are you won't have any either.

HILLBILLY (see also Yokel)

A backwoods woman, the soles of whose feet had been toughened by a lifetime of shoelessness, was standing in front of her cabin fireplace one day when her husband addressed her.
HUSBAND: You'd better move your foot a mite, Maw; you're standing on a live coal.
WIFE: Which foot, Paw?

The hillbilly hadn't taken a bath for a long, long time. The situation grew so bad that his family finally deputized a committee to force him to take a bath.
The mountaineer objected strenuously. He kicked, and he squawked, but finally they succeeded in undressing him. After removing several garments he was down to his long flannel underwear. Under this, much to his surprise, was a sweater. "Can yer imagine that?" he drawled. "And here I've bin searchin' high and low fer that sweater fer over two years!"

HISTORY

"Do you know what happened to Pompeii?"
"Sure—he died of an eruption."

"My brother swallowed my history book. Now he has hiccups all the time."
"That shows history repeats itself."

"I'll find out what you know about history. Who were the Puritans?"
"Huh?"
"Who were the Puritans? Who were the people who were punished in stocks?"
"The small investors."

"What is an emperor?"
"I don't know."
"An emperor is a ruler."
"Oh, sure, I used to carry an emperor to school with me."

"Now, what did Caesar exclaim when Brutus stabbed him?"
"Ouch!"

HOLLYWOOD (see also Actors, Agents, Movies, Motion Pictures, Films)

She wins a beauty contest. She arrives in Hollywood. She appears in a picture. She starts receiving publicity. She orders a clipping service. She learns to read.

A Producer is the guy who gives the public what they want—and then hopes they want it!

(Knock) "I'm from the Selznick Office. We're producing *Gone With The Wind* and we'd like to sign you up."
"You really mean it? You want me to act?"
"No. *Blow.*"

After listening to how many writers were let go by the various studios, Kaufman said, "I see they're taking the writers away from the secretaries."

Hollywood is the place where half the population is on a diet because they're in pictures and the other half is on a diet because they're not in pictures.

"Could you make up Ned Sparks?"
"Yes, one good lipstick would bring out his lips, one good eye pencil would bring out his eyes, and one good rouge would bring out his cheeks.
"What will bring out his teeth?"
"One good sneeze."

"Call Frank Buck and see if he has an extra cage."
"Why, aren't you sleeping at home anymore?"

"I don't like all my scenes in the shadows."

"What's the matter?"
"All my fan mail comes from spiders."

"Go and see my picture and you'll leave the theatre a happier man."
"Yes, I always do feel much better after a good sleep."

A new film is so bad, they say, that the Chinese Theater is afraid to book it for fear the cement footprints will walk out of the lobby.

The South Sea Island we used to shoot a lot of the scenes on was lovely and nobody there speaks English.
We have an island like that right here.—Coney Island.

The woman in front of me took off her shoes too, and when I got up I put on her open-toe shoes by mistake. As I was walking up the aisle, one of my big toes said to the other, "This is all new stuff to me—we must have come in through a tunnel."

Really, it was such a scarey picture that the ushers found five toupees that were ignored in the excitement.—I don't know whether my hair stood up or not but the dandruff on the back of my head kept hollering "Down in front."

I went to the première of my new picture last week and when my name came on the screen there was a burst of applause, but the usher came down and made me stop.

I was talking to the cutters the other day and they said they liked to work on you, but when they're through there's so much film on the floor that there's a fire-hazard.

1ST GIRL: You won first prize and a movie contract. . . . What did you enter?
2ND GIRL: A producer's apartment. . . .

Hollywood is where if a guy's wife looks like a new woman . . . she probably is.

1ST GIRL: Hollywood certainly is a man's world.
2ND GIRL: Well, I don't mind living in it as long as I'm a woman.

In Hollywood many a starlet has made it to the top because her clothes didn't.

A third-rate Hollywood producer died and went to heaven. He was called before St. Peter immediately.
ST. PETER: I want you to produce a picture for me.
PRODUCER: Me? But I'm a third-rater. You've got great men up

here. Why me. . . . When there's Ratoff and DeMille . . . ?

ST. PETER: Because I've got confidence in you. Now Will Shakespere will write the scenario, music by George Gershwin and lyrics by Oscar Hammerstein. Your leading men will be Clark Gable and Gary Cooper and your leading ladies will be Jean Harlow and Carole Lombard. Will you do it now . . . will you produce this picture?

PRODUCER: Will I? Sure, I'll do it.

ST. PETER: Good. Now there's this cute little girl I know. . . .

HOMES (see also Marriage)

Why do you have your front door leading right into your dining room?

So my wife's relatives won't have to waste any time.

"It ain't sanitary to have the house built over the hog pen that way," said the careful farmer to his less fastidious friend.

"Well, I dunno. We ain't lost a hog in fifteen years," he answered.

LANDLORD: I want you to pay your rent.

STRUGGLING ARTIST: Let me tell you this—in a few years' time people will look up at this miserable studio and say,

"Doakes, the famous artist, used to work there."

LANDLORD: If you don't pay your rent by tonight, they'll be able to say it tomorrow.

"How much are they asking for your apartment rent now?"

"About twice a day."

RALPH: I'm homesick.

LOUIS: Isn't that your home?

RALPH: Yes, but I'm sick of it.

HONESTY (see also Crooks, Thieves)

Jack and Jim were discussing the wife of an absent friend.

"He doesn't trust her any more."

"How is that?"

"One morning he sneaked in the kitchen of her home and kissed her on the neck. Without turning around, she said, "All right, just leave a quart of milk and a pint of cream.""

Two college friends met after a long separation. Said the first, "What are you doing nowadays?"

"Trying to earn an honest living," answered the second.

"Well, you certainly won't have much competition."

JACK: Come with me and we'll sit beneath that pine tree.

ETHEL: Not me!

JACK: Why—can it be you don't trust me?

ETHEL: Well—I trust you—and I trust myself—but I can't trust the two of us together.

Never trust a girl who says she loves you more than anybody else in the world. It proves that she has been experimenting.

HOPE, BOB

I'm glad President Kennedy is President. His father gave him a choice. He said, "Either you can run for President or go to camp."

I was in Arizona and it was so dry people were putting stamps on envelopes with pins. I saw a tree chasing a dog. I cried, and three people started to lick my face.

The Pentagon in Washington has a new emblem—crossed shovels on a field of red tape.

Think of it, it took the wagon train six months to get cross-country. Today they send rockets millions of miles into space and back in fifteen minutes. But nobody's watching. They're all home watching *Wagon Train* on television.

Boy, those jets travel fast. And they sure serve fast meals. I don't mind mashed potatoes on a stick, but when they serve lamb chops with their panties half down—that's too much.

I didn't win an Academy Award again. So look for me at the dinner afterwards. I'll be sitting with Dick Nixon and Arthur Miller.

Marlene Dietrich's mother and father won the Nobel Prize for architecture.

Adlai Stevenson is going to South America to visit all our friends.—He'll be back the same day.

President Kennedy is golfing now. You'd think when he has a little free time he'd want to get away from politics.

HORSEBACK RIDING (see also Horses)

"Why didn't you ride on the bridle path?"
"I thought that was only for newly-married couples."

"Have you a riding habit?"
"No, I haven't been riding long enough to get the habit."

"Do you prefer an English saddle or a Western?"

"What's the difference?"

"The Western saddle has a horn."

"I don't think I'll need the horn. I don't intend to ride in heavy traffic."

"I was horseback riding yesterday and from the aftereffects I think I'll learn to ride sidesaddle."

"Why do that?"

"It saves a little place where you can sit down the next day."

"That horse has never had anyone on him."

"I've never been on a horse— so we start off even."

"That was a beautiful horse you were riding Sunday, but why did you have that piece of iron tied to her tail?"

"Well, I felt sorry for her. She kept switching the flies off with her tail. So I tied the iron on her tail so she could kill 'em and then they couldn't come back to bite her."

HORSEPLAYER (see also Horse Racing, Racetrack)

So this horseplayer died last week and a friend called another friend who was in residence at Gulfstream. He told the pal in the South about the funeral arrangements and then admitted he couldn't remember the name of the cemetery. "It doesn't make any difference," he finally decided. "When you get to La Guardia, take a cab and it's the third cemetery on the way to Aqueduct."

HORSE RACING (see also Players, Racetrack)

"The other day I picked a horse that I thought could win in a walk."

"And did it?"

"The other horses double-crossed it and outran him."

"I'm betting on a horse that's starting 20 to 1. And I can't lose."

"What do you mean, you can't lose?"

"I can't lose. The horse is starting 20 to 1, and the race doesn't start until one."

"I bet on a horse once."

"Did he win?"

"No, I think he just ran out of curiosity!"

"What do you mean—out of curiosity?"

"The only reason he was in the race was to see if the other horses had tails."

Animals are superior to human beings. There are thirty horses in a race and fifty thousand people go to see it, but put thirty people in a race and not one horse would go to see it.

"Last week he won a race.— He was head and head with another horse."
"If he was head and head with the other horse, how did he win the race?"
"In order to finish right, he stuck out his tongue."

"Were you lucky at the races yesterday?"
"I should think I was. I found a dollar after the last race, so I didn't have to walk home."

"Is it wrong to bet on the horses?"
"It is—the way I do."

"I lost fifty dollars on that tip you gave me for the horse race. You told me that horse could win in a walk and he finished last."
"He could have won in a walk, but it was a running race."

HORSES (see also Horseback Riding)

"There's quick dough in playing horses."

"Quick dough?"
"Sure. I lost twenty bucks in two minutes. Ain't that quick?"

A race track is a strange place. There the windows clean people.

"That horse mustuv been a police horse at one time."
"Why do you say that?"
"In the middle of the race he stopped to direct traffic."

"I used to ride horses bareback but I didn't like it."
"Why not?"
"Too chilly."

"Did you ever try spurs on your horses?"
"Yeah, but they keep slipping off his hooves."

"I've got a brother who is a horse's aide."
"A horse's aide?"
"Yeah, he works at the stables twelve hours a day for two dollars."
"He's no horse's aide . . ."

"Now there's a man who knows horse flesh . . ."
"Is he a trainer?"
"No, a butcher."

"Do you use spurs on that horse?"
"I don't have to; I have long toenails."

HOSPITALS (see also Doctors, Physicians, Illness)

Two newborn babies were lying in their respective cribs in the hospital when one of them turned to the other and said, "I'm a little boy," to which the second baby replied, "I don't believe it."

First baby said, "Is that so? Well, you just wait till the nurse leaves the room and I'll show ya." Just as the nurse left the room, he kicked off the blankets, lifted his foot in the air and said, "See, blue booties!"

"How can I get to the emergency hospital?"
"Stand in the middle of the street."

Did you hear about the panhandler who worked in the hospital?

HOT

It's been so hot lately, burglars are only breaking into air-conditioned apartments.

It's so hot, on Wall Street watered stock is evaporating.

It's so hot, everybody is reading fan mail.

It's so hot Indians are wearing sheets instead of blankets.

It's so hot I took a four-way cold tablet and it didn't know which way to go.

HOTEL (see also Motel, Rooms)

A sailor went to a hotel. He was about to register when suddenly he threw down the pen and yelled for his bags.

"What's the matter?" sez the clerk.

"Only this," bellowed the flattie, "I've found bugs in the beds, on walls, on the floors but never before have I seen one crawl up on the register to see the number of my room."

LANDLORD: This room was formerly occupied by a chemist. He invented a new explosive.
PROSPECTIVE BOARDER: I suppose those spots on the wall are results of his experiment?
LANDLORD: Well, indirectly, yes. You see, that's the chemist.

I was getting a room at the Buldgemose last week when a young couple from upstate approached the clerk and asked for a room.
CLERK: Inside or outside room, sir?
VISITOR: Inside, it looks like rain.

DINER: You seem to keep the hotel remarkably clean.

WAITER: I'm glad you think so, sir.

DINER: Yes, everything I've eaten tastes of soap.

An upstate hotel received a reservation request for next season from a Brooklynite who wrote: "Please reserve a suitable room where I can put up with my wife."

Phil Schwiedel, the travel agent, heard this one from one of his clients: The man complained to the manager of a small-town hotel about his accommodations. "This is the best we have," said the manager defensively. "This is the royal suite." The man cracked, "The last royalty that slept here must have been King Kong."

I just came back from a hotel so ritzy that when the guests pitch horseshoes, they have to wear riding habits.

The owner was at his desk in the hotel when the salesman checked in. He tried to be courteous and asked, "Do you want the clerk to call you in the morning?"

"No, thanks, I always wake up every morning at seven."

"Then," said the owner, "would you mind calling the clerk?"

The honeymoon couple was checking out of the hotel. "What's this item, a hundred dollars for meals? We never came down for dinner. You know we're on our honeymoon."

CLERK: We're on the European plan here. It was there for you. If you didn't use it, it's not our fault.

MAN: Well, then, we're even, because you owe me a hundred dollars for making love to my wife.

CLERK: I never touched your wife.

MAN: Well, it was there for you. If you didn't use it, it's not my fault.

Herb Shriner described the only hotel in his home town. "It wasn't much, but at least it had a bridal suite. That was the room with the lock on the door."

HOUSES (see also Rooms, Apartments)

BUYER: Is the house built of well-seasoned lumber?

BROKER: It must be . . . see how the termites enjoy eating it.

HUSBAND: Why pay a paperhanger when I could put the wallpaper on myself?

WIFE: Because it would look better on the wall.

Modern houses feature things hidden in the walls. Well, my

house is twenty years old and it has things hidden in the walls, too. . . . Mice.

I saw a model home last night . . . but she wouldn't let me in.

HUSBAND: I told your brother that he could use our house as though he owned it.
WIFE: That was nice of you.
HUSBAND: Oh yeah. Well, he sold it yesterday.

BUYER: Isn't this house a little strange? How come it's 2 feet wide and 220 feet long?
BROKER: Well, it was originally intended to be a bowling alley.

1ST WOMAN: We cut the cost of building the house by use of a new method that does away entirely with electric wiring.
2ND WOMAN: What's this new method?
1ST WOMAN: Candles.

Our house was bounded by a shoe factory on the east, a stockyard on the west, a glue factory on the north and a chemical plant on the south. One good thing about our location—you knew which way the wind was blowing.

HUNTING (see also Big Game)

1ST MAN: I went hunting in Africa and I bagged a lion.
2ND MAN: You bagged a lion?
1ST MAN: Sure, I bagged him and bagged him he should please go away.

1ST MAN: Some woodsman. I'll bet you wouldn't know what to do if you came face to face with a skunk.
2ND MAN: If I meet a skunk, that's the way I want to meet him . . . face to face.

1ST MAN: I went hunting alligators with my brother-in-law.
2ND MAN: Did you catch one?
1ST MAN: See this wallet?
2ND MAN: Alligator?
1ST MAN: No, brother-in-law.

Cannibals are the most ambitious people in Africa . . . they're always trying to get a head.

HE: Do you know what it's like to be lost in the Sudan?
SHE: No, but I've had some pretty rough times in a coupe.

MAN: I was just hunting. I'm sorry I killed your cow. Can I replace it?
FARMER: Don't know. How much milk can you give?

1ST MAN: I love hunting. Me and my brother used to get up at

four in the morning to go hunting.
2ND MAN: What did you go hunting for?
1ST MAN: Father.

1ST MAN: Last time I went bear
hunting, I had a frightful experience. I was suddenly confronted by a tremendous bear.
We stood there, face to face.
It was a big she-bear. She threw
her arms around me and
hugged me. She squeezed me.
2ND MAN: What did you do?
1ST MAN: What could I do? I
kissed her.

FATHER: Moby Dick lunged at
the whale. Then the whale
lunged at Moby Dick.
SMALL SON: Then what hap-
pened?
FATHER: They had "lunge" together.

COUNTRY FRIEND: Well, why are
you back so soon?
HUNTER: I'm after more dogs.
COUNTRY FRIEND: More dogs!
Those were good dogs I gave
you.
HUNTER: I know, but I've shot
all those dogs already.

"How can you tell the difference between ducks and geese?"
"A duck goes quack quack and
a goose goes honk honk. Now, if

you were hunting and a flock of
birds came into sight and went
honk honk, what would you do?"
"I'd step aside and let them
pass."

He's a big dame hunter.

"You're going hunting?"
"Yes."
"But where are your pants?"
"That's what I'm hunting for."

HUSBAND (see also Wife, Mar-
riage, Married, Matrimony)

"Silence is golden."
"I guess my wife is on the
silver standard."

"Sir, I would like to marry your
daughter."
"Young man, have you seen my
wife?"
"Yes, sir, but I still prefer your
daughter."

"Oh, please help me to find
my husband. I've lost him in the
crowd."
"How will I know him?"
"He has a mermaid tattooed
on his stomach."

"Really, Bill, your argument
with your wife last night was most
amusing."
"Wasn't it though—and when

she threw the axe at me I thought I'd split."

"May I marry your daughter?"
"What is your vocation?"
"I'm an actor."
"Then get before the foot-lights."

A matrimonial martyr is the henpecked husband who has to drive the car home all by himself because his wife is asleep in the back seat.

HYPNOTISM

Hypnotism is getting a man in your power and making him do what you want.

That's not hypnotism, that's marriage!

HYPOCHONDRIAC (see also Health, Illness)

It's easy to spot a hypochondriac. He's the guy who can read his doctor's handwriting.

❖❖

I

ICELAND

In Iceland I saw a sign that read BEWARE OF POLAR BEAR, Signed *Friendly Eskimo*. Then I went farther and I saw another sign that read DISREGARD FIRST NOTICE, Signed *Hungry Polar Bear*.

Have you heard about the northern Eskimo who said to the southern Eskimo, "Glub glub glub" and the southern Eskimo said, "Glub glub glub, you-all."

ICE-SKATING (see also Sports)

McNulty looked rather dejected as he was taking off his ice skates. "What's the matter?" asked his friend.

"I've been trying to make a fancy figure for two hours."

"What happened?" prompted the friend.

"She slapped me in the face," said McNulty.

ILLNESS (see also Health, Doctors, Physicians, Hospital)

PHYSICIAN: Shall I give her a local anesthetic?

NOUVEAU RICHE: No. I'm rich—give her the best. Give her something imported.

One man-about-town met another, who asked, "Weren't you in the hospital last week?"

"Yes, I had a terribly high fever."

"What did they give you to slow down your heart action?"

"An elderly nurse," he snorted.

Three blood transfusions were necessary to save a lady patient's life at a hospital. A brawny young Scotchman offered his blood. The patient gave him fifty dollars for the first pint; twenty-five dollars for the second pint; and the third time she had so much Scotch blood in her she only thanked him.

A Madison Avenue bus was unusually crowded one morning. A passenger sitting next to the window suddenly buried his head in his arms. The man next to him asked, "Are you ill? Can I do something for you?"

"It's nothing like that," the other assured him. "I just hate to see old ladies standing."

Paul Winchell tells about the two germs who were talking. One said to the other, "Don't come near me, I just got shot with penicillin!"

"Doctor, there is someone waiting for you. He's sitting on pins and needles."

To which the doctor answered, "Well, dress his wounds and send him in!"

A woman was seriously ill. Her husband summoned the doctor, who dashed inside the sickroom and came out a minute later asking for a chisel. The stunned but anxious husband didn't ask questions and found a chisel. Minutes later, the doctor poked his head out and asked, "Y'got a hammer?" The husband was puzzled, but not wanting to doubt the doctor gave him a hammer. Five minutes later, out came the doc with another request, this time for a hacksaw. The husband was upset and screamed hysterically. "Doctor, you asked for a hammer, chisel and a hacksaw. What the hell are you doing to my wife?"

The doctor said, "What wife? I'm trying to open my satchel!"

INCOME TAX (see also Taxes)

"What do you do when you get a letter from the income people?"
"I finish reading it on the train."

This letter came to the Income Tax Bureau: "Gentlemen, I have not been able to sleep at night because I cheated on last year's income tax. Enclosed find my check for a thousand dollars. If I find I still can't sleep, I'll send you the balance."

An angry man ran into the post office and shouted to the postmaster, "For some time I've been pestered with threatening letters. I want something done about it!" "I'm sure we can help," soothed the postmaster. "That's a Federal offense. Have you any idea who's sending you these letters?" "I certainly do," barked the fellow. "It's those pesky income tax people."

I don't mind paying income taxes, but I'd like to know which country it's going to.

You should file your income tax, not chisel it.

FRIEND: Which of your works of fiction do you consider best?
AUTHOR: My last income tax return.

Tax collectors and psychiatrists are giving out the same advice: It's no good for a man to keep too much to himself.

HARRY: Poor Sam, he was ruined by untold wealth.
SOL: Yeah, he should have told about it in his income tax report.

New income tax forms are being printed on Kleenex. That's to make it comfortable for you when you pay through the nose.

If you pay your income tax you go to the poorhouse and if you don't pay, you go to the jailhouse.

Income tax forms: Blankety blanks.

HUSBAND: Wait a minute, you can't deduct your hats from our income tax.
WIFE: Why not? They're overhead.

1ST GIRL: This year pay your income tax with a smile.
2ND GIRL: I tried that, but they wanted money.

"I sent in my estimated tax but I didn't sign my name to it."
"Why not?"
"If I have to guess how much I'm going to earn—let them guess who sent it in."

"How come you're putting down your baby as a dependent? It hasn't been born yet."
"I know, but it was part of last year's work."

"Look you've got miscellaneous expenses listed five times. What's this miscellaneous?"
"The name of my bookie."

"How can you deduct your gambling debts as sickness?"

"Don't you think gambling's a sickness?"

INDIA

It seems that two Englishmen boarded a train on a very slow trip through India. Now India is a very uninteresting, flat country, so after traveling for two or three days, a conversation finally got started. The first man said, "British?" and after a while the second one said, "Yes."

Nothing more was said for two days when the first man in the same low tone with no animation or interest drawled out, "Foreign service?" . . . Another pause and the other answered in the same low, draggy, drawly voice, "Y-e-s."

Two days later, the first one spoke up again and asked, "Stationed in Delhi?" and after a long, hesitating pause, in the same drawly tone, "Yes."

Several more days passed and another question: "Sexual pervert?" Another long pause and the answer was, "No."

Two more days went by and the first Britisher, without raising the tone of his voice, mumbled. "Pity."

Oil rich Indian entering the Copacabana is stopped by the maître d'.

MAITRE D': Do you have a reservation here sir?

INDIAN: Nope. Just have one back in Oklahoma.

"There I was surrounded by Indians. Indians to the right of me, Indians to the left of me, Indians in front of me, Indians behind me."

"What did you do?

"I bought a few blankets."

Tonto and the Lone Ranger were surrounded by Indians when the Lone Ranger turned to Tonto and said, "We're in trouble, Tonto."

To which Tonto replied, "You mean you're in trouble, white man."

"After I learned the Indian dances the members of the tribe gave me an Indian name."

"What was that?"

"Clumsy."

INDIAN: Me big heap Indian Chief.

ADAMS: Me big heap comedian.

INDIAN: No, you just big heap.

INDIANS (see also Cowboys, Western)

INFLATION (see also Money, Inflation)

Americans are getting stronger. Twenty years ago it took two people to carry ten dollars' worth of groceries. Today, my child can do it.

INNOCENT (see also Law, Judge)

"I'll teach you to make love to my daughter."
"I wish you would. I'm not making much headway."

"Then there was the girl who was so dumb that she thought assets were little donkeys."

"That's good, clean fun."
"Well, what good is it?"

"Daddy, why do they call them the virgin forests?"
"My son, only God can make a tree."

"Am I the first girl you have ever kissed?"
"Now that you mention it— you do look familiar."

"What kind of a dress did Sue wear to the party last night?"
"I think it was checked."
"Baabee! That must have been a real party."

INSANE ASYLUM (see also Insanity, Nut, Moron)

An important official who was visiting an insane asylum made a telephone call but had difficulty in getting his number. Finally, in exasperation, he shouted to the operator, "Look here, girl, do you know who I am?" "No," she replied calmly, "but I know where you are."

An inmate in the asylum insisted upon standing in his room completely naked except for a hat. The doctor asked him why he didn't get dressed.
The guy said, "Why, no one is coming in here to see me."
"But why the hat?" asked the doctor.
The inmate replied, "Somebody might."

An inmate in the asylum was standing over a washbasin filled with water with a fishing pole, and he was fishing. The doctor, wanting to humor him said, "Catch anything?"
The inmate replied, "Don't be silly, in a washbasin?"

Late at night in the asylum one inmate shouted, "I am Napoleon." Another said, "How do you know?" First guy said, "God told me." Just then, a voice from the other end shouted, "I did not."

A do-gooder visiting the asylum saw one inmate building a

wall with bricks. She was very impressed with his style as a mason and said, "Look, I don't believe you're crazy. I'll hire you to come build me a barbecue pit in my yard. Here's my address. Don't forget—this Sunday you'll come to my house."

The inmate said, "Thank you" and as the woman was walking away he picked up a brick and threw it at her, belting her in the head and knocking her out cold. When she finally became conscious he was standing over her and said, "Remember, this Sunday!"

The doctor called the police. "Listen—a crazy man escaped. He weighs three hundred pounds and is three feet, four inches tall. The cop said, "Are you kidding?" Doctor said, "I told you he was crazy."

INSANITY (see also Insane Asylum, Nut, Moron, Stupid)

Insanity is hereditary. You can get it from your children.

A farmer passed the insane asylum with a wheelbarrow of fertilizer, when an inmate asked him what he was going to do with it. "Put it on my tomatoes," said the farmer.

"And they call me nuts because I put mustard in my milk," answered the inmate.

DOCTOR: Why, that patient's floating in air.
ATTENDANT: Yeah . . . the nut think he's an astronaut and this is one of his weightless moments.

DOCTOR: Why do you keep hitting yourself in the head?
PATIENT: Just trying to break up this cold.

ATTENDANT: There's a man outside who wants to know if we've lost any of our men inmates.
DOCTOR: Why's that?
ATTENDANT: Seems someone has run off with his wife.

DOCTOR: Why do you say you're Wilbur Wright? Yesterday you were Thomas Edison.
PATIENT: Yesterday I didn't know how to fly.

DOCTOR: You say you like me better than your last doctor?
PATIENT: Yeah, you seem more like one of us.

DOCTOR: Well, you're cured. You may go now.
PATIENT: Well, then kiss me quick.
DOCTOR: Kiss you! I shouldn't even be lying on the couch with you.

INSECTS (see also Animals)

Two caterpillars were munching away on a cabbage leaf. A butterfly fluttered in the air above them. One caterpillar noticed the butterfly and said to the other, "You'll never get me up in one of them things."

"Do you wanna keep these moth balls?
"No, throw them away. The moths are tired of playing with them anyway."

"Do you know why the bees buzz?"
"Yeah, you'd buzz, too, if someone took your honey and nectar."

You can learn a lot from the bees.
They go to work while the Queen sits home with the hives.

"What do silkworms live on?"
"What difference does it make? I've never seen a worm who couldn't make both ends meet."

"You've got two worms for pets and one is a boy worm and one is a girl worm. How can you tell the difference?"
"The worm that turns is the boy worm."

As the lightning bug said when he got his tail caught in the pencil sharpener, "I'm de-lighted . . . no end."

"I didn't sleep a wink last night . . . this fly kept sitting on my nose."
"Why didn't you brush him off?"
"I didn't know he was dusty."

INSTRUMENTS (see also Music, Musicians, Band)

"So you prefer a piano?"
"Oh, yes. You can't lay a cigarette on a violin. It rolls off."

"I just killed a saxophone player."
"That can't be a capital offense. What do you think you'll get?"
"Some sleep."

"Remember how I used to play my accordion in Hollywood? And how the crowds used to gather?"
"Yes, up to the time your monkey died."

"Have you ever played any concerts?"
"I have played with (names several cities) Philharmonics."
"What about Washington?"
"He had a tough winter at Valley Forge."

"Is it true you never took a lesson on the accordion?"

"It's true and I can prove it."
"You just did."

"Did you ever notice that he closes his eyes when he plays?"
"Yes, he's so kind-hearted he doesn't want to see us suffer."

I asked him to take them out to hear some music and he took them to hear his father's organ recital. Four of them were bitten by a monkey.

I don't know what to do. You tell me to practice and the neighbors tell me to stop.

"While I was unpacking your musical instruments I found an old tuba."
"Can I take it home to my uncle, who's a floorwalker?"
"He can't play it."
"I know—he wants to soak his feet in it."

"Are you fond of musical instruments?"
"No, but I'll say one thing for a trombone. It looks better in a derby than I do."

"They say she attained her present prominence by pulling wires."
"Really?"
"Yes. She plays the harp."

"Do you make a living playing that thing?"

"No, I just play to kill time."
"You've got a powerful weapon there!"

"You know, you remind me of a clarinet."
"But a clarinet is a wind instrument."
"Well??????"

"I'm a musician. I got an organ and a monkey."
"Have you still got them?"
"No, the monkey took one look at me one day and went into business for himself."

"What's better than a broken drum?"
"I don't know; what?"
"Nothing. It can't be beat."

An English horn is a bazooka with a college education.

"People take off their hats to my accordion playing."
"Oh, are you quite accomplished?"
"No, all I can play is *The Star Spangled Banner.*"

"I make forty dollars a night playing the violin. That's ten dollars a string."
"Aren't you sorry you didn't learn to play the harp?"

"Have you a zither?"
"No, but I've got a couple of brothers."

"Why does he always throw his horn on the floor when he's finished?"

"He doesn't want to be caught standing there, holding the evidence."

"He has 108 cats."
"108 cats?"
"Yes, he grows his own fiddle strings."

She went to the doctor for an examination and he asked if she played an instrument. When she said, "Yes," he said it must be a wind instrument. He said he could tell by the condition of her lungs and throat. Then she just died laughing.
Why?
She plays an accordion.

To open his new West End Avenue apartment the owner decided to have an expensive ten-piece orchestra. On the eventful evening he stood in the foyer to welcome the arriving guests. Finally he called to the butler, "Hoibert, go and see—why ain't the orchestra playing?"

"They're just tuning up, Mr. Grubmick."

" I hired them two weeks ago —and they're just tuning up?"

"What key does she play in?"
"Skeleton key."

"What is a skeleton key?"
"The key that fits anything."

My brother used to play the cornet, but he had to stop. His teeth were so loose that people used to accuse him of shooting beans at them.

"How did you happen to take up the oboe?"
"The neighbors complained of the baby crying so I took up the oboe and that got rid of the neighbors."

"Why do you play a zither? I like the piano better."
"Yes, but a piano is a little harder to play in a canoe!"

"You get a lot of music out of an instrument."
"Yes, and I think they got all there was out of that one before they sent it."

"You certainly put your heart and soul into those solos."
"About time he put a little music into it."

"Could I take home that big stringed-harp for my wife?"
"She doesn't play the harp."
"I know. She just wants to slice the hard-boiled eggs."

"Why on earth did you encourage your wife to quit playing the piano and start playing the clarinet?" demanded one neighbor of another.

Whereupon the other explained, "Because she can't sing while she's playing the clarinet."

"Remember that fellow who used to play the harp in the band?"

"Whatever happened to him?"

"He fell from a fifth floor window."

"I don't suppose he plays the harp anymore."

"Oh yes, he plays a harp, but now he doesn't have to belong to a union."

INSULTS (see also Hecklers)

Will you please follow the example of your head and come to the point.

Listen, lady, if you ever become a mother will you give me one of your puppies?

You're a comedian of the first water—a big drip.

Lady, why don't you sue your brain for non-support?

Do you have a chip on your shoulder, or is that your head?

Madame, you're a buried treasure. Too bad they dug you up.

If I had your face I'd hire a pickpocket to lift it.

If Moses had seen your face there would have been another commandment.

There's a guy who is dark and handsome. When it's dark he's handsome.

You have a very striking face. How many times were you struck there?

Yes, sir, you have a brain in your head. It's little things like that that count.

INSURANCE

A fellow who lives in the city most of the year but summers in Maine was surprised one winter day when he received a call from the caretaker of his summer place.

"There's a bad forest fire up here," he was informed, "and it looks like your house might get burned down."

"My goodness!" the homeowner exclaimed. "Is there anything I can do?"

"Well," the caller replied, "I thought maybe you might want to put more insurance on the house."

A man went into the insurance office to report that his car had been stolen and he would like to get his money. The insurance executive was polite but firm: "Sorry, we do not give you money, we replace the car with a new one."

The man answered indignantly, "If that's the way you do business, you can cancel the policy on my wife."

When I was sick my husband sat up all night and read to me— my insurance policy.

Insurance is like a football game . . . relatives sit around and wait for you to kick off.

I have hair insurance . . . if all my hair falls out my policy covers my head.

I have theft insurance—in case I should steal.

I have nose insurance . . . not only does it pay for injuries to my nose but it's also made out of kleenex.

My insurance man asked me if I wanted a ten year term, a twenty year term or life. I didn't know if I was getting insurance or a jail sentence.

The broker said he was going to plan my estate. I don't even

have my own room and he's planning an estate.

Did you know that statistics show that most accidents happen in the home? If you have an argument with your wife and you win, that's an accident—and you can collect from her—in a lump sum.

I have this new hospitalization insurance—black and blue cross.

INTEGRATION (see also Dick Gregory, Nipsy Russell)

During the bus trouble in Alabama Nipsy Russell, one of the great Negro comedians, said, "The Negro's had better luck with the bloodhounds than with the Greyhounds."

A guy walked into a Chinese restaurant and saw a Negro waiter· Surprised, he asked what was the special of the house. The Negro waiter said, "Pizza."

The guy said, "Pizza in a Chinese restaurant?"

Waiter said, "Well, this is a Jewish neighborhood."

The above Mr. Nipsy Russell, a great Negro entertainer, also speaks about his club dates entertaining in the South. "I had a sensational run in Tennessee and quite a following in Alabama. . . .

I played a club called the "Noose"—quite a swinging place . . . but really they were nice and afterwards we had a nice time barbecuing chickens over burning crosses. . . ."

INVENTIONS

I just invented a new kind of fur. I crossed a fox with a mink and got a fink.

They laughed at Edison, they laughed at Marconi, they laughed at Fulton. I wonder who wrote their material?

"Benjamin Franklin wasn't so smart."
"But he invented electricity."
"Yeah but the guy who invented the meter made all the money."

"I combined an electric iron with an electric toaster and an electric blanket."
"What did you get?"
"Third degree burns."

I just invented a new kind of racing form . . . it unfolds into a pair of pants so you can have something to walk home in.

"I took a fender from a Buick, the chrome from a Chrysler, and the hub caps from a Thunderbird . . ."

"What did you get?
"Ninety days."

I put Mexican jumping beans in pancake flour so that they turn over by themselves.

I crossed Metrecal with soap and made a new shampoo for fatheads.

A guy invented a new kind of cigarette lighter. When you press the button, an arrow pops up and points to guy with a match.

Jonathan Winters invented a new way to fly: Scotch tape pigeons to your arms.

A scientist invented a new kind of rocket that saves the government a lot of money: It blows up in the factory.

A gambler invented a new way to beat the gambling tables at Las Vegas: When you get off the plane, walk into the propeller.

IRELAND (see also Irish)

Pat walked into a bar in Dublin, his face beaten to a pulp. "And who did that to you?" asked the bartender. "I had a fight with Mike Shannon." "What?" asked the bartender. "You let a little guy like that beat you up? You should be ashamed of yourself, a little good-for-nothing runt like Mike." "Hold on there," said Pat, "don't be talking disrespectfully of the dead."

An Irishwoman who had reached the age of 102 was giving an interview about her longevity when one of the reporters asked her if she had ever been bedridden and she said, "Oh yis, many times, me bye . . . and once on a sleigh."

A priest once saw a small boy in an Irish town standing on tiptoe trying to reach a doorbell, so the priest climbed the stairs and rang the bell for the lad, who said, "Thanks, Father, now let's run like hell."

IRISH (see also Ireland)

An Irishman was telling his friend of a narrow escape in the war.

"The bullet went in me, chist and came out me back," said Pat.

"But," answered his friend, "It would go through your heart and kill you."

"Me heart was in me mouth at the time," came the quick reply.

PAT: Begorra, Oi couldn't pay me three dollars foine and Oi had to go to jail for six days.

MIKE: And how much did yez spend to get drunk?

PAT: Oh, about three dollars.

MIKE: Three dollars? Yez fool, if yez had not spent yer three dollars for drink, ye'd had yer three dollars for yer foine.

IRISHMAN (dining in restaurant): Why does this lobster have a claw missing?

WAITER: He was in a fight, sir.

IRISHMAN: Take this one back and bring me the winner.

MR. RILEY: Why are ye decoratin', Mr. Murphy?

MR. MURPHY: Me b'y Denny is coming home this day.

MR. RILEY: I t'ought it was for foive years he was sint up?

MR. MURPHY: He was; but he got a year off for good behayvure.

MR. RILEY: An' sure, it must be a great comfort for ye to have a good b'y like that!

"Good morning, Mrs. Kelly," said the doctor, "Did you take your husband's temperature, as I told you?"

"Yes, doctor, I borrowed a barometer and placed it on his chest; it said "very dry" so I brought him a pint o' beer an' he's gone back to work."

Once upon a time there were two Irishmen. There are lots of them now.

An Irishman was selected to be the donor of blood for a former English king who had been seriously ill. The first transfusion seemed to help, so a second was given and to make matters just right, the third was in progress when the King sat up in bed and yelled, "The Hell with the King of England!"

Did you hear about the Irish psychiatrist who used a Murphy bed instead of a couch?

St. Patrick's is a day on which the Irish march up Fifth Avenue and stagger down Sixth Avenue.

ISRAEL (see also Jewish)

Much of Israel's rumor reflects the day-to-day affairs and tensions under which the Israelis live. It is not surprising, therefore, that many Israeli jokes have to do with war and violence—and even the youngsters reflect the tensions of this new country.

There is the story of the little Israeli boy who came home from school and his mother said to him, "What are you doing home so early?" He answered, "Well, I put some dynamite under the teacher's chair."

His mother frantically shouted at him, "What a terrible thing to do! You go right back to school."

His noncommittal answer was, "What school, where's school?"

While the Israelis have made a name for themselves with outstanding feats of bravery, they love to kid themselves. They tell the story about the young Israeli soldier who was sent on reconnaissance to investigate the possibility of crossing a bridge. He came back tattered and bleeding and said, "To the right there are tanks and artillery and infantry in heavy numbers. To the left there are numerous atomic war heads and machine guns. I am sure we can go either to the right or to the left, but I'm afraid we cannot cross the bridge."

When asked, "Why not?" he said, "They've got a big black dog at the other end."

Rabbi Charles E. Shulman, of the Riverdale Temple, tells of visiting Israel and asking a native guide whether there were any golf courses there. "Golf?" shrugged the guide. "In a country as tiny as ours, a good golf drive could become an international incident."

Former Ambassador James G. McDonald tells this one. An Israel philharmonic was playing one of the long-haired *avant garde* compositions. Mrs. Ben-Gurion nudged her husband. "See, over there, Ben Zvi is sleeping." "For that you have to wake me?" replied Ben-Gurion.

Israel is the greatest place in the world for people. Especially for a millionaire. Why? No millionaire has died there yet.

Someone who recently waited her turn in a grocery queue in Jerusalem passed along this story to the *Jerusalem Post*: A housewife was trying to buy more than one bottle of a popular detergent, of which the grocer had just received a long-awaited supply. She could only have one, she was informed.

Whereupon the housewife began a harrowing account of her soap shortage, its effect on the health of her small children, and so on. Finally the grocer softened. "All right," he said, "I'll let you have two if you give me two empty bottles." The happy woman turned to her young daughter and said, "Quick, darling, run home and get two bottles of X from the kitchen."

In a few minutes the child returned clutching two full bottles.

An aunt from town visited a *Kibbutz* and arrived just in time to see the kindergarten tots playing in the swimming pool—stark naked. "Aren't you ashamed?" she asked her nephew, aged four.

He didn't know what she was talking about. A week later, a parcel arrived from the city with a small pair of swimming trunks inside.

The little boy put them on and when asked in the pool what the strange garment was for, he replied, "So I can be ashamed."

Not long ago in Tel Aviv a frustrated lover, who had been threatening to kill the girl and her family, jumped off her third-floor balcony when the police approached. By a miracle he escaped injury.

Police promptly seized and searched him, finding a pistol and a dollar bill. He was charged with illegal possession of foreign currency.

A rather inexpert father, anxious to make himself useful around the house, undertook to put his small son to bed, a housewife told the *Jerusalem Post* recently. She put supper on the table, trimmed the oil stove and sat down to worry about her next day's chores. Still her husband did not emerge. Then the bedroom door opened softly and the little boy crept out, hushing her, finger to mouth. "Well, Ima (mama)," he said, "the old man is asleep at last."

A public taxi was traveling from Tel Aviv to Haifa. One of the six passengers was an old lady, a new immigrant, who kept asking the driver to tell her when they passed Athlit. She asked him so often that he got nervous, and when they reached Athlit kept right on going before he checked himself. He apologized to the other passengers, turned around and drove back. Turning to the old lady he said, "Here is Athlit; now you can get out."

Whereupon she said to him, "Who wants to get out?" The driver, startled, answered, "But you did." "No," answered the old lady, "my daughter told me when I left Tel Aviv that when I pass Athlit, I should take my medicine."

During the time of the war of liberation, there were not enough guns and ammunition to go around—let alone uniforms. An American volunteer tried to join the Israeli Army. He passed his medical with flying colors, but when he asked for his uniform he was told, "We are a poor country. We cannot afford uniforms."

Whereupon the American said he would try the Air Force. He then asked couldn't he at least have a cap or insignia. He again was told no uniforms—this request also could not be fulfilled. So he decided to join the Navy where a uniform is not important on a ship.

When he was being interviewed, he was asked if he could swim, whereupon he got up and screeched, "My God, don't you even have ships here?"

The brashness of Israeli youth is not confined to the Army, it is also reflected in civilian life. One little boy boarded a crowded bus where he had to stand with no place to hang on. He reached up and held on to the beard of an old man near him. After riding this way for a half hour the gentleman said to him, "Look, son, you will have to let go." Whereupon the boy in astonishment replied, "What's the matter—are you getting off here?"

One kid came late to school and his excuse was they had a family situation that had to be taken care of. He went on to explain that his father had to take the bull to the cow. When the teacher replied, "Couldn't your father do it himself?" the boy's answer was, "I guess he could, but the bull would do it better."

ITALY

A plane was flying over Italy, then over the Bay of Naples, when the pilot turned to his passenger and said, "Pardon me, but have you ever heard of the expression "See Naples and Die?"

The passenger answered, "Yes, I have, why?"

Then the pilot said, "Take a good look, the propeller just came off."

Sign in an Italian shop window: DON'T BE MISTAKEN FOR AN AMERICAN TOURIST . . . WEAR ITALIAN-MADE CLOTHES.

The Italian composer, Rossini, went to see his doctor. After examining him, the doctor said, "Your trouble stems from wine, women and song." Rossini suggested, "Well, I can get along without the songs, since I compose my own." The doctor said, "Well, which of the other two are you prepared to give up?" And Rossini replied, "That depends entirely on the vintage."

This is a story about a warrior of ancient Rome. He was called off to war and, fearing for the safety of his beautiful young wife, locked her in armor and then summoned his best friend and handed him the key. He said, "My friend, if I do not return in six months, use the key. To you, and only you, do I entrust it." Then he galloped off to battle. He hadn't gone but five miles when he heard hoofbeats in back of him, and looked around; through a cloud of dust his friend rode up and very excitedly cried, "Stop! You gave me the wrong key."

Mascagni, the composer, once heard an organ grinder under his window in Naples playing excerpts from his opera *Cavalleria Rusticana*. The tempo was much too slow and the dragging notes almost drove the composer to distraction. Finally, unable to stand it any longer, he rushed into the street and told the musican, "Here, I am Mascagni. I will show you how to play this music correctly." Thereupon he gave the crank handle of the barrel organ a few rapid turns, thus speeding up the tempo, and said, "There, that is the tempo in which you play."

The next day Mascagni heard the organ grinder playing again. Looking out of his window, Mascagni saw that the organ grinder had the following sign hanging over his hurdy-gurdy: PUPIL OF MASCAGNI.

❖❖

J

JAIL (see also Crooks, Cop, Police, Thieves)

VISITOR: What is your name, my good man?
PRISONER: 9742.
VISITOR: Is that your real name?
PRISONER: Naw, dat's just me pen name.

PRISONER: Ha, ha, ha, ha.
VISITOR: What's so funny?
PRISONER: They're giving me the chair tomorrow, and I'm the wrong guy.

1ST CONVICT: I wonder if I could get a pardon?
2ND CONVICT: What ya in for?
1ST CONVICT: Killin' the Governor's mother.

WARDEN: And the governor is giving one hour with grace.
PRISONER: All right, bring her in.

"What are you in jail for, Harry?"
"Taking a picture, Galahad."
"What?"
"Yeah, they caught me just as I was getting down from the wall."

JAPAN

An American official in Tokyo had occasion to write to a Japanese businessman there, and thinking to give his letter the flowery Oriental touch that would make for good public relations, closed with these words: "May Heaven preserve you always"—to which the Japanese man replied: And may Heaven pickle you, too!

Three American Red Cross girls shared a house in Yokohama where they employed a Jap butler by the name of Togo who, at one time, had served on an ocean liner and clung to the idea that all visitors were to be announced as passengers. The girls took him in hand and briefed him, telling him not to announce the guests as passengers but as callers or visitors, or company. Togo assured the girls he knew the proper word and for the girls not to worry.

That evening the girls were having a little party and the living room was filled with guests when the doorbell rang. When Togo saw two male visitors standing there, he turned and rather proudly announced: "Miss Prentiss—two customers for you."

JEALOUSY (see also Wife, Girls)

Little boy saying his prayers: "God bless mommy, God bless daddy, God bless my new baby brother. . . . and get him out of here."

1ST WOMAN: My husband is so jealous . . . he hired a detective to follow every move I make.
2ND WOMAN: That's dreadful.
1ST WOMAN: Yes, but if he ever hires another detective to follow the first detective, I'm sunk.

GIRL: What do you see in that Dorothy that you can't find in me?
MAN: Nothing. Only with you I gotta look a little longer.

MAN: How can a guy be married to you and want to devote an entire night going out with the boys?
GIRL: Well, he figures when he's out with the boys, they can't possibly be out with me.

Then there was the bride who was so jealous she had male bridesmaids.

JETS (see also Airplanes)

I heard recently of a pilot who was suspended by his company for walking up and down a line of ticket buyers reading a book entitled in large letters: *How to Fly a Jet in Ten Easy Lessons.*

A gentleman was taking his first trip by jet and was scared stiff. When the motors began to roar, he gripped the arms of his seat and closed his eyes tightly for about five minutes. Then he opened his eyes, looked out of the window and said to his companion: "My, look at those tiny people below. They look just like ants."
"They *are* ants," said the man in the seat next to him, "we haven't left the ground yet."

After completing a trip in a jet plane, the little old lady sought out the pilot: "I want to thank you," she said, "for both those rides."
"What are you talking about?" replied the pilot, "we only made one trip."
"Oh, no," said the little old lady, "two. My first and my last."

WIFE: What kind of day did you have, dear?
JET PILOT: Oh the usual . . . New York, London, Paris, Rome.

JEWELRY

MAN: That ring once belonged to a millionaire.
GIRL: Which one . . . F. W. Woolworth?

1ST GIRL: Is that a new string of pearls you're wearing?
2ND GIRL: What did you think it was, moth balls?

1ST GIRL: This is a blue diamond in my ring.
2ND GIRL: It should be blue . . . it's sad looking.

My watch is on the bum . . . my husband's wearing it.

MAN: This may be a small diamond but it hasn't one rough flaw.
GIRL: In that diamond there's no room for a flaw.

JEWELLER: These are cultured pearls.
CUSTOMER: Look, we just want to buy pearls, not pay for their education.

WOLF TO GIRL: Here's my gift, a string of pearls, but I must warn you there's a string attached.

JOBS (see also Employment)

I have a wonderful job as a lifeguard in a car wash.

"I hear in South America they're making dresses out of glass."
"So long, I'm going to South America for a job."
"Are you a glass blower?"
"No, I'm a window washer."

Fellow had an odd job. All winter he'd eat mothballs and then during the summer he got jobs breathing on overcoats.

JUDGE (see also Lawyers)

"Why don't you settle this case out of court?" the judge asked the two men before him. "That's just what we were doing," replied one fellow, "when the police came and interfered."

The noted jurist was asked how he comes to a decision. "Oh," he said, "I listen to the plaintiff and then I make my decision." "Don't you ever listen to the defendant?" he was asked. "I used to," he said, "but that mixes me up."

An old Southerner who could trace his ancestry back to the time when Lee fought Grant was hauled into court for vagrancy. Brought before the judge, he was asked his name. "It's Colonel Zeth

Eaton," he replied. "And what does the 'Colonel' stand for?" the man on the bench asked. "That 'Colonel' is kinda like the 'Honorable' in front of your name," the old man answered. "It doesn't mean a damn thing!"

A Michigan circuit judge tells about a divorce suit he handled recently. "I think you might as well give your husband a divorce," he advised the wife. "What!" shouted the lady. "I have lived with this bum for twenty years, and now I should make him happy?"

A fellow in the New Jersey Court of Chancery recently asked for a divorce on the grounds that his wife didn't love him. The judge asked the husband for proof. "Well, Your Honor," he replied, "only yesterday I was painting our cellar door and when I missed my footing, crashed to the bottom of the steps. My wife rushed to the scene, stared down at my half-conscious form and said, 'While you're down there, Henry, put some coal on the furnace.'"

JUVENILE DELINQUENCY
(see also Kids, Cops)

I heard one father state that Juvenile Delinquency is the result of parents trying to train children without starting at the bottom.

POLITICIAN: There is no such thing as juvenile delinquency in this town. Why all we have is some rock and rollers.

VOTER: Yeah . . . but those kids hit you over the head with a rock and then roll you.

The delinquents of today are the same as the delinquents of fifty years ago, only they have better weapons.

A town was having a juvenile delinquency problem. The kids kept having gang wars in the alleys. So the city fathers built three beautiful playgrounds. Now they have the gang wars in the playgrounds.

A small community in Long Island had the parents meet every weekend to find out the problem causing juvenile delinquency. They finally found out. The problem lay in the fact that the parents were never home on weekends.

A young delinquent walked into a grocery store and held it up. As he was going out, the grocer pulled out a gun and shot him in the arm. The kid ran four blocks, slipped in a puddle, ripped his pants on a nail, and finally, with a last breath, staggered to his home and rang the bell. His mother opened the door—saw the bedraggled son and said, "First you'll eat—then we'll talk."

The jury foreman stood up, cleared his throat and said, "We're all of one mind . . . temporarily insane."

The man was suing the city and was on the witness stand. "I'm walking on the sidewalk when I fell in a hole."
JUDGE: Were you walking east or west?
PLAINTIFF: I'm walking on the sidewalk when I fell in a hole . . .
JUDGE: Were you walking toward the drive or away from it?
PLAINTIFF: I'm walking on the sidewalk wh—
JUDGE: Why do you avoid my question?
PLAINTIFF: Because if I move one inch from the hole, I lose my case.

In his chambers, the judge was talking to the convict and counselled, "You'll have to carry your plea for clemency along . . the governor has been indicted himself."

K

KANNON, JACKIE

Did you ever get the feeling you were walking up a gangplank and there was no ship?

So there was this girl with a beehive hairdo and I wanted to get at the honey.

The first man President Kennedy wanted to send up in the rocket was Jimmy Hoffa. Hoffa didn't want to go to the moon because he's afraid there'd be nobody there to organize.

Russians will never land in New York. They'll never get a parking place.

Are you ladies celebrating anything or are you just out boozing it up?

Wanna drive your wife crazy? Don't talk in your sleep; just lay there and smile.

My book *Poems for the John* is selling like hotcakes. I wish it was selling like a book.

KIDS (see also Children, Adolescent, Baby, Offspring, Parents and Children, Youth)

A three-year-old was struggling with the back button on his new long winter underwear. Finally he gave up, trotted up to his mother and said: "Mommy, open my bathroom door, please."

Did you ever hear the cutie about the lady who sent her four-year-old son to a progressive summer camp? On visiting day she found him all agog about having gone swimming in the camp pool. "But how did you do that?" She asked. "I forgot to pack your bathing trunks." "We went in naked!" the tot explained. "Did the little girls go in naked, too?" asked the mother excitedly. "Goodness no, Mother!" the tyke replied. "They wore bathing caps."

"All the neighbors complain about our Freddy," said his mother, "and unfortunately they've got good cause because he's a little rascal!" "Then I'd better buy him a bicycle," said his father. "Why, do you think that will improve his bad behavior?" asked Mother. "Well, no," said Father, "but it will distribute it over a wider area."

A father asked his twelve-year-old son to make a list of the nine greatest men in America. The lad began writing. A few minutes later, the inquisitive parent asked, "Well, how're you getting along?" "I've got eight of them already," the kid smiled, "but I can't make up my mind who to put down for third base."

A little boy asked his mother if he could watch the solar eclipse. "Okay," she replied, "but don't go too close."

A little boy looked at his mother's fur coat and remarked, "How that poor beast must have suffered so that you might have that coat." His mother answered, "Shut up, you shouldn't talk about your father that way."

A little boy asked his father, "Daddy, who gave me my bicycle for Christmas?" "Santa Claus, of course." "Well, Santa was here this morning and said another installment is due."

"Why, I'm ashamed of you, my son," the father screamed at his lazy offspring. "When George Washington was your age, he had become a surveyor and was hard at work."

"And when he was your age," shot back the lad, "he was President of the United States."

Two kids came downstairs during a bridge game without a stitch of clothes on. The mother dropped her cards on the table and screamed, "What do you mean by coming down undressed?" "See, smarty," one kid said to the other, "I told you Ma's vanishing cream wouldn't work."

The thoughtful nephew smiled as he asked his rich aunt, "Did you like the chocolates I sent you?" "To tell the truth," she replied, "they haven't come back from the chemist's yet."

Two kids were discussing a young woman who was in the family way. "She ate too much yeast," the first one said loud enough for her to hear him. Annoyed, she barked at him, "Sonny, if your mother had eaten a little more yeast before you were born, you'd be better bread."

The little bud asked Mamma Rose, "Mother, where did I come from?" And Mamma Rose answered, "The stalk brought you."

A little rich boy was picked on by a big rich boy. Said the little rich boy in a fit of pique, "Well anyway, my analyst can lick your analyst."

A young kid was being enrolled for a progressive school and received an application blank. At the top was the question, "Is your child a leader?" His mother wrote, "No, but he's a good follower." A week later the mother got a letter from the school. "Your child has been accepted for the class of '62, which is comprised of fifty-eight leaders and your son."

Two kids were on the corner and a little girl walked by.
One said, "Her neck's dirty."
Other one said, "Her does?"

The little girl's mother scolded her, "If you don't stop sucking your thumb, you'll swell up and bust." The thought of such a sad ending stayed with her.
A couple of weeks later a friend of the mother's was visiting. The friend was about to become a mother. With her mommy's warning still ringing in her ears, the little girl blurted out, "I know what you've been doing!"

KID: Mama, can I go out and play?
MAMA: With those two holes in your socks?
KID: No, with the kids across the street.

The eight-year-old was asked by his grandfather, "What is the first thing you notice about a girl?" The lad, with a knowledge beyond his years, said, "That all depends on which direction she's facing."

A mother told her daughter the story of the princess and the frog and how the frog spent the night in the princess' room and then turned into a handsome prince. The child looked at her mother and said, "I don't believe it and I bet her mother didn't either."

FATHER: When I was your age, I got up at five every morning, walked 10 miles with my dog, and thought nothing of it.
SON: Well, dad, I don't think much of it either.

FATHER: Where are your manners? Haven't you learned anything watching your mother and me at dinner?
SON: Yeah . . . never get married.

1ST KID: My old man didn't want me to go to the burlesque show. He said I'd see something I shouldn't. But I went anyway.
2ND KID: Did you see something you shouldn't????
1ST KID: Yeah . . . my old man.

TEACHER: After you finish your homework what do you do for recreation?
KID: What's recreation?
TEACHER: Recreation is having fun. For example—when your daddy is through working what does he do?
KID: That's what mommy wants to know.

KINDNESS

BOY SCOUT: Oh, I always do a good deed every day.
SCOUTMASTER: That's fine—what good deed have you done today?
BOY SCOUT: Why, there was only castor oil enough for one of us this morning, so I let my little brother have it.

"You know, I think everyone should divide his wordly goods with the other fellow," said one office worker to another.
"That's a good idea. If you had two thousand dollars, would you give me one-half?"
"Sure."
"And if you had two automobiles, would you give me one?"
"Sure."
"And if you had two shirts, would you give me one?"
"No."
"Why?"
"Because I've got two shirts."

KING, ALLAN

The new Israel Airlines is great. They don't have stewardesses. They have little old ladies giving out fruit.

I love the Con Edison people. They come, dig a hole in the street, put up lanterns, then go away and you never see them again.

I love those helicopters that give traffic statistics. They say "Traffic on the highway is moderate." Well, up there it's moderate. Down here it's jammed.

I got so mad at my kid I told him to go play in the traffic.

I love the move to the suburbs. Covered wagons headed toward the Long Island Sound with mink stoles hanging out of them.

My kid loves television so much when all the programs are over for the night he watches the little white dot in case it does something.

The stewardess on the Israel airlines comes over the loudspeaker and says—"Your stewardesses are Mrs. Rose Goldberg and Mrs. Fannie Kennan and, of course, my son, the pilot."

A little old lady was on a park bench in the Bronx. A neighbor admired her two little grandchildren and asked how old they were. The little old lady said, "The lawyer is four and the doctor is six."

KISSING (see also Osculating, Romance, Love, Lovers, Spooning)

"Say, pretty, do you shrink from kissing?"
"No, if I did I'd be nothing but skin and bones!"

"How many times have I kissed you tonight?"
"Only three times—you remember mother came in once and I answered the phone once."

"Don't let my mother see you kissing me."
"But I'm not kissing you—"
"I thought I'd tell you, just in case."

There's a girl who never kisses a man with whiskey on his breath. It has to be imported champagne or nothing.

Probably a girl shuts her eyes when she kisses a man because she is trying to remember his name.

"Just one more kiss, darling."
"On an empty stomach?"
"Of course not! Right where the last one was."

"What kind of a girl is Alice?"
"Well, she can be kissed on two occasions."
"So? What are they?"
"When it rains, and when it doesn't."

"Jack wanted to kiss me last night."

"What did you say?"
"Same old thing."
"What did he do?"
"Same old thing."

Kissing her is like scratching a place that doesn't itch.

"John, dear, I wouldn't let anyone else kiss me like that."
"My name isn't John, lady."

I got a warmer kiss from the high school principal when I graduated.

"Do you believe kissing is unhealthy?"
"I couldn't say, I never—"
"You've never been kissed?"
"I've never been ill."

"How many times did that fellow kiss you?"
"Oh, I don't know. I'm a singer, not an accountant."

Speaking of kissing—there's one thing on which my girl friend and I always agree.
What's that?
Her sofa.

"That fellow kisses every girl in the class."
"Gosh, how does he do it?"
"Very nicely."

"Didn't I kiss you at Bill's house last Wednesday?"
"About what time?"

"Don't you dare kiss me. You've been drinking varnish again."
"Why can't I kiss you?"
"Lips that touch lacquer shall never touch mine."

MUSICIAN; Kisses are words in the language of love.
SINGER: Oh, goody, do you know some nice long words?

Women may be divided into two classes—those who close their eyes when you kiss them, and those who keep them open to see if you do.

NIGHT WATCHMAN: Young man, are you going to kiss that girl?
YOUNG MAN: No.
NIGHT WATCHMAN: Here, then, hold this lantern.

HE: When did you learn to kiss like that?
SHE: I used to blow up footballs.

She's such a hot kisser, she melts the gold in a guy's teeth.

The guy walked into a bar with a black eye and a swollen lip. "I got beat up for kissing a bride." he said.
"I thought that was permissible."
"But this was two years after the ceremony."

HE: Kiss me!
SHE: What? Remember I'm a lady.
HE: I know, if I wanted a man, I'd kiss my father.

KNOCK-KNOCK JOKES

Knock, knock
Who's there?
Domino
Domino who?
"Domino Cowhand."

Knock, knock
Who's there?
Butcher
Butcher who?
"Butcher Arms Around Me, Honey, Hold Me Tight."

Knock, knock
Who's there?
Frankfurter
Frankfurter who?
"Frankfurter Memories."

Knock, knock
Who's there?
Eddie
Eddie who?
Eddie Fisher

Knock, knock
Who's there?
Elizabeth
Elizabeth who?
Elizabeth Taylor. Didn't I just see my husband come in here?

KNOWLEDGE (see also University, College)

"When you went to school, didn't you learn the three R's?"
"Yeah—Rah! Rah! Rah!

"Well, Bobby, and how do you like school?"
"When it's closed."

"Papa, vat is science?"
"My, how could you be so dumb! Science is dose things vat says: NO SMOKING."

"Do you like school, Tommy?"
"Golly, missus! If it wasn't for school we wouldn't get any holidays."

"What did you learn in school today, Clarence?"
"How to whisper without moving my lips."

L

LABOR

1ST GIRL: I lost my job because of illness and fatigue.
2ND GIRL: That's too bad.
1ST GIRL: Yeah, my boss got sick and tired of me.

BOSS: Have you anything to say before I fire you?
EMPLOYEE: Yes. How about a raise?

WIFE: Why are you so afraid of work?
HUSBAND: I'm not, haven't I fought it successfully for years?

INTERVIEWER: What's your husband's average income?
GIRL: Oh, about 1 A.M.

1ST BOY: My father got a job this morning.
2ND BOY: Doing what?
1ST BOY: We don't know yet. My mother doesn't start work till next Monday.

1ST MAN: I'll have you know I have a B.A., an M.A., and a Ph.D.
2ND MAN: What good is that if you don't have a J.O.B.?

LANDLORDS (see also House, Rooms, Apartments)

"When I left my last place the landlady wept."
"But I won't. You have to pay in advance here."

As a well-known landlady once said; "Go and never darken my bathtub again."

"Young lady, your rent is way past due. You'll either pay or get out!"
"All right, darn it. I'll go out with you!"

"Look here, young man, you've been here three months and haven't paid any rent yet."
"But I thought you said it would be like home here."
"I did, but what of it?"
"Well, I never paid any rent at home."

I want to tell you, Grandpaw had an answer for everybody. One time a man complained of the soup. He told Grandpaw, he says, "I told you I wanted chicken soup and you brought me vegetable soup." Grandpaw went over and looked down at the soup and he says, "What's that floatin' around on top?" And the man looks and says, "That's a piece of celery top." And Grandpaw says, "Well, that's what fooled me—I thought it was a feather."

Was your landlord put out when you asked him to trust you for another month? No indeed, I was.

The landlady was over to the house and she gave Father three days to pay the rent.
What did he do?
He took Fourth of July, Easter and Christmas.

Guy called the landlord and said, "Hey, my whole house is flooded with six inches of water." Landlord said, "So what, for your lousy forty dollars a month rent—whatta ya want, champagne?"

LANGUAGES (see also Geography)

TEACHER: The British language is composed of vowels and consonants.
PUPIL: What, no words?

MRS. BROWN TO SCHOOL PRINCIPAL: Now I want my Archie to receive an all round education, including Latin.

PRINCIPAL: Of course, though Latin is, as you know, a dead language.
MRS. BROWN: So much the better. You see, Archie's going to to be an undertaker.

LAS VEGAS (see also Betting, Gambling)

During a recent convention of atom scientists at Las Vegas, one of the professors spent all his free time at the gambling tables. A couple of his colleagues were discussing their friend's weakness.
"Costa gambles as if there were no tomorrow," said one.
"Maybe," commented the other, "he *knows* something!"

Sign on entering Las Vegas: "Keep Las Vegas Green: Bring Money."

Definition of Las Vegas: Where the odds are you won't get even.

EDITOR: When I read your stuff I think of Las Vegas.
WRITER: You mean it has excitement, daring, adventure— or do you mean to print it would be a gamble????
EDITOR: Neither. I just think it's a lot of crap.

A gambler just back from Las Vegas told his friend he'd undergone Las Vegas surgery. "I had my wallet removed painlessly."

LATE LATE SHOW (see also Television)

Saw a late late TV movie last night that was made before they made movies.

Some of the movies on the Late Late Show are too old to be kept up that late.

In England the Late Late Show shows old American films.

I saw an old Late Late Show Western that was so old the Indians won.

LATENESS

1ST MAN: You're late again. Don't you ever do anything on time?
2ND MAN: Sure. I bought my car on time.

1ST WOMAN: My husband came home late again last night. He knocked down the tree in the back yard and crashed through the garage door.
2ND WOMAN: Did he wreck the car much?
1ST WOMAN: Who said he was driving?

BOSS: You're ten minutes late. Don't you know when we start working around here?
EMPLOYEE: No sir, when I get here everybody's already working.

1ST MAN: I'm sorry I'm late but I ran into this beautiful blonde.
2ND MAN: So that's why you're out of breath.
1ST MAN: Yeah, I ran into her husband, too.

WIFE: I've been waiting for two hours. Where were you????
HUSBAND: I've been buried in the sand waiting for the sun to go down.
WIFE: Isn't that silly.
HUSBAND: Not when you've lost your bathing trunks.

LAUNDRY

The only trouble with some of these laundries is that they don't leave enough shirt on the cuffs.

"Here, look what you did."
"I can't see anything wrong with that lace."
"Lace? That was a sheet!"

"Our new minister is so wonderful. He brings things home to you that you never saw before."
"I have a laundryman who does the same thing."

"Your laundry is back."

"Oh, thanks."

"Yeah, they refused it."

LAWYER (see also Judge, Jail)

The story is told of the lawyer's wife who was complaining about the way their home was furnished. "We need chairs, a dining room set and a new lamp."

"Listen," her spouse told her, "one of my clients is suing her husband for divorce. He has a lot of money and as soon as I finish breaking up their home, we'll fix ours."

A lawyer is a fellow who is willing to go out and spend your last cent to prove he's right.

A recent story concerns the old lady who tottered into a lawyer's office and asked for help in arranging a divorce. "A divorce?" asked the unbelieving lawyer. "Tell me, Grandma, how old are you?" "I'm eighty-four," answered the old lady. "Eighty-four! And how old is your husband?" "My husband is eighty-seven." "My, my," myed the lawyer, "and how long have you been married?" "Next September will be sixty-two years." "Married sixty-two years! Why should you want a divorce now?" "Because," Grandma answered calmly, "enough is enough."

The lawyer representing the insurance company lost the case to a man who he was convinced was faking his injury. Indignant over this travesty on justice the lawyer spoke to the faker.

LAWYER: You may have cost my Company $100,000 but I'm going to follow you wherever you go to make sure you're not faking.

FAKER: Who cares? You won't be able to prove a thing . . . because I'm taking the $100,000 and going to England to see those big specialists. They won't be able to help me. Then I'm going to Germany to see some more specialists. They won't be able to help me. Then I'm going to France, to Lourdes, and you're going to see the biggest miracle of your life.

CLIENT: I'm going to the electric chair in ten minutes. Can't you tell me something that may save my life?

LAWYER: Sure—don't sit down.

Two lawyers met with their clients to try and settle an accident that occurred on the golf course out of court.

1ST LAWYER: My client was hit in the head by your client's golf ball and we won't settle for anything under $10,000.

2ND LAWYER: But it wasn't my

client's fault. He yelled, "Fore."
1ST LAWYER: We'll take it.

LAWYER: I'll handle your case for $500 and twelve hamburgers.
CLIENT: What's the twelve hamburgers for?
LAWYER: When I plead a case I have the jury eating out of my hands.

When lawyers play baseball there are twelve umpires because they're more at home with a jury making the decisions.

Who is the best lawyer in town?
Henry Brown, when he's sober.
And who is the second best lawyer in town?
Henry Brown, when he's drunk.

Martin had just opened his law office, and immediately hired three good-looking stenographers to work for him.
"But how," a visiting friend inquired, eyeing the three, "do you expect to accomplish anything?"
"Simple," Martin replied and grinned, "by giving two of them the day off."

Tombstone: "Here lies a lawyer and a honest man." Whoever thought two people could fit in that little coffin?

A lawyer tore excitedly into court and asked that a new trial be granted a client found guilty the day previous. "I've uncovered new evidence," declared the lawyer. "Of what nature?" asked the judge.
"My client," the lawyer told him, "has an extra six hundred dollars. I only found out about this morning."

The lawyer had just won a speedy acquittal for a wealthy businessman charged with bigamy.
"You're a free man" said the lawyer, "Go on home to your wife."
"Which one?" enthused the acquitted.

LAZY (see also Loafer)

His feet have been known to fall asleep while running after a streetcar.

Father says, "Son, go out and see if it's raining" and the son is so lazy he answers, "Oh, Paw, call in the dog and see if he's wet."

Uncle Ed, on relief and employed on a Vermont highway project, complained to the foreman that he wanted a shovel. The foreman told him not to worry about having a shovel, that he'd get paid anyway. "But I want a shovel," insisted Uncle Ed. "Everybody but me's got somethin' to lean on."

Nathan's wife tells of his discomfiture the time the sheriff's funeral passed their gate. "It was a grand sight," she said. "Nathan was restin' in the hammick when it went by. I come out and told him who all was in the carriages and autymobiles, and his kinfolk wavin' to him. Nathan was kinda peeved. 'Just my luck,' he said, 't'be facin' th' other way.' "

There's the story about the lazy playboy who had so little vitality he stood with the cocktail shaker in his hands waiting for an earthquake.

Has the seven years' itch and is already nine months behind in the scratching.

Two characters were off on a binge. "I'm going to leave this job soon and I want you to come with me," said one of the boys after his eighth drink. "I know a place in Australia where there's a lot of gold just lying around waiting for someone to pick it up." "I knew there was a catch in it," replied the friend. "What's the catch?" "You've got to bend over."

PAT: Say, what caused the explosion at the plant the other day?
MIKE: Oh, Casey was carrying a load of dynamite and the whistle blew.

"It sure is hot."
"Yeah, see that shady tree over there?"
"Yes."
"I'd give anything if I were under it."

He's so lazy that when he worked on a farm they had to sharpen every tree stump.

He's so lazy he gets in a revolving door and waits.

One of the laziest men in the world lives in Lumberton, North Carolina. One day his cousin drove by the man's farm and noticed his barn was on fire.
"Your barn's burning down," he yelled.
"I know it," said the lazy man, "I'm sittin' here prayin' for rain."

LEGS

IRATE MAN: Your dog bit me and I'm going to sue you.
SHREWD MAN: Never mind! I'll give you fifty dollars to settle out of court.
IRATE MAN: Okay. I'll take the money. Say, what are you laughing at?

SHREWD MAN: That's a counterfeit bill. What are you laughing at?
IRATE MAN: I've got a wooden leg.

FIRST FAKE: Would you rather be lame or blind?
SECOND FAKE: I'd rather be lame.
FIRST FAKE: Why?
SECOND FAKE: Because when I was blind people were always giving me counterfeit money.

JOHNNIE: I've got an uncle with a wooden leg that drinks.
SUSIE: Is that so?
JOHNNIE: Yeah.
SUSIE: Does it injure the finish?

"I've got a cedar chest," she told him.
"Wonderful!" he conceded. "I've only got a wooden leg."

"My uncle has a wooden leg," Jeanie told her teacher.
"That's too bad," her teacher sympathized.
"Yeah, and it pains him just awful," continued her pupil.
"How could a wooden leg pain him?" asked her mystified teacher.
"His wife hit him over the head with it," explained Jeanie.

I won't say she's bowlegged but she used to model for doughnuts.

Now there is a girl who is well-heeled . . . and they're on both of her arms.

1ST MAN: She has two of the most beautiful legs in the world.
2ND MAN: How do you know????
1ST MAN: I counted them.

WOMAN: You said these nylons were guaranteed not to run.
SALESMAN: Now that I see your legs I'm going to run, too.

One of her legs is knock-kneed and the other one is bow-legged. When she walks you don't know if she's coming or going.

"I want you to know that I can match my legs with Dietrich."
"How can you match your legs with Dietrich when your legs don't even match each other?"

"Don't they make a handsome couple. He with his bow tie and she with her bow legs?"

She's so bowlegged that she's the only girl I know who can walk out of a taxi from both ends.

The last time I saw a leg like that it had a message tied to it.

LEONARD, JACKIE (see also Hecklers, Insults)

Sir, someday you're going to find yourself and you're going to be disappointed.

I never forget a face but with you I'll make an exception.

And now Ray Bloch will play a song he recently recorded on his tape recorder.

Ed Sullivan lights up a whole room when he walks out of it.

I saw this man play Shakespeare and Shakespeare lost.

I remember you from ten years ago, lady. I don't remember the face but I remember your dress.

Now let's give him a big hand right across his mouth.

Don't feel bad, sir; a lot of people have no talent.

"Mommy, Mommy, I don't want to go to Europe."
"Shut up, kid, and keep swimming."

Jack Carter has a great comedy style—mine!

On Steve Allen: "I could be funny for hours on your show, Steve, but I don't wanna change the format."

There's Nick Kenny—Maxie Rosenbloom with a typewriter.

There's Harry Hershfield, one of the few living witnesses to the parting of the Red Sea.

LETTERS (see also Mail, Telegrams)

"I received a letter from my girl friend in the East."
"I'll bet she is glad."
"That she's my girl friend?"
"No—that's she's in the East."

"I wrote her a letter every day for three years."
"What happened?"
"She married the mailman."

(Reads postcard):
"Am having great fun. In the next room to me in the hotel is a honeymoon couple. Wish you could hear!"

Everyone was licking stamps and addressing packages at the post office to send for Xmas. I reached for a pen and when I got my hand back, it had a dozen Xmas seals on it.

P. O. CLERK: Is this package for you? The name is obliterated.
MAN: No, that can't be mine. My name is O'Brien.

BILL: How are we going to mail it? We haven't even got the price of a stamp.
WILL: Just drop it in the mailbox when nobody is looking.

"How much does it cost to send a telegram?"
"Where to?"
"Betty."

"Shall I put a stamp on myself?"
"No, on the letter."

"I always kiss the stamps on your letters because I know that your lips have touched them."
"You're wrong there, I moisten the stamp on Fido's nose—it's always wet."

"As a matter of fact, I have received letters from ladies in almost every place in which I appeared."
"Landladies, I presume."

LEVENSON, SAM

Yosheh Phivel brought a package to the post office but the clerk refused to accept it.
"What's the matter?"
"It's too heavy; you'll have to put more stamps on it."
"And if I put more stamps on it that will make it lighter?"

My Uncle Hirshel solved his vacation problem in a cute way. His wife had been nagging him all year long for a trip to the Thousand Islands. He compromised by taking her 1,000 times to Coney Island.

I use the word "farblundjet" sometimes and I'd like to explain it. "Farblundjet" can be defined as a "kosher butcher in Scarsdale."

The excuses kids used to give me when they were late for school were amazing. One kid once told me—"I was late because there's eight kids in my family and my mother only set the alarm for seven . . ."

I once asked the question in class—"What's the difference between a king and a president?" One kid handed in this answer: "The king has to be the son of his father . . ."

And mothers are great. When I was teaching a mother once wrote me a note about her son. It said, "If Gregory is a bad boy, don't slap him. Slap the boy next to him. Gregory will get the idea."

LEWIS, JOE E. (see also Alcohol, Liquor)

They asked me about doing a Western series for TV. They're going to call it "Frontier Drunk."

They did the story of my life in the movies but they couldn't do the true story. Paramount Pictures didn't have a liquor license.

In the movie of my life story there's one scene in which I refuse a drink. They had to get a stuntman to play me.

I told my doctor I drank to quiet my nerves. He said, "Nobody's nerves are that noisy. . . ."

I never drink on New Year's Eve. That's Amateur Night.

I've donated my liver to science after I die . . . They were thrilled. They were so happy to get one already pickled.

Someone asked me what my drinking capacity was. Well I don't know for sure, but I'm about 2000 swallows ahead of Capistrano . . .

I woke up at the crack of ice and I've been cold drunk all day. My pianist, Austin Mack, is the one who really drinks. He was so drunk, as I was leaving the club last night on the way out he stepped on my fingers. I hate a guy who falls on top of me when he's drunk.

I used to be a test pilot for Seagrams.

When my doctor took my blood test he offered me sixty dollars a case.

LIES (see also Fibbing, Liar, Lying)

"It feels great to be well again."
"Have you been sick?"
"Sick? I was lying at death's door for two weeks."
"That's courage for you."
"Huh?"
"At death's door and still lying."

"Can you guess where I've been?"
"I can. But go on with your story."

"Our author down the hall has at least had a story accepted."
"No!"
"Yes; he got home at 2:00 AM this morning, and told his wife a story and she actually believed him."

"Have you seen one of those instruments to detect falsehoods?"
"Seen one? I married one."

"Can you tell by your husband's face if he's lying?" asked one wife of another. And the other snorted, "Yes, if his lips are moving, he is."

"That man is going around telling lies about you!"

"I don't mind—but I'll break his head if he begins telling the truth."

LINDY'S (see also Restaurants, Waiters)

The new hillbilly star decided to enjoy his new-found show business wealth and fame, so he went into Lindy's to eat dinner. This was the first time in his life he had ever eaten in a restaurant. The star liked everything about Lindy's and was careful to eat according to rules presented in Emily Post. As he left Lindy's he took a toothpick from the counter, used it for a while and then replaced it. The cashier looked at him unbelievingly.

STAR: I bet some people who come in here steal those things.

Lindy's is a restaurant where all the Broadway stars eat. If you're a star of stage, screen and TV they treat you like a king and you sit at the front table. If you are a star of records they treat you like a prince and seat you at the second table. If you are a star in night clubs they treat you like a duke and you sit at the third table.

COMIC: So how do they treat you, Joey?

ADAMS: Like one of the family . . .

COMIC: Like one of the family?

ADAMS: Yeah. I eat in the kitchen.

A renowned waiter at Lindy's died, and some of his show business regulars were so saddened by his loss that they decided to visit a spiritualist to try and communicate with their long-lost friend.

The spiritualist advised, "Just knock on the table as you did when he was alive and he shall appear."

The friends knocked on the table but the waiter didn't appear. They knocked again and still no waiter. Finally they banged on the table and called his name.

Then in a puff of smoke the waiter appeared in his uniform and a cloth over his arm. "Why didn't you first appear when you heard us knocking?" they asked.

"Wasn't my table," answered the waiter.

The headwaiter at Lindy's spotted a customer with a napkin tucked into his collar and asked a waiter to explain as courteously as possible his bad manners. The waiter walked up to the customer and discreetly asked, "Shave or haircut, sir?"

LIAR (see also Fibbing, Lies, Lying)

MOTHER: I don't like the way you tell lies.
JOHNNY: Well, I don't know any other way.

HUSBAND: I've noticed you've been telling quite a few fibs lately.
WIFE: I thought it was a wife's duty to speak well of her husband occasionally.

NEWSPAPER EDITOR: So you'd like a job on our paper?
CUB REPORTER: Yes sir.
EDITOR: Have you ever told a lie?
REPORTER: No, but I'm willing to learn.

1ST MAN: Today I saw a lie detector for the first time.
2ND MAN: That's nothing . . . I'm married to one.

JUDGE TO DEFENDANT: You are lying so badly that I would advise you to get a lawyer.

FATHER: How can you make up such lies?

YOUNG MAN: It sure ain't easy.

LIQUOR (see also Alcohol, Booze, Drunk)

Whiskey has killed more men than bullets. Maybe so, but wouldn't you rather be filled with whiskey than with bullets?

A Westerner entered a saloon with his wife and a three-year-old boy. He ordered two straight whiskies. "Hey, Pa," the kid asked, "ain't Mother drinking?"

"Let's go through those swinging doors."
"Those ain't swinging doors, that's two customers."

"I'm so thirsty, I could drink water."
"Me, too. Am I parched! My throat feels like a dust storm wearing a collar and tie."

He drinks so much the mosquitoes bring along a cup of water before they bite him. They can't take it without a chaser.

"Do you ever feel your liquor, honey?"
"Of course not, why should I get my fingers wet?"

Here's one elephant who got so drunk he saw pink men.

HUSBAND: We had a drinking contest at the club today, dear.
WIFE: Who won second prize?

The surest way to lose your health is to keep drinking other people's.

That's not a flask, that's her hip!

He can't drink any more waiter. Better pour it over him.

"How many beers does it take to make you dizzy?"
"Oh, four or five, but don't call me Dizzy."

Young man, I found a pint of Scotch and a bottle of ginger ale in your overcoat. What am I to make of that?
A couple of highballs.

This stuff is twenty years old. Don't let it live another minute.

Without a cent in my pockets I went into a bar and got a straight shot of whiskey.
And what did you do for a chaser?
The bartender.

Is this good stuff?
Yes, it's government alcohol.
What government?

So Jack is against prohibition? Against prohibition? Why he's so wet that every time you blow on him he ripples.

He ought to stop drinking.
Oh, he's cut down now. Last night he came home a quart and a half earlier.

He had to have his pick-me-up every morning. It was generally a policeman that did the picking up.

MAN: Drinking makes you beautiful.
GIRL: But I haven't been drinking.
MAN: I know, but I have.

WIFE: Don't you know that liquor is slow poison?
HUSBAND: That's all right . . . I'm in no hurry.

SIGN IN BAR: The customer is always tight.

WIFE: Can't you do anything but drink?
HUSBAND: Sometimes I hiccup.

HUSBAND: I'll drive.
WIFE: You're in no condition to drive.
HUSBAND: Well, I'm in no condition to walk.

1ST BOY: My old man dropped some Scotch into the fish bowl.
2ND BOY: What happened?
1ST BOY: We had pickled herring for breakfast.

WIFE: Marriage hasn't changed you at all . . . you drink just as much as before.
HUSBAND: Yes, but then I used to drink out of pleasure . . .

DRUNK: Waiter . . . hic . . . bring me a dish of prunes.
WAITER: Stewed?
DRUNK: Thash none o' your business.

JUDGE: Now, George Jones, you are charged with habitual drunkenness. What have you to say to excuse your offense?
JONES: Habitual thirst, your honor.

1ST DRUNK: Say, know what time it is?
2ND DRUNK: Yeah.
1ST DRUNK: Thanks.

LOAFER (see also Lazy)

"Your father is very lazy."
"Maybe so, but he never raised his hand to me."
"That's because he's afraid he'll break the cobwebs that's been spun under his arms."

The premium lazy man does his reading in the Autumn, because the season turns the leaves.

"I can't drink coffee in the morning."
"Why not?"
"Because it can keep me awake all day."

The college boy who is too lazy to write home for money.

I was just thinking that I wish I was a coal miner so I could go on strike with them others.

"What are you doing there?"
"I'm just fishing."
"Well, don't you know that there couldn't be any fish there?"
"Yes, I know that, but this place is so handy."

His feet have been known to fall asleep while running after a street car.

When the committee arrived to present Nathan with the $10 prize for being the laziest man north of the Massachusetts line, Nathan was distressed. "Boys," he said, "ef y're set on givin' this to me, d' y' mind rollin' me over and putting it in my backside pocket?"

There's the story about the man who had so little vitality he stood with the cocktail shaker in his hands waiting for an earth-quake.

Has the seven years' itch and is already nine months behind in the scratching.

LOANS (see also Banks, Money, Cash)

"Can I put the nab on you for $125—I want to get a pair of shoes."
"But you can get some for $5."
"Not for my feet. I want four new ones for my car."

"I need $100 for some X-ray pictures."
"But X-ray pictures only cost $10."
"But mine turned out so well I ordered a dozen."

"Suppose you loan Red $10 and he agrees to repay you at the rate of a dollar a week? How much have you after seven weeks?"
"Nothing."
"Nothing? You don't know math."
"You don't know Red!"

Everybody out here is so pros-perous the loan companies are putting in floor shows to attract business.

"Hello, Tommy, what's new?"
"How about that twenty you owe me?"
"Nothing new, eh?"

"Would you give ten cents to help the Old Ladies' Home?"
"What! Are they out again?"

"I wanna put the bite on y' for $10,000—I wanna pay for a tur-key."
"That's silly,—I can produce a turkey for six dollars."
"The turkey *I* produced was in three acts."

"I could loan you money, but loaning money only breaks friend-ship."
"Well, we never were very good friends."

"Could I borrow $200?"
"Why don't you borrow from some of the other relatives?"
"You wouldn't want me to hang around that bunch of chis-elers, would you?"

"Could I put the bite on you for $800? I want to get a gallon of gas."
"Why, you can get a gallon of gas for two bits."
"Yeah, I know, but I've got to have a car to go with it."

Two men sat in a restaurant. At the end of the meal one requested a loan.

"Can you lend me a ten spot for a week?"

"Sure," replied the other, counting out the money.

As they rose, the second man spoke again.

"Remember," he reminded, "that is only for one week."

The borrower turned a vivid red. "You'll get your money!" he screamed. "Stop hounding me!"

"I'm looking for someone to lend me ten dollars."

"Well, you've got a nice day for it."

"Do you believe that lending money breaks up friendship?"

"I certainly do."

"Well, lend me $200 and break up."

"You wanted to borrow $50.00 and they offered you $2? What did you do?"

"I took the $2. I was in no mood to dicker."

"Give me a nickel."

"I gave you a nickel last week."

"I know, but I overate on it, and now I've got to see a doctor."

"Haven't you forgotten that you owe me a hundred dollars?"

"I should say not. Didn't you see me trying to duck into that hallway?"

The man who is always asking for a loan is always left alone.

"Thanks awfully for this quarter, old man. I'll send it back to you next week. By the way, what's your address?"

"Oh, er, send it to Woodlawn Cemetery."

"Why, hang it; that's not your address."

"No; but that's where I shall be by the time you send it back."

"You must have a wonderful memory to keep all that knowledge in your head."

"Yes, I never forget when it is once in my head."

"Well, old man, how about the five dollars I lent you some time ago?"

"Ah. That's different. I put that in my pocket."

"I say, old man, could you lend me fifty cents?"

"I'm a little deaf in that ear; go around to the other one."

(Changing his mind) "Could you lend me five dollars?"

"Lend you what?"

"Five dollars."

"Oh, you had better go back to the fifty-cent ear."

Joe Lewis tells about the guy, a casual race track acquaintance, who said: "Could you lend me ten bucks?" Lewis took a chance, and at the end of the day received his ten spot back. The next day, the same bloke made another request —this time for $20, and after the seventh race, refunded the loan. . . . On the third day when he asked him for $30, Joe waved him away. . . . "Nuthin' doin!" said Joe, "you fooled me twice!"

LOST

"Did you lose your wallet?"
"No."
"Then lend me $20."

"Lost a dime and my brother found it."
"What are you doing now?"
"Looking for my brother."

"Anything happen to you today?"
"Did it? I found a $10 bill. Is that hard luck?"
"Yes, for the guy that lost it."

"What are you looking for?"
"I lost a five-dollar bill at Broadway and Thirty-third St."
"But this is Broadway and Forty-second St."
"I know. But there's more light up here."

"I want to know what happened to the money."
"I was carrying it home with me and I was held up."

"You were held up?"
"Yes, eight men sprang out at me."
"Eight men?"
"From two alleys."
"I might have fought them off if there were six of them, but there were eight."
"Go on —"
"Interesting, eh?"
"They held me up and divided the money among them."
"Yes, but eight into four dollars goes to fifty cents apiece. What happened to the rest?"
"There's a discrepancy? Eh?"
"What happened to the other fifty cents?"
"They thought I was such a good guy, they gave me a cut on it, too."

LOVE (see also Lover, Romance, Courtship, Marriage)

BIG SISTER: Snoop, have you been prowling through my diary again?
KID SISTER: Sure, I've read it from lover to lover.

They say that love is blind and that the home is an institution. Therefore marriage must be an institution for the blind.

Making love is like baking bread. All you need is lots of dough and plenty of crust.

"Do you go for the quiet type of women?"

"No, I'm in love with my wife."

It must be love. She looks at him as if he's a coat she can't afford.

She said she wanted to be loved to pieces. She got her wish, and now she's all broken up.

"Frank's in love."

"That's nothing. Hoboken's in New Jersey."

He fell in love with me. He wrote to me every week—for one week.

He loved the girl so much that he worshipped the very ground her father discovered oil on.

Love is valued highest during the days of courting and the days in court.

Love is like the measles. It's worse when it comes late in life.

Love is a sweet dream, and marriage is the alarm clock.

"How's your love affair?"

"It's all off."

"I thought everything was settled."

"It was. I told her my uncle was a millionaire."

"What happened?"

"Now she's my aunt."

SHE: After we are married I will share all your troubles and sorrows.

HE: But I have no troubles and sorrows.

SHE: Well, you will have after we are married.

Business is like making love—when it's good it's very good and when it's bad, it ain't bad.

If all the world loves a lover, how come they have cops in Central Park?

He showed her a lot of love and affection. He took her to a drive-in movie and let her peek into the other cars.

An historian was telling his friend that here are no such things as modern and old-fashioned lovers. "Actually," he said, "the art of courting hasn't changed in more than two thousand years. Then, too, Greek maidens used to sit and listen to a lyre all night."

A couple celebrating their twentieth anniversary were seated at the movies watching one of those torrid foreign films. When they got home that night, the wife turned to her spouse and purred, "Why is it that you never make love to me like all those men in the movies?" "Are you crazy?" he roared. "Do you know how much they pay those fellows for doing that?"

Love is the only game that is never postponed on account of darkness.

Love is the wine of life, and marriage is the morning after.

Hollywoodites will go in for pretty near anything as long as it isn't too much trouble and doesn't call for too much risk. The other day on the set, a couple of extras were talking to me and told me they were going to get married. I said, "Well, are you sure you love each other?" and the boy says, "Well, not exactly, but it won't cost nothin,—my father's a preacher." So I asked the girl if she was sure she loved the boy and she says, "No, but what have I got to lose—my father is a lawyer."

"I don't know why your father don't like me." "Neither do I. After all, money, brains and looks aren't everything."

Love is just a lot of dame foolishness.

He wants to take her away from it all—and she wants to take it all away from him.

He has a soft spot in his head for her.

This week's motto: It is better to have loved and lost than to have run into the house detective.

If love is blind, maybe that's why you see so many spectacles in the park.

A woman set out to reform her fiancé. She got him to give up smoking, then swearing—drinking—chewing tobacco and gambling, and when she finally finished with him. HE decided she wasn't good enough for him—so he jilted her.

It's better to have loved and lost—yeah, lots better.

To fall in love with her, you must have an open mind . . . a hole in the head!

At the liquor shop the two friends were arguing. One said, "Aah, you don't know anything about making love." The second man answered, "I don't, huh? Ask your wife!"

HUSBAND: Honey, will you put that book down and go to sleep! It's late.

WIFE: But I'm just reading a fascinating article . . . *Casanova's Ten Rules for Successful Lovemaking.*

HUSBAND: Well, the first rule is turn out the light.

GIRL: You're a man after my own heart.
MAN: That's not all I'm after . . .

SHE: Lots of men have fought for my hand.
HE: What happened when they saw the rest of you?

SHE: Will you love me when I'm old and grey?
HE: Why must I wait that long?

1ST MAN: Yesterday I went into the Tunnel of Love . . .
2ND MAN: Did you have a girl with you? ? ?
1ST MAN: What for? I'm not afraid of the dark.

BOY: I love your hair, your teeth, your lips, your nose . . .
GIRL: Well then kiss me and stop taking inventory.

I could marry a girl with $100,000 . . . Why don't you??? I don't have $100,000.

LOVER (see also Love)

"Can you love two girls at once?"
"Yes, sir, immediately."

Ah! Puppy love! Those nights when we sat on the back porch and she scratched my head and I licked her hand.

"Don't tell anyone, but I had your name tattooed on my arm."
"Oh, let me see!"
"Wait 'till I roll my sleeve up—there!"
"But my name isn't Rose!"
"Oops, wrong arm."

Love is what you shout to the world and whisper to me.

Love is when two people with their eyes shut can see heaven.

They're as inseparable as a screen test and a proposition.

"I'm in love with a banker and every time he kisses me, he makes me a present of a bond."
In other words, dearie, you're getting your education by lips and bonds.

"Do you love me alone?"
"Yes."
"Will you always adore me?"
"Yes."
"Will you always be faithful and true to me?"
"Sure."
"Then let's elope and get married tonight."
"I can't—I have a date."

"I gave up love."
"Why?"

"My girl had bad eyesight."
"Bad eyesight?"
"Yes, she said she couldn't see me from a hole in the wall."

"What do you know about love?"
"Plenty. I drove a taxi for five years."

"She turned her back on love, so she got it in the neck."

"I'll love you only, if I live to be eighty years old."
"Yes, and then I suppose you'll start chasing out with other women."

LUCK

He had tough luck. He had a check for ten dollars and the only person who could cash it was a fellow to whom he owed nine dollars.

An engineer friend of mine, when taking his shower slipped on the soap. Then he tore his shirt while he was putting it on. On the way out of the house he fell down the stairs. He finally got out on his run, and as he was traveling 60 miles per hour he looked ahead, and there he saw another train coming toward him at the same speed on the same track. He turned to the fireman and said,

"Joe, have you ever had one of those days when everything went dead wrong?"

LYING (see also Lies, Liar, Fibbing)

WIFE: Frederick, when you came home last night you told me you had been to the Grand Hotel with Mr. Wilson, and Mrs. Wilson just called and said you were both at the Trocadero. Why did you lie to me?
HUSBAND: When I came home last night I couldn't say "Trocadero."

The first lie detector was made out of the rib of a man. No improvement has ever been made on the original machine.

BIBLE PROFESSOR: I will lecture today on liars. How many of you have read the twenty-fifth chapter?
(Nearly all the members of the class raise their hands.)
PROFESSOR: That's fine. You're the group to whom I wish to speak. There is no twenty-fifth chapter.

"Don't you think that Wordsworth was right when he said: Heaven lies about us in our infancy?" asked a poetry-loving matron.

"Yes," replied her cynical friend, "but he forgot to add that everybody lies about us in our maturity."

LITTLE GIRL: Mama, what is a second story man?
MOTHER: Your father's one. If I don't believe his first story, he always has another one ready.

MAN OF THE HOUSE: How dare you tell my wife what time I got in this morning—especially when I told you not to tell?
MAID: I didn't tell her what time you came in. She asked me and I just said I was too busy getting breakfast to notice.

"There is only one thing that keeps you from being a barefaced liar."
"What's that?"
"Your mustache."

LAWYER: Remember, when they put you on the witness stand, you must not lie.
WITNESS: I wouldn't lie—my uncle told a lie in court once.
LAWYER: Your uncle told a lie? What happened to him?
WITNESS: He won the case.

A witness was being questioned on the stand in court.
WITNESS: I've been wedded to the truth from infancy.
PROSECUTOR: Is the court to imply from this statement that you are now a widower?

He claims the country is getting along—progressing. He says George Washington couldn't tell a lie and now almost everybody can.

BACHELOR: At the hospital I saw one of these machines that tell if a man's lying.
BENEDICT: Pooh!
BACHELOR: Pooh? Did you ever see one?
BENEDICT: See one? I married one.

"Nothing that is false ever does anybody any good."
"You're wrong, stranger. I have false teeth and they do me a lot of good."

FRANCES: Can you tell by your husband's face if he's lying?
LAURA: Yes. If his lips are moving, he is.

❖❖❖

M

MAIL (see also Letters, Telegrams)

"I want a stamp."

"Do you know the difference between a stamp and a burnt match?"

"No, I don't."

"Well, here's a burnt match, then."

"Your letter just balances, miss; if it weighed any more you would have had to put on another stamp."

"I'm glad I didn't sign my middle name."

This pen is so bad it belongs in the post office.

"Just think—my wife received another anonymous letter today."

"From whom?"

"The postmaster gave you a dirty look when he handed out your mail."

"My friends are such poor writers he can't read the cards that come for me."

"Berlin, U.S. November 22nd."

"Wait a minute, Berlin is in Germany and not in the U.S."

"Sure, but the U.S. in this letter doesn't mean United States."

"What does it mean?"

"Upstairs."

She cried when she was readin' your letter. She almost fell off the fellow's lap.

"Post Office—Are there any letters for Brown?"

"Not one."

(Cries loudly) "Every day the same thing. No letters, NO LETTERS. Hey—what am I crying for? My name isn't Brown."

"Does that rich young man of yours write convincing letters?"

"I can't say. The case hasn't gone to the jury yet."

MAKE-UP (see also Girls)

HE: My wife is just as beautiful today as she was 20 years ago when we first met. It just takes her longer.

1ST GIRL: Did you hear about that new lipstick they just put out? It's made out of Bourbon.

2ND GIRL: Out of bourbon?

1ST GIRL: Yes, it's kissproof, smearproof and 100 proof.

My wife puts so much grease on her face at night you'd think she was going to swim the English Channel.

1ST GIRL: Did Mary inherit her looks?

2ND GIRL: Yes, from her father. He left her a drug store.

HE: You certainly do a good job with your make-up.

SHE: I do? Thanks.

HE: Yeah, you can hardly tell where your face ends and Elizabeth Arden's begins.

MANNERS (see also Etiquette)

My uncle blew on his soup so hard once, that he started the windmill on an old Dutch painting.

"What did you do?—The hostess never wants to see you again."

"I didn't do anything. I just fed her dog under the table."

"That wasn't her dog, that was her husband."

My folks eat so fast that they start on their dessert before the echo of their soup has died away.

"Charlie never raises his hat to a lady."

"No manners?"

"No hair."

"Now, when you're there for dinner, show your versatility—go out in the kitchen and offer to help."

"But suppose they have lamb chops? I wouldn't know what kind of panties to put on them."

"Some like lace panties and then some like coaties and vestees."

"Well, how do you tell a boy from a girl lamb chop?"

"That should be of interest *only* to another lamb chop."

There were twelve of us at the table and thirteen pieces of meat and I told them no matter how hungry they were they were not to touch it it, and sure enough they remembered what I said, and no one touched it.

Just then, the lights went out and there was a terrible clatter of silverware and when the lights went on, there was the guest of honor with eleven forks stuck in the back of his hand.

"George, what are you reading?"

"Don't bother me—dammit, shut up and get the hell out of here. Can't you see I'm studying this book of etiquette?"

He just came back from a vacation, where he almost died of

thirst. The hotel didn't have any saucers.

"Now men, don't swear before the little lady."
"Oh, beg your pardon. We didn't know she wanted to swear first."

"I hope you don't do the same thing tonight that you did at the hotel the other day. You did nothing but sit there and eat soup all through the meal."
"The ceiling had a leak in it and I had to eat soup or drown."

A bird in the hand is bad table manners.

"Is my face clean enough to eat with?"
"Yes, but you better use your hands."

She's very proper. She won't even look at things with a naked eye.

So polite that when she threw a cup of hot coffee at him, she took the spoon out first.

He embarrassed us—he drank his soup and six couples got up and danced.

My boyfriend is so polite he always knocks on the oyster shells before he opens them.

MARRIAGE (see also, Husband, Wife, Married, Matrimony, Newlyweds)

My wife will put on most anything for dinner except an apron.

"What did you do before you were married?" The husband answered, "Anything I wanted to."

A multimillionaire was telling how he attained his fortune. "I never hesitate," he said, "to give my wife full credit for her assistance." "And just how much did she help?" he was asked. "Frankly," confessed the wealthy one, "I was curious to see if there was any income she couldn't live beyond."

I finally discovered the perfect way to get rid of dishpan hands— I let my husband do the dishes.

There's nothing like a dishtowel for wiping that contented look off a married man's face.

The husband complained, "You promised to love, honor and obey.—Right now I'd settle for any one of them."

Married men may not be the best-informed men, but they are the most.

The husband asked his wife angrily, "Another new hat! Where will I get the money to pay for it?" She answered, "Whatever my faults, dear, I'm not inquisitive."

There's buried treasure in this country. If you don't think so, listen to some women talk about their first husbands.

A friend tells us about Sam, a successful dress manufacturer, who had to make a trip to the West Coast on business. Sadie, his loving wife, resented the trip bitterly because it meant celebrating their anniversary alone. Plead as she might, Sam couldn't avoid the trip and left his tearful Sadie behind. Every night he called from the Coast and every conversation ended with pain and sobs.

Sam had to do something special to prove his own anguish and great love, so one evening he phoned and said, "Sadie dear, I'm sending you two wonderful presents—a Picasso and a Jaguar." And he did.

A few days later, Sam asked Sadie during one of their phone conversations, "Didn't the Picasso and the Jaguar arrive yet?" "Not both, Sam," answered Sadie. "only one of them came." "Good! Wonderful!" Sam exclaimed. "Which one?" "Who knows?" answered Sadie.

1ST MAN: I think I'll see the doctor today. I don't like the way my wife's looking.
2ND MAN: Good idea. I'll come with you . . . I can't stand the sight of mine, either.

1ST MAN: My wife is a magician.
2ND MAN: Really?
1ST MAN: Yeah, she can turn any-anything into an argument.

Marriage is a three-ring circus . . . Engagement ring, wedding ring and suffering.

WIFE: You're such a wonderful husband. Even if Rock Hudson asked me to run away with him, I wouldn't forget you.
HUSBAND: You wouldn't?
WIFE: No, I'd write you every week.

1ST MAN: My wife is always nagging.
2ND MAN: Mine too. She is always talking about her last husband.
1ST MAN: Mine is always talking about her next husband.

HUSBAND: Let's go out on the town tonight and really have some fun.
WIFE: Okay and whoever is home first should leave the light on in the hall.

1ST MAN: My wife's been nursing a grouch.

2ND MAN: I didn't know you were sick.

WIFE: Tell the truth. . . . if you had to do it over again, would you marry me?
HUSBAND: If I had to.

1ST MAN: I hear in India a man doesn't know his wife until after he marries her.
2ND MAN: Same thing in the States.

WIFE: Now that we're married, your mother is my mother and my mother is your mother. Isn't that wonderful?
HUSBAND: Gee . . . I hope Pop appreciates the change.

1ST MAN: My wife is always complaining she has nothing to wear about the house.
2ND MAN: What do you do about it?
1ST MAN: I pull down the shades.

MOTHER: I don't think you're taking this marriage of yours seriously.
DAUGHTER: Well, after all, Mother, it's only my first.

"Was your married life happy?"
"I should say. Married ten years and never had a fight in our house."
"How nice."

"Yes, we always went out in the yard."

Marriage is a game of give and take. What you don't give, she takes.

JOE: Yessir, I want to get married.
JIM: Don't. You're not wise enough?
JOE: When will I be wise enough?
JIM: When you get over the idea that you want to get married.

"Are you going to marry her?"
"Should I?"
"Why not? Every day, all over the world, people are getting married."
"You think I'm a copy cat?"

"We made an agreement when we were married. She would decide on the little things and I would decide on the big things."
"How did it work out?"
"So far no big things have come up."

"What do you know about married life? You're single."
"But I live in a bungalow court."

"I've been married for fifteen years."
"It must be nice to live in marital bliss that long."
"No, we live in Boyle Heights."

"My razor's awfully blunt, dear. I can scarcely shave with it."

"Why, Charles, you don't mean to tell me your beard is tougher than the linoleum."

"So you and your wife have finally come to terms?"
"Yes, hers."

"What do you mean, you were tricked into marriage?"
"The gun wasn't loaded."

"What did your wife say when you came home last night?"
"The darling never said a word. And I was going to have those two front teeth pulled out, anyhow."

"Who introduced you to your wife?"
"We just met. I don't blame anybody."

"She had been married before hadn't she?"
"Yes, I'm her third husband."
"There's nothing like doing business with an old established firm."

"When are we going to get married?"
"As soon as I save up enough money."
"Go on, you ain't got room in your sox for your feet now."

It's too bad a girl can't get married without dragging some innocent man to the altar with her.

"There you go again, buying electric sweepers, electric washing machines, mixing machines —!"
"But, darling, what is home without a motor?"

"No wonder I'm sick of marriage! Tommy hasn't kissed me once since the honeymoon."
"Why not divorce him?"
"But Tommy isn't my husband."

"I want you to stop picking on Kay—the man who marries her will get a prize."
"Well, if I were a man I'd make her show me the prize first."

"This note says that a man is planning to run off with my wife."
"And will you shoot him?"
"Yes! If he changes his mind."

"I have to take my wife's dog for a walk every day."
"What's the matter with your wife? She's strong and husky."
"Exactly. That's why I have to take the dog for a walk."

"Darling, we've only been married twelve months."
"It seems more like a year to me."

"I understand the government is going to handle marriages."

"Yes."

"Wonder what department they'll be in?"

"The War Department."

"Are you married?"

"I don't know, the jury is still out."

"What happened to you? You used to be such a dude."

"I got married."

"I see, sub-dude."

"Marriage is like a sweepstakes ticket."

"No, in a sweepstakes you can always tear up the ticket."

"I told him I wasn't going to marry him."

"Did he ask you?"

"No, but he looked like he was going to, but I was wrong. He was only going to sneeze."

"Did you and your husband find a peaceful place to spend the summer?"

"No, we went together everywhere."

"I was so embarrassed starting our second honeymoon by going to jail."

"But it isn't anything compared to the first time—don't you remember how you told your corsage how beautiful it looked and threw your bridesmaid downstairs?"

MOVIE DIRECTOR: Unmarried?

APPLICANT: Twice.

"Are you sure you'll love me when I'm old and ugly?" pouted the nagging wife.

And, the husband bristled and snapped, "Who says I don't?"

BORESOME HUSBAND: Let's have some fun this evening!

BORED WIFE: OK., and please leave the light on in the hallway if you get home before I do.

Two unhappily married stars are so mad at each other they're not even speaking about a divorce.

You can always surprise your friends by getting married, and then once again by staying married.

"Now that your father has sent us that check, we can buy a car and visit my family more often."

"What made you think of that?"

"Well, you know you never will visit my family unless you're driven to it."

MAY: Ever since Jack got married he's been having trouble with another woman.

FAY: What, an old flame?
MAY: No, his mother-in-law.

"I hear Rowley is getting married next week."
"Good! I never liked the fellow."

MRS. HAMMER: So Phoebe has gone back to live with her husband again?
MRS. SLAMMER: Yes, she couldn't bear his having such a good time.

UNCLE: You boys of today want too much money. Do you know what I was getting when I married your aunt?
NEPHEW: Nope! And I bet you didn't, either.

"Do you know your wife is telling around that you can't keep her in clothes?"
"That's nothing. I bought her a home and I can't keep her in that either."

Have you heard of the absentminded play producer who married and sent out invitations for the first night?

"Just as the widow and I started up the aisle to the altar every light in the church went out."
"What did you do then?"
"Kept on going. The widow knew the way."

"Sorry, madam, but licenses are issued only when your form is filled out properly."
"Why, I like your nerve, sir. We can get married no matter what I look like."

BRIDE: But darling, if I marry you, I'll lose my job.
GROOM: Can't we keep our marriage a secret?
BRIDE: But suppose we have a baby?
GROOM: Oh, we'll tell the baby, of course.

EDDIE: Yes, I married that girl because she saved my life.
JERRY: Yes, what did she do?
EDDIE: She told her dad not to shoot.

We know a married couple who are just like a pair of love birds— always flying at each other.

WIFE: Have you missed me, dear?
HUSBAND: Er-er-no, dear. I've been listening to a lecture on the radio.

"Were you surprised when Chester said he wanted to marry sister?"
"Was I? The shotgun nearly fell out of my hand."

HUSBAND: The shirt you bought me is too big.

WIFE: Of course it's too big. You didn't think I'd let the storekeeper know I'd married a little shrimp like you!

Happy married couple—another guy's wife out with another dame's husband.

Support her? I should say not! Why buy the cow when the milk is so cheap?

We know of a Hollywood couple who have been married for so long that their lawyers are starving.

"You say your wife caused you to grow that long beard?"
"Yes, she started buying my neckties."

"Willie tells me that he saw you kissing the cook."
"Don't be absurd, dear. She attacked me with a rolling pin for criticizing the biscuits and I had to bite her to protect myself."

Marriage originates when a man meets the only woman who understands him. So does divorce.

"Max, darlink, today is guess what?"
"Don't bodder me."
"You silly little boy. Twenty-five years today we are togedder."

"Howz about a hug, a skviz vit some kisses?"
"No. Go jump from the vinder."
"Max, how could you tritt me like diss?"
"Because, ven I tink how if I had bomped you uff on de foist day—de most I could get vould be 15 years—and for 10 years already I vould be single."

"Why the worried look?"
"I'm thinking, but I can't for the life of me decide whether to spend this month's bonus on a new coat of paint for the car or to have my wife's face lifted."

"And when you get tired of your husband, I suppose you'll see your lawyer?"
"Oh no, he doesn't appeal to me one single bit."

"And what were you before you married?"
"A housemaid."
"And the change is a pleasant one?"
"The change isn't much—I just work for nothing now."

"What brave act did you ever do?"
"Prevented you from dying an old maid."

"Here is an invitation to my golden wedding."

"Your golden wedding?"

"Yes, I am going to marry the only son of a millionaire."

"I understand your wife is a hard worker."

"She is all of that. Why, after she sings the baby to sleep, she comes and talks me to sleep."

"Have you a marriageable daughter?"

"Have I? I'd like to see the one that got married any oftener."

"Married people don't wink."

"Oh, yes—but not at each other."

"I married for sympathy."

"Well, you've got mine."

Just because his wife crowns him doesn't mean a man is king in his own house.

"Before we were married George kissed me whenever we went thru a tunnel."

"And now?"

"Now he takes a drink."

"Say, Wallace, why don't you settle down and take a wife?"

"I would, but I don't know whose wife to take."

"Didn't I see you with your husband last night?"

"Yes."

"But I thought he had two more years on his term."

"Oh, they let him out for good behavior."

"It must be a comfort to be married to such a good man."

"You're looking fit. Been exercising?"

"Yeah. Every morning I get my radio exercises. My wife turns it on for hers, and I get up and turn it off."

"Honey, I'm going over to the radio and get something that will put you in a romantic mood."

"Oh, is that where you keep your liquor now?"

"My wife is like George Washington; I don't believe she could tell a lie to save her soul."

"You're lucky. Mine can tell a lie the minute I get it out of my mouth."

"Look here, I'm not going to stand this sort of thing any longer. That brother of yours called me a fool today and right in public, too."

"That's just like Tom. He's always blurting out family secrets."

"Offisher, you'd better lock me up. Just hit my wife over the head with a club."

"Did you kill her?"

"Don't think so—thash why I want to be locked up."

MARRIED (see also Marriage)

"Your wife is telling it all around that you cancelled your life insurance."

"Yes, I got tired of her telling her friends that I was worth more dead than alive."

"What makes you think you are qualified for a position in the Diplomatic Corps?" demanded the examiner.

"Well," answered the applicant, modestly, "I've been married twenty years and my wife still thinks I have a sick friend."

"Are you married?"

"No. Just naturally discontented."

"I'm buying a washing machine for my wife as a birthday present."

"That will be a surprise, eh?"

"You bet! She's expecting a new car."

"Did you give your wife that little lecture on economy you spoke of?"

"Yes."

"Any result?"

"Yes—I've got to give up smoking."

For breakfast I get a three minute egg and a five minute argument.

WIFE (referring to guest): He's a most attractive man; is he married?

HUSBAND: I dunno. He's a reserved chap—keeps all his troubles to himself.

"I'm leaving for Chicago tonight. I'm supposed to get married tomorrow."

"Where, in Chicago?"

"No, here in New York."

"How long have you been married?"

"Long enough to learn that there are some things you can't say with flowers."

"You have no excuse for staying out so late."

"Haven't I? Watcha s'pose I've been standing at the corner thinkin' about for the last half hour?"

"What's the penalty for bigamy?"

"Two mothers-in-law."

"Do your daughters live at home?"

"No—they're not married yet."

They are married and she fights with him all the time and one night she says, "Wouldn't it be delightful to have friends in?"

"Even an enemy would be a pleasure."

"Johnson has matrimonial dyspepsia."

"What's that?"

"His wife doesn't agree with him."

"I regret the day I was married."

"Say, you're lucky. Mine lasted a whole week."

"If you marry two women it's bigamy."

"What is it when you marry one woman?"

"Monotony."

"How do you find marriage?"

"During courtship I talked and she listened. After marriage she talked and I listened. Now we both talk and the neighbors listen."

"John, we're going to the theatre tonight."

"We are not!"

"What?"

"Excuse me, dear—I was just playing boss."

"John—John—"

"What is it?"

"There's a burglar in the house."

"What do you want me to do— get up and run the risk of being killed?"

"No; but if you find in the morning that somebody has gone thru your pockets don't blame me."

"A pretty time of night for you to come home."

"A pretty time of night for you to be awake."

"I stayed awake for the last four hours waiting for you."

"And I have been keeping myself awake for the last four hours at the club waiting for you to go to sleep."

Marriage is like a game of cards. It takes a pair to open, he shows a diamond, she shows a flush and they end up with a full house.

"Has your wife made home happier since she went to cooking school?"

"Much happier. We've both learned to appreciate plain, simple restaurant food."

"So you were only seventeen when you were married? You didn't have to wait long for a husband."

"Not then, but I do now. He's at the club five nights a week."

"I can't imagine how you get money out of your husband."

"Oh, I simply say I'm going back to mother and he immediately hands me the fare."

"Who's boss in your house, you or your wife?"

"I am, of course."

"Really? What do you do when she talks too much?"

"I tell her to pipe down and shut up."

"You don't say."

"Well, not exactly, but I think."

"Well, I guess if the worst came to worst, we could go and live with your parents."

"That wouldn't be possible; they're living with their people."

MATRIMONY (see also Marriage)

"I'm a musician."

"Where do you play?"

"On my family's sympathy."

"I had bad luck with both my wives."

"How is that?"

"The first eloped and the second didn't."

"How long have you been married, Jim?"

"Oh, for about two pouting spells and a hysterical attack."

"During the earthquake his wife lost her head and ran out of the house."

"Yeh?"

"Then he lost his head and went out and brought her back."

"Was you ever in love, Dusty?"

"Yes, once when I was a young squirt I was in love."

"Well, you never did get married, did you?"

"Nope. I never did marry."

"How did it happen?"

"Well, it was like this. The gal I was in love with wouldn't marry me when I was drunk and I wouldn't marry her when I was sober."

"I suppose the next thing you'll want is the world with a fence around."

"You don't have to bother about the fence."

"Who did you marry?"

"A woman."

"Well, did you ever hear of anyone that didn't marry a woman?"

"Yes."

"Who?"

"My sister."

"It wouldn't be much trouble for us to marry. My father's a minister, you know."

"Well, let's have a try at it— my dad's a lawyer."

"Where have you been?"

"No place, I just got married."

"That's good."

"No, that's bad. I'm stepfather to nine kids."

"That's bad."

"No, that's good. My wife has plenty of money."

"That's good."

"No, that's bad. She owns a big house."

"That's good."

"Not so good. It burned down last night."

"That's bad."

"Not so bad—she burned with it."

"That's good."

"Yeah! Man—that's good!"

(Arriving home and finding wife sewing on tiny garments.)

"Darling, you don't mean—"

"Don't be silly—this is my new dinner gown."

"We live on a budget."

"I live on my father-in-law."

When I married, my wife was a grass-widow, and I was a grass-widower. Now the question arises —if my wife was a grass-widow and I a grass-widower—would our children be grasshoppers?

It is better to marry for money than for no reason at all.

One way of making your wife sit up and take notice is to talk in your sleep.

"Believe me, I've been pinching and scraping at the office."

"Yes, pinching the steno's cheeks and scraping the lipstick off your own."

"It looks like a storm—you had better stay for dinner."

"Oh, thanks, but I don't think it's bad enough for that."

"How old is your wife?"

"Forty."

"How would you like to change her for a couple of 20's?"

"How did this marriage turn out today?"

"Not very well.—The preacher was cross-eyed and he married the groom to the best man, kissed the ten dollars and put the bride in his pocket."

Eavesdropped at Club Bail: "They're celebrating their tin anniversary—five years of eating out of cans."

"How in the world did they ever come to get married?" someone asked.

"Same old story, probably," said Lionel Royce. "They started out to be good friends—then suddenly changed their minds."

"You come right here and marry me!"

"I can't I have one wife now. —Come to think of it, I have two wives."

"You can't have two wives. —There is a law against it."

"Ah yes! Non-Harem forming, isn't it?"

"I want a man that is as rich as Rockefeller, as strong as Joe Louis, as handsome as Rock Hudson."

"If there were such a man he'd be crazy to marry you."

"Say, he could be crazy, too."

"I used to be a social butterfly before I married you."

"Yes, and you must have turned into a moth from the way you go thru my clothes."

"You told me before we were married, that I should never want for anything."

"But that was before I knew how much you could want."

"I think I'll get married as soon as I find some girl who will have me."

"Well, take it from me, no one is going to be injured in the rush."

"Last night when I got home, my wife had my chair drawn up before the fire, my slippers ready for me to put on, my pipe filled, and . . ."

"How did you like her new hat?"

"Gosh, if I had a million dollars, do you know where I'd be?"

"Yeh, we'd be on our honeymoon."

MEALS (see also Cooking, Food, Diet)

DINER: How do the foreign dishes compare with American ones?

WAITER: Oh, they break just as easily.

JUDGE: What do you mean, selling the unsuspecting public horsemeat?

MAN: It wasn't all horse meat— I mixed it half and half. Half horse and half rabbit.

JUDGE: How many rabbits to one horse?

MAN: One rabbit, your Honor, to one horse.

"Waiter," complained the customer in a waterfront restaurant, "these are very small oysters."

"Yes, sir," agreed the waiter.

"And," added the customer, "they don't appear to be very fresh."

"Then it's lucky they're small, ain't it, sir?" answered the resourceful waiter.

"How do you keep the smell of onions off your breath?" asked the onion-lover of his waggish friend.

"Well, it's a long story. First, I peel carefully, then slice them with perfect precision; pepper and salt sufficiently to taste—then add a little vinegar and a few drops of salad oil—and then I throw them away."

"What's your favorite dish?"
"A clean one."

"This butter is so strong it could walk around the table and say 'Hello' to the coffee," said one truck driver to another in a roadside eatery.
"Well, if it does the coffee is too weak to answer."

MEAN

You're so mean you only give one finger when you shake hands.

When I cut my finger she cried over it—just so she could get salt in the wound.

He throws Mexican jumping beans to the pigeons in the park.

He's very mean. A man was drowning while he was fishing.

My uncle watched him go down twice and when the man came up for the third time, my uncle said. "When you go down the next time, see if my bait is still on the hook."

He's so mean he'd send a get-well card to a hypochondriac.

He's so mean that if he killed himself he'd get the right man.

"Honestly, if I could trade places with Rock Hudson or Tab Hunter right this minute, I wouldn't do it."
"I know you wouldn't. You never do anything to please me."

He is so mean he tears the month of December off his calendars to fool his children.

He was so mean he put a tack on the seat of the electric chair.

A Russian was being led off to execution by a squad of Bolshevik soldiers on a rainy morning. "What brutes you Bolsheviks are, to march me through the rain like this."
"How about us? We have to march back."

Speaking of public enemies, I know a guy who gets up at 4 A.M., leans out the window and whistles to wake up the birds.

MEMORY

1ST GIRL: My husand is so forgetful.

2ND GIRL: So I've noticed. At the party last night I had to keep reminding him that he's married to you and not to me.

MAN IN RESTAURANT: Waiter, about an hour ago I ordered a steak. Did you forget it or have I eaten it already?

1ST MAN: My wife has the worst memory in the world.

2ND MAN: Forgets everything?

1ST MAN: No, she remembers everything.

HUSBAND: I saw the doctor today about my loss of memory.

WIFE: What did he do?

HUSBAND: He made me pay him in advance.

HE: I know I proposed to you last night but I can't remember whether you accepted or not.

SHE: I knew I said 'No' to someone last night but couldn't remember to whom.

MEN

"What sort of a chap is Johnson?"

"Well, if ever you see two men in a corner, and one looks bored to death, the other is Johnson."

He came in like a lion and went out like a lamp!

At a tea, Darryl Zanuck was discussing with an elderly femme author the difficulty of properly casting a part in a picture. "I want a young fellow, who looks like Lindbergh, who is tall and blue-eyed. He must have good manners, sex appeal, a grand sense of humor, a pleasing speaking and singing voice, and an air of distinction."

"So do I," sighed the lady.

He was only a dentist's son, but he had a lot of pull.

He respects old age only when it comes in bottles.

"Men are like toothpaste tubes."

"How's that?"

"You've got to give them a squeeze before you can get anything out of them."

"He's a wiry little chap."

"He doesn't look it. What does he do?"

"Connects telephones."

There were four men. The first was a banker, the second was also in jail, the third was a college graduate and the fourth couldn't get a job, either.

I knew he had a lotta dames on a string, but the one with him looks like she should be on a leash.

"What makes him act so grouchy?"
"Oh, he's teething."
"Teething?"
"Yes . . . they keep slipping out."

"What's the noise?"
"The barber is shaving himself."
"What's the conversation?"
"He's trying to talk himself into a shampoo."

Our idea of a kindhearted man is one who orders a ton of soft coal when the cat insists on sleeping in the coal bin.

Men are just like children. They prefer blondes because they're afraid of the dark.

A gentleman is a fellow who won't strike a woman with his hat on.

He's gone around with more women than Macy's revolving doors!

"How long you been shaving?"
"Four years now."
"G'wan."

"Yes sir, cut myself both times."

A smart man is one who hasn't let a woman pin anything on him since he was a baby.

When you're with him you're as safe as a Scotch highball at an American Legion Convention.

A fellow had three suits—nonsupport, separation and breach of promise.

A bachelor is a guy who didn't have a car when he was young.

He's a Jack of all trades, and he's out of work in them all.

Some fellows carry a torch for a gal simply because they aren't so bright.

And one guy who's always down in the dumps is the garbage collector.

My uncle is an outdoor man— all he needs is a straw to sleep on, a crust of bread to eat and a direct wire to his bookie.

The kind of man who remembers your age but forgets your birthday.

He's a prominent man. As prominent as knees in Scotland.

He's the only guy I ever met who has a falsetto burp.

He has a wonderful head on his shoulders—I wonder whose it is?

That guy's as annoying as a busy-signal.

He looks like a kid of eighteen until you're in his roadster.

He's an athlete all right—he can throw a wet blanket 200 yards over any party.

Is he important? Why—the mob hears from him.

He's the answer to a maiden's stare.

"Paul is the most bashful man I ever married."
"What makes you say such a thing?"
"He took along mistletoe on our honeymoon."

He's not mean. Why he wouldn't hurt a fly. He'd give it novocaine before swatting it.

MEXICO

A wealthy American, touring through a remote section of Mexico, stopped at a lonely little ranch house to ask directions and was surprised to come face to face with what was obviously a hundred per cent American cowboy. He was seated on a magnificent black stallion with the brand Bar-H burned into his skin.

The visitor said, "That's a mighty fine horse you have there. If you could only rub out that brand mark I'd give you $2,000 for him."

The cowboy answered, "Mister, if I ever could rub out that mark I'd still be living in Amarillo, Texas."

MIND

"Isn't it funny, when I stand on my head the blood rushes to my head, but when I stand on my feet the blood doesn't rush to my feet," said the freshman to a senior in the college gym.

"Well, frosh," quipped the senior, "Your feet aren't empty."

LOIS: Well, I'm falling in love and I think I should go to a palmist or a mind reader. Which would you suggest?
DORIS: You'd better go to a palmist—you *know* you've got a palm.

INNOCENT: Your husband looks like a brilliant man. I suppose he knows everything.
SOPHISTICATE: Don't fool your-

self, he doesn't even suspect anything.

"My uncle has a lot of horse sense," remarked a local citizen of the town's outstanding old ne'er-do-well.
"I'll say he has. You can lead him to water but you can't make him drink," retorted his disapproving nephew.

MODESTY

He is so modest he carries extra fuses around with him just in case his girl's lights go out.

She's so modest she blindfolds herself while taking a bath.

She's so modest she pulls down the shade to change her mind.

He told her he wasn't himself tonight, so she beat him up because she doesn't allow strangers in the house.

OLD MAID: This isn't your room.
DRUNK: That's all right, I'm not myself tonight.

MONEY (see also Cash)

The salary we used to dream of is the one we can't live on today.

Morris Uchitel, the shoulder-pad man, stuffed me with: Be sure and save your money—you never know when it may be valuable again someday.

Even if money could buy happiness, think what a luxury tax there would be on it.

United States money not only talks—it has learned to speak every foreign language.

You can't see his hidden charms—his money is in Swiss banks.

A man, after buying a ticket to a show, walked off without picking up his change. The customer next in line asked the cashier what she did in a case like that. "I rap on the window with a sponge," she replied.

A certain producer brags about the fact that he came to this country without a dime in his pocket—and now he owes more than $50,-000.

Money may talk but it seems to be very hard of hearing when you call it.

"Your wife says she only asks for pin money?"
"Yes, but the first pin she

wanted had twelve diamonds in it."

"Money doesn't bring happiness."
"Can you prove it?"
"Sure, you take a guy with forty million dollars. He ain't happier than a man with thirty-nine million."

Having a little financial trouble —I'm two cents overdue on my library card.

Everything is foolish—even the dollar hasn't the same sense it used to have.

Louis Wolfson, the big businessman, who knows his money, cashed in on this one: "It's called cold cash because we don't keep it long enough to get it warm."

What is the height of being mercenary? Marry Brigitte Bardot for her money.

If a pickpocket would go through my pockets now, all he would get is exercise.

I've been saving for a rainy day. Well anyway, it was a drizzle. Three days of constant rain and I'd be a bum.

He's money mad. He hasn't got a cent . . . that's why he's mad.

Girls don't only marry for cash . . . they'll take checks.

Money means nothing, so she spends it to get rid of it.

The Scotsman asked the bank for a loan of a dollar and was told that he would have to pay 4% interest at the end of the year.
"That's 4¢, eh?" asked the Scotsman.
"What do you have for security?" asked the banker.
"Fifty thousand dollars in U.S. Bonds."
The bank accepted the bonds and gave him the dollar. At the end of the year, the Scotsman was back with a dollar and four cents to clear up his debt, and asked for the return of his fifty thousand in bonds.
As he returned the bonds, the banker asked, "I don't want to get personal, but if you have all these bonds, why did you have to borrow a dollar?"
"Well," said the Scot, "do you know any other way I can get a safety deposit vault for four cents a year?"

"I don't know, Max," said Harry, "do you have the same trouble with your wife?"
"What trouble?"
"There's no end to it. All the time she keeps nagging me for

money, money, money, more money . . ."

"And what does she do with all the money?"

"Who knows? I never give it to her."

Money can't buy happiness, but it will get you a better class of enemies.

He makes as much money as a hat check girl in a nudist colony.

Two friends in the Bronx met on the street one day. One said to the other, "Sam, lend me $5 till I come back from Florida."

His friend said, "When are you coming back?"

The first one replied, "Who's going?"

Making big money was the cause of my downfall. I was making it two inches too big.

Money is the root of all evil, but so far no one has found a better route.

Song Title: "I'd Give a Thousand Dollars to Be a Millionaire."

United States money not only talks—it has learned to speak every foreign language.

1ST MAN: How can you tell me that you're going to marry a woman worth ten million dollars and still insist it's a love match?

2ND MAN: It is . . . I love money.

1ST GIRL: What's the use of money? You can't take it with you.

2ND GIRL: If I can't take it with me, I ain't going.

1ST MAN: I had a million dollars once but I lost it.

2ND MAN: How d'you do that?

1ST MAN: I had a hole in my pocket.

He has all his money tied up in U.S. Blondes.

HE: I wish I were a millionaire.

SHE: Don't worry about it . . . you have something no millionaire's got.

HE: What's that?

SHE: No money.

1ST MAN: Love is something money can't buy.

2ND MAN: That's true . . . but it sure puts you in a good bargaining position.

1ST MAN: Since he lost his money half his friends don't know him anymore.

2ND MAN: And the other half?

1ST MAN: They don't know yet that he's lost it.

"What's your husband's average income?"

"Oh, around midnight."

"You spent $50,000 in one day? How did you spend $50,000 in a day?"

"I was hungry."

"What's this item? Twenty cents."

"Entertainment."

"That must have been some fling."

HUBBY: I got our relief check today.

WIFIE: Good. Now we can get a new car.

"Your wife says she only asks for pin money?"

"Yes, but the first pin she wanted had twelve diamonds in it."

He's been doing business with one bank for twenty years and he has yet to meet the paying teller.

SHE: It says in this paper that the Eskimos use fishhooks for money.

HE: Gee! It must be tough on their wives getting fishhooks out of hubby's pocket while he's sleeping.

SHE: Oh, well, the nights are six months long up there, dear.

"She won $50,000. Her ship finally came in. Tell me, did you ever win anything before?"

"Just ten dollars."

"Well, that was only a canoe."

"I'm getting $500 tomorrow in the mail."

"Why don't we have breakfast at your house then? Set the table near the mailbox."

"Money doesn't bring happiness."

"Can you prove it?"

"Sure, you take a guy with forty million dollars. He ain't any happier than a man with thirty-nine million."

"It cost 1000 buttons."

"Did you have a hard time keeping up the payments?"

"No, I had a hard time keeping up my pants."

(Knock)

"Are you the young lady who found the wallet with $800 in it?"

"Yes, but you'll have to describe it before you get it back."

"Well, I only want the cardboard that's inside."

"Why do you only want the cardboard?"

"Because it's raining outside and I've got a hole in my shoe."

"My husband has taken all the cash out of the baby's money box."

"Oh."

"And there was nearly enough for my new hat, too."

"You owe for your last 100 cigars."

"Oh! How much?"

"A dollar and a quarter."

"How did you make all your money?"

"I formed a partnership with a rich man."

"How did you do it?"

"He had the money and I had the experience."

"And was it a successful business for you?"

"Immensely so. When we dissolved a year later, I had the money and he had the experience."

"Here's a tip."

"Man, look at that buffalo squint at the light."

He makes something like $40,-000 a week, and yet there are those poor misguided youths who dream of becoming president some day.

"When I came to New York I had only a dollar."

"How did you invest the money?"

"I used to send a wire home for more money."

It's called cold cash because we don't keep it long enough to get it warm.

"My brother's a coin collector."

"Is that so?"

"Yes, he robs telephone booths."

We don't know the scientific name for it, but the popular name for it would be athlete's palm.

MORONS (see also Nuts, Insane Asylum, Insanity, Stupid)

1ST GUY: I'm so scared of the dark, I put my pillow over my head when I go to sleep.

2ND GUY: Don't you suffocate?

1ST GUY: No, but I get behind in my breathing.

GRANDFATHER: Read the paper to me.

GRANDSON: But you know I can't read.

GRANDFATHER: So what . . . I can't hear anyway.

She's so dumb, she thinks band-aid is a charity organization for musicians.

SHE: If we wait much longer to get married, George, our children will older than us.

BANK CLERK: Mr. Brown, you are overdrawn on your checking account by $5.15.
MR. BROWN: That's okay . . . I'll write you a check.

TEACHER: Now, children, who can tell me what comes before March?
JOHNNY: Forward?

1ST GUY: When do you think a boy should put on long pants?
2ND GUY: When he gets up in the morning.

MOTEL (see also Hotel, Rooms)

Xavier Cugat tells the story about the girl, wearied by a long drive, who stopped into a motel looking for a room. The clerk told her that the last room had just been occupied but that there was a couch there and if the man didn't mind her lying down on the couch, it was all right with him.

In desperation, she knocked on the door and said to the man, "Look, you don't know me. I don't know you, we don't know them, they don't know us. Can I please bunk on your couch for a while? I won't bother you."
"Sure," he said, and went back to sleep.

A little later, she woke him up and said, "Look, you don't know me, I don't know you, we don't know them, they don't know us, do you mind if I just sleep on top of the bed? I won't bother you."
"Okay," he said, and fell asleep again.

A short while later, she said, "Look, I don't know you, you don't know me, we don't know them, they don't know us, whaddya say we have a party?"

"Look," the man said, "if I don't know you, you don't know me, we don't know them, they don't know us—who the hell we gonna invite to the party?"

MOTHER-IN-LAW (see also Marriage)

Have you heard of the lad who didn't try to win the forgiveness of his mother-in-law for eloping with her daughter because if he did he feared she'd begin visiting them?

"I get on with my mother-in-law."
"Does she live with you?"
"No, she lives in Chile."

"Don't you think we ought to get mother a little present to take back home with her?"
"What about a nice, big jar of vanishing cream?"

"How's your mother-in-law?"
"Oh, fair to meddling."

"My mother won't stay in this house another moment unless we get rid of the mice."

"Say, where are you going?"

"To get rid of the cat."

"My mother-in-law is staying with us this week."

"She's your house guest?"

"Sure! Did you think she was staying in the garage?"

"My mother-in-law broke my best golf club."

"Now, now, you can buy another one."

"Yes, but that won't make my head stop hurting."

"Do you believe that people follow the same occupations in the next world as they do on earth?"

"My mother-in-law won't. She makes ice cream."

"You brute! You ought to be ashamed to talk about mother the way you do. For two cents, I'd send her a letter and ask her never to visit us again."

"Hah! I'll give you seven cents. Send it Air Mail."

When my mother-in-law was sick, I went to her bedside, and began to cry.

She said, "Don't cry, we will meet in the other world." I began to go to church right away.

"Hello, Higbee. Off on a pleasure trip?"

"Yes, I'm taking my mother-in-law home again."

"You ask me if I've got nerve? Why, listen I even tore into my mother-in-law last night and told her what I thought of her."

"Over what?"

"Over a long distance telephone."

"What's wrong? You look sad."

"I just wrote a good mother-in-law joke."

"Didn't the editor like it?"

"I don't know. My mother-in-law saw it first."

Adam had no mother-in-law. —That is how we know he lived in Paradise.

"John, mother was so pleased with all the nice things you said about her in your letter. You see, she opened it by mistake."

"Yes, I thought she would."

LOOSE-TONGUED BARFLY: I knew your mother-in-law in the old days and I tell you she was a burlesque dancer. Why, I've seen her wearing nothing but a smile.

GENT: I can't believe it.

LOOSE-TONGUED BARFLY: You mean you can't believe that she ever danced in the nude?

GENT: No, I can't believe she ever wore a smile.

Smith's mother-in-law rushed to him in great excitement on his return from business one evening.

"Oh, John, that great, horrid, heavy grandfather's clock in the hall has just fallen with a dreadful crash on the very spot where I'd been standing only a moment before."

"Humph," muttered Smith, "I always said that clock was slow."

"Daddy's mother-in-law is visiting us."

"I suppose your daddy doesn't like that?"

"Oh yes he does; he keeps giving her presents."

"Presents? What kind of presents?"

"Well, he gave her a traveling bag and yesterday he gave her a railroad ticket."

"Will you donate something to the Old Ladies' Home?"

"With pleasure. Help yourself to my mother-in-law."

"Yesterday while we were out hunting you almost shot my mother-in-law."

"Sorry, here's my gun. Take a shot at mine."

"My wife threatened to go back to her mother. I said 'Is that a threat or a promise?' "

"What's the difference?"

"If she goes back to her mother, that's a promise. But if she says she's going to bring her mother home—that's a threat."

My mother-in-law was kidnapped last week. The kidnappers said if we didn't send twenty-four thousand dollars quick we would have to take my mother-in-law back.

"Have you a car?"

"I have a new car—a mother-in-law special.

"A mother-in-law special?"

"Yeah—the crank is in the back seat."

"Do you mean to tell me you've been married for five years and your mother-in-law has only been to visit you once?"

"Yeah. She came the day after we were married and never left."

"Do you know what the penalty for bigamy is?"

"Two mothers-in-law."

WIFE: Mother says she nearly died laughing over those stories you told her.

HUSBAND: Where is she? I'll tell her some funnier ones.

"George, what do you think? Mother wants to be cremated."

"Right! Where is she? Tell her to put her things on."

The shortest distance between two points—is the route a groom takes when driving his mother-in-law home.

The daughter called her mother and cried that she wanted to come home to her house. "How will that punish him?" she asked. "I'll come to your house."

My mother-in-law is a very good cook. I usually get two of her favorites: "Cold Shoulder" and "Hot Tongue."

"Did I actually hear Tommy say that his mother-in-law has the skin he loves to touch?"
"That's right; it's sunburned and he likes to hear her holler when he touches it."

If you're taking your mother-in-law along fishing, be sure to bring an extra hook, line and "sinker."

1ST WOMAN: We're sending my mother-in-law to New York for a vacation.
2ND WOMAN: Won't the weather disagree with her?
1ST WOMAN: It wouldn't dare!

My mother-in-law always call me son . . . but she never finishes the sentence.

WIFE: I suppose you wish I'd go home to mother.
HUSBAND: Oh no, I wouldn't wish that on anyone.

NEW BRIDE: George is perfectly wonderful to me, mother. He gives me everything I ask for.
MOTHER: That merely shows that you're not asking enough.

1ST MAN: Your dog bit my mother-in-law yesterday.
2ND MAN: Oh dear, I suppose you're going to sue?
1ST MAN: Heck, no! What will you take for the dog?

MOTION PICTURES (see also Hollywood, Movies, Films, Actors)

"How did you get a start in pictures?"
"I started as a villain. First I was a mean villain, then a comic villain and then a dignified villain Then I began to be a success. They started hissing me."
"Gosh, I must be a success too. I've made five pictures and they're hissing me."

"You know, my screen test for United Artists came out so well, I was offered a job by Twentieth Century."
"You were offered a job by

Twentieth Century? Really. What did they want you to do?"

"Make up the berths."

Then shot the picture in a hurry—previewed it and then shot the director.

I made a couple of pictures while I was out there but I had to stop. My Brownie broke.

I dropped in to see your latest picture—I wanted to be alone.

"Would you like to be my assistant?"

"Well, yes and no."

"Never mind. I can't use you. You talk too much."

I saw your latest picture, but the seats were so uncomfortable, I couldn't sleep.

Can we use your brother, your uncle and two cousins? This is a play and not a family reunion. Oh, your uncle can't speak English? Then we'll let him be the supervisor.

"What did Juliet say to Romeo when she saw him in the balcony?"

"Why the hell didn't you get seats in the orchestra?"

She didn't get a chance in pictures. Her son-in-law was the cutter.

"I'm going to be very funny in the movies."

"Who's going to double for you?"

About the woman who took her five year old kid to a preview. At the door she presented only one ticket, and the doorman said: "The kid'll have to have a ticket." The woman answered: "Aw, he'll fall asleep in five minutes."

"My father saw your last picture and he's going to sue you."

"Sue me? What for?"

"He saw your last picture and almost choked to death."

"But no matter how funny a picture is, he didn't have to choke to death."

"No? You try holding your nose for an hour and a half."

(After great rave—)

"I think it's great too, and when you get it finished, do you know what you can do?"

"What?"

"Take the celluloid, cut it up, and sell it for mandolin picks."

"We ought to make this bedroom scene twice as good."

"That's easy. Put in a double bed."

Wants $600 to play role of Indian so they give him $300 because it's the role of a half-breed.

"You say you want me to play a mob scene in my next picture?"
"Yes, you're to meet all your former lovers."

You have to interview fifty good actors before you can find one who can be depended on to spoil a role.

The star's double walked under a ladder to give the star bad luck.

She had a quiet wedding with only the press agents of the immediate family present.

Hollywood: Where movie stars wear dark glasses to night spots so they won't be inconspicuous.

"Have you any friends in Hollywood?"
"I won't know until after my picture is previewed."

"Do you have lines to speak in the picture?"
"No, I take the part of the husband."

You should see all the native girls in the picture, and all the clothes—they could have worn.

Once made a picture so bad that when they put it up on the shelf the film next to it moved away.

"What part of the picture did you like best, little girl?"
"The part where Mr. Jones was thrown out."
"Did you like the rest of it?"
"I didn't like the Mickey Mouse."
"There was no Mickey Mouse."
"I know—that's the part I didn't like."

Met an absent-minded producer at Central Casting who was looking for a couple of extras as bookends.

A visiting Hollywood quickie producer didn't have enough money to tip at the Stork Club— so he gave the waiter the lead in his next picture.

"Remember that scene where I looked into your eyes, took you in my arms and you kissed me?"
"Yes, and for the same money, I'd do it again."

I had a half-hour contract with ten-minute options.

"Our next pix will be for the kids. Let's figure—there are five million kids and they won't go to the movies alone, they will bring a friend, that makes ten million kids, and the friends won't come alone, they'll bring a friend, that makes fifteen million."

"But there are only thirteen million kids in the U.S."

"Well, some kids have Mexican friends."

I used to have trouble getting into the studio. But not anymore. Now I just walk in with the scrub-woman.

"Who was the midget you had with you?"

"Well, he was the movie critic for the *Reader's Digest*."

"I'm acting in shorts."

"Aren't you ashamed?"

Walt Disney never has trouble with his film stars. When he doesn't like a performer he doesn't tear up the contract—he tears up the actor.

Hollywood trade unions are all-powerful. In my picture, I say, "I feel as fit as a fiddle." That same afternoon I was told I had to join the Musicians' Union.

"What company will I work for —Twentieth Century Fox?"

"No, Nineteenth Century Skunk."

"What's the name of this picture?"

"It's a sequel to *The Rains Came*. It's called, *The Sewers Backed up*."

(At director's office) "I want to see Mr. Blank. I'm George Green."

"Green?"

"Yes."

"Here's your pay check."

"But I haven't done any work yet."

"Quiet, radical."

"I understand you just finished *The Hunchback of Notre Dame*. How was it?"

"It wasn't easy at all.—I had to make myself even *more* hideous. My clothes were in rags and tatters; I was a mess. It took me four hours every day to make up."

"You needn't have wasted all that time. All you'd have to do would be to walk into Times Square Subway Station at rush hour."

"It was a sad picture—why I even cried *before* the picture."

"Why?"

"I missed the price change by one minute."

"When are they going to release your picture?"

"They're not going to release it; they are going to *parole* it."

"I played two bit parts while I was in Hollywood."

"Goodness, you didn't make much money at those rates, did you?"

"Remember that party we went to in Hollywood and we went out on the veranda? And we were afraid the moon wouldn't come out?"

"In Hollywood it's gotta come out—it's under contract."

The only star that picture will get will be on the sheriff's vest.

There's one thing about Hollywood—at least you can starve without an overcoat.

You ought to get in easy. You have a new face. I have a head that's hardly been used!

"That was some realistic battle they had between the North and the South, wasn't it?"

"Yeah, during the intermission a bunch of Southerners went out and beat up a blue Chevy."

I went to see the première of *Ben Hur* but I got there a little late—I missed the first two days.

"I heard that there weren't any people at the theatre to see your picture."

"That's not true, the people were lined up clear around the corner."

"What was playing around the corner."

My idea of a square is a guy who goes to a Brigitte Bardot movie and complains because the picture doesn't have a plot.

1ST GIRL: There was a man in the movies annoying me.
2ND GIRL: Really? What was he doing?
1ST GIRL: Nothing.

1ST MAN: Why do you keep buying tickets to the same movie? You only need one.
2ND MAN: I know, but that jerk at the door keeps tearing them up.

WIFE: Why don't you ever make love to me like Gregory Peck did to that girl in the movie?
HUSBAND: Do you know how much they have to pay him for doing that?

MOVIE ACTOR: Darling, will you marry me?
GIRL: I do like you, George, but it frightens me to hear you've been divorced five times.
MOVIE ACTOR: Oh you really mustn't believe those old wives' tales.

FRIEND: I'm so sorry I couldn't come to your wedding.
MOVIE ACTRESS: Never mind . . . You'll come to my next one.

1ST MOVIE ACTRESS: That's a very unusual necklace you're wearing.

2ND MOVIE ACTRESS: Yes, I made it entirely out of my old wedding rings.

MURRAY, JAN

Just about the only thing you can borrow without collateral is trouble.

Guy came to work all beat up and bandaged. Friend said, "What's the matter?" Guy said, "It's my seenus." Friend said, "You mean, sinus," Nope said the guy—"Seenus. I was kissing this girl and her husband came home and seenus."

"I've been on daytime television so long when the sun goes down I lose my sense of humor.

Nothing confuses a man more than driving behind a woman who does everything right.

MUSEUMS (see also Art)

"Here is a statue of a Roman Gladiator."

"But look, one of his arms is broken off, his leg is ending at the knee, his helmet is dented, and there are several patches over his eyes."

"Yes, we know that. This statue represents Victory."

"He represents Victory?"

"Yes."

"If that's the fellow that won, I'd like to see the guy that lost."

"This is the skull of a man who was shipwrecked for two years on a desert island with a couple of chorus girls."

"How did he die?"

"He wore himself out tearing down the signals they'd put up."

"I come here every afternoon with my husband. He's interested in some old fossil."

"Well, don't worry. It's probably a harmless flirtation."

"You know what that aquarium looks like to me?"

"What?"

"Like a flooded fish market."

Mabel and Ted were going thru the museum. Wide-eyed, they passed slowly from one glass case to the other reading the inscriptions on them.

Finally they came to a case that was unmarked and its contents puzzled them.

It was a model street scene, carefully worked out and designed by some plastic artist. It represented a deserted section of a city street.

"Why, dear what is this anyway?" asked Mabel. For a moment Ted seemed stumped; then he said brightly, "Why, dear, this is a parking space."

"The glaciers were large pieces of ice that came down and brought huge rocks and stones."

"That's right. And where are the glaciers now?"

"They've gone back for more stones."

"These mummies are all dated. This says 609 B.C. Do you know what that means?"

"Yes, that's the number of the car that hit him."

They will merge the aquarium with midgets and raise shrimps.

For a long time the visitor to the great museum stood gazing at the Egyptian mummy swathed in bandages. "Tell me one thing," he ventured.

"What is it sir?" asked the guide.

"Was it a motor or an airplane accident?"

MARIE: Why don't you like to visit the zoo?

MAZIE: It makes me sad to see those fashionable furs practically going to waste.

"These are dinosaurs."

"They must be wonderful animals when they're finished. They've got the framework up now."

"What do you learn from looking at Venus?"

"Not to bite your fingernails."

"I went to the museum."

"Did you see the fish?"

"I saw the electric eels, alternating on direct current. And I saw an octopus. It looked like a bunch of snakes in a huddle."

MUSIC (see also Musicians, Band, Instruments)

1ST MAN: Look at Mozart. At the age of four he was already composing symphonies.

2ND MAN: Well, what else could he do? He was too young to go out with girls.

1ST MAN: That's not a Caruso record. The man is singing in German.

2ND MAN: Yes . . . the record was translated.

HUSBAND: My wife used to play the piano a lot, but since the children came she doesn't have time.

GUEST: Children are a blessing, aren't they?

WIFE: The paper says that the concert we went to last night was a great success.

HUSBAND: Really? I had no idea we enjoyed it that much.

MAN: Madame, I'm the piano tuner.

WOMAN: But I didn't send for you.

MAN: No, but the neighbors did.

Rock 'n roll music makes me long for the good old days of radio when all you got was static.

"I have music in my very soul!"

"Yes, I thought I heard your shoes squeak."

"What is your occupation?"

"I used to be an organist."

"And what made you give it up?"

"My monkey died."

"Give me Beethoven's First, Mozart's Second and Brahms' Third."

"What about me?"

"You can play shortstop."

I used to *love* violin music, until I found that it was produced merely by dragging the tail of a horse across the interior of a cat.

"Do you know anything about music?"

"You can't fool me on music; I know every bar from the Battery to 125th Street."

Musicians who play by ear should remember that we listen the same way.

"He's a music arranger."

"I wish he'd do something for my brother."

"What would you like him to arrange for your brother?"

"To get his saxophone out of the pawnshop."

"Are you fond of music?"

"Yes, but keep right on playing."

"Where is your brother, Freddie?"

"He's in the house playing a duet. I finished first."

"I appeared in Carnegie Hall, and when I was finished, the entire audience rose, as one man, and applauded."

"YESSIR! You went right down in front and shook hands with him."

Talk about rapid progress in music! We knew a fellow who two months ago couldn't carry a tune. Now he's a piano mover.

I've heard quite a bit about your playing—from you.

"Isn't this music heavenly?"

"Heavenly? You've got your directions mixed."

He said he's had a tune running through his head all evening. Well, there's nothing there to stop it.

MUSICIANS (see also Orchestra, Band, Music)

They were returning from a concert given by local talent.

HE: I envy the man who sang the tenor solo.

SHE: Really? I thought he had a very poor voice.

HE: So did I, but just think of his nerve.

MUSICIAN: Why do you always play the same piece?

STUDENT: It haunts me.

MUSICIAN: It should; you've murdered it often enough.

The old man was applying for admission to a charity institution.

"What is your occupation?" asked the manager.

"I used to be an organist," answered the old man.

"And why did you give it up?"

"The monkey died."

FRIEND: Your voice surprises me.

VOCALIST: I studied and spent one million dollars to learn to sing.

FRIEND: I would love to have you meet my brother.

VOCALIST: Is he a singer, too?

FRIEND: No, he's a lawyer. He'll get your money back.

STRANGER: Does your orchestra ever play by request?

ORCHESTRA LEADER: A lot of times.

STRANGER: Ask them to play pinochle.

N

NAMES

Then there's the story about the fellow who excitedly approached a man walking innocently down a street, slapped him enthusiastically on the back, and shouted,

"Abe Minkofsky! Am I glad to see you! But tell me, Abe, what in the world happened to you? Last time I saw you, you were short and fat; all of sudden you're tall and thin. Last time you—"

The bewildered man finally was

able to interrupt long enough to say, "Look, mister, my name is not Abe Minkofsky." "Ah," boomed the undaunted greeter, "changed your name too, eh?"

1ST GIRL: My boy friend's name is Rex.
2ND GIRL: What's his last name?
1ST GIRL: He hasn't any. His mother wanted a dog.

POLICEMAN: What's your name?
OFFENDER: John Smith.
POLICEMAN: Come on. None of that. Give me your real name.
OFFENDER: Well, put me down as William Shakespeare.
POLICEMAN: That's better. You can't fool me with that Smith stuff.

1ST HILLBILLY: Here, sign here.
2ND HILLBILLY: Okay . . .
1ST HILLBILLY: Wait a minute, you usually sign "x" . . . why did you put down "y?"
2ND HILLBILLY: That's my new pen name.

1ST MAN: What's the name of your new girl friend?
2ND MAN: Gloria Vander . . . Vander . . . Vander . . .
1ST MAN: Vanderbilt?
2ND MAN: She sure is.

1ST WOMAN: Why do you call your husband Automatic Sam?

2ND WOMAN: Because he's shiftless.

TEACHER: What is your father's name?
LITTLE GIRL: Daddy.
TEACHER: Yes, but what does your mother call him?
LITTLE GIRL: She doesn't call him anything . . . she likes him.

NATURE

1ST MAN: My entire family loves nature. For example, my brother says he's completely happy with the earth as his pillow and the sky as his cover.
2ND MAN: He's found peace of mind?
1ST MAN: No, he's lost his apartment.

1ST MAN: Canada is known for its flora and fauna.
2ND MAN: What about the wild life?
1ST MAN: That can be found in Montreal.

1ST MAN: Ah, the air is like rare wine . . . I could breathe Spring forever . . . it's champagne . . .
2ND MAN: Take it easy . . . One more sniff and you'll have a hangover.

1ST GAMBLER: His father was a naturalist.

2ND GAMBLER: Only rolled 7's, huh?

1ST MAN: You look great. You must have spent a wonderful vacation.
2ND MAN: Phooey I did! Nature played me a dirty trick. It rained my entire vacation.
1ST MAN: But where did you get the sunburn?
2ND MAN: Sunburn? Ha, that's rust.

NECKING (see also Courtship, Kissing, Osculating)

"One of my kisses would make you feel ten years younger," boasted the bachelor to the spinster. The latter cooed. "Then give me three of them and we'll have a swell evening."

"Darling, I must confess, your kisses remind me of another."
"Oh, pshaw!"
"No, McGillicuddy."

"He didn't say more than three words last night."
"Honestly, you shouldn't let him kiss you so much."

"Would you call for help if I tried to kiss you?"
"Do you need help?"

"I hear she makes a practice of kissing boys."

"Listen, dearie, she hasn't had to practice in years."

"Oh, Madelon, I have a cold chill running down my back."
"So that's what happened to my Good Humor."

"Have some peanuts."
"Thanks."
"Wanna kiss?"
"No."
"Gimme my peanuts back."

"Do you remember when you kissed me for fifteen minutes?"
"Yes."
"By any chance did you find a pivot tooth?"

"Is it easy to kiss Jane?"
"Like falling off a log."
"Where did you get the black eye?"
"I fell off a log."

"The Americano asked me for a kiss last night."
"I hope you weren't influenced by what he had to say."
"No, I was influenced by what he gave me to drink."

"Thank you for the hug and the kiss."
"The same to you—the pressure was all mine."

"Aha, my pretty maiden. Would you let a stranger kiss you?"

"No, my friend."

"Did you get my check for a thousand kisses?"
"Yes, the iceman cashed it this morning."

NEIGHBORS

WIFE: Why do you walk outside every time I start to sing?
HUSBAND: I just want to show the neighbors I'm not beating you.

HUSBAND: A neighbor just told me that the milkman who delivers here makes love to every woman in this building but one.
WIFE: Yeah, it's that snooty Mrs. Lerner on the third floor.

HUSBAND: That couple across the street certainly are in love. Every morning Mr. Green kisses Mrs. Green on the steps of their house.
WIFE: Why don't you ever do that?
HUSBAND: How can I? I don't even know her.

MAN IN HARDWARE STORE: I want three lawn mowers, three rakes and three hoses.
CLERK: Certainly sir. Are you buying these for the golf club?
MAN: No. You see I have two neighbors.

MAN: Say, can I borrow your lawnmower?
NEIGHBOR: No; firstly because it's your lawnmower and secondly because I lent it to Harry.

NEWHART, BOB

I started out as an accountant but I didn't work out so well. I mean I figured if you came within two or three numbers of it, it was good enough.

Somebody once figured out that if you took an infinite number of monkeys and an infinite number of typewriters and let the monkeys type for an infinite number of times —they would write all the great books ever written. If they did this they would, of course, have to have overseers watching the monkeys. It would maybe go like this —

"Hey, Harry, come here a minute, this monkey here seems to have gotten something. He's typing along pretty good. Let's see what he wrote—'To be or not to be that is the siglelackoffcuk tor. . . .'"

NEWLYWEDS (see also Marriage, Elopement, Courtship, Engagement)

A man who had just checked out of a hotel room discovered

that his umbrella was missing. By the time he got back to the room, it was already occupied by a newly married couple. Listening at the door, he heard the following conversation:

GROOM: Whose lovely eyes are those darling?

BRIDE: Yours, sweetheart.

GROOM: Whose lovely, gorgeous lips are those?

BRIDE: Yours, lover.

GROOM: And whose precious swanlike neck is that, baby?

BRIDE: Yours, dearest.

At this point the man yelled through the keyhole, "When you get to the umbrella—it's mine!"

A famous maestro had a tough time deciding whether to marry a very beautiful but stupid girl or a rather painful-looking creature who was blessed with a magnificent voice. Art triumphed. He married the soprano. The morning after their nuptials, he woke, took one look at his bride, nudged her and shrieked, "For God's sake—sing."

As they walked down the aisle the bride shyly turned to the groom and said, "It won't be wrong now."

The bride was very much disconcerted at seeing twin beds in their bridal suite. "What's the matter, dearest?" asked the bridegroom. "Well, I certainly thought we were going to get a room all to ourselves!"

It was the day after their wedding. He took her in his arms and said, "Darling, now that we're married, I must tell you a few little defects I've noticed about you."

"Well," she answered, "it was those little defects that kept me from getting a better husband!"

They were honeymooning in England. He left the hotel room . . . after all, y'gotta eat sometime.

When he returned he noticed, frantically, that there were no numbers on any doors. In trying to find what he thought was his room, he knocked on a door gently, purring, "Honey, honey. Oh, honey, honey."

From within came an answering bellow, "Go away, you blooming idiot. This is a bathroom, not a beehive!"

The newlyweds tried to be nonchalant about their first night together as they checked into the hotel. The clerk in the hotel in Niagara Falls tried to make them comfortable. "Do you wish a corner room?"

"I do," said the groom.

"Do you wish an adjoining bath?"

"I do," said the bride.

"I now pronounce you room and bath!"

NEWSPAPERS (see also Advertisements)

Letter to subscription department. *The New York Times:* "My son has been reading *The Times* since his confinement to a mental institution. Now that he is cured, I wish to cancel his subscription."

Vital statistics note in a small-town newspaper: "Due to the shortage of paper a number of births will be postponed until next week."

1ST MAN: Have you seen the newspapers lately?
2ND MAN: Only the first page.
1ST MAN: Why?
2ND MAN: The newsboys keep chasing me away.

CHIEF EDITOR: On this paper, every reporter must suit his job. For sports we have an athlete; for advice to the lovelorn we have a romantic young woman . . .
JOB APPLICANT: Who writes the obituaries?
EDITOR: Oh, we always manage to dig someone up.

ADVERTISEMENTS: 1) Wanted . . . Secretary. Also slight knowledge of typing. Bring a friend.
2) Man with trailer would like to meet girl with car. Object: Latch on.

JOB APPLICANT: I understand you need a reporter.
EDITOR: Yeah, you're hired.
APPLICANT: What do you pay?
EDITOR: Don't be silly, this is a free press.

1ST MAN: I started my career as a leg man on a newspaper but I was fired for being too conscientious.
2ND MAN: You were fired for being too conscientious?
1ST MAN: Yeah, I followed every pair of legs in town.

REPORTER: Do you think I should put more fire into my articles?
EDITOR: No, vice versa.

The reporter came back from covering the campaign trail.
EDITOR: Well, what did the candidate have to say today?
REPORTER: Not a thing.
EDITOR: Good, then we can keep it down to a column.

Obituary Editor receiving a phone call: "You say our paper reported you as having died yesterday? Ah . . . tell me . . . where are you calling from?"

NEW YEAR (see also Yuletide)

"I'll bet you didn't keep your New Year's resolution about necking when you went out with that saxophone player last night."

"Sure I did—I kept it to myself."

January second is the day on the calendar when you break New Year's resolutions.

A rich exclusive couple at a New Year's Eve party were regaling friends with details of the sensational holiday week they had provided for their offspring—the giant tree laden with trinkets, the fabulous presents, the round of theaters and parties, the special 30 piece orchestra engaged to play for the last night of vacation.

Suddenly the wife gave an unearthly shriek.

"Harry, Harry," she cried, "I just remembered. Our children never came home from prep school."

In the liquor industry they call New Year's Eve Amateur Night.

NEW YORK

1ST SOUTHERNER: How did you like New York? Did you feel at home there?

2ND SOUTHERNER: Yessir. Why I got so comfortable I could keep my seat in the subway and not give a second thought to the ladies standing around me.

TEACHER: Now children, who can tell me where in the world the most ignorant people live?

JOHNNY: In New York, miss.

TEACHER: (puzzled): In New York?

JOHNNY: Yes . . . you said yourself that's where the population is most dense.

RICH BUSINESSMAN: Yessir, when I first came to New York, I only had $1 in my pocket.

INTERVIEWER: And how did you invest that $1 sir?

BUSINESSMAN: Why, I sent a telegram home asking for more money.

NIGHT CLUBS (see also Hecklers, Comedians)

1ST MAN: I was at the Latin Quarter yesterday when I saw Sophia Loren . . . so I sent the waiter over to ask her to dance. . . .

2ND MAN: So what happened?

1ST MAN: She danced with the waiter.

1ST MAN: I went to El Morocco yesterday and the place was

empty. How do they manage to stay in business?

2ND MAN: El Morocco empty? That's funny. What night were you there?

1ST MAN: Night? I was there yesterday morning. . . .

WAITER: For $50 you get a meal trés magnifique, for $30 you get a meal trés elegant, for $20 you get a meal trés superb.

CUSTOMER: What do I get for $10?

WAITER: For $10? Oh you get the tray.

Doorman in front of the Stork Club on a rainy night: "Why stay outside in the rain, folks, when you can go inside and get soaked?"

1ST MAN: I'm going to open up a night club in Madison Square Garden.

2ND MAN: But that's where they have the fights.

1ST MAN: So isn't that a good place for a night club?

1ST MAN: You say this night club was small???

2ND MAN: Small? It was nothing but a large ash tray and a bartender.

I took her out last night to a night club and my check only came to $10. . . . Of course hers was much larger.

NOSES

"Do you know I've had my nose to the grindstone for a year?" said the Washington bureaucrat to a friend.

"You had your nose to the grindstone for a year?"

"Of course. Why are you laughing?"

"I'll bet it was a beauty when you first started!"

BUSYBODY: You must think my head is soft.

LONG-SUFFERING NEIGHBOR: No, but I know your nose isn't soft."

BUSYBODY: How do you know my nose isn't soft?

LONG-SUFFERING NEIGHBOR: Because when you stick it in my business, it won't break off.

NOVELS (see also Books)

"Did you ever read Tolstoi's *Goodbye*?"

"I didn't even know he was leaving."

"What do you know about the works of Ingersoll?"

"I know he makes a darn good watch for a dollar."

"You know that pet bookworm I have? You won't see him for some time. He left yesterday. He's taking a two-year trip through *Gone With the Wind*.

"Is this a free translation?"
"No, sir, the book will cost you two dollars."

"Do you know Poe's *Raven*?"
"No, what's he mad about?"

"Can I see that book I had last week?"
"I guess so. Was it fascinating?"
"No, but it's got my girl friend's telephone number in it."

"Whatcher been doin' this even'?"
"Reading *Ben Hur*."
"Oh, readin' racy literature nowadays."

NUDIST COLONY

You can always spot a Peeping Tom at a nudist colony. He's the guy sneaking looks at the girls passing by outside.

It's easy to spot the psychiatrist in a nudist colony. He's the guy who's listening instead of looking.

NUDISTS

FRIEND: How are things at your nudist colony?

OPPORTUNIST: Well, pretty good. I opened up a little store out there. I'm selling underthings to the nudists.
FRIEND: What kind of underthings could you sell to nudists?
OPPORTUNIST: Cushions.

And then there was the conscientious nudist who drove into the nudist colony and stripped his gears.

"What happened to your husband?" asked Mrs. O'Toole.
Mrs. O'Hara smiled proudly. "He has a new job. He is out at the nudist colony. He's teaching horseback riding. He's teaching the nudists how to ride bareback," she said.

He's as careful as a nudist crossing a barbed wire fence.

BOB: My uncle is champion golfer at the nudist colony.
BESS: What makes you think he's champion golfer out there?
BOB: Because yesterday he went around the whole course in nothing.

NURSE (see also Hospital, Doctor, Physician)

The nurse entered the professor's room and said softly: "It's a boy, sir."

The professor looked up from his desk. "Well," he said, "What does he want?"

PRETTY NURSE: Oh, Doctor. Each time I take this person's pulse it beats faster and faster. What should I do?

DOCTOR: Blindfold him.

PATIENT: I'm in love with you, and I don't want to get well.

NURSE: Never fear. The doctor is in love with me, too. He saw you kiss me this morning.

NURSE: Mr. Jones, you are the father of quadruplets.

JONES: What! One of them things that runs around on four legs?

BILL: How's Benny doing in the hospital?

BUD: Fairly well, but I don't think he will be out as soon as expected.

BILL: How did you find out—see the doctor?

BUD: No! I saw his nurse.

The Head Nurse was showing the pretty young graduate from nursing school the hospital. As they were walking, the Head Nurse stopped in front of a door of the Men's Convalescent Section. "This is a really dangerous ward," she remarked; "these patients are almost well."

The nurse was nicknamed "Appendix" because all the doctors wanted to take her out.

NUT (see also Insane, Stupid, Moron)

A nut hopped into a psychiatrist's office and kept snapping his fingers and growling in low, rumbling tones. "Calm down," said the doctor, "what are you doing that for?" "It keeps away the elephants," was the nut's reply. "There aren't any elephants around here." "See?" said the nut happily, "it works."

❖❖❖

O

OFFICE (see also Boss, Secretary)

A young miss just out of business school was filling out an application form (her own form was already filled out) in one of New York's larger advertising agencies. She went through it fine, but when she came to the heading called

"Sex" she hesitated. Finally, she decided to answer. "Once in a while," she wrote.

OFFSPRING (see also Kids, Children, Adolescent, Parents and Children)

LADY: (to little boy) My dear, does your mother know you smoke?
SMALL BOY: Madam, does your husband know you speak to strange men?

"Dad, you were born in California, weren't you?"
"Yes."
"And mother was born in New York?"
"Yes."
"And I was born in Indiana."
"Yes, son."
"But, Dad, isn't it funny how we all got together here?"

"Where's your mother, sonny? I've come to wash her bay window."
"You're too late, mister. She took a bath last night."

TEACHER: Now, Johnny, what stirring speech did Paul Revere make when he finished his immortal ride?
JOHNNY: Whoa.

OLD AGE

"My grandfather is ninety-five years old and every day he goes horseback riding—except during the month of July."
"Why not during July?"
"Cause that's when the man who puts him on is on his vacation."

He's been smoking since he was fourteen. Now at ninety he's giving it up. He doesn't want to get the habit.

An eighty-five-year-old man was complaining to his friend, "My stenographer is suing me for breach of promise."
His friend answered, "At eighty-five, what could you promise her?"

He's so old he gets winded playing chess.

OLD MAIDS (see also Bachelor)

Old Maid (calling fire department): "A man is trying to get into my room."
"You don't want the fire department—what you want is the police department."
Old Maid: "I don't want the police—I want the fire department —a man is trying to get into my

room—and we're on the second floor and he needs a ladder."

Imagine my embarrassment, when, according to my usual habit, I looked under the bed before retiring—and I had forgotten that I was in an upper berth.

An old maid rang the fire alarm and twenty firemen responded. When they arrived, she said: "There's no fire, so nineteen of you can go back."

Tillie and Millie met for lunch and were discussing what had occurred in their lives since their last meeting.

Millie asked, "You say, Tillie, you were engaged to a promising young lawyer?"

"Yes, but he didn't keep his promise."

The old maid was asked which she liked most in a man, brains, money or appearance, and she answered, "Appearance—and the sooner the better."

The old maid found a thief under her bed. She held a gun on him and called the police. "Please send a cop over—in the morning."

An old maid is a girl whose father never owned a shotgun.

An old maid was attending a wrestling match when one of the wrestlers was thrown in her lap. She refused to give him up and kept yelling, "Finders keepers!"

Did you hear about the mean ventriloquist who went around throwing his voice under the beds of old maids?

Two old maids ran a drug store. A man walked in and said, "I'd like to see a male clerk."

One old maid answered, "I'm a registered pharmacist. You can tell me all your troubles."

The customer explained, "I'd like some sort of pill to calm me down. I have a terrible habit. Everytime I see a girl, I wanna make love to her. What can you give me?"

The old maid replied, "Just a minute, I'll discuss it with my sister."

About five minutes later she returned. "Well?" said the man.

"My sister and I," said the old maid, "decided to give you the drugstore and seven hundred dollars."

Two old maids were sitting in the insane asylum. One said, "Y' know, I feel like having a man hug me and kiss me and make love to me!" to which the other replied, "Oh, now you're talking sense. You'll be outta here soon!"

OPERA (see also Music)

"Tell me, how do you remember all the words in the opera?"
"I just tie a little string around my finger."

"We'll have to go over to the Opera House and rehearse for *Carmen.*"
"I'm ready for her if she's ready for me."

"Can you hear the music?"
"No. These are good seats."
"I had better seats last year.— They were behind a post."

"In the opera I stab him and then put a candle at his feet."
"It's not bad enough that you stab him—you've got to give him a hot foot?"

"I was at the opera last night."
"Grand opera?"
"Oh, I should say, splendid."

As far as the performance was concerned, it was some of the best bracelets we ever heard. We spent the first act looking at ermine and for the rest we just let our eyes slum a bit. It was truly a night at the opera, but personally we enjoyed it much better with the Marx Brothers.

Two film actresses went to the opera. One actress said to the other, "If you close your eyes, can't you just imagine you're at home with the radio on?"

"How are you getting along with your opera?"
"Not so good, I don't know whether I'm *Carmen* or goin'."

"What is your favorite opera?"
"*The Golden Goose!*"
"Was it a hit?"
"It laid an egg."

"It's a tribute to you, making a living at opera. On the side I'm a contortionist."
"A contortionist?"
"Yes, I have to do something to make the ends meet."

OPPORTUNITY

A gent called at the box office of a hit show to purchase a seat. "Not a ticket in the house—you can't buy one for love or money," came the turndown. But this was a persistent customer: "You mean to tell me that if Mayor Wagner wanted to see this show tonight, you couldn't manage to scrape up a ticket for him?" "Yes," came the admission, "if Mayor Wagner needed a ticket, we'd have one for him." "Well," shot back the insistent one, "I got news for you —Mayor Wagner isn't coming and I'd like to have his seat."

You know why I'm a failure? The one time and the only time Opportunity ever knocked on my door, I didn't answer. I thought it was the House Detective!

Opportunity knocks, but last night a knock spoiled my opportunity.

H. L. Mencken once said, "Most people don't recognize Opportunity when it knocks because it comes in the form of hard work."

OPTIMIST

An optimist is a man who goes to the window in the morning and says, "Good morning, God." A pessimist goes to the window and says, "My God, it's morning!"

Harry Weisbaum, of Beau Brummel Ties, got me in knots with this gag: An optimist is a guy who thinks his wife quit cigarettes, because when he came home he found cigar butts all over the house.

An optimist is a guy who falls off the Empire State Building and on the way down he keeps thinking, "Well, I'm not hurt yet."

An optimist is a college professor who sits in the last row of

the gallery and winks at the chorus girls.

ORATORS (see also Speakers, Speech)

If you want to know what an orator is, I'll explain: If you meet a man and ask him how much is 2 and 2 and he says it's 4—he's not an orator. But if you ask another man the same question and he says, "When in the course of human events it becomes necessary to take the second numeral and superimpose it upon the figure two, then I say unto you and I say it without fear of successful contradiction, that the consequential result amounts to four"—Brother, that's an orator!

An orator complained, "When I talk, nobody listens. When money talks—everybody listens."

ORCHESTRA (see also Musicians, Band, Instruments)

"This is just a B.V.D. orchestra."
"What do you mean?"
"Oh, it's only one piece."

"What are the boys in the band doing these afternoons?"
"Playing poker."
"Playing poker? Don't they re-

hearse? Yes, but no matter how much they rehearse they can only win when they deal."

At an orchestra rehearsal the members had just finished playing "My Old Kentucky Home." The leader, seeing a gentleman weeping, inquired in a sympathetic voice, "Are you a Kentuckian?"

To which the man replied, "No, sir, I'm a musician."

"Didn't that number pep you up?"

"What number?"

"The number you didn't expect to hear."

"Didn't you hear it?"

"No, but then I didn't expect to."

"That was very good."

"Would you like to hear us play another number?"

"Oh, come now, it wasn't that good."

"Last night I listened to a sympathy orchestra."

"Symphony, fool, not sympathy."

"Well, doesn't sympathy mean 'Sorry for someone?' "

Several Broadwayites heard a certain maestro's recordings the other day. Said one, "If he's a conductor I want a transfer."

"Have you seen my baton?"

"It's in your right hand."

"No wonder I couldn't find it. I usually carry it in my left hand."

"I like an orchestra that makes my hips swing, that sets my blood to running fast, that makes my blood tingle."

"You don't want an orchestra, you want a body massage."

The orchestra is from the grill room of the Automat.

"I had a band once."

"I didn't know you were a musician."

"I didn't have to be—I was the leader."

"I used to have a band."

"You did?"

"Yes, it was only two pieces."

"That was unique."

"And we played over the TV. The only trouble with us was that while the band was playing one of us liked to go into the control room and listen to how the band sounded. The whole thing broke up when I met the other member of the band coming out of the control room while I was going in."

"Pardon me, fellers, but there is a gentleman in the house who requests 'I'm Alabama Bound.' "

"Okay," he replied. "It's an old

number, but we can arrange to play it for a customer." He turned to his men. "A customer wants 'I'm Alabama Bound', boys," he asserted. "Let's give it to him—train whistle and all."

The drummer started off with the train whistle and the band went into the chorus. Suddenly, the waiter rushed over and grabbed the orchestra leader's arm, "Leave out those train whistles," he panted.

The leader swung around, "What are you talking about?" he snapped. " 'Alabama Bound' starts off with a train whistle."

"You've got it all wrong," he howled. "This customer is going by bus!"

"What's the idea of all the noise at this hour of the night?"
"I need practice on my trombone. I've been letting it slide too much lately."

"You know, I heard you on a phonograph record last night."
"Oh, so that's where I was last night? I wondered what made me so dizzy!"

ORGANIZATION

Mr. Cohen belonged to an organization with many social benefits. Each person in the club was asked to buy a plot at a reduced rate—sort of a group plan so they could have a place to live when they died. When the organization found that it wasn't paying off too well, they asked the president to talk to the delinquent members. Cohen was first to be called. "You bought a plot twenty-five years ago," the president began, "and you haven't paid for it yet." The member looked askance. "I didn't use it," he answered. "Who stopped you?" was the topper.

OSCULATING (see also Kissing, Romance, Love, Spooning, Necking)

Never let a fool kiss you and never let a kiss fool you.

"And what did Flo say when you kissed her?"
"What do you think she is, a ventriloquist?"

"I could never let a man kiss me unless I was engaged."
"Darn it! Just my luck."
"But I am engaged."

It's no fun to kiss a girl over the telephone—unless you're right in the booth with her.

"His kisses are talent."
"On what amateur program?"

"If you make another mistake in grammar, I'm going to kiss you."

"You ain't, neither!"

A kiss is something which once given cannot be taken back, but is often returned.

"Aren't my kisses like something electric?"

"Yeah, a Frigidaire."

"Darling, stop kissing me. Here comes my mother and three of my old maid aunts!"

"Well, they'll just have to line up and wait their turn."

"Louise, your hair is all mussed up. Did that young man kiss you against your will?"

"He thinks he did, Mother."

"If I should kiss you would you scream for your folks?"

"No, not unless you want to kiss the whole family."

"May I kiss you?"

"Sure—help yourself."

"It will be much nicer if you help, too."

"Aren't you ashamed of yourself?"

"Not yet."

P

PAAR, JACK

I grew up to be the kind of kid my mother wouldn't let me play with when I was a kid.

Little girl told her mother, "Mommy, I want my own mirror, I'm tired of making up in doorknobs."

José Melis will tell you the story of the girl who took a bath in lemon juice and puckered to death.

President Kennedy wanted to have an egg-rolling contest for his family but he couldn't get an okay to rent Soldiers' Field.

You can always tell the tourists —they're the ones who wear hats.

Hugh Downs is a little stuffy. If Hugh was chaperone for Adam and Eve—there'd be no world.

You all know the Paar Law: "If something bad is going to happen—it will."

As my Daughter Randy says, "May I thank you from the top of my heart and my bottom."

Charlie Weaver is the only man I know who receives CARE packages from Hurley's Bar.

My wife has an "Artichoke Hairdo." I don't know whether to kiss her or serve her.

PARENTS AND CHILDREN (see also Kids, Offspring, Children)

"Mommy, mommy, what's an Oedipus complex?"
"Shut up and kiss me."

"Your face is clean," the mother said, "But how did you get your hands so dirty?"
"Washing my face," replied the young boy.

A father found his small son looking very unhappy.
"What's wrong?" he asked. "I can't get along with your wife," the boy replied.

"Mommy, why do I only walk in circles?"
"Shut up or I'll nail your other foot to the floor."

The mother said to her little boy, "Don't bang on the floor, the stork is visiting Mrs. Jones downstairs."
The boy replied, "I hope he doesn't scare her, she's pregnant, you know."

Some young boys were bragging about their fathers. One said, "My father's a great magician. He can walk down the street and turn into a saloon."

A young boy boasted about his father to his friends. "My father was the first man to fly 10,000 feet with a stick in his hands." "Oh, was he a flyer?" "No," the boy said, "the poolroom blew up."

The worried mother told the doctor, "My son insists on emptying ashtrays." "Well, that's not unusual," the doctor said. "Yeah," the mother said, "but in his mouth?"

PARTNERS (see also Business)

"Sam," his dying partner wheezed, "I have a confession to make. I robbed our firm of $100,-000. I sold the secret formula to our competitors. I took the letter from your desk that your wife needed to get her divorce, and, Sam, I . . ."
"That's all right," said Sam, "it was me that poisoned you."

Two partners decided to take a trip to Florida. Just as they got on the train and were seated comfortably, one of them jumped up and screamed, "My God! I left the safe open!" The other partner shrugged his shoulders and replied, "What are you worried about? We're both here, ain't we?"

A feller called his partner from Miami and said, "Sam, this is Max, how's everything in New York?"

SAM: Very good.

MAX: How's the weather up there?

SAM: The weather's how it should be.

MAX: How's business in the shop?

SAM: Very good, but I got bad news for you.

MAX: What's the matter?

SAM: We've been robbed.

MAX: Don't be silly, PUT IT BACK!

I wouldn't say Dean Martin drinks a lot but it was two months before he realized he was on the stage without Jerry Lewis.

PEDESTRIANS (see also Traffic)

OFFICER: Where's the driver that hit him? Get him!

TRAFFIC VICTIM: Wait, Mr. Policeman, wait. I was trying to cross the street and the driver stopped and motioned me to go across. The shock was too much. I fell down.

IRATE MOTORIST: The way some pedestrians walk you'd think they owned the streets.

IRATE PEDESTRIAN: Yeah, and the way some motorists drive, you'd think they owned their cars.

YANK: I read where a kangaroo was run over by an automobile today.

AUSSIE: What about it?

YANK: It's most discouraging. You know how a kangaroo can leap.

AUSSIE: Yes, I know.

YANK: Well, what chance has a pedestrian got?

Two hitch-hikers were trying to get a ride.

ONE: Why don't you try hailing a few cars?

OTHER: I'm saving my thumb for the ride back.

PESSIMIST

Must tell you about the man who was looking so glum and despondent that a friend asked, "Morris, what's eating you? You look like last month's balance sheet." "What's eating me, he asks! Remember two weeks ago, my Tante Razel died and left me $50,000?" "Yeah, I remember, so what's so awful?" "What's so awful, he asks! Remember last week my Uncle Chaim died and left me $75,000?" "I remember that too, but what's bad about that?" "What's bad about it? . . . This week nothing!"

PHYSICIANS (see also Doctors, Hospitals)

DOCTOR: Are you taking the medicine regularly?
PATIENT: I tasted it; I'd rather have the cough.

SERVANT: The doctor's here, Sir.
ABSENT-MINDED MAN: I can't see him. Tell him I'm sick.

PRETTY NURSE: Oh, Doctor, each time I take this person's pulse it beats faster and faster. What should I do?
DOCTOR: Blindfold him.

DOCTOR: I have been treating men for ten years and have never heard a complaint. What does that prove?
SHE: Dead men tell no tales.

DOCTOR: The best thing you can do is give up cigarettes, liquor and women.
PATIENT: What's the next best thing?

DOCTOR: Nurse, how is that little boy who swallowed a quarter this morning?
NURSE: No change yet.

DOCTOR: (looking at patient's eye) I see indication of liver ailments and Bright's disease.
PATIENT: Try again, Doc, that's my glass eye.

If the person who stole the alcohol out of my cellar in a glass jar will return Grandma's appendix, no questions will be asked.

DOCTOR: What is the most you ever weighed?
NEW PATIENT: One hundred fifty-four pounds.
DOCTOR: And what is the least you ever weighed?
NEW PATIENT: Eight and a quarter pounds.

"I'd like my tooth extracted, please."
"I'm sorry, young lady, but I'm out of gas."
She walked five miles home.

PIANO (see also Instruments, Music)

"You still study the piano?"
"Sure. Three lessons a week."
"Making any progress?"
"Oh yes, I'm progressing by leaps and bounds."

"Oh, that's what makes your music sound that way."

"I know a girl who plays piano by ear."

"That's nothing. I know an old man who fiddles with his whiskers."

"The fact that I am a good musician was the means of saving my life during the flood in our town a few years ago."

"How was that?"

"When the water struck our house my wife got on the folding bed and floated down the stream until she was rescued."

"And what did you do?"

"Well, I accompanied her on the piano."

Willing to have his neighbors think he was a fine musician, Brown installed a mechanical piano near a front window of his home, where he spent hours each day pedaling out melodies. "Your father is a great piano player, isn't he?" one of the neighbors remarked to Brown's boy William one afternoon.

"Yep, but it makes his feet awful sore."

"He ate an onion before he sat down to the piano."

"He wanted to flavor us with a song."

"We had a piano concert."

"Is that so?"

"A duet."

"What did your concert consist of?"

"Mozart and mistakes."

"Girlie, when I walk up to a piano, they don't laugh."

"Oh, a musical genius."

"Wrong again. I'm the installment collector."

"Before I'm through, you'll know such terms as *allegro,* etc."

"What kind of language is that?"

"Italian."

"For ten dollars a lesson you could at least give me lessons in English."

"As soon as you started playing the piano at the party, twenty people stopped talking."

"Is that so?"

"They fell asleep."

"I've got to go home now and get my piano."

"We've got a piano here in the studio."

"Yeah, but my piano's got my music on it."

"We'll send home to get your music."

"That's no good. The music's carved on the piano."

"I love the piano."

"Me too, except when my wife

plays it and then I realize what a wonderful musical instrument the riveting machine is."

"Have you done your piano practicing?"
"I practiced yesterday."
"I didn't hear the piano."
"I was practicing rests and pauses."

PICNIC (see also Family)

This is about the family that went picnicking on a Sunday afternoon. They found a lovely green spot in the country, spread out the tablecloth and covered it with sandwiches, hard-boiled eggs, etc. Impressed by the beauty of the place, they were puzzled by the flags with numbers they saw at various points in the distance.

Midway through their picnic, a gentleman strode angrily toward them. "Just what do you think you are doing?" he exploded. "Don't you realize you are sitting on the fifteenth green of the most exclusive golf club in the country?"

Papa swallowed his hard-boiled egg and sarcastically answered, "So, is this the way to get new members?"

PILLS (see also Illness, Health)

Have you heard about the lad who complained of chronic headaches and was told by his doctor he had a brand-new, simply wonderful cure? An atomic pill. "It's really powerful. You take one now," urged the medico, "and call me back in about an hour. Let me know how it worked."

An hour later the patient phoned. "Doc," he moaned, "come over right away and pick me up." "Where are you?" asked the doctor. Came the answer: "On 5th Avenue and 50th Street. You know, where Saks Fifth Avenue used to be—until about a few minutes ago!"

PLAYBOY (see also Bachelor)

A handsome young playboy showed up at his favorite bistro swathed in bandages. "What happened to you?" asked a friend. "I held up a train," said the playboy. "You?" exclaimed his friend. "Held up a train?" "Yeah," came the laconic answer. "It was a bride's train and it seems I held it up too high!"

An amorous playboy had cornered his girl in the back seat of the sedan and was eagerly trying his hand at her. She kept resisting and pushing him away. But still he persisted. Finally, she became annoyed and gave him a violent shove. "Lester," she said, smoothing her skirt, "I don't know what's come over you. You've always been so restrained and so gentlemanly." "Yes, I know," said Lester apologetically, "but I just can't help it. I'm trying to give up smoking."

PLAYS (see also Theatre, Actors)

"I only saw one act and I left."
"Why didn't you see Act Two?"
"The program said, Act Two same as Act One."

WIFE (an ardent theatre patron): Aren't the acoustics fine?
HUSBAND (a businessman, pure and simple): You bet. I'll have to congratulate 'em before we leave.

THEATREGOER: Did you see him in *Hamlet?*
CRITIC: Yes. He played the king as though he expected somebody to trump him.

TEDDY: My sister's practicing to be an actress.
NEDDY: She is?
TEDDY: Yeah, and so far she's learned how to sleep until eleven o'clock in the morning.

POLICE (see also Cops, Crooks, Thieves)

POLICEMAN: How did you come to get hit by that car?
SMALL BOY: I didn't come to get hit. I come to see my aunt.

POLICEMAN: And did you save the girl?
FIREMAN: Yes, for another time.

POLICE SERGEANT: You here again?
HE: Yeah. Any mail?

GIRL: Stop that man: he wanted to kiss me.
COP: That's all right, miss. There'll be another along in a minute.

CHIEF: So you saw the guy at the safe, eh? Did you get the drop on them?
POLICEMAN: Did I? They bought six tickets to the Policeman's Ball before I let them go.

POLICEMAN (to motorist who nearly collided): Don't you know that you should always give half the road to a woman driver?
MOTORIST: I always do, when I find out which half of the road she wants.

COP: Hey, there's no red light on your car!
GIRL: No, sir! It's not that kind of a car.

COP: Who was driving when you hit that car?

DRUNK: (triumphantly) None of us. We were all in the back seat.

COP: Did you ever hear of the Mann Act?

STUDE: No, where's it playing?

NIGHT WATCHMAN: Young man are you going to kiss that girl?

YOUNG MAN: No Sir.

NIGHT WATCHMAN: Here, then, hold my lantern.

COP: Have you read the traffic rules?

MOTORIST: Yes, what would you like to know?

WARDEN: Well, young man, they're about to give you the juice. Have you any last request?

CONDEMNED: Yeah, make it orange juice.

"You're wanted for a safe-cracking job."

"Fine! I'll take the position."

A policeman stopped a woman for passing a red light and was about to give her a ticket.

WOMAN: I wouldn't give me a a ticket if I were you. I know some important people like Jack Javits, Robert Wagner, Frank Hogan. . . .

POLICEMAN: Do you know Carl Phillips?

WOMAN: Why, no.

POLICEMAN: Well, then, here's your ticket. Phillips is the one you should have known. . . .

WOMAN: Who's he?

POLICEMAN: Me!

POLICEMAN (standing at traffic light as woman sits in car as light goes from red to green to yellow to red to green): What's the matter, lady, didn't you see any color you liked?

(Policeman giving driving test).

POLICEMAN: Read the first line on that chart on the wall.

DRIVER: Always drive carefully.

POLICEMAN: Okay. . . . now read the last line.

DRIVER: I want some tickets to the Policeman's Ball.

POLICEMAN: Fine. How many?

POLITICS (see also Democrats, Republicans)

Franklin D. Roosevelt claims that this is the most popular joke sweeping the political corridors in Washington. Senators Barry Goldwater, Jack Javits, and Stu Symington were swapping chitchat in the Senate lunchroom when the latter said: "I had a real nice dream last night. I dreamed that God touched me on the back and said, 'Stu, you are going to be the next President of the United States.' "

"That's a coincidence," Javits interrupted. "I had almost the identical dream. I dreamed that God touched me on the back and said, 'Jack, I have decided that you will be President.' "

Goldwater, who remained silent through this exchange of dream talk, finally smiled and offered a comment. "I hate to spoil your dreams," he said, "but I think I ought to tell you that I wasn't near enough to touch either of you on the back last night!"

A politician was making a speech about the conservation of natural resources. "I'd be willing to wager that there isn't a person in this crowd who has done a single thing to help conserve our timber." No one spoke for a few seconds. Then, a meek-looking fellow in the back stood up, raised his hand and said, "I once shot a woodpecker."

"What do you think is to blame for all our problems with the countries in Europe?" asked the interviewer of the Senator. "The trouble with American foreign relations," replied the Senator, "is that they're all broke."

A member of Congress insisted that he never made a mistake.

"I'm always right," he told an associate, "and furthermore, I'd rather be right than President." "Don't worry," smiled his companion, "you'll never be either."

FRANCES: I wonder why they don't ever have a woman for president?
ELEANOR: A president has to be over forty years of age and a great leader of men, and you know as well as I do, Fanny, that no man would follow a woman after she's forty years old.

"He makes money on election day. He is sort of a taxidermist."
"What is that?"
"He stuffs the ballot boxes."

He was an unsuccessful politician, poor but dishonest. He went to his ward leader. "I have thirty votes in my family and I control two hundred more. Why can't I be an assemblyman?"

After a little persuasion, the leader ran him for office and he was elected. Two years later he was back again with a request to become a congressman. The leader granted this request, too, and he was elected. Four years later he asked to be run for governor. Again the leader consented and again he won.

Soon he was back again and

said to the Boss, "You must do me another favor."

"What now?" screamed the head politician. "I made you an assemblyman, I made you a congressman and I made you a governor. What do you want me to do now? Make you President?"

"No, whimpered the governor, "make me a citizen."

The politician was campaigning the middle West, trying to get the Indian votes. At one reservation, he promised schools and colleges for all the Indians, to which they stood up as one and yelled, "Hoya! Hoya!" With that he became more inspired and promised hospitals, fully-staffed clinics and the like for each tribe. Again the entire body stood up, chanting "Hoya! Hoya!" This continued throughout his speech.

Later, he went on a tour of the camp and came upon a field he wanted to inspect. The guide told him it was the pasture for the horses and that he could go through if he wished, but counselled him to be careful not to step in the hoya!

MOM: What makes you think our son will be a politician?
POP: He says more things that sound well and mean nothing than any other boy on the block!

One politician to another: "I liked the straightforward way you dodged all those issues."

One Republican told another of one method of getting votes. "Give every taxi driver a big tip and tell him to vote Republican."

The other said, "I have a better method. I give them no tip at all and tell them to vote Democratic."

FIRST CITIZEN: It must be terrible for two great political leaders to split.
SECOND CITIZEN: Not if they split 50-50.

POOR (see also Broke, Loan)

There is one good thing about being poor—it's inexpensive.

POPULARITY

CARRIE: What makes you so popular?
MARY: It's my line.
CARRIE: What is your line?
MARY: The line of least resistance.

"My girl's father doesn't like me," stated Bill.

"He doesn't? On what grounds does he object to you?" asked Bob.

"On any grounds within ten miles of the house."

He's the kind of guy who, when you first meet him, you don't like. But when you get to know him, you hate him.

PREACHER

PREACHER: If there is anyone in this congregation who likes sin, let him get up. What, Stella, do you like sin?
STELLA: Oh, excuse me, preacher, I thought you said sin.

Don't you know it's wrong to shoot craps?
Yes, sir, and I'm sure paying for my sins.

MAN: Father, forgive me, for I kissed a pretty girl.
PRIEST: How many times did you commit this terrible sin?
MAN: Father, I came here to confess and not to brag.

"Well, my boy," said the new minister to the three year old, "what did Santa Claus bring you?"
"Aw, I got a little red chair," said the kid, "but it ain't much good. It's got a hole in the bottom of it."

"Please pray for my father's floating kidney."
"But I can't pray for any one thing like that."

"Well the other day you prayed for the loose livers."

"Can you tell me what grace is, son?"
"No, sir."
"Surely you can. Your father says it before each meal."
"Oh yes, it's 'Go easy on the butter, it costs sixty cents a pound.'"

PRESENTS (see also Gifts)

"See these stockings? I just paid five dollars for them. They're a gift for my girl. Think she'll like them?"
"Why, there's a run in each stocking."
"Yeah—I did that—I wanted to get a run for my money."

"Why not buy him a couple of book ends?"
"Oh, he won't have time to read them."

"I came in here to get something for my wife."
"What are you asking for her?"

" Here's a present for you."
"Oh, I think it's wonderful—it's just what I needed—isn't it grand!"
"Well, I'm glad you like it."
"Yeah—but tell me—what is it?"

"What are you going to give me for Christmas?"

"Close your eyes and tell me what you see."

"Nothing."

"That's what you're going to get for Christmas."

"That mouth organ you gave me for my birthday is easily the best present I've had."

"I'm glad you like it."

"Yes—mother gives me a quarter a week not to play it."

"What shall we get Dad for Christmas?"

"I hear he's buying us a car—let's get him a chauffeur's outfit."

PROPOSALS (see also Courtship, Newlyweds, Engagements)

ADA: Did Joe propose?

MAIDA: Yes, but I turned him down on account of the book I was reading.

ADA: What could your reading a book have to do with refusing him?

MAIDA: Well, my sister's husband proposed to her while she was reading *The Three Musketeers* and she had triplets.

ADA: I don't see the connection.

MAIDA: When Joe proposed, I was reading *The Birth of a Nation!*

TIMID MAN: (proposing over phone): Miss Simkins?

WOMAN: Yes, Miss Simkins speaking.

MAN: Well—er—will you marry me, Miss Simkins?

WOMAN: Yes! Who's speaking?

MISS GOTROCKS: You! You want to marry me?

YOUNG MAN: Yes.

MISS GOTROCKS: But, my dear boy, you've only known me three days.

YOUNG MAN: Oh, much longer than that, really! I've been two years in the bank where your father has his account.

MADGE: "What made you quarrel with Merlin?"

MADELINE: "Well, he proposed to me again last night."

MADGE: "Where was the harm in that?"

MADELINE: "My dear, I had accepted him the night before."

FATHER: "So you want to marry my daughter? You know that she has a perfectly good home?"

SUITOR: "Exactly, sir, and I think it would be rather cruel to take her away from it, don't you?"

PROSTITUTES

A voluptuous redhead walked up to the window in the bank and plunked down fifty twenty dollar gold pieces. A big grin appeared on the teller's face and he said, "Naughty girl, you've been hoarding haven't you?"

"Listen, wise guy," snapped the redhead, "It's none of your business how I earned this money; all you got to do is deposit it!"

The girls in the profession keep the wolves from the door . . . by picking them up in the street.

Abe was fifty-eight years old and his doctor just told him that either he retired or expired. Confronting his fifty-five-year-old wife, Molly, with this tale and the fact that they had nothing in the bank depressed Abe.

MOLLY: Don't worry, Abe. I'll support us.

ABE: But Molly, you're fifty-five and you never did a day's work in your life. What are you going to do?

MOLLY: I'll walk the streets. That every woman knows how to do.

With that remark Molly left the house and returned at 5 A.M. and handed Abe a roll of bills and some change. Gleefully and surprised Abe counted the money of her night's work.

ABE: Eighteen, nineteen, twenty . . . dollars and four pennies. You did all right Molly. But tell me, who gave you the pennies?

MOLLY: They all did. . . .

A successful Madam was telling an interviewer about her profession and why she had to leave the field.

MADAM: I had twenty of the most beautiful girls in New York and business was great for five years but then the customers stopped.

INTERVIEWER: Why was that.

MADAM: I guess they were tired of seeing the same old faces!

PSYCHIATRIST (see also Analyst)

The psychiatrist said to the comedian, "Lie down and tell me everything you know." He did and now the psychiatrist is doing the comic's act in Chicago.

A guy went to the psychiatrist and complained about feeling inferior because of his height. The psychiatrist reminded the short fellow about the great men in history, such as Napoleon and Lautrec, who were great men in spite of their height.

The little man felt completely cured after talking to the psychiatrist and everything would have worked out fine, but a cat ate him.

A man said to the psychiatrist, "Doc, I can't remember anything, I have such a poor memory." The psychiatrist said, "How long have you had this trouble?" "What trouble?" the man said.

The man relaxing on the couch said, "You know the girl whose hair I used to stick in the ink-well?" "Oh yes," The psychiatrist said, "Ever see her?" "Only when I want to fill my fountain pen," the man said.

A psychiatrist reported half his patients went to him because they weren't married, while the other half went to him because they were.

Two psychiatrists passed each other on the street and one said, "Good morning, how are you." And the other one said, "I wonder what he meant by that?"

The psychiatrist asked the troubled man how long he had been thinking he was a dog. "Since I was a puppy," the man replied.

Not too long ago I was feeling quite distraught and nervous, whatever that means, so I went to visit my psychiatrist. He said to me, "Joey, give up smoking," I said, "Why?" He said, "Listen to me, Joey, give up smoking!" I said, "What for? It's not bad for me." He said, "I know, but you're burning my couch. . . ."

This fellow awoke one morning and discovered lilies growing right out of the top of his head. He ran straight down to his psychiatrist's office. The head shrinker stared at the flowers. He said, "Why, this is fantastic. Now where on earth do you suppose those flowers came from?" The guy yelled, "Look at the card! See who sent them!"

A man dressed in mid-nine-teenth-century garb approached a psychiatrist and told him, "I'm Abraham Lincoln." Then he whispered, "Doc, I've got a serious problem. I think my wife's trying to get rid of me. She keeps insisting that I take her to the theater."

A man visited a psychiatrist because he thought he was Colonel Nasser. The head shrinker assured him that it wasn't too serious a delusion. "A lot you know," moaned the man. "I happen to be Jewish."

A psychiatrist was explaining to her patient, "Now, you mustn't continually say you're Adam. It's just nonsense and an absurdity of your mind. You couldn't have been the first man." "Skip the long talk, Doc, that's what caused all the trouble between me and my wife."

Young man to psychiatrist: "My trouble is, I'm from Texas—and I'm ashamed of it."

A very distraught businessman went to a psychiatrist and told him that he was very jumpy and upset and couldn't sleep nights. "I've got a plan," said the psychiatrist. "Where do you live?"

"The Bronx."

"All right. How do you get to work?"

"I take the subway."

"You'll have to stop. Here's what you do: get yourself a hoop and a stick and every morning roll the hoop in to work and every night roll the hoop home."

"Isn't that a little silly?"

"A little, but it will give you something to do, keep your mind occupied and tire you physically so you'll sleep."

"Okay, I'll try anything."

The next morning, he rolled his hoop into work and that evening he rolled it home. He kept it up for two weeks and began to feel better. He ate better and slept very well. One day when he went to the garage where he parked his hoop, the attendant greeted him with a long face. Since the attendant had a long face anyway, the businessman wasn't worried. However, the attendant said, "Mr. Jones, I have bad news for you. Some guy came in here driving a big Cadillac and before we could stop him he ran over your hoop."

"Oh," said the man, "that's awful. How'm I going to get home?"

One chap had a distinct fear of telephones. When they rang, he just wouldn't answer. But the psychiatrist took care of that. After considerable analysis the man was cured. Now he answers the phone whether it rings or not.

A beautiful girl walked into the psychiatrist's office and he leaped at her, kissing her. When he pulled away he said, "Well, that takes care of my problems; now what's on your mind?"

"Do you believe in child psychiatry?" asked a troubled man. "Yes, I do," said his friend. "Why don't you visit mine, he's only eleven years old?"

Q

QUARRELS (see also Fight)

They had been quarrelling for the twenty-five years of their married life. On their silver anniversary, she said, "Well, old man, how are we gonna celebrate?"

"How about two minutes of silence?" he suggested.

They reached the point where they had a mutual feeling . . . they hated each other.

This is silly, and I know it, but did you hear the one about the dentist who married a manicurist and they've been fighting tooth and nail ever since?

The seven children were sitting around arguing about the division of the estate that was left by their father, when their mother walked in, saying, "Children, I suppose I must tell you this sometime. Your father and I were never legally married."

There was silence for a moment, when the youngest one stood up, looked at the other six and announced, "I don't know what the rest of you bastards are doing . . . I'm going to Hollywood!"

QUESTIONS (see also School)

An elderly lady was introduced to Dr. Klein at a party. At her first opportunity she cornered the gentleman and said, "Doctor, I'm so glad to meet you. Let me ask you a question. Lately I get a terrible pain here in my side when I raise my arm like this. What should I do about it?" The gentleman answered, "I'm very sorry, madam, but you see, I'm not that kind of a doctor. I happen to be a doctor of economics." "Oh," said the old lady. "So tell me, Doctor, should I sell my General Motors?"

A man was seen walking around on a very warm day wearing a heavy overcoat. A friend stopped him and asked why he was doing such an obviously silly thing. "My dear friend," answered the perspiring fellow, "there are some things you and I know. There are some things only I know. There are some things only God knows. That I am wearing a heavy overcoat on a hot day, you know and I know. That I have a big hole in the seat of my pants only I know. And when it will be fixed, only God knows!"

"Dad," asked the boy, "what's the difference between 'anger' and 'exasperation'?" "Well," answered the father, "it's mostly a matter of degree. Suppose I show you an example and then you won't forget." The father went to the telephone and dialed a number at random. To the man who answered the phone, he said, "Hello, is Boris there?" The man answered, "Mister, there's no Boris here. Won't you please look up the number before you dial?" The father turned to his son. "See?" he pointed out. "That man wasn't a bit happy with our call. He was probably very busy with something and we annoyed him. Now watch . . ."

He dialed the number again. "Hello," said the father calmly, "is Boris there?" "Now look here!" came the heated reply, "you just called this number and I told you there's no Boris here! You've got a lot of nerve calling. You better look up the right number this time!" The receiver slammed hard.

The father turned to his son and said, "You see, son, that was anger. Now I'll show you what 'exasperation' means. He again dialed the same number, and when

a violent voice roared "HELLO," the father calmly said, "Hello, this is Boris. Any calls for me?"

QUESTIONS AND ANSWERS

Marriage?—Declaration of War.
Divorce?—Declaration of Peace.
Alimony?—Taxation without Representation.

QUIET

Their little baby was very quiet. It never spoke. They were pleased while he was a baby but as he grew up he was also quiet and never once spoke. Finally, when the kid was eight years old and had never uttered a sound, all of a sudden the child said, "Pass the salt." Shocked, the father said, "How come in eight years you never spoke?" The kid replied, "Well, up to now everything was all right."

QUIZ (see also Stupid)

When a quizmaster asked a contestant, "If you win this $500, what are you going to do with it?" the contestant said, "Count it!"

Have you ever noticed that few chorus girls go to quiz shows? That's because they can always get a mink coat by merely answering only ONE question!

A contestant was asked on a quiz show to name some famous Russells. The contestant said, "Lillian" and the quizmaster said, "That's one"; and the contestant continued and said, "Jane" and the Quiz Emcee said, "That's three . . ."

They have a new twist in quiz shows now—they call you up and if you are home, they borrow $20 from you.

QUOTATIONS

I never married and I wish my father never had. (Anon.)

She is intolerable, but this is her only fault. (Talleyrand)

When a man takes a woman to be his wife, it's the highest compliment he can pay her and it's usually the last. (Rowland)

Morality is simply an attitude we adopt toward people whom we personally dislike. (Oscar Wilde)

Experience is not what happens to a man. It is what a man does with what happens to him. (Aldous Huxley)

I once knew a fellow who spoke a dialect with an accent. (Irvin Cobb)

Amusement is the happiness of those who cannot think. (A. Pope)

A critic is a man who writes about things he doesn't like. (Anon.)

A cigarette is the perfect type of pleasure; it is exquisite and leaves one unsatisfied. (Oscar Wilde)

Blessed is he who expects nothing, for he shall never be disappointed. (Alexander Pope)

I never read a book before reviewing it. It prejudices me so! (Sidney Smith)

A humorist is a man who feels bad but who feels good about it. (Don Herold)

I'm not interested in facts, I want the truth. (Talleyrand)

He is so good, that he is good for nothing. (Italian proverb)

A critic is a legless man who teaches running. (Channing Pollock)

The ten best years in a woman's life come between 28 and 30.

A woman's word is never done.

A man is only as old as he looks—and if he only looks, he's old.

Pretty soon all the drive-in theatres will be open and people will quit watching movies again.

I've got the son in the morning and the father at night.

Do unto others before they do unto you.

French actor Maurice Chevalier telling how it feels to be seventy: "It's not so bad—especially when you consider the alternative."

Novelist Somerset Maugham, commenting on British cooking: "If you want to eat well in England, eat three breakfasts daily."

❖❖❖

R

RACE TRACKS (see also Horse Racing, Gambling)

Now they have a special window for the women bettors—a $1.98 window.

I have a system to beat the first four races at the track every day —don't show up till the fifth.

I don't play the horses for money. I play strictly for laughs. Last week I laughed away my car and my home. . . .

In the spring everything is green. Then the tracks open and all the green is gone.

"For three nights straight I dreamed about salami, baloney and liverwurst. Is a hunch, no? I go to the track and in one race is running a horse named "Salami" a horse named "Baloney" and a horse named "Liverwurst." So I bet all three to win. Coming in the stretch is running dead heat— "Salami," "Baloney" and "Liverwurst."
"Which horse won?"
"A long shot named "Cold-cuts.""

Herman was an ardent baseball fan but one day his friends talked him into going to the track. He bet on a horse named "Strikeout" and as the horse came down the stretch "Strikeout" was second and coming up fast. As they neared the finish it was neck and neck and Herman couldn't control himself any longer. He screamed —"Slide, you bum, slide!"

"On my days off I usually go walking in the park."
"Where?"
"Belmont."

RADIO (see also Television, Actors)

Radio . . . you remember radio . . . that's TV with the picture tube blown.

"I've got job in radio."
"Oh, yeah? What do you do?"
"I put out the bottles for 'Milkman's Matinee' . . ."

I went to visit my mother last week and found her in her kitchen listening to seven different radios going at the same time. I said, "Ma, what are you doing listening to seven radios at the same time?"
"Shh," she said, "I'm listening to 'One Man's Family.' "

1st Woman: Oh those radio commercials send me . . .
2nd Woman: Where do they send you?
1st Woman: They send me to the grocer . . . they send me to the movies . . . they send me everywhere. . . .

1st Woman: Radio nowadays is terrible. You turn on the radio and all you hear is rock'n' roll.
2nd Woman: So why do you listen to it?
1st Woman: What should I do then . . . watch it?

RAILROADS (see also Transportation)

On a certain railroad whose trains were notoriously late and slow, a young woman passenger gave birth to a baby. It took the entire staff and most of the facilities to bring her and the child through. When the ordeal was over and the mother and child were resting in one of the drawing rooms, the conductor finally gave vent to his annoyance. He said, "Young lady, you never should have boarded this train knowing you were in that condition." The young mother said, "Sir, I'll have you know that when I got on this train, I was not in that condition."

A district railroad superintendent always made a special point of insisting that all station masters send in an immediate report of any accident, no matter how small it might be. One morning he got a message: "Man fell from station platform in front of moving train. Details later." He sweated it out for good until he got the second message which read: "Everything okay, nobody hurt . . . engine going backwards."

RAIN

WEATHERMAN: Put down rain for a certainty this afternoon.
ASSISTANT: Are you sure, sir?
WEATHERMAN: Yes . . . I've lost my umbrella, I'm planning to play golf, and my wife's giving a lawn party.

1ST MAN: I'm worried; it's raining and my wife is downtown.
2ND MAN: Oh, she'll probably step inside some store.
1ST MAN: That's just it.

WIFE: Darling, it's raining so heavily,—wouldn't it be a good idea to stop the car and wipe the windshield?
HUSBAND: Wouldn't do a bit of good—I've left my glasses at home.

Contrary to all rumors, the boys at the Weather Bureau do seem to know what they're doing. Asked at the beginning of the summer to choose their vacation period, they all pulled out the charts and asked for the same three weeks.

REAL ESTATE

A sign in front of a real estate office: WE HAVE LOTS TO BE THANKFUL FOR!

This afternoon I went over to the real estate office to see a model home but she had already left.

When a real estate agent asked a woman if she wanted to buy a home, she said, "What do I need a home for? I was born in a hospital, educated in a college, courted in an automobile and married in a church. I live out of paper bags and delicatessen stores. I spend my mornings at the golf course, my afternoons at the bridge table and my evenings at the movies. And when I die, I'm gonna be buried at the undertaker's. I don't need a home—all I need is a garage!"

RECOGNITION (see also Famous)

FIRST GOB: Say, I remember you. Weren't we messmates in the navy?
SECOND GOB: Sure. You used to get into the same messes I did.

SARA: Tell me, did any of your friends admire your engagement ring?
SALLY: They did more than that. Two of them recognized it.

RELATIONS (see also Family, Relatives)

He's my own flesh and blood
—he's got the flesh and I got the
blood.

JUDGE: So you want a divorce
from your wife? Aren't your
relations pleasant?
HUSBAND: Mine are . . . but hers
are horrible.

A harassed husband runs frantically into a drug store.
HUSBAND: Quick give me some
arsenic for my mother-in-law.
DRUGGIST: Have you got a doctor's prescription?
HUSBAND: No I haven't . . . but
here's a photograph of her.

The patient lay on the psychiatrist's couch and explained to his
doctor that he was haunted by
visions of his departed relatives.
PATIENT: These ghosts are
perched on the tops of fence
posts around my garden every
night. They sit there and watch
me and watch me and watch
me. What can I do? What can
I do?
PSYCHIATRIST: That's easy. Just
sharpen the tops of the posts.

Harry had to drive his wife and
his mother-in-law from Brooklyn
to the Catskills and all along the
way the two women in his life
were giving him advice on how to
drive. Finally Harry couldn't take
it any more and pulled the car to
the side of the road and furiously
turned to his wife in the back
seat . . .
HARRY: All right. Now let's get
this straight once and for all.
Who's driving this car. You . . .
or your mother?

The red-eyed wife was complaining to her mother-in-law
about her husband.
WIFE: And your son can't drink,
and he can't gamble.
MOTHER: You call that faults?
Why that just shows you what
a fine man he is.
WIFE: You don't understand. He
can't but he tries to.

RELATIVES (see also Rela- tions)

My mother always went shopping with a baby carriage and it
was two years before I found out
a head of lettuce wasn't my
brother.

1ST ENGLISHMAN: My cousin has
been staying at my house for
six months.—I just can't seem
to get rid of him.
2ND ENGLISHMAN: Maybe you
should drop him a hint or two?
1ST ENGLISHMAN: Oh, I do . . .
Every time I see him I run up
to him and say "Well, so long."
He just stands there smiling and
says "Well, hurry back, old
man."

1ST MAN: Have you any poor relations?

2ND MAN: Not one that I know.

1ST MAN: Have you any rich relations?

2ND MAN: Not one that knows me.

FRIEND: Was your uncle's mind sane and vigorous up to the very last minute?

HEIR: I don't know . . . they're not reading the will until tomorrow.

RELIGION (see also Church, Heaven)

Preacher Simmons says things are getting better because he's getting much better buttons in the collection.

PREACHER: There will be weeping, wailing and gnashing of teeth among the wicked who pass on to the next world.

MEMBER OF THE CONGREGATION: What about those who haven't any teeth?

PREACHER: Teeth will be provided.

Yesterday I saw a man knocked right up in the air. He lay stretched out under the telegraph wires unconscious, and when he woke up he found the wires all around his wrists. He said,

"Thank goodness, I've led a clean life. They've given me a harp."

Do you believe that a missionary goes to Heaven and a cannibal that eats people goes to the other place?"

"Of course I believe it. A missionary always goes to Heaven."

"But answer this question, 'What happens when the missionary is inside the cannibal?' "

"Say Dad, our lesson in Sunday school told about the evil spirits entering the swine."

"Yes, my son. What do you wish to know?"

"Was that the way they got the first deviled ham?"

MOTHER: Why did you strike your little sister?

JOHNNIE: Well, we were playing Adam and Eve and instead of tempting me with the apple, she ate it herself.

SERGEANT: Hey, there, you Mose! Come back here! Suppose you do get killed, what of it? Heaven is your home.

MOSE: Yes, suh, Sarge, Ah knows dat. But right now Ah ain't homesick.

Two old-timers were reminiscing and comparing notes.

"Yes, I have had some terrible disappointments," said one. "But none stands out over the years like one that came to me when I was a boy."

"And what was it?" asked his friend.

"When I was a boy I crawled under a tent to see the circus, and I discovered it was a revival meeting."

Little Clarence, climbing a tree, began to fall swiftly toward the ground: "Oh, Lord, save me! Save me!" . . . (pause) . . . "Never mind, Lord, my pants caught on a branch."

REMINISCENCE (see also Memory)

WIFE: When I was young I could have married a real caveman.
HUSBAND: When you were young . . . that's all there were.

1ST MAN: Where did you live when you were a kid?
2ND MAN: Over a laundry, and they'd hang the wash out on the line every day. I was twelve years old before I found out the sun didn't have a flap on it.

1ST MAN: So you were a tough kid?
2ND MAN: Were we tough! Why, I played football for ten years before I found out you were supposed to use a ball.

When I was a kid we lived on the wrong side of the tracks—underneath.

WIFE: Oh if I had my life to do over.
HUSBAND: So what would you do?
WIFE: I'd do it over you.

1ST MAN: Hey, Harry, remember when we were kids? We'd go dancing every Saturday night.
2ND MAN: Yeah. Didn't we have fun?
1ST MAN: And we would've had more fun if we had girls.

1ST MAN: When we were kids we use to hitch a ride on the ice wagon. Every day we'd sit on the ice for two hours.
2ND MAN: You kids use to sit on the ice for two hours?
1ST MAN: Yeah . . . they called us the Dead End Kids.

REPUBLICANS (see also Politics, Democrats)

One day Franklin D. Roosevelt gleefully told this story:

An American Marine, ordered home from Guadalcanal, was disconsolate because he hadn't killed even one of the enemy. He stated his case to his superior officer, who said, "Go up on that hill over there and shout: 'To hell with Emperor Hirohito!' That will bring the Japs out of hiding." The Marine did as he was bidden. Immediately a Jap soldier came out of the jungle shouting, "To hell with Roosevelt!"

"And of course," said the Marine, "I couldn't kill a Republican."

A Westchester Republican Committeewoman returned from downtown New York to Party Headquarters dishevelled and distraught. When asked what had happened she related this tale:

"I happened to be in the garment district at the time Kennedy was campaigning in that area. The mobs were thick and disorderly. Suddenly, two thugs grabbed me and pulled me into a hallway. They tore my clothes and attacked me. It was horrible."

"Didn't you scream?" asked a fellow woman Republican.

"What, and have the Democrats think I was cheering for them?"

RESTAURANTS (see also Lindy's, Waiters, Food, Tipping)

CUSTOMER: Is there any soup on the menu?
WAITER: No sir; there was, but I wiped it off.

CUSTOMER: Waiter, I just found a button in my soup.
WAITER: Oh thank you sir—I've been looking all over for it.

WAITER: How did you find the steak, sir?
CUSTOMER: Oh, quite by accident . . . I moved the potato and there it was underneath.

DINER: Have you any wild duck?
WAITER: No sir, but we can take a tame one and irritate it for you.

CUSTOMER: I see you advertise an unlimited variety of sandwiches. Give me an elephant steak sandwich on rye.
WAITER: I'm sorry sir, we can't start an elephant just for one sandwich.

CUSTOMER: Do you serve crabs here?
WAITER: Certainly, we serve anyone. Sit down.

Two men both grab for the check after lunching together.
1ST MAN: Either you're losing your grip, or I don't know my own strength.

1ST MAN: Did you ever hear of a good After-dinner Speech?
2ND MAN: As a matter of fact, I have. Last night I was dining with a friend and afterwards he said "Waiter—Give me the check."

CUSTOMER: Do you serve ladies here?

WAITER: Yes, sir.

CUSTOMER: Bring me a nice, tall blonde.

1ST MAN: How d'you like this little restaurant?

2ND MAN: Well, it could use a little atmosphere . . . a little band . . . a little fire . . .

Everybody comes to Sam's delicatessen . . . that is, everybody but the Health Inspector.

WAITER: We're all out of frogs' legs, sir. I can bring the next best thing, though—toadstools.

1ST MAN: Why do you always eat in a cafeteria?

2ND MAN: The doctor told me always to take long walks and get plenty of exercise before meals.

DINER: I want some oysters, but they mustn't be too large or too small; they must neither be too old nor too tough; they must not be salty. I want them cold and I want them right away.

WAITER: Yes sir . . . with or without pearls?

DINER: Do you have pickled herring?

WAITER: No, but we have stewed tomato.

1ST MAN: I went to the Automat yesterday. I put in a nickel and got coffee, then I put in another nickel and another nickel and another nickel and another . . .

2ND MAN: Why did you put in so many nickels?

1ST MAN: Why should I stop when I'm on a winning streak?

DINER: I have a complaint.

RESTAURANT PROPRIETOR: Complaint? This is a restaurant, not a hospital.

CUSTOMER: What does this Mean? There's a fly at the bottom of my teacup.

WAITRESS: How should I know? I'm a waitress not a fortune teller.

WAITRESS: Tea or coffee?

CUSTOMER: Coffee, without cream.

WAITRESS: You'll have to take it without milk—we're all out of cream.

A gal ordered a filet mignon, the most expensive dish on the menu. The waiter looked at her escort and said, "What do you wish, sir?" "I wish I hadn't brought her," moaned the guy.

Two men wandered in for dinner and ordered the most expensive dishes and the finest champagne. They looked well-groomed but they didn't have a penny between them. When the check arrived, one said to the other, "Let's split the check—you wash and I'll dry."

When a customer complained to the waiter that the chicken he served him had one leg shorter than the other, the waiter said, "Look, are you gonna eat it or rhumba with it?"

The chef told Jack E. Leonard: "I put my heart into this clam chowder." Jack snapped, "Never mind your heart—put a few clams into it."

I told the waiter I didn't like the looks of the codfish and he said, "If it's looks you want, why don't you order goldfish?"

When I ordered some Russian dressing, they brought me a picture of Khrushchev putting on his pants.

I said, "Hey, waiter, how long did these eggs boil?" and he said, "Five seconds." I said, "Five seconds? But I want 3-minute eggs." He said, "I'm sorry, the chef can't hold them in the water for 3 minutes—burns his hand!"

The restaurant is so swanky, before you use the finger bowls you have to wash your hands.

The Stage Delicatessen does such a terrific business they are now calling it "Fort Lox."

The food is so bad there, instead of a check, the waiter gives you a citation.

I asked him how much was the Nova Scotia salmon. He said, "$7.50 an order." I said, "Look, I wanna buy salmon—not Nova Scotia."

"What's wrong?" asked a stranger at the next table.
"I forgot my teeth."
"Try this pair."
"They're too loose."
"How about this pair?" he offered from another pocket.
"They're not comfortable."
"I think these should fit you."
"Thanks!" said the man. "They do! Where's your office, Doc? I've been looking for a good dentist."
"I'm not a dentist. I'm the local undertaker."

The customer was annoyed by the waiter who kept scratching his stomach and finally asked, "Do you have eczema?"
The waiter replied, "No special orders, just what's on the menu."

RETAIL (see also Wholesale, Business, Salesman, Clerks)

Once upon a time, there was a boy named Jack Beanstalk. His mother told him to take the cow to market and sell it since they needed the money. As they were crossing a railroad track, the train came along, hit the cow, and knocked her tail off. So, Jack had to sell the cow wholesale because he couldn't *retail* it.

A Forty-Second Street retailer wrote to a publisher the following note: "What the book industry needs is a good five-cent illustrated sex manual."

Husband looking up from newspaper to wife, "What's happened between you and the retail merchants, dear? I see they say business is off."

RICH (see also Wealth, Snob)

1ST MAN: I'll have to buy a new Cadillac this week.
2ND MAN: What's wrong with the one you have?
1ST MAN: The ashtrays are full.

MAN: I'm independently wealthy. I own a gold mine but it's no good.
GIRL: Why?
MAN: Oil keeps coming out.

1ST MAN: I was born with a silver knife in my mouth.

2ND MAN: You mean a silver spoon.
1ST MAN: No, knife. My family had more money than manners.

GOLD DIGGER: He's tall, dark and has some.

1ST GIRL: If we were rich, we'd spend six months of the year in California, six months in Florida and six months in Europe.
2ND GIRL: But that makes eighteen months in one year.
1ST GIRL: Ain't it wonderful what money can do?

1ST MAN: On my estate I'll have three hundred cows.
2ND MAN: So what? Plenty of estates have that many cows.
1ST MAN: In the refrigerator?

BEGGAR: Lady, can you spare a dime for a poor, starving man? . . . Hurry up, lady, I'm double parked.

And then there was the sultan who bought a Cadillac. He paid for it with a ten thousand dollar bill and said, "Give me my change in Volkswagens."

It's easy to spot a rich man at a football game. He's the guy who brings an electric blanket.

RIDDLES (see also Questions)

QUESTION: What is a misleading figure?
ANSWER: A woman in a girdle.

QUESTION: What did the wallpaper say to the wall?
ANSWER: You may be a little cracked but I still have designs on you.

1ST MAN: Did you hear the story about the broken pencil?
2ND MAN: No . . . what about it?
1ST MAN: Ah . . . there's no point to it.

1ST MAN: What do they call frozen ink?
2ND MAN: Iced ink. . . .
1ST MAN: You said it.

QUESTION: Why do the bees buzz?
ANSWER: You'd buzz too if someone stole your honey and nectar.

1ST MAN: How many birds are there in the sky?
2ND MAN: I don't know.
1ST MAN: How many bees make honey?
2ND MAN: I don't know.
1ST MAN: How many dwarfs were with Snow White?
2ND MAN: Seven.
1ST MAN: How come you don't know about the birds and bees yet you know about the fairies?

TEACHER: If I laid two eggs on the chair and three eggs on the table, what do I get?
PUPIL: Your picture in "Believe It or Not."

ROMANCE (see also Kissing, Love, Lovers, Osculation, Necking, Spooning)

SHE: I'm itching for love!
HE: Okay, Toots . . . where do you want to be scratched?

If love is blind maybe that's why you see so many spectacles in the park.

SHE: The greatest lover in town tried to flirt with me last night.
HE: It's a lie! I didn't even see you last night.

"What makes you suspect she loves another?"
"Last night she said that I'd have to leave before the milkman came."

He's been carrying the torch so long, his heart must have a heluva tan by now.

DAUGHTER: The name William means "good" and the name James means "beloved." I wonder what George means?
FATHER: I trust that George means business.

I'll never forget the night my first husband discovered my great love.
Did he beat him up?

The minute the average fellow discovers that a girl is hungry for love he starts feeding her a line.

When a girl loves in a breezy manner, the boys soon get wind of it.
Some girls fall head over heels in love with a fellow, while others go ahead and fall in love with heels.

The only way to tell if a girl is ripe for love is to squeeze her.

"Is your roommate in love?"
"Is he? He's so bad off he makes me wake him up every fifteen minutes after he's gone to bed so can go to sleep again thinking of his girl."

The young man approached the counter where Valentine cards were being sold.
"Have you anything real sentimental?"
"Here's a lovely one, 'To the only girl I ever loved.' "
"That's fine. I'll take four, no, six of those please."

ROOMS/HOUSING SHORT-AGE (see also Hotels, Motels, Landlords)

He was so desperate for a place to live . . . he had his appendix removed so he could get a night's sleep.

1ST MAN: There's one good thing about living underground.
2ND MAN: What's that?
1ST MAN: When you die they don't bury you . . . they just close the door.

There's a sensational new idea to solve the Veterans' Housing problem and it's free. It's called "Re-enlistment."

People who live in glass houses at least have some place to live.

LANDLADY: I must remind you that I will not tolerate children, dogs, cats, parrots, piano playing, radio or television.
TENANT: That's okay but I think you should know that my fountain pen scratches a little.

TENANT: I want you to get rid of the mice in my apartment.
LANDLORD: Not me . . . If they don't like it here, let them move.

LANDLORD: I'm going to raise your rent.
TENANT: Go ahead, because I can't.

TEACHER: Lincoln lived in a log cabin. If you had a log cabin with no heat, no light and rain coming through the roof, what would you do?

JOHNNY: I'd rent it for $500. a month.

ROOSTER (see also Farm)

A rooster found a hole in the fence and crawled through into the next farm. It was an ostrich farm and there were many nests there. He walked over, looked into one and noticed that some ostrich eggs were at least ten times as big as any he'd ever seen.

He went back to his farm, got all his hens together and took them back with him. He led them to the nest, pointed and said, "Ladies, I didn't bring you here to scold you and I don't want to sound unreasonable, but I just wanted to show you what's going on in the world outside our farm."

ROYALTY (See also King)

My family is so blue-blooded, we never use fountain pens when we write . . . we just cut our fingers.

1ST MAN: I was presented to the Queen of England.
2ND MAN: Really? What happened?
1ST MAN: She refused me.

1ST MAN: Do you know how to address a high official?
2ND MAN: I don't even know how to undress a sober one.

RUSSIA (see also Communist)

1ST MAN: In Russia they sing through their noses.
2ND MAN: Why's that?
1ST MAN: No one's allowed to open his mouth.

MOVIE STAR: I've been married to everyone but a Russian . . . I can't get one to say "Yes."

1ST MAN: I hear the people in Russia are starving.
2ND MAN: But they have chickens there, don't they?
1ST MAN: Yes, but they only let them eat the left wings.

Someone broke into the Kremlin and stole next year's election results.

1ST MAN: I'm a White Russian.
2ND MAN: I'm a Blue Russian.
1ST MAN: There's no such thing as a Blue Russian.
2ND MAN: Yes there is. It's cold where I come from.

In Russia there are two editions of *Who's Who*. One is called *Who Was Who;* the other is called *Who Is Still Who*.

❖❖❖

S

SAHL, MORT

I like Governor Faubus although I wouldn't marry his sister.

I think I'm a pacifist except in wartime when I think you should be sensible and get a commission.

During his campaign Governor Rockefeller was promising the kids Little League polo.

I bought a sports car—because I mean how else are you going to get sexual gratification?

I was pondering Admiral Strauss's statement on radioactivity. He seems to be saying there is no increase in radioactivity but not to plan large families.

I'm going to remind you to see the movie *On the Beach*. It's an escapist film—it'll take your mind off the birth control issue.

If we're lucky the Russians will steal some of our secrets and then they'll be two years behind us.

In regard to Shelley Berman— his search for the perfect telephone call is like my search for the perfect woman, and I know I've looked from one end of the bar to the other.

Did you ever date an airline stewardess? You know, they wear flats in the car and then when they get out of the car they put on their heels.

SALARY (see also Employment, Money)

"Hello, I'm glad to see you here."
"I'm glad to be here. After all, money's not everything."
"Who told you that?"
"My boss."

It was their price or mine so we tossed and I won. So they tossed again.

"Wages. Wages. What does your father get every Saturday night?"
"Drunk."

I'd raise your salary, if I didn't forget things like that so easily.

"You'll have to forget next week's salary."

"For the amount you pay me, I won't have to join the Foreign Legion."

"Dorothy is getting a man's wages."

"Yes, I heard she was married."

"Here's the money, dear—I'll take a short walk while you count it."

"Say, you're ten cents short—what's that for?"

"Well, the boss docked me for a nickel—by mistake and I drank out of his Dixie cup, and then I bought some gum on sale, two for a nickel."

"I don't believe it—I think you're taking some woman to a night club."

"Say, the only thing you can get at a night club is dishwater hands."

"Here you squander your money and I *never* get any clothes."

"How about the outfit you bought last week?"

"I don't mind wearing it in the house, but if you expect me to wear a sarong on the streetcar, it's too much."

SALESMAN (see also Clerks, Business)

A new cough medicine is now on the market. It is called Laxalax —and the slogan is, "Six tablets and you don't dare cough."

A man went into a store and ordered a tie. The clerk wrapped up the one he selected and handed it to him.

"I believe I'll trade this for a pair of socks instead," said the man.

"All right."

The customer picked out his socks, and after they were wrapped started to leave.

"You didn't pay for those," yelled the clerk.

"I traded the tie for them," said the man.

"Yes, but you didn't pay for the tie!"

"I didn't take the tie!"

BOSS: How long do you want to be away on your honeymoon?
BOOKKEEPER: (timidly) Well, sir—er—how long would you say.
BOSS: How do I know? I haven't seen the bride.

SALESMAN: Hello, little boy. Is your mother at home?
LITTLE BOY: Hell, man! Do you think I'm cutting the grass for my health?

The old lady was looking for something to grumble about. She entered the butcher shop with the light of battle in her eyes.

OLD LADY: I believe you sell diseased meat here?

BUTCHER: Worse.

OLD LADY: (Astonished) What do you mean, worse!

BUTCHER: The meat we sell is dead.

CAR SALESMAN TO CUSTOMER: Madam, it's a buy. You'll never get another opportunity like this in your entire life.

WOMAN: How much is it?

SALESMAN: The price? Why, it's priced just over the car which is priced a few dollars above the car which costs no more than some models of the lowest price cars.

1ST SALESMAN: I'd like to learn the secret of your success as a house-to-house salesman.

2ND SALESMAN: Oh, it's easy. The minute a woman opens the door I say "Miss, is your mother in?"

SALES MANAGER: I think it's a good time to sell the Joneses a car.

SALESMAN: What makes you think so?

SALES MANAGER: Their neighbors just got a new one.

SALES MANAGER: What's this big item on your expense account?

SALESMAN: Oh, that's the hotel bill.

SALES MANAGER: Well, don't buy any more hotels.

BOSS: I'm surprised at you! Do you know what they do with boys who tell lies?

OFFICE BOY: Yes, sir. When they get old enough, the firm sends them out as salesmen.

"I'm an independent salesman."

"Yeah?"

"Yeah—I take orders from no one."

"You should never touch a live wire. It's dangerous."

"Then why do they sell them?"

"Nobody sells live wires."

"Certainly they do. I saw an ad in yesterday's paper and it said: 'Wanted, a live wire salesman.'"

"Is he a good salesman?"

"I'll say—he could sell the foot-hills a pair of shoes."

"Did you ever have any real exciting experiences while you were a traveling salesman?"

"About twenty years ago—I was ordered out of a Wyoming town by a notorious two-gun man who didn't like the cut of my clothes."

A high-pressure auto salesman told his customer, "Do you realize that while you're standing here dickering, your car is depreciating?"

SALOONS (see also Bartenders, Drunks)

A guy at the bar ordered a beer and downed it as soon as the beer hit the bar. He ordered another and downed it as the bartender let it out of his hand . . . then he ordered another.

BARTENDER: Hey, how long have you been drinking beer like that?

DRUNK: Ever since my accident.

BARTENDER: Accident? When was that?

DRUNK: About two years ago. I ordered a glass of beer and some drunk standing next to me knocked it over before I could drink it.

NEW BARTENDER: You have a children's party here every Christmas?

BOSS: Yeah, when the kids come down here to get their fathers.

DRUNK: Ahg . . . this liquor of yours is slow poison . . .

BARTENDER: Than why do you drink it?

DRUNK: I'm a patient man.

BARTENDER: I want you to know that this is the toughest saloon in town.

DRUNK: It can't be so tough. Look at the clean sawdust on the floor.

BARTENDER: That ain't sawdust. That's the furniture from last night.

BARTENDER: I went to bartending school for two years and I can't get a job.

FRIEND: Why not???

BARTENDER: I can't fix a TV set.

SCHOOLS (see also Teachers, College, Campus, University)

"What did they teach you at school today, sonny?" asked the proud mother.

"Oh, teacher told us all about Columbus who went two thousand miles on a galleon," answered her pride and joy.

"She did, did she? Well, don't believe all she tells you about those foreign cars, my boy."

AUNTIE: Are you going to the movies after the program tonight?

NEPHEW: No, I ain't going.

AUNTIE: What grammar! You should say: I'm not going, they're not going, he's not going, she's not going. Get the idea?

NEPHEW: Sure—nobody ain't going.

FRIEND: What's your boy going to be when he finishes his education?

DISCOURAGED PARENT: An octogenarian, I think.

PROFESSOR: Don't you know the difference between ammonia and pneumonia?

MEDICAL STUDENT: Sure, one comes in bottles and the other in chests.

LITTLE BOY: What part of the body is the fray?

TEACHER: What part of the body is the fray? What are you talking about?

LITTLE BOY: Well, right here in the history book it says—"the general was shot in the thick of the fray."

PROFESSOR: Give for one year the number of tons of coal shipped out of the United States.

SMART ALECK: Fourteen ninetwo—none.

TEACHER: Can you tell me what the former ruler of Russia was called?

STUDENT: Tsar.

TEACHER: Correct. And what was his wife called?

STUDENT: Tsarina.

TEACHER: Right. What were the Tsar's children called?

STUDENT: Tsardines!

INSTRUCTOR: If I tear a piece of paper into four pieces, what do I get?

STUDENT: Quarters.

INSTRUCTOR: And if I divide it into eight?

STUDENT: Eighths.

INSTRUCTOR: And if I divide it into eight thousand parts?

STUDENT: Confetti.

(Switch: Substitute steak for paper and the answer is hamburger)

"What would your father have to pay if he owed thirty-four dollars to the grocer, forty dollars rent, and fifteen dollars to the milkman?" the fifth grade teacher asked little Willie.

"Nothing—he'd move!" said Willie.

SCIENCE

My outline for a science-fiction tragedy. It concerns a hero who falls in love with an electronic brain, then ends up in jail. Seems he had to rob a bank so he could keep paying her electric bills. . . .

You now this is the age of science and one of its newest discoveries is an electric car; you plug it in a socket in your house and the other end in your car. I know one fellow who did this and traveled all the way from California to New York, and didn't spend a cent for gas—but it cost him four thousand dollars and twenty-six cents. He had to get a long cord.

SCOTCH (see also Scotland)

"What's the Scotch football yell?"
"Get that quarter back, sir."

A Scot was engaged in an argument with a conductor as to whether the fare was five or ten cents. Finally the disgusted conductor picked up the Scotchman's suitcase and tossed it off the train, just as they passed over a bridge. It landed with a splash.

"Mon," screamed Sandy, "isn't it enough to try to overcharge me, but now you try to drown my little boy?"

"Stand behind your lover," said the Scotchman to his unfaithful wife, "I'm going to shoot you both."

Then there was the Scotch farmer, the father of two daughters, who brought home a double-barreled shotgun.

Then there's the story about the Scotsman that spanked his children and then put them out in the flowerbed to cry.

A Scotchman was once run over by a beer wagon and for the first time in his life the drinks were on him.

"My Scotch boy friend sent me his picture."
"How does it look?"
"I don't know, I haven't had it developed yet."

What Scotland needs is a good five-cent box of cigars.

Scotch gangster took his victim for a hitchhike.

Sign on a Scotch golf course:
MEMBERS WILL KINDLY REFRAIN FROM PICKING UP LOST GOLF BALLS UNTIL THEY HAVE STOPPED ROLLING.

"What started the Grand Canyon?"
"A Scotchman lost a penny in a ditch."

Then there was the Scotchman who went out into his back yard with his shotgun on Christmas morning, shot three times into the air, and returned to tell his children that Santa Claus was dead.

"Goodbye," said Mcintosh, "and don't forget to take little Donald's glasses off when he isn't looking at anything."

A Scotsman went into a store and bought an attaché case.

CLERK: Shall I wrap it for you?

SCOTSMAN: No, thank you. Just put the paper and string inside.

1ST SCOTSMAN: Did ye hear about Sandy MacPherson findin' a box of corn plasters?

2ND SCOTSMAN: No, did he?

1ST SCOTSMAN: Yes . . . so he went and bought a pair of tight shoes.

1ST ENGLISHMAN: Is old Angus a typical Scotsman?

2ND ENGLISHMAN: He certainly is. Why he's saved all his toys for his second childhood!

Did you hear about the Scotsman who bought only one spur? He figured that if one side of the horse went, the other was sure to follow.

1ST SCOTSMAN: I hear you and Maggie have made up and are to be married after all.

2ND SCOTSMAN: Aye. Ye see Maggie has put on weight an' we couldn't get the engagement ring off her finger.

SCOTLAND (see also Scotch)

I don't believe the sick, sick story of the Scotsman who murdered his parents so he could go to the orphans' picnic.

They stopped the crime wave in Scotland by putting up a sign over the jailhouse saying: ANYONE CAUGHT AND PUT IN JAIL WILL HAVE TO PAY HIS BOARD AND LODGING.

In Scotland they had to take the "Pay-as-you-leave" cars off the streets; they found two Scotsman starving in one of them.

Scotland—where the cows give condensed milk.

In Scotland, all horse races are very close.

When you ask a Scotch girl if she's free for any night she's bound to say, "No, but I'll be reasonable."

Scotland, where they borrow a pipeful of tobacco and then can't light it because it's packed too tight.

London isn't the only town that gets foggy in Great Britain. They say it was so foggy in Scotland one day a Scotsman milked three cows before he found out he wasn't playing the bagpipes.

You can always tell when you're flying over Scotland.—*No Garbage Cans. . . .*

The way they teach a Scotsman to swim in Scotland in one lesson:

they pin a dollar bill to his bathing suit and throw him in the water.

Please don't misunderstand—some of my closest friends are Scotsmen. . . .

SEASONABLE

"Say, are you Santa Claus?"
"No, why?"
"Then leave my stocking alone."

Santa Claus is only one I know of who runs around with a bag all night and doesn't get talked about.

Things are so bad this year that Santa is only going to wear a mustache.

CYNIC: I trust no one. Even my parents took advantage of me.
DOUBTFUL: How was that?
CYNIC: They told me there was a Santa Claus before I was old enough to know better.

"My girl's down on me for good."
"How come?"
"I sent her a present on Mother's Day."

"Take the case of George Washington. Do you remember my telling you of the great diffi-culty George Washington had to contend with?"
"Yes, Ma'am," said the little boy. "He couldn't tell a lie."

INDIGNANT FATHER: Do you think it is fair, Bobby, after I told you that there wasn't any Santa Claus to go and tell the neighbors that I laid your Easter eggs?

SUNDAY SCHOOL TEACHER: Who was the son of Abraham?
BRIGHT PUPIL: Lincoln.

How did Thanksgiving day originate?
It was instituted by the parents whose sons survived the football season.

They were serving the turkey.
"Is that white meat good?" asked the visitor.
"Yes," replied the hostess, "It's the very breast."

SECRETARY (see also Business, Office)

An energetic secretary came into her office, smiled at a co-worker and asked, "And how are you this lovely morning?" Her friend, who'd had a bad night, raised her head slowly and said, "What you need is a good case of tired blood."

1ST SECRETARY: Look at that IBM Calculator. Do you know it replaced 25 men?
2ND SECRETARY: Yeah. . . . darn it.

1ST SECRETARY: I wonder where Alice suddenly got that Southern accent?
2ND SECRETARY: Probably drinking from a Dixie cup.

1ST SECRETARY: So you thought I was going to marry the boss, huh? Well, I just broke our engagement.
2ND SECRETARY: That's too bad. What happened???
1ST SECRETARY: Well, I saw him in his swimsuit and he looked so different without his wallet.

SERVANTS (see also Rich)

HOUSEWIFE: I see a spider web in the corner, Mary. Why is that there?
HOUSEMAN: The spider put it there, Ma'am.

BUTLER: Mr. Marmaduke, I regret to tell you that I must give notice. I cannot get along with the Madam.
MR. MARMADUKE: Oh, is she too demanding?
BUTLER: Yes sir. Mrs. Marmaduke forgets I can leave any time I like and orders me around just as if I were you.

HOUSEWIFE: What's the meaning of this, Bridget? Only cheese for lunch?
COOK: Yes, the cutlets caught fire and it spread to the apple pie, so I had to use the soup to put it out.

(Mistress was explaining routine to the new cook.)
MISTRESS: And on Wednesday we lunch precisely at one, as on that day we go for a spin in the car at two.
COOK: Very good ma'am, but I shall have to leave the washin' up till we gets back again.

MISTRESS: I shall be very lonely, Bridget, if you leave me.
BRIDGET: Don't worry, ma'am. I'll not go until ye have a houseful of company.

MISTRESS (to new maid): Be careful when you dust these pictures, Mary, they're all Old Masters.
MAID: Good gracious! Who'd ever think you'd been married all these times, ma'am.

MISTRESS: Now, when you wait on the guests at dinner, I want you to be very careful not to spill anything.

NEW MAID: Don't worry, I won't say a word.

NEW MAID: Now, Mary, you must always remember to serve from the left and take the plates from the right. Is that clear?
NEW MAID: Yes ma'am.—What's the matter—you superstitious or something?

SHAGGY DOG (see also Stories)

After a man had had a few dry Martinis, he praised the bartender.
MAN: Such genius deserves a reward. (With this remark he takes a live lobster out of his pocket.) Here, take this with my compliments.
BARTENDER: Why thanks. Can I take it home for dinner?
MAN: No, no. He's already had dinner. Take him to a movie.

A tired-looking actor marched into a vaudeville house with a kangaroo and asked for a job.
BOOKER: A job? What does the kangaroo do? Can he sing, dance, tell funny stories?
ACTOR: He doesn't do anything.
BOOKER: Then why did you bring him here?
ACTOR: I had to . . . he's my agent.

The alligator boarded the train heading for Chicago when a redcap came up to him.

PORTER: Carry your bag, sir?
ALLIGATOR: Sure, but be careful . . . that's my wife.

Did you hear about the porcupine who walked into a cactus bush in the desert and yelled: "Hey, is that you, Dad?"

A dachshund and a cocker were talking about their health.
DACHSHUND (with German accent): Ach, I'm so nervous lately, I can't sleep.
COCKER: (with Spanish accent—after all he's a spaniel): Well, amigo, why don't you see a psychiatrist?
DACHSHUND: How can I? I'm not allowed on the couch.

A fellow walked into a bar and ordered two drinks. The fellow poured one in his breast pocket and drank the other. After he had done this four times the bartender said: "What are you, some sort of a nut?"
Insulted, the man put up his fists and said, "Come out from behind that bar and I'll punch you in the nose."
As the bartender walked from behind that bar, a tiny mouse popped out of the fellow's breast pocket and said: "And that goes for your cat, too."

SHARK (see also Fish)

"I saw a man-eating shark at the aquarium."

"That's nothing; I saw a man eating herring in the park."

"Can I buy a live shark here?"

"Gosh, lady, what do you want with a live shark?"

"A neighbor's cat has been eating my goldfish and I want to teach him a lesson."

FIRST SHARK: What's that funny two-legged thing that just fell in the water?

SECOND SHARK: I dunno, but I'll bite.

SHIFTLESS (see also Loafer, Lazy)

"You say that your folks will be late?"

"I know they will be if that lazy brother of yours is driving them."

"What? He isn't so lazy."

"Why, he's so lazy that he drives over a bump in the road to knock the ashes off his cigar."

We've heard of the man who was too lazy to walk in his sleep—he hitchhiked.

"Did you save anything for a rainy day, shiftless?"

"Yes, the watering of the lawn."

"Why is a lazy dog like a hill?"

"I surrender."

"A slow pup!"

"Why do you have to take your brother to the doctor with you?"

"I stick my tongue out and he puts it in again."

He hasn't energy enough to make his own coffee in the ordinary way. At breakfast, he just puts the coffee grounds in his mustache and drinks hot water.

SHOE BUSINESS (see also Business)

"How much are your four dollar shoes?"

"Two dollars a foot."

"The soles of my shoes are so thin I could step on a dime and tell whether it's heads or tails."

SICK JOKES

"Your father just fell into the fireplace."

"Well, poke him up. It's chilly in here."

"Must be getting close to town. We're hitting more people."

"Mommy, how come daddy is so pale?"

"Shut up and keep digging."

There was a guy who sent his girl a heart for Valentine's Day —and it was still beating.

"But Henry, that isn't our baby."
"Shut up. It's a better carriage."

Sign on electric chair. "You can be sure if it's Westinghouse."

"Mommy, can I watch television?"
"No, you know it'll hurt your eye."

Mama Cannibal: "How many times have I told you not to talk with someone in your mouth?"

The kid came home from school crying, "Mommy, the teacher said I look like a monkey." "Shut up!" his mother hollered. "And comb your face."

SIGNS

Sign on a midtown bar ceiling: WHAT THE HELL ARE YOU LOOKING WAY WAY UP HERE FOR? .

Sign on the tailor shop: WE'LL CLEAN FOR YOU. WE'LL PRESS FOR YOU. WE'LL EVEN DYE FOR YOU.

Sign in a casting office: THINGS ARE TOUGH ALL OVER. EVEN THE CHORUS IS KICKING.

Sign in brassière shop: WHAT GOD HAS FORGOTTEN, WE STUFF WITH COTTON.

Sign in a Hollywood charm school—THINK MINK.

Sign posted in a midtown New York office: THE EASIEST WAY TO MAKE ENDS MEET IS TO GET OFF YOUR OWN.

Sign in a brassière shop: WE FIX FLATS.

Sign in a French antique shop in New York: ENGLISH AND FRENCH SPOKEN—CASH UNDERSTOOD.

SINGER (see also Vocalist, Warbler)

"I started taking singing lessons but I can't sing."
"What's the matter, did you lose your voice?"
"No, somebody else is in the bathroom."

She embarrassed all of us when she led the community singing.
How did she do that?
Well, she was leading the singing and she said, "Now I want just the tenors to sing the first part and when we come to the Gates of Hades, that's where I want you all to come in."

"O Le Aye Le Whoo."

"My gosh, what are you doing?"

"I'm singing. I've paid $1000 for some lessons."

"I'll take you to see my brother."

"No. I've got a teacher now."

"My brother is not a teacher. He's a lawyer and he can get your money back."

"You can't sing on this program. We're supposed to be presenting professional talent."

"You fooled me!"

"How was your song?"

"I was terrific."

"Why don't you be a little modest?"

"Okay, I was barely sensational."

"We sing like the angels."

"If those are angels—heaven can wait."

"I can't think why they make so much fuss about Miss Smith's voice. Miss Jones has a much richer one."

"Yes, but Miss Smith has a much richer father."

"For thirty years I sang at the Trocadero."

"Thirty years ago there was no Troc. The place was all desert."

"Ahhh. No *wonder* there were camels applauding."

"I want you to sing this song with gusto."

"Aw, gee, I wanted to sing it alone."

The headwaiter at a New York night spot told a singer that a customer had a request for her. When the singer asked what it was, the garçon replied, "to leave town."

"That was 'Lilacs in the Rain' and your vocal was beautiful—I could almost smell the lilacs."

"What about the music?"

"That, too!"

"When I sing, my voice fills the studio."

"Yes. I noticed that some of the people got up and left to make room for it."

"You sang that wonderfully."

"You played it nicely."

"That was because I was inspired."

"Here use my handkerchief. It *is* warm in here."

"Is he a virtuoso?"

"Well, I wouldn't know, I didn't go into his personal life."

"Watch your expression."

"When I sing I sing in front of a mirror."

"That's the only way you can get an audience."

"What's he singing about?"

"He says he wishes he was in Dixie."

"I wish he was, too."

"You're a baritone singer?"

"Yes."

"One of the Baritones of Wimpole Street?"

"Marvelous. I'll make you a diva."

"But you forget I don't swim."

"Your voice makes me think of sailors."

"Why should it make you think of sailors?"

"It has a tendency to die at C."

SKELTON, RED

I used to catch sparrows in the park, color them with iodine, and sell them as canaries.

Two pigeons were flying over a parking lot and one said to the other, "Let's make a deposit on that Cadillac."

A drunk was driving up a one-way street the wrong way. Cop stopped him and said, "Where do you think you're going?" Guy said, "I don't know but I must be late—everyone else is coming back!"

Two nuts were walking along late at night and they came to a big wall.

One said, "How are we gonna get over it?"

Other guy said, "Well, I'll shine this searchlight up there and you climb up the searchlight beam."

First guy said, "Oh, no, I'll get halfway up and you'll turn it off!"

Beautiful girl walked by and I said, "Are you a model?" She said, "No, I'm full-scale."

A drunk was lying in the gutter with one arm on the curb, yelling, "I'll get over this wall if it takes me all night!"

SLEEP (see also Lazy, Loafer)

HUSBAND: Why did you wake me up? It's still dark.

WIFE: Well, open your eyes.

WIFE: No wonder you're cold. Your feet are sticking out. Put them under the covers.

HUSBAND: Oh no. I'm not gonna stick those cold things into bed with me!

WIFE: How can you sleep so much?

HUSBAND: I just can't stay idle. I must be doing something all the time.

1ST MAN: If you're a light sleeper, you should try sleeping at the edge of your bed.
2ND MAN: Will that help me to sleep?
1ST MAN: Sure, you'll drop right off.

1ST MAN: Do you go to sleep on your left side or your right side?
2ND MAN: Both sides. All of me goes to sleep at once.

1ST WOMAN: To wake up my husband in the morning is just like starting a jalopy.
2ND WOMAN: Why?
1ST WOMAN: I have to wind him, crank him and then jump back.

WIFE: I can't sleep, dear. I keep thinking there's a mouse under the bed.
HUSBAND: Well, start thinking there's a cat under the bed and go to sleep.

TEACHER: You can't sleep in my class.
STUDENT: If you didn't talk so loud I could.

SMOKING (see also Habits)

TEACHER: Where do you find tobacco?
PUPIL: Tobacco is found in North Carolina, South Carolina, Kentucky, and once in a while in a five-cent cigar.

SAM: I never saw you smoke a cigar before.
BO: No, I just picked it up recently.

SNOB (see also Rich)

A snobbish Park Avenue matron walked into a pet shop and ordered the proprietor to give her the finest dog he had in the store. He showed her several of his prize animals but she was dissatisfied. Finally, he picked up an adorable little pup and handed it to her. "Is he pedigreed?" she asked haughtily. "Pedigreed?" smiled the dealer. "If this dog could talk, he wouldn't speak to either of us."

A haughty socialite died and arrived at the gates of Heaven. "Welcome," St. Peter greeted him, "come right in." "I will not," sneered the snob, "any place where a perfect stranger can get in without a reservation is not my idea of Heaven."

SONGS

"Love song—'I Loved Her for All She Was Worth!' "
"Who wrote that?"
"The Income Tax collector."

"What number do you like best?"

" 'The Old Spinning Wheel In The Corner' "

"How does it go?"

"You work it with your foot."

"Do you know the Gorilla song?"

"Why no, I don't believe —"

" 'Gorilla My Dreams I Love You.' "

"What is your favorite musical number?"

"I have five of them."

"Five? What are they?"

" 'Three Blind Mice' and 'Two Sleepy People.' "

"So you're a song writer? How do you write your tunes?"

"Well—in the old days, I picked out the songs on the piano with one finger."

"And now?"

"Now everything has been modernized. Now—I use two fingers."

SONGSTER

"Who was that girl that just sang?"

"My daughter; do you like her?"

"Mmmmmmmm, most unusual; most unusual."

"She got her voice from me."

"You were darned lucky to get rid of it."

"Are you familiar with Mendelssohn's 'Wedding March'?"

"Am I? Four times."

"What can I do with my voice now that it is trained?"

"Well, if there's ever a conflagration in your neighborhood you can yell 'Fire.' "

"I believe every person should sing at his work."

"My brother can't."

"Why not?"

"He's a trombone player."

"She used to sing in a cage full of lions, but she had to retire."

"Why?"

"The ASPCA made her stop."

"My uncle studied voice in Italy, in a controversy."

"You mean in a conservatory?"

"The way my uncle sings, it's a controversy."

"He also went to Switzerland to yodel."

"Didn't he have to learn?"

"No, he's gotta system. He drinks a lot of beer and lets his stomach take it from there."

"He sings in a duo."
"A duo?"
"Yes, a quartette of two men."
"You mean half a quartette."
"Yes, a pint."

"She sings. How do you like her range?"
"Very well. In fact, I like her whole kitchen."

"We had you down for a song, Lucille. Do you think you can do it?"
"I was told by two people that I shouldn't sing."
"Two doctors?"
"No, one doctor and one musician."

"Did you go to see the famous singing teacher?"
"Yes, and he said he couldn't see me."
"He and I have something in common."

SOUTH AMERICA

South America has so many revolutions, the Cabinet meets in a revolving door.

My advice to any South American president—"Don't have any personal stationery made."

Things are so quiet in South America, it's about time we sent former Vice-President Nixon down there on another good-will tour.

SPACE JOKES (see also Astronauts)

A Martian landed in New York's Central Park at midnight and got mugged.

The Martian walked up to the clerk in a bookstore and said, "Take me to Lolita."

A truck went around the corner too fast and a carton dropped out of the back. The Martian chased the truck up the street yelling, "Hey lady, you dropped your purse."

The moon man whispered to his girl friend: "Look honey, a full earth tonight."

Two outer space monsters came to the city and began devouring garbage cans waiting to be picked up by the garbage collectors.
"You know," said one of the monsters, belching, "the crusts are good, but the fillings are too damn rich."

A Martian saw UNIVAC and said: "She's not only beautiful, but she's got brains, too."

A Martian was approached by a bum. "Can you spare a dime fella?" the bum said. "What's a dime?" said the Martian. "You're right," replied the bum, "Make it a quarter."

Sign on highway to Cape Canaveral: Watch out for falling rockets.

Sign on doorknob of Army Rocket Center: Out to Launch.

SPAIN

A modern neurotic is a guy who doesn't build castles in Spain. He builds ranch houses there.

In an arena in Spain one angry bull came charging out of the pen. The bullfighter raised a green cape and waved it wildly at the bull. "What are you doing?" shouted a man in the grandstand. "What's the idea of a green cloth? If you want the bull to charge, you should use a red cloth." The matador looked up and shook his head. "Red makes him stop. This bull was raised by an American traffic cop."

SPEAKER (see also Banquets, Dais, Speeches)

The speaker had agreed to address the monthly meeting of a small but active group of nice elderly ladies. The evening turned out to be miserable—one of those snow-sleet-wind combinations that make home-sweet-home seem even sweeter than usual. Arriving at the scheduled time, the speaker found the meeting only halfway through its agenda. He sat politely by while the ladies reported at length on their activities. After an hour or so, the chairlady called the business meeting to a close, and in a formal and dramatic voice announced, "Ladies, we want to welcome our guest speaker. We appreciate that he is with us. Not even a dog would go out on such a night and he did it!

"This man," she stated with sincerity and enthusiasm, "is a true example of sacrifice and courage. Nothing has been too much for him. Call him late at night and with no notice at all, he's on a plane traveling hundreds of miles to cover a meeting. Ask him for help of any kind and he's right on the spot. As a matter of fact, I don't know how he keeps it up— he must have a heart of granite!"

And believe it or not, at another meeting on the same day, a committee was deciding on a speaker for an important national conference. Several suggestions were made but none seemed to fill the bill properly. Finally, in some exasperation and complete innocence, the chairman observed, "Well, it certainly is hard to pinhead the speaker."

SPEECH (see also Banquets, Speakers, Dais)

If all the people who sit through after-dinner speeches were lined up three feet apart, they would stretch.

SPEAKER: There are so many ribald interruptions I can scarcely hear myself speaking.
MAN: Cheer up, Guv'nor—you ain't missin' much."

An after-dinner speaker gushed on and on. Deacon Miller nodded and presently rested his head on the tablecloth. The chairman reached over and bumped him lightly on the head with his gavel.
DEACON MILLER: Hit me harder —I can still hear him.

SPELLING (see also School, Kids)

"I couldn't learn to spell."
"Why not?"
"My teacher was always changing the words."

"So your sister got fired?"
"Yeah—but she was going to leave anyway. Her boss is so conceited—he thinks the words can only be spelled his way."

"Johnny—you mispelled most of the words in your composition."
"Yes'm—I'm going to be a dialect writer."

"Now, if I write n-e-w on the blackboard, what does that spell?"
"New."
"Now, I'll put a 'k' in front of it and what have we?"
"Canoe."

"Spell the word neighbor."
"N-e-i-g-h-b-o-r."
"That's right. Now, Tommy, can you tell me what a neighbor is?"
"It's a woman that borrows things."

SPOONING (see also Kissing, Necking, Osculating)

"Last night I was kissed sixty times in one hour."
"By the clock?"
"No, over by the radio."

"Why does a girl raise one foot when she's kissed?"
"Oh, I suppose so she can kick the guy if he backs out."

"Oh, where did you learn to kiss like that?"
"I used to be a tester in a bubble-gum factory."

"If I were to throw you a kiss what would you say?"
"That you were the laziest man I'd ever met."

"Did your last boy friend give you long kisses?"
"Yes, once on a lonely country road he kissed me, and when I opened my eyes they had put up a skyscraper across the street."

"I kissed at least a dozen girls at that party."
"Drunk, I suppose?"
"Yes, every one of them."

"Why are you always talking about the good old days?"
"Well, then you could kiss a girl and taste nothing but girl."

"Every time I'm kissed it upsets my nerves. If you were a doctor what would you give me?"
"A nervous breakdown."

"If you kiss me, I'll scream."
"Oh, you will, will you?" (kisses her)
"Well, why don't you say something?"
"Don't interrupt me."
"Don't interrupt you? Why?"
"I'm screaming."

"A submarine kiss."
"What's that?"
"It's all wet, and never comes up for air."

"Let's turn out the lights, dearie, and pretend we're in heaven."
"But honey, I'm no angel."
"I know—that's why I turned out the lights."

"Where did you learn to pucker up your lips like that?"
"Used to thread needles for my grandmother."

"Do you think there are any statistics on how many kisses are stolen?"
"No, those things are kept pretty much in the dark."

SPORTS (see also Baseball, Basketball, Football, Golf)

1ST MAN: I was great in sports when I was young—I had the body of an athlete.
2ND MAN: Well, you still have the feet, anyway.

1ST MAN: You know nothing about sports.
2ND MAN: Yes I do. Why, I had boxing gloves on when I was two years old.
1ST MAN: Wait a minute, why would you wear boxing gloves when you were two years old?

2ND MAN: So I wouldn't suck my thumb.

He broke the underwater record by staying under for three hours and twenty-five minutes. Funeral services will be held tomorrow.

WIFE: John, what becomes of a ball player when his eyesight starts to fail?
HUSBAND: They make an umpire of him.

1ST MAN: I used to play hockey.
2ND MAN: Why did you quit?
1ST MAN: I ran out of things to hock.

At baseball game:
SHE: What's the man running for?
HE: He hit the ball.
SHE: I know. But does he have to chase it, too?

REPORTER: May I speak to Mr. Brown, the boxer?
MRS. BROWN: I'm sorry, he's not up yet. Since he turned professional, he never gets up before the stroke of ten.

KIND OLD LADY: And what is your name, little boy?
JOCKEY'S SON: I'm Jerry Glutz, by Bill Glutz out of Sadie Schmidt.

HE: You know, Henrietta, every time I see you my heart beats

faster. I feel the urge to do bigger and better things. I feel so strong and virile. Do you know what that means?
SHE: Sure. It means in about five minutes you and I are going to have a wrestling match.

"Can you do any card tricks?"
"Well, I'm pretty good at keeping from being a fourth at bridge."

"My son was hit by a bowling ball."
"That's what you get for letting him play in the alleys."

COME-TO-GRIEF AIRMAN: I was trying to make a record.
FARMER: Well, you've made it. You be the first man in these parts who climbed down a tree without having to climb up it first.

IRATE PLAYER: I wasn't out.
SARCASTIC UMPIRE: Oh, you weren't? Well, you just have a look at the newspaper tomorrow.

SPORTS CARS (see also Cars, Auto Traffic, Transportation)

I saw this sports car from Italy and it had real continental styling . . . fenders with cuffs . . . tapered doors and a button down grill. There was one drawback . . . the exhaust smelled like garlic. But what economy. . . . It can go 40 miles on a gallon . . . not of gasoline but of Chianti. Come to think of it, I can go 40 miles on a gallon of Chianti.

Then I saw this French sports car. You could tell it was French because its tail light was uncovered and its gears were stripped. Its engine was all souped up . . . that's what it ran on—onion soup.

The carburetor was fed by fuel injection. This is the only car I know that's on the needle.

This car has tremendous horsepower . . . so much, in fact, that you have to be a jockey to drive it.

This car is small but it seats two comfortable people . . . and makes them uncomfortable. This car is so small that when I got out of it I hit my head on the curb. It's so low to the ground the only way you can get into it is through a manhole cover.

They're making those cars so small I stuck out my hand for a left turn and one of them sports cars ran up my sleeve.

Those sports cars are so small I stuck my arm out for a left turn and ruptured a cop.

I couldn't get my foreign car out of the garage this morning— it was stuck on a piece of gum.

Those sports cars can stop on a dime. But then, the problem is getting over the dime.

A sports car was in a bad accident—a pedestrian fell on it.

Hotel had sign in lobby—NO PARKING BABY CARRIAGES OR SPORTS CARS IN THE LOBBY.

I got a compact car that can fit in a compact.

New sports car is the Mafia— it's got a hood under the hood.

SPRING (see also Love, Sports)

I know spring is here—my wife just made a pass at me.

Spring is a little late this year— it couldn't find a parking space.

Spring must be here. Out on the sidewalk I just saw a robin sitting on a bridge chair with a Good Humor popsicle.

Song: "If the Bed Caves in I'll See You in the Spring."

SQUELCH (see also Hecklers, Insult)

A Bostonian visited San Antonio, Texas, and asked a native, "What is that dilapidated-looking ruin over there?" "That, suh, is the Alamo. In that building, suh, 136 immortal Texans held off an army of 15,000 of Santa Ana's regulars for four days."

"Um-m-m," said the Bostonian, "and who was that man on horseback on that hill over there?"

"That, suh, is a statue of a Texas ranger. He killed 46 Apaches in singlehanded combat and broke up 47 riots in his lifetime. Where you from, stranger?"

"I'm from Boston. We have our heroes there, too. Paul Revere, for instance—"

"Paul Revere!" snorted the Texan. "You mean that man who had to ride for help?"

Any comedian worth his weight in laughs should be able to handle a heckler, on or offstage, at the drop of a gag. Your proper line can be a rope around the neck of your opponent if it's used at the right place at the right time. Here are some good squelchers to be put away in your brain file, so that you will always be prepared for battle:

I couldn't warm up to you if we were cremated together.

It isn't that we have something against you personally—you just happen to be the kind of jerk we don't want hanging around the premises.

You may be a social lion to your friends but you're just an animal cracker to me.

Why don't you gargle concrete and let it get hard?

What a combination—corny and illiterate.

You're the sort of guy who talks penthouses and takes subways.

He's the kind of guy who picks his friends—to pieces.

They're about as compatible as ham and matzoths.

He's an intellectual. He can bore you on every subject.

You're snappy on the comeback—like your checks.

Don't you ever get tired of having yourself around?

Stay with me. I want to be alone.

Why don't you send your wits out to be sharpened?

Are you a self-made man, or do you want to blame someone else?

Why don't you go on a diet and quit eating my heart out?

There was something I always liked about him—but he spent it.

His idea of an exciting night is to turn up his electric blanket.

Most of our top-drawer actors are amiable folks—approachable, tolerant, often eager to help new-comers. The old-timers held themselves more aloof. Perhaps the most irascible, sharp-spoken was the late Wilton Lackaye—a great performer but not the most amiable gentleman. Once, after his opening night in The Pit, he came into the Lambs Club and was approached by an eager young hopeful who exclaimed enthusiastically, "How does it feel, Mr. Lackaye, to receive all that wild acclaim for your great acting?" Lackaye stared at him coldly and snapped: "You'll never know!"

STENOGRAPHERS (see also Secretary, Boss, Office)

Boss came in early and found his bookkeeper kissing his stenographer.
Boss: Is this what I pay you for?
BOOKKEEPER: No . . . this I do free of charge.

1ST VICE PRESIDENT: Say, Dick, you've got the latest thing in stenographers.
2ND VICE PRESIDENT: I'll say. She never gets here on time.

CLERK: Sorry madame, but Mr. Goldberg has just gone to lunch with his wife.
MRS. GOLDBERG: Is that so? Vell, just tell him his stenographer called.

Boss: What's the difference between a beautiful stenographer and a dumb stenographer?
ASSISTANT: You can fire a dumb stenographer.

Boss: Every time I want you, you're on the phone, Miss Flurd!
STENO: They were all business calls sir.
Boss: Oh yeah . . . well in the future don't address my clients as darling.

STENO: Boss, will you advance me my next week's salary?
Boss: Of course not. I never make advances to my stenographers.

STOCK MARKET (see also Money, Business)

My brother-in-law is a stock broker. That's a blood sucker in an ivy league suit.

They call him a broker, because after you see him you are.

"I'm telling you there's money to be found on Wall Street."
"Good, I'll go down there now with my searchlight."

"What do you know about the bears and bulls?"
"Nothing, but I know about the birds and bees."

He works for a stock brokerage house called Button, Button and Zipper. Zipper replaced one of the Buttons.

"I'd have to be an idiot to buy stock in that company."
"Good. How many shares do you want?"

"Put your money in oil."
"Are you crazy? Who wants oily money?"

"Why are you watering that stock?"
"It's a growth stock and it needs water to grow."

STONE, HARVEY

When I was a kid we were so poor we didn't have underwear. My mother painted buttons on us, And, of course, we always had two painted in the back . . . or else you're trapped.

Every kid in my school carried a blackjack in his pencil box.

We were all honor students . . . you know, "Yes Your Honor; no, Your Honor; three days, Your Honor?"

In Miami Beach everybody is rich, even the poor people. I saw a woman with a cashmere car and mink dental floss. Then one day I went to the hotel pool to get an estimate on a swim.

Seems like yesterday I got married. I wish it was tomorrow. I'd call the whole thing off.

My wife used to say to me "OK, so I like to spend money. Name one other extravagance."

When I was in the army they used to wake us at four o'clock in the morning. The first thing I used to do is run out and shake a tree. I figured if I'm awake why should the birds sleep.

I was the only guy in the army who was awarded the yellow heart.

STORES (see also Department Stores, Clerks, Salesman, Business)

"What do you mean by arguing with that customer? Don't you know our rule? The customer is always right."
"I know it. But he insisted that he was wrong."

"Gimme a dime's worth of asafetida. Dad wants you to charge it."
"All right; what's your name?"
"Shermerhorn."

"Take it for nothin' . . . I ain't going to spell asafetida and Shermerhorn for no dime."

"Is this a second-hand store?"
"Can't you see it's a second-hand store?"
"Well, I want a second hand for my watch."

WOMAN: (Talking over telephone) Send up a bale of hay.
MERCHANT: Who's it for?
WOMAN: The horse.

"I bought it at the fifteen cent store."
"You mean, the five and ten."
"Well, five and ten makes fifteen."

"Your opening sale has closed. What now?"
"Our closing sale opens."

A pharmacist is a man in a white coat who stands behind the soda fountain selling dollar watches in a drug store.

"He is a great druggist, isn't he?"
"He is—but don't you think he makes his chicken salad a little too salty?"

MAN: I want a mustard plaster.
DRUGGIST: We're out of mustard; but how about mayonnaise?

Did you hear about the man who bought a Louis XIV bed? It was too small for him so he sent it back and asked for a Louis XVI?

YOUNG LADY: I'd like to see some gloves, please.
CLERK: What kind, kid?
YOUNG LADY: Sir, how dare you!

CUSTOMER: I'd like to try on that suit in the window.
SALESMAN: Sorry, sir, but you'll have to use the dressing room.

LADY (in pet shop): I like that dog but his legs are too short.
SALESMAN: Too short! Why, madam, they all four reach the floor.

GENTLEMAN: (in ladies' lingerie store): I want a corset for my wife.
CLERK: What bust?
GENTLEMAN: Nothing. It just wore out.

CUSTOMER: I want a toy for a little boy whose father is very fat and unable to do any kneeling.

STORIES (see also Shaggy Dog)

The wife was always antagonized by her husband going out at night. His departing words, which especially angered her, were always, "Good night, mother of three."

But one night she could stand it no longer, and when he took his hat, started out the door, and called out cheerfully, "Good night, mother of three," she responded, quite as cheerily, "Good night, father of one."

Now he stays home at night.

"—then I said, 'No, sir, I won't marry your daughter. I defy you to lay a hand on me. Come one step nearer and I'll tear you limb from limb.' "

"Well, how did it all turn out?"

"Oh, I married his daughter."

"Hello, Bill. How are ya?"

"Well, good and bad, Joe. I'm suffering pretty much from body odor, and I've had a crick in my neck for the past two weeks. I had a bad toothache last night, and do you know that I frequently have dizzy spells and spots before my eyes? That rheumatism has been bothering me again lately, too. My hair's falling out pretty fast now, and I think I'm catching athlete's foot. I'm just getting over a pretty bad cold, but I guess I can't complain. How are you Joe?"

"Oh never mind."

They were some distance from shore when the boat filled with water and sank.

"Do you think you can swim to that buoy?" he asked.

"If I can't, it will be the first buoy I haven't made," she said.

The stingiest man was scoring the hired man for his extravagance in wanting to carry a lantern in going to call on his best girl.

"The idea!" he scoffed, "When I was courtin' I never carried a lantern; I went in the dark."

The hired man proceeded to fill the lantern.

"Yes," he said, sadly, "and look what you got."

The extremely homely girl approached the information desk at the tourist park and asked for a road map.

"Here's your copy," said the attendant.

"Well, I hope I won't go wrong," replied the tourist.

"With that map of yours," retorted the attendant, "I don't see how you could."

The class in public speaking was to give pantomimes that afternoon. One frosh got up, when called on, went to the platform and stood perfectly still. "Well," said the prof, after a minute's wait for something to happen, "What do your represent?"

"I'm imitating a man going up in an elevator," was the quick response.

We have heard countless tales about girls who walked back from airplane rides, but what we'd like to know is what happened to the girl who was taken out walking.

An aviator took an old man and his wife for an airplane ride and told them it would cost nothing if neither made any sound when he did the loop the loop and the barrel roll. They agreed and the aviator did some breathtaking stunts.

As they landed he yelled back at them, asking how they liked it.

"Fine," returned the old man, "but I thought I'd yell when the old lady fell out."

"Say," said one little boy to another, "how do you teach a girl to swim?"

"Oh, dat's easy," said the other kid, "you take her gently by the hand, an' you leads her down to de water, an' you says to her, 'Don't be afraid, I ain't goin' let nothin' hurt you,' and"—

"Heh," interrupted the first one, "what are you givin' us? Dis is me sister I'm talkin' bout."

"Aw shove her off de dock."

Mr. Jones returned from the office before lunch, and entered the house by the kitchen to surprise his wife. Mrs. Jones was busy with the dishes. As he kissed the back of her head, what was his dismay when, without looking around, she said, "One bottle of milk and a pint of cream."

An absent-minded professor was walking down the street one day with one foot in the gutter and the other on the pavement. A friend, meeting him, said:

"Good morning, professor; and how are you?"

"I was very well, I thought, but now for the last ten minutes I've been limping."

A large map was spread upon the wall and the teacher was instructing the class in geography.

"Horace," she said to a small pupil, "when you stand in Europe facing the north, you have on your right hand the great continent of Asia. What have you on your left hand?"

"A wart," replied Horace, "but I can't help it, teacher."

An old maid went to have her picture taken and the photographer noticed her tying a piece of clothesline around the bottom of her skirt.

"What's the idea of that?" he asked. "I can't take your picture that way."

"You can't fool me, young man," said the old girl. "I know you see me upside down in that camera."

A gentleman slightly soused was having some trouble with a revolving door. Each time he got started, he was whirled around, and landed out in the street again. He stood gazing at it in awe and wonder, when a man came along and went in. The door spun around. Out came a young lady. The souse blinked "Thash a pretty good trick, all right," he said, "but I don't see yet what he did with his clothes."

There were two men standing on a corner whose names were Wood and Stone. A pretty girl with short skirts walked by and Wood turned to Stone and Stone turned to Wood, and then both turned to rubber and the girl turned into a drugstore.

We are twins and look alike. When we were at school my brother threw an eraser and hit the teacher. She whipped me. She didn't know the difference, but I did.

I was to be married, but my brother arrived at the church first and married my girl. She didn't realize but I did.

But I got even for all that. I died last week and they buried him.

A fond mother, whose daughter had not come home at the usual time, grew worried at her absence, so she telegraphed five of her daughter's best friends, asking where Mary was. Shortly after her daughter's return, the answers to her telegrams arrived. Each one read, "Don't worry, Mary is staying with me tonight."

This is the story of a young lady who had to undergo an operation at the hands of a young doctor. He nonchalantly told her to remove her clothes and lie down on the operating table. Noticing her embarrassment, the doctor spread a sheet over and wheeled her into the operating room, then departed in search of his necessary instruments.

Standing about the room were a number of young men in white uniforms. One of them walked forward, raised a corner of the sheet, smiled, and returned to the side of the room. A minute later another of the white-uniformed men did the same thing. The young lady by this time was blushing a terrific scarlet, and even the thought that hospital internes were used to seeing such things failed to ease her mind. When still another of the white-uniformed young men walked forward to repeat the actions of his predecessors she could stand it no longer.

"For heaven's sake," she blurted out, "When are you going to operate?"

The young man looked at her in surprise.

"Why, I don't know, Miss. You'll have to ask the doctor. We're the painters here."

Mrs. Smith took her freshman son to the zoo with her not long ago. When the lad passed the cage of storks, he paused. His exasperated mother finally found out that he was only trying to see if the stork remembered him.

Two stuttering blacksmiths had finished heating a piece of pig iron, and one placed it upon the anvil with a pair of tongs.

"H-h-h-h-h-h-hit it," he stuttered to his helper.

"Wh-wh-wh-wh-wh-where?" asked the other.

"Ah, h-h-h-h-h-h-ell, we'll 'ave to heat it again now."

The weighing machine was out of order. A fat lady clambered on and inserted a penny. An inebriated gentleman standing in the vicinity saw the scale register 75 pounds "My God," he whispered, "she's hollow."

The waiter in the Greasy Spoon sidled up to the man who had just parked on a stool at the counter. "I'll have a bowl of chicken soup, please," said the diner.

"Chickenzoup!" the waiter bawled back to the kitchen.

"No, on second thought, I believe I'll have pea soup."

"Make the chicken pea!" boomed the waiter.

"Er-never mind," gulped the diner. "Maybe I'd better just have a hamburger."

A certain little boy expressed a wish for a baby brother. His mother advised him to ask God for one. Each night he asked in his prayers for a baby brother. After a time he became discouraged and told his mother that he had quit praying for one.

One morning his father took him to his mother's room where two new baby brothers were awaiting his inspection. His first comment was, "Gee dad, isn't it lucky I stopped praying when I did?"

Two ladies stopped at a livery stable and asked for a gentle horse to drive.

The liveryman brought out one, saying: "This horse is perfectly gentle so long as you don't let the rein get under his tail."

Within a few hours they returned. "How did you get along?" asked the liveryman.

"Oh, we got along just fine. Had a couple of showers while we were out, but we took turns holding the parasol over the horse."

A Hebrew storekeeper's show window, to the surprise of his

brethren, was suddenly adorned with a gorgeous new blind.

AARON: Nice blind you have.

ISAAC: Yes, Aaron.

AARON: Who paid for it, Isaac?

ISAAC: The customers paid, Aaron.

AARON: What, the customers paid for it?

ISAAC: Yes, Aaron, I put a little box on my counter, "For the Blind," and they paid for it.

Saint Peter was interviewing the fair damsel at the pearly gate.

"Did you, while on earth," he asked, "indulge in necking, petting, smoking, or dancing?"

"Never!" she retorted emphatically.

"Then why haven't you reported sooner?" asked Peter. "You've been dead a long time."

STUPID (see also Insane Asylum, Insanity, Nut, Moron)

A Negro with his ears stopped up was reading a letter to another when the boss came along.

BOSS: What kind of horseplay are you two fellows up to?

NEGRO: He done got dis yere letter dat his gal writ him, boss, but he kain't read, so he gets me to read it fo' him, but stops mah ears up so I kain't hear what his gal done writ him.

NAGGING WIFE: What a sap to let a man sell you a dead horse for twenty dollars.

HUSBAND: Yeah? Well, I sold the horse for one hundred dollars.

NAGGING WIFE: How?

HUSBAND: I raffled him off. I sold a hundred tickets for a dollar apiece.

NAGGING WIFE: What did the fellow say who won?

HUSBAND: Well, he made an awful fuss about it, so I gave him his dollar back.

A man was counting pigeons on the roof of the City Hall when a fellow came along and said: "Say, buddy, that's going to cost you one dollar apiece for counting pigeons on the City Hall."

The man handed him fourteen dollars.

Later he confided to a friend: "Yeah, but the joke is on him— I'd already counted fifty pigeons."

BLOTTO: You got drunk last night and sold the Chrysler Building.

SOTTO: Well, why are you so sad about it?

BLOTTO: I bought it.

You want her to write Happy Birthday on the cake. For three hours she tries to get the cake into the typewriter.

The woman had been out all day. When she returned she spoke to her new maid.

WOMAN: Did you clean out the refrigerator as I told you?
MAID: Yes, ma'am . . . and everything was delicious.

An American manufacturer was showing a prospective customer from an Iron Curtain country through his plant. When the noon whistle blew and thousands of men hurried away, the visitor was aghast. "They're all escaping," he cried. "Can't you stop them?" "Don't worry," the manufacturer said. "They'll come back." The visitor looked at him skeptically, but, when the starting whistle blew, the men returned and set to work.

Later in the day the manufacturer broached the subject of business. . . . "Now," he said, "about those machines you were interested in buying . . ." The Iron Curtain customer interrupted him. "We'll talk about that afterward," he said, " but first tell me how much you want for that whistle!"

The husband and wife went to see the latest Brigitte Bardot movie at the drive in. They were late arriving and as they drove up to the attendant the husband said, "Will we get to see a complete performance?" "No sir," he said, "you won't. But I reckon you'll come closer to it than in any other movie I can think of."

The movie was a touching story of the hardships of the average family during the French Revolution. But one young woman was unimpressed. She said to her escort, "If they were so poor, how could they afford all that antique furniture?"

STUTTERING

BETA: Did you make the debating team?
PHI GAM: N-n-n-n-no. They s-s-said I w-w-w-wasn't t-t-t-tall enough.

Two soldiers who had been buddies before they were separated by the fortunes of war met again on foreign shores.

"Whatever became of Henry?" inquired the first about a third pal.

"He was dishonorably discharged," said the second.

"How did it happen?"

"He was loading a bunch of soldiers on a boat, marching them onto the dock. Four hundred of them went over the side and got drowned before he could say 'Halt.' You know how he stuttered."

SUBURBS (see also Allan King)

An American city is a place where by the time you've finished paying for your home in the suburbs, the suburbs have moved twenty miles farther out.

You go into the suburbs nowadays and every house has wall-to-wall carpeting. When I was a kid living in a tenement we were lucky to have wall-to-wall floors.

A fellow walked into a suburban bar and ordered a martini. Before drinking it, he removed the olive and carefully put it into a small glass jar. Then he ordered another martini and did the same thing. After an hour, when he was full of martinis and the jar was full of olives, he staggered out. "Well," said a customer, "I never saw anything as peculiar as that."

"What's so peculiar about that?" the bartender said. "His wife sent him out for a jar of olives?"

SUCCESS (see also Ambition, Rich)

CITY MAN: The suit you had on the other night was about three sizes too big for you.
SMALL TOWN FRIEND: I know it doesn't fit me here, but when I'm home it fits just right.
CITY MAN: Why shouldn't it fit you here?
SMALL TOWN FRIEND: Well, you see, I'm a much bigger man in my home town.

Two friends who had not seen each other for several years met. "I hear your son is getting on," one remarked to the other.

"Rather," answered the father. "Two years ago he wore my old suits—now I wear his."

SUPERSTITION (see also Luck)

TRAVELING SALESMAN: I knew I would have hard luck. We had dinner on the train and there were thirteen in the party.
FRIEND: That's only superstition. What makes you think thirteen at dinner is unlucky?
TRAVELING SALESMAN: I had to pay the check.

BOOKIE: I had a hunch today. I got up at seven, had seven dollars in my pocket, there were seven at lunch, and there were seven horses in the race—I picked the seventh.
JOCKIE: So he came in the winner?
BOOKIE: No, he came in seventh.

SWIMMING (see also Sports, Fish)

A timid woman approached the lifeguard at a crowded beach.
"Can you swim?" she demanded.

"Only at times, ma'am," responded the guard.

"Only at times? How strange. And when do these moments of ability come to you?"

"In the water, ma'am."

A pompous gentleman puffed down to the waterfront at a fashionable resort. His only child was stretched on the beach attended by two perspiring lifeguards.

"What are you doing to my daughter?" he shouted.

"She nearly drowned and we're giving her artificial respiration," was the response.

"The heck you will. There's going to be nothing artificial about it. You give her the genuine. I can afford it."

SWITZERLAND

Two Cincinnati sightseers were mountain climbing in the Swiss Alps when they lost their way, somehow. 'Midst the drifts of ice and snow they yoo-hoo'd, holloo'd and yodeled. Nothing happened; for hours they wandered. They roamed so long even the guarantees on their Swiss watches were used up. Then from around the corner came a St. Bernard, dragging a beaker of cognac around his neck. "Hallelujah," cried one, "we're saved. Here comes man's best friend." "Yeah,

and look at the size of the dog carrying it."

When I was in Switzerland, I saw a big Swiss Cheese who was such a great ice skater that he had and accountant following him around, adding up his figure eights.

In Geneva the hotels are so ritzy that when you request fresh milk in the dining room, they bring the goat to your table.

Sign in Switzerland at one of the resorts: ATTENTION, ALL SKI-ERS. WHEN YOU BREAK AN ARM OR LEG, HAVE YOUR FRIENDS WRITE THEIR NAMES ON THE CAST. WHEN YOU HAVE THE CAST REMOVED, SEND SAME TO US AND WE WILL TRANSFORM IT INTO A BEAUTIFUL INDESTRUCTIBLE VASE OR LAMP OR AN UMBRELLA RACK AND IT WILL BE A TREASURED HEIRLOOM POSSESSION AND SOU-VENIR OF SWITZERLAND.

In Switzerland I found out what Swiss cheese really is—just a bunch of holes strung together.

I love Switzerland for its skiing —what a wonderful sport! One day of glorious skiing and six months in the hospital.

A Swiss left his beloved Switz-erland for America and opened a jewelry factory in Greenwich Village where he is now making watches with "Swish" movements.

In Switzerland there's a man who raises St. Bernard dogs just for the brandy.

❖❖❖

T

TAILORS (see also Business, Clothing)

A tailor was complaining about his business on account of the warm weather setting in so early when he should be selling heavier garments. He said, "Mine suits are better than money. Money you can get rid of."

My tailor sold me a suit he said would wear like iron, and he's right. I can't even sit down in it!

TALKING (see also Girls, Marriage)

SMITH: Have you noticed how a woman lowers her voice whenever she asks for anything?
JONES: Oh, yes. But have you noticed how she raises it if she doesn't get it?

"They say her husband's words are sharp and to the point."
"Maybe that's the only way for him to get a word in edgeways, now and then."

GEORGE WASHINGTON JONES: I come from a very truthful family—a lie never passed my father's lips.
FRIEND: How do you know?
GEORGE WASHINGTON JONES: He talked through his nose.

BROWN: Can you keep a secret?
GREEN: Sure.
BROWN: I need to borrow some money.
GREEN: Don't worry. It's just as if I never heard it.

Two walls were talking and one said to the other, "Hold me up, I'm plastered."

Two toes were talking and one said to the other, "I think there's a heel following us."

"One tonsil said to the other, "We must be in Capistrano. Here comes another swallow."

The mayonnaise said to the icebox, "Close the door, I'm dressing."

One fly said to the other, "I was up all night walking the ceiling with the baby."

One frog said to other, "I think I have a man in my throat."

A broom told another broom, "My wife and I were just swept together."

Two ducks were talking on a sunny day and one said, "It's nice weather for people."

One appendix said to other, "What this country needs is a good five-cent scar."

TAXES (see also Income Tax, Money)

This is a funny world. If you do wrong you get fined—if you do right you get taxed.

A merchant got into trouble with the income taxers so he went to the office to explain his records which were full of shorthand and mysterious markings. They told him they only wanted to know how much he spent, how much he took in and how much he profited. He said, "That's all? I wouldn't even tell that to mine partner."

Nowadays we don't make money, we just hold it for the government between tax collections.

The difference between death and taxes is that death doesn't get worse every time Congress meets!

Ad in newspaper: Man with income tax blank would like to meet lady with income.

The tax collector must love poor people he's creating so many of them.

I wrote the Income Tax Bureau to have a heart, and they wrote back and said, "We'll take it!"

With taxes taking everything, you work like a dog all your life so you can live like a dog.

I found out that it's the Ways and Means Committee which takes care of your taxes—if you have the Means they'll find the Ways to get it!

The income tax is the Government's version of *Instant Poverty*.

In Europe they have a new form of tax collection. In Rumania, a girl in Bucharest heard the doorbell ring and when she opened the door and saw the tax collector, so she shouted to her mother upstairs, "Ma, the tax collector is here." And her mother shouted, "I'll be right down, give him a chair." The girl shouted back, "A chair won't do, he wants *all* the furniture!"

TAXI (see also Taxicabs)

1ST MAN: I had a terrible accident in a taxi the other day.
2ND MAN: What happened?
1ST MAN: The taxi hit a bump in the road and the meter jumped three dollars. Luckily my insurance covered it.

RIDER: Hey driver . . . the meter's clicking off dollars instead of nickels.
CABBIE: Well, naturally, we're passing through a ritzy neighborhood.

A New York cab driver took a farmer from Grand Central to a hotel one block away by a very circuitous route. At the end of the ride the meter read $15.45.
FARMER: You can't play me for a sucker. I've been driven to this hotel before from Grand Central and last time the fare was only $11.90.

RIDER: Driver, you're passing a red light.
CABBIE: That's okay . . . I'm color blind.

MAN: Driver, are you engaged?
CABBIE: No, but I'm going steady.

MAN: Driver, please take us to the station.
CABBIE: Sorry, I never take anyone to the station.

MAN: Why not?
CABBIE: I can't stand saying goodbye.

RIDER: Say, driver, can you see what's going on in back through your rear-view mirror?
CABBIE: Ha! Why d'you think I took the job?

TAXICABS (see also Taxis)

This is a Hy Gardner classic: It all started in front of the Waldorf-Astoria. A mink-befurred, lorgnette-dangling dowager, with trunks and suitcases stacked up like planes over Idlewild, was helped into a cab while a second taxi took care of her excess. "Mrs. Whittlestick," the uniformed doorman said, "wishes to be driven to Pier 8. She's sailing on the s.s. *United States*." The hackie nodded, dropped the flag and beckoned with his little finger to have the baggage car follow.

In no longer than it takes to read a union contract, the cabs arrived at the pier, the baggage was checked into staterooms A through X, and the passenger spoke to the cabby. "If you're single and want to double your income, I'd like to offer you a proposition to see the world through your own windshield. I simply loathe hailing strange cabs in strange places. How would you like to drive me around Europe, all expenses paid?"

The hackie's mouth opened, but no words came out. Finally he nodded. In a few minutes arrangements were made to have the cab hoisted into the hold of the ship, where it remained till the ship berthed in Le Havre. From there they drove to Paris, then Nice, then Monte Carlo, then back to Paris for the channel crossing to England, then to Rome, Berlin and through the Scandinavian countries. Like the cab's two occupants, the meter never stopped running. Eventually, the party retraced its tire treads, the *United States* docked again at the point of origination, Pier 8. The cab was hoisted out of the hold and plunked on terra firma.

"Well, my good man," the fatigued dowager sighed, paying the $12,457 clicked on the clock, "we're on native soil again, thank goodness. Now will you please drive me home?" "Where is home, ma'am?" the hackie smiled. "It's near Prospect Park, in Brooklyn," his benefactor replied. "Brooklyn!" the hackie snorted, slamming the door. "Are you nuts? You'll have to take another cab. Every time I go to Brooklyn I have to come back to Manhattan empty!"

This guy was in a cab. The cab driver said, "Where you wanta go?" The guy answered, "Anywhere." The driver stopped and said, "Get out, I got a schedule to make."

A little couple from the Bronx and their four children were downtown and decided to take a taxi home. Approaching the cab driver the husband demanded, "How much will you charge to drive us to the Bronx?"

"I figure two dollars apiece for you and your wife," said the driver, "and I'll take the four kids along for nothin'."

The husband turned to his kids and said, "Jump in children, and have a nice ride home. Mamma and I will take the subway."

Two stuffy old dowagers were sitting in a cab. One turned to the other and said, "These cab drivers make so much money they all have homes on the Island." The two women went on talking about how wealthy the driver should be. He remained silent. Finally one of the matrons said to the other— "Hump, some service. There's not even an ashtray back here."

At this point the driver turned and said, "Oh, just throw it on the floor, I have a woman who comes in once a week."

A cab driver who knocked down a pedestrian was being bawled out by a cop. "Wassamatter" the officer yelled, "Ya blind?"

"Wassamatter," replied the cabbie, "I hit her, didn't I?"

I know a guy who is so rich he takes taxicabs to go to the drive-in movies.

TEACHERS (see also Schools, College, University)

TEACHER: Bobby, can you tell me where the elephant is found?
BOBBY: Well, teacher, the elephant is such a large animal that is is hardly ever lost.

TEACHER: Willie, what are you drawing?
WILLIE: I'm drawing a picture of God.
TEACHER: But Willie, you mustn't do that; nobody knows what God looks like.
WILLIE: Well, they will when I get this done.

FATHER: And how did Johnny do in his history examination today?
MOTHER: Oh not very well, but it wasn't his fault. Why they asked him things that happened before the poor boy was born.

TEACHER: Johnny, why are you late for school every morning?

JOHNNY: Well, every time I come to the corner a sign says "School—Go Slow."

TEACHER: Johnny, where was the Declaration of Independence signed?
JOHNNY: At the bottom, I guess.

MOTHER: Well, Jimmy, do you think your teacher likes you?
JIMMY: I think so, because she always puts a big kiss on all my homework.

MOTHER: Well, dear, what did they teach you on your first day at school?
LITTLE GIRL: Nothing much; I've got to go again.

TEACHER: Johnny, did your father write this essay for you on "Why I love teacher?"
JOHNNY: No, he didn't; mother stopped him.

FATHER: Why were you kept late at school today?
SON: I didn't know where the Azores were.
FATHER: Well, in the future just remember where you put things.

TEACHER: Now, who can tell me what Caesar exclaimed when Brutus stabbed him?
TOMMY: Ouch!

TEACHER: And what is your name?
NEW BOY: Charles.
TEACHER: Charles what?
NEW BOY: Oh that's all right; just call me Charles.

FATHER: I got a note from your teacher today.
SON: That's all right Dad, I won't tell anyone.

TEACHER: When was Rome built?
TOMMY: At night.
TEACHER: Who told you that?
TOMMY: You did. You said Rome wasn't built in a day.

TEACHER: How was it your homework sums were all correct for once?
PUPIL: Dad is away from home.

TEACHER: Who can tell me where we can find mangoes?
PUPIL: Yes, miss . . . wherever woman goes.

TEACHER: And what was Nelson's farewell address?
JOHNNY: Heaven, ma'am.

TEETH (see also Dentist)

1ST MAN: She has teeth just like pearls.
2ND MAN: Yeah . . . she and Pearl got them at the same dentist.

1ST MAN: I know where you can get false teeth for one dollar.
2ND MAN: That's impossible.
1ST MAN: Didn't you ever hear of buck teeth?

PATIENT: Do you extract teeth painlessly?
DENTIST: Not always . . . the other day I nearly dislocated my wrist.

PATIENT: Have you been a dentist very long?
DENTIST: No, I was a riveter till I got too nervous to work high up.

PATIENT: Hey, that wasn't the tooth I wanted pulled.
DENTIST: Take it easy. I'm coming to it.

I believe the members of the dental profession are the only men who can tell a women to open or close her mouth and get away with it.

TELEGRAMS (see also Letters, Mail)

Max was sitting in his office when the intercom buzzed. Max flipped the switch and his partner Sam in the next room said, "Listen I got an important telegram."
MAX: So go ahead and read it.

SAM: Wait. The secretary's here; she'll read it.

MAX: Go ahead, darling.

SECRETARY: Must have ten gross ... stop ... Ladies' gloves stop ... Assorted colors ... stop ... Pay top price ... stop ...

MAX: Sam, will you leave that girl alone and let her read the telegram ... this is business ...

Husband and wife vaudeville team were backstage after opening night at the theater when a Western Union boy arrived and handed the wife a telegram:

HUSBAND: What did you get— a *billet doux* from an admirer?

WIFE: No ... a bill due from the phone company.

A lawyer wired his client, "Your mother-in-law passed away in her sleep last night. Shall we order burial, embalming or cremation?" Back came a reply to the lawyer, "Take no chances, order all three."

HUSBAND: That telegram is from Western Union.

WIFE: Oh, did I marry a genius. How did you know?

HUSBAND: I recognized the writing.

TELEPHONE

"Hello, is this the city bridge department?"

"Yes, what do you want?"

"How many points do you get for a little slam?"

"Is this the Weather Bureau?"

"Yes."

"How about a shower tonight?"

"It's all right with me; take it if you need it."

VOICE OVER PHONE: Is this the lady that washed?

SOCIETY SNOB: Indeed not, I should say not.

VOICE OVER PHONE: Why, you dirty thing.

OPERATOR: The number you called is out of order.

MAN: That's strange—she was all right last nite.

Did you see where the man from San Francisco and the Hollywood girl were married by telegraph?

Yeah, it was a western union.

In Teheran when you use the phone you make what is known as Persian to Persian calls.

The meek little man completed the phone call, hung up and then chuckled as his dime clinked back into the slot. Suddenly the telephone rang. "Are you the man who just made a call?" the operator asked. "Well, then, by mistake

I returned your dime. Will you please redeposit it?"

"Sorry, ma'am," the caller said in a typical telephone operator's monotone. "I can't do that, but if you send me your name and address I'll be glad to send the dime to you in stamps."

The owner of a tavern received a phone call at 5 A.M.
DRUNK: Hey, buddy, when do you open your joint?
OWNER: You can't get in until noon.
DRUNK: I don't want to get in. . . . I want to get out.

WIFE: (calling husband at home. Husband has been waiting for her for hours.)
WIFE: Darling, I'm in the car now and I'll be home in ten minutes.
HUSBAND: If you're in the car how come you're phoning me?
WIFE: I took a short cut through a drug store.

Drunk makes a phone call at the bar.
DRUNK: Hello Charlie.
VOICE: This isn't Charlie. You have the wrong number.
DRUNK: Oh I'm sorry. . . . I hope I didn't wake you up.
VOICE: Oh that's all right. I had to get up to answer the phone anyway.

Boy calls the house of a girl who has just broken off with him . . . and finds the girl's mother on the other end of the line.
BOY: Hello, is Jane in?
MOTHER: Who's calling?
BOY: This is Arnold.
MOTHER: Jane's not in.
BOY: Do you know when she'll be back?
MOTHER: Wait a second . . . I'll ask her.

HARRY: What were you doing in that phone booth for a half hour?
CHARLIE: I was talking to my girl.
HARRY: Who's that coming out of the booth now.
CHARLIE: Oh that's my girl. . . .

TELEVISION (see also Late, Late Show, Radio, Actors)

Did you hear about the TV announcer's kid saying his bedtime prayers? The kid said, "Please make me a good boy until my birthday—and now a short commercial about an electric set."

Entertainment is all right for some, but we prefer television programs that make you stop and think. Our favorites are "Network Difficulties" and "One Moment, Please."

The difference between television and vaudeville.—In vaudeville, if you lay an egg in Boston, you make up for it by doing well in Providence the following week; but on television, if you lay an egg you lay it all over the country —it's an omelet!

A man sitting at a television show was trying to watch the monitor, but a woman sitting in front of him was wearing a hat that blocked his view.

MAN: Hey, lady, will you please remove your hat? I can't see the comedian.

LADY: That's all right. Just laugh when I laugh.

Overheard at the Garry Moore show:

MOORE: I quit . . . I quit.

KIRBY: Garry, you can't quit the show.

MOORE: Oh those sponsors. They always order me around. Moore do this . . . Moore do that . . . Moore . . . Moore . . . There's only one way to make them stop.

KIRBY: Change your sponsor?

MOORE: No, change my name.

TV rating service called a man who answered the phone—

RATING SERVICE: Who are you listening to right now, sir?

MAN: My wife.

Union official to new TV performer:

OFFICIAL: Were you ever in AFTRA?

PERFORMER: No . . . but I was in India.

Fight Manager to Fighter:

MANAGER: You gotta get knocked down in the 4th round.

FIGHTER: Why?

MANAGER: I sold a spot commercial on the soles of your shoes for that time.

Everything on TV nowadays is canned. There's canned laughter, canned applause, canned crying. . . . A can opener and a little ham and you've got a show. Last week I opened a can of tuna and out came "Sea Hunt."

GROUCHO: What does your husband do for a hobby?

WIFE: He's a do-it-yourself taxidermist.

GROUCHO: A do-it-yourself taxidermist?

WIFE: Yes. Every night at dinner he stuffs himself.

. . . TV or not TV, that is the question. . . . Alas, poor radio, I knew it well. . . .

A guy who didn't have a TV set drilled a hole through to his neighbor's apartment and watched wrestling every night . . . until he found out they had no television set, either.

Television shows are so bad these days that one fellow sold his bar.

Drunk watching wrestling on TV: "This is a lousy picture! No plot."

TEXAS

Texan viewing Niagara Falls with a friend who lives in Buffalo:
FRIEND: Look at that beautiful sight. I bet you don't have anything in Texas to match the Falls.
TEXAN: Nope, but we got a plumber in Dallas who could stop that leak in ten minutes.

A Texan was rather worried to receive his check back from the bank marked "Insufficient Funds" . . . until he saw a further notation reading: "Ours—not yours."

Did you hear about the Texas child who walked up to Santa Claus and said "What can I do for you?"

A Texas oil tycoon went to a dentist who told him quite honestly, "Your teeth are in perfect shape. There's no work necessary—they don't even need polishing." "Start drilling," ordered the tycoon, "I feel lucky today."

Did ya hear about the Texan who wanted his son to learn to spell, so he hired a college marching band to spell out words for him?

Texas is where the men yell "Remember the Alamo" and the women yell "Remember the Alimony."

A Texan was asked how much land he owned.
"Oh, just about fifty acres. Small little piece!"
"Where is it located?" he was asked.
"In downtown Dallas."

A Wall Street financier asked a Texas oil tycoon, "How's business holding up in your part of the world?"
"Son," drawled the oil man, "in Texas we do more business by accident than you do on Wall Street on purpose."

When you find a pair of boots on the floor with a big ten gallon hat on top of them, what have you got? . . . A Texan with all the hot air let out of him.

THANKSGIVING

"So you had a nice Thanksgiving?"

"Yeah."

"Well, I wanted to come over to your house for dinner, but I couldn't make it. What did you have to be thankful for?"

"I was thankful you couldn't come over for dinner."

"I like turkey all right, but that turkey skeleton is going to last for weeks."

"You shouldn't say skeleton—it's a carcass."

"It may be a carcass when you get through with it, but when I get through with it, it's a skeleton—the inside is out and the outside is off."

"I suppose you got the best part of the turkey?"

"You bet. But I was fourteen years old before I knew a turkey had anything else but a neck."

"So you had Thanksgiving dinner at your house? Did you like the turkey?"

"Well, that turkey couldn't have gone any faster if it had been streamlined."

ICEMAN: What have you been eating?

COOK: Some giraffes left from Thanksgiving.

ICEMAN: I thought you had turkey.

COOK: We did. It might just as well be giraffe—I just had a neck.

The poor turkey, he's hit in the neck, loses his head, they break his legs, knock the stuffing out of him, cut him to the heart, and pick on him for weeks.

THEATRE (see also Agents, Actors)

1ST MAN: How are the acoustics in the new theatre?

2ND MAN: Great. The actors can hear every cough.

1ST MAN: Did the new play have a happy ending?

2ND MAN: Sure. Everybody was glad it was over.

1ST GIRL: No matter what they say about actors and their temperaments, I think they're the best-hearted and most charitable in the world.

2ND GIRL: Charitable? I suppose you're right. I never heard of one yet who wouldn't take the other's part if he had a chance.

The story is told about a man who stood in line so long for tickets to *My Fair Lady* that he ended up with three instead of two; two for the show, one for parking.

1ST MAN: Do you know how much that singer earns?
2ND MAN: No, how much?
1ST MAN: At least $75,000.
2ND MAN: Why, that's as much as the President of the United States makes!
1ST MAN: Yeah, and the President can't even sing a note.

A man went to the theatre for the first time and walked over to the box office and asked for a ticket.
TICKET CLERK: Do you want one downstairs for $5.80 or one upstairs for $2.50?
MAN: Why, what's playing upstairs?

I've always had the theatre in my veins—sometimes I wish I had blood.

My advice to stage-struck young ladies who want to break into show business: Change your hair style, learn how to walk, buy a sexy wardrobe and before you know it—you'll be married and have six kids and forget all about the mishmash.

The theatre is my home. Where else can you get an apartment nowadays?

I know one theatre that would definitely be safe in case of an atomic attack—it never had a hit.

During the height of the vaudeville era when Alexander Pantages owned a chain of theatres, his Salt Lake City theatre was a coveted booking. One song-and-dance team was disgruntled because of losing the Salt Lake booking, so they threatened to cancel the rest of the Pantages bookings and wired Pantages: EITHER PLAY US AT SALT LAKE CITY OR COUNT US OUT. They received the following wire in reply: ONE, TWO, THREE, FOUR, FIVE, SIX, SEVEN, EIGHT, NINE, TEN! ALEXANDER PANTAGES.

THIEVES (see also Crooks, Jail, Cops, Police)

DAN: My cousin is learning to steal.
ANN: Learning to steal—but why?
DAN: So he can follow in his father's fingerprints.

VICTIM: But my watch isn't a good one. Its value is only sentimental.
BURGLAR: That doesn't matter—I'm sentimental.

ROSE: What does your husband do?

MARY: He's interested in uplift business.

ROSE: Uplift business?

MARY: Yes, he goes around and says, "Stick 'em up."

THOMAS, DANNY

In today's modern times the last thing a woman does by hand is put her finger in the wedding ring.

The firing squad was lined up. They put the blindfold on the political prisoner. The head of the firing squad raised his hand for the men to shoot, when all of a sudden the prisoner started to shout, "Fidel Castro is a bum." The captain of the firing squad stopped everything, walked over to the prisoner and said, "Listen you wanna get yourself in trouble?"

There was a long line waiting in the early morning in front of a clothing store that advertised a special sale. A man walked to the front of the line. The people grabbed him and pushed him to the end. Again he walked to the front and they beat him up and shoved him to the back. Once more he headed for the front of the line and they kicked him and pushed him into the gutter. Finally, he got up, brushed him-

self off, and said to a man at the end of the line, "If they do that once more—I'm not opening the store."

Guy saw a sign on a restaurant that said, Elephant Ear on a Bun. Guy went in to try it. Ordered from the waiter. Five minutes later the waiter came back and said, "I'm sorry, we can't serve you the sandwich." Guy said, "Aha! It's a lie. You really don't have elephant ears here. You're out of them. Fake!" Waiter said, "No, sir, we have the elephant ears—but we're out of buns."

TIPPING (see also Waiter, Restaurant)

CUSTOMER: Does your firm allow you to take tips?

CLERK: No sir, but if they asked if you gave me one, I'd lie like anything to protect you.

1ST GUEST: I'm sure I don't know why they call this hotel The Palms. I've never seen a palm anywhere near the place.

2ND GUEST: You'll see them before you go. It's a pleasant little surprise the whole staff keeps for the guests until the last day of their stay.

AMERICAN TOURIST TO BUTLER (after looking over historic

castle): I've made a stupid mistake. I tipped his lordship instead of you.

BUTLER: That's awkward, sir. I'll never get it now.

DINER: And here's something for your pains, waiter.

WAITER: Thanks . . . but what is it?

DINER: A band-aid.

If you can't get away for a vacation, you can get the same feeling by tipping every second person you see.

TITLES

Song Title: Since I Put a Bar in the Back of My Car . . . I've Been Driving Myself to Drink.

Book Title: Since My Wife Left Me I've Been Going to Pieces.

Book Title: The Stages of Man, or From Infancy to Adultery.

Song Title: We Were All Out of Firewood . . . so Father Came Home With a Load.

Book Title: Case of The Missing Ring or . . . Who Washed Out the Bathtub?

Book Title: Life in a Pickle Factory or Down By The Old Dill Stream.

She Was Only the Stableman's Daughter but All the Horse Manure.

She Was Only a Trainman's Daughter . . . Loco With No Motive.

Book: The Swiss Alps by O. Leo Layie.

She Was Only the Baker's Daughter but She Knew What to Do With Her Dough.

TOUGHNESS

During a practical exercise at a European Military Police base in Germany, the instructor was giving a class on unarmed self-defense. After presenting several different situations to the class, he asked a student:

"What steps would you take if someone were coming at you with a knife?"

"Big ones!" he replied.

A young boy was preparing to go on his first overnight hike with the Boy Scouts. It was March and still chilly, but they were planning to use sleeping bags.

"Would you please put my electric blanket on three tonight, Mom? I've got to start toughening up for roughing it."

TRAFFIC (see also transportation, Auto, Cars, Pedestrian)

"What are your taxi rates, sir?"

"Well, we charge 25¢ the first mile, then 10¢ for each additional mile."

"I'll walk the first mile; you can pick me up the second mile."

"You know, my speedometer is broken."

"Why you're crazy. It's working perfectly."

"That's funny. The last time I stopped to look at it, the thing wouldn't even register."

SHE: I didn't like to ride with you, you're too reckless.

HE: Yes, we have had some tight squeezes, haven't we?

WIFE: You missed that last red light.

HUSBAND: (angrily) Well, what do you want me to do—go back and hit it?

HILLIARD: Does your girl know much about automobiles?

CLYDE: Gosh, no. She asked me if I cooled the car by stripping the gears.

POLICEMAN: How did the accident happen?

MOTORIST: My wife fell asleep in the back seat.

"Want a ride, lady?"

"No, thanks, one is all I can walk back from in one night."

The traffic was so bad that rescue planes had to drop supplies and food to the Good Humor man.

I read where a man is knocked down by a car every five minutes, in traffic. That guy must be made of iron.

The only time a pedestrian has the right of way is in an ambulance on the way to the hospital.

A rookie cop was asked by his sergeant what he was doing away from his corner, where he was supposed to be directing traffic. He said, "I want another corner, Sarge. The traffic at my corner is always getting balled up."

TRAILERS

The guy who invented the trailer probably got the idea from his grandmother's bustle, because it's something that's tied on behind.

TRAINS

"For the east is east, and west is west,"

"And never the train he'll meet."

CONDUCTOR: I've been on this road ten years now, and I know what I'm talking about—

PASSENGER: Ten years, huh? What station did you get on at?

OLD DEACON (to profane young man sitting near him on train): Young man, you are on the straight road to perdition.

CHAP: Just my infernal luck—I bought a ticket to Reading.

1ST MAN: I always eat garlic before I go on a train ride.

2ND MAN: Why's that?

1ST MAN: I breathe in the conductor's face and he gives me a wide berth.

CONDUCTOR: This train only goes eight miles an hour.

PASSENGER: Is it a regular train or a milk train?

CONDUCTOR: What's the difference? D'you want to ride it or milk it?

MAN: Is Train #85 on time?

CONDUCTOR: No, we paid cash for it.

FATHER: Are there half-fares for children?

CONDUCTOR: Yes, under fourteen.

FATHER: That's all right. I only have five.

PASSENGER: Why did they build this station so far out of town?

CONDUCTOR: They wanted to get it near the railroad.

TRAMPS

THE LADY: I gave you a piece of pie last week, and you've been sending your friends here ever since.

THE TRAMP: You're mistaken, lady. Them were my enemies.

1ST MAN: Y'aint y'self no more. Watsa matter? Sick or somethin'?

2ND BUM: Got insomnia. Keep wakin' up every few days.

TRAMP: Would you take a fellow's last cent for a pack of cigarettes?

MERCHANT: Yes, sir, I have none to give away.

The tramp gently picked up the cigarettes and left his penny on the counter.

HOBO: Boss, will you give me a dime for a sandwich?

GENT: Let's see the sandwich.

A wealthy gentleman approached, and on being accosted by a bum, replied, "I will give you a nickel if you will tell me what you are going to do with it."

The tramp replied, "First I will go across the street and get a swell feed; then I will go down to the

Ford Agency and buy me a car in which I will ride out to one of the exclusive sub-divisions nearby and buy myself a villa; then I will purchase a yacht and tour abroad."

The gentleman drew a quarter from his pocket and said, "Take this, my friend and live in happiness for the remainder of your days."

OLD LADY: Are you really content to spend your life walking around begging?
HOBO: No, lady. Many's the time I wished I had an auto.

"I wish I were in your shoes."
"Why?"
"Mine leak."

"Do you know they have over a thousand beds in the ranch?"
"Aw, that's a lot of bunk."

"I beg pardon, lady, but what do you do for vermin at this place?"
"Not anything, brother, scram."

TRANSPORTATION (see also Trips, Railroad)

"Can I get out at Pudsea?" inquired the fussy old gentleman, who wanted to go there.

"You can, sir," replied the guard, "but I shouldn't if I were you. The train doesn't stop there."

"Lady, you'll have to pay half fare for that boy."
"But, conductor, he's only four years old."
"Well, he looks like a six-year-old."
"Sir, I have been married only four years."
"Lady, I'm not asking for a confession; I'm asking for a half-fare ticket."

PASSENGER: What makes this train go so slow?
IRATE CONDUCTOR: If you don't like it, get off and walk.
PASSENGER: I would, only I'm not expected until train time.

"My aunt was killed because she got out of wrong side of the bed."
"How in the world was she killed? That's usually not fatal."
"Well, you see she was in the upper berth."

The locomotive was not behaving as a true locomotive should. First it would move forward a hundred yards or so, and then, with a good deal of puffing, it would shift back to its original position. For ten minutes this had been going on, while the passengers raved all along the train.

At last one of them, unable to contain himself any longer, hailed the conductor.

"What on earth is the matter?" he demanded.

"Well," the conductor said, "I'm not sure, but I think the engineer is teaching his wife how to drive."

PORTER: Shall I brush you off, sir?
PASSENGER: No thanks, I'll climb off like the rest of the passengers.

The young woman kissed the man goodbye before boarding the train. As she sat down in the Pullman, she burst into tears. Noticing that she had a wedding ring on her finger, the sympathetic conductor said, "Does it distress you so much to leave your husband?"

"I'm not leaving my husband," she sobbed, "I'm going back to him."

JOE: Say, can you tell me why there are fewer railroad accidents than automobile accidents?
JIM: Well, perhaps not exactly, but I think it is because the engineer isn't always hugging the fireman.

"What's the first thing to do, when you park with a girl?"
"Well, I set the emergency brake and clutch."

Sign at a busy small town filling station:
"Automobiles Washed: One Dollar"
"Austins Dunked: Fifty Cents"

CHAUFFEUR: Sir, I feel sure that we just ran over a human being.
TOURIST: Excellent, Hawkins, then we are still on the right road.

We heard of the man who stepped out in the road and asked for a lift. An accommodating motorist obliged him by lifting him several feet.

And we know that men still die with their boots on . . . yeah, on the accelerator.

Aw, he's too drunk to ride in the back seat, let him drive.

TRAVEL (see also Transportation, Trips, Geography)

After looking at a prospective tourist's passport photo, a fellow at a travel bureau commented, "If the owner really looks like that, he's too sick to travel."

I heard that Washington is so economy-minded these days that Vice-President Johnson is flying Tourist.

When my wife packs for a trip, the only thing she leaves behind is a note for the milkman.

TRIPS (see also Travel)

"I went to a hotel for a change and rest."

"Did you get it?"

"The bellboy got the change and the hotel got the rest."

"Did you enjoy your weekend trip?"

"The trip going was terrible."

"Have a flat tire?"

"Yeah—but I made her walk home."

"Don't you ever take a vacation?"

"I can't get away."

"Why? Can't the firm do without you?"

"Quite easily. That's what I don't want them to find out."

TRUTH

Overheard in a Western saloon:

1ST MAN: I believe in calling a spade a spade.

2ND MAN: That's right, friend. There was a man who nearly lost his life here by gettin' into a game an' tryin' to call a spade a club.

1ST MAN: Well, and did the fortune-teller tell you the truth about yourself?

2ND MAN: Yeah, but it was a waste of time . . . my wife's been doing it for years.

1ST SALESMAN: I suppose I'll be up all night. I have to make out my expense account.

2ND SALESMAN: Why don't you tell the truth and get a good night's rest?

A tax delinquent's conscience bothered him, so he wrote the following letter to the Bureau of Internal Revenue:

Gentlemen:

I haven't been able to sleep at night because I cheated on last year's income tax.

Enclosed find my check for $1,000. If I find I still can't sleep, I'll send you the balance.

One woman to another:

"If you stop telling lies about me, I'll stop telling the truth about you."

TURKEY

They must have a girl's ball team in the Sultan's harem. One day one of the girls asked the Sultan if she was in tomorrow's line-up.

The fact that Turkish women are covering their faces only proves that the men don't count on their faces—they rely on figures.

TWINS AND TRIPLETS (see also Babies, Kids)

At the christening of newborn twins the clergyman asked the parents what names they had chosen.

"Steak and Kidney," replied the father.

"You fool," cried his wife, "it's Kate and Sydney."

HUSBAND TO WIFE: Just because you had twins, doesn't mean you now have to go through life exaggerating.

Mr. Jones recently became the father of triplets. The minister stopped him on the street to congratulate him.

MINISTER: Well, Jones, I hear the stork has smiled on you.

JONES: Smiled on me! He plum laughed out loud!

Little Dorothy had just seen triplets for the first time and came running excitedly to her mother:

"Oh, Mummy, just imagine. I saw a lady that had twins—and a spare."

❖❖

U

UGLY

I asked the girl in front of me at the movies to remove her hat. She became very angry. She wasn't wearing any. I liked her face. It reminded me of my home —especially the front stoop. I began talking to her and commented favorably about her wavy hair. Later, I found out that her hair was straight, but her head was wavy.

His second wife is so ugly that two weeks before he took her home he told his children ghost stories so they wouldn't be frightened when they saw her.

She had a real shady background.—Why not? She had hips like a beach umbrella.

Sylvia had blue eyes, red lips and thirteen white teeth. When she smiled, she looked like the

Colonial flag. That wasn't bad—but when she laughed she looked like George Washington.

There was one gal named Abigail Schwartz who had a beautiful face except for her nose. She had to lift it up to eat. But a girl's face isn't everything. Listen to this: Abigail's measurements were 38–23–38.—Those were her leg measurements.

An acquaintance tells of a wise guy husband saying to a visiting friend, "Yes, that was my wife who opened the door for you—do you think I would hire a maid that homely?"

Some girl I never went with was so ugly that when she came into a room the mice jumped on the chairs.—She used to model bicycle pumps. And what charm! When she left the room, she gave it an added glow. She was a good dancer, though. They called her "crazy legs." She had four of them. She used to be an Arthur Murray dance instructor but she finally gave it up. She couldn't teach Arthur how to dance. But when you come right down to it (and you had to—she was four feet tall), she had everything a man desires—muscles and a beard.

Her head sticking out of a cellar door would start a hockey game in anybody's neighborhood.

She's so ugly she rents herself out for Hallowe'en parties.

She's so ugly her face looks like it's done up in curlers.

She was too ugly to have her face lifted so they lowered her body instead.

She used to do scarecrow work by appointment only.

If all the girls are sisters under the skin, I wish she'd go back under there and send out her sister.

UNDERTAKERS (see also Funeral, Death)

He looks as if an undertaker started to work on him and was suddenly called away.

Sign in an undertaker's window: DRIVE CAREFULLY—WE CAN WAIT.

A kid stole a sign from a nursery and stuck it in front of an undertaking parlor. It read: LET US DO YOUR PLANTING FOR YOU.

The boss had been keeping the girl on salary for years . . . even after she stopped working in the office. When he died he left her money to buy a stone. After she bought the five-karat ring, she had enough money to arrange for the funeral, but she wanted to conserve it.

The undertaker arranged for a five-hundred-dollar service in which he would furnish an orchestra, choir, ten limousines with chauffeurs, and all would be in tuxedos; but she didn't want to spend that much.

For $250 the undertaker arranged for the cars, but no chauffeurs, he'd wear a plain blue suit, and the orchestra would be replaced by a phonograph record. Still, she didn't think she could afford it. He offered her the $100 funeral, where he'd wear sports clothes and the congregation would hum, but she didn't think so . . .

Finally he said, "For $25, I come out in my pajamas, but I oughtta warn you, I get a couple of laughs!"

Gambling is rampant in Las Vegas. The undertaker was complaining to his friend that business was terrible. "With the exception of a few night club comics, nobody's been dying here recently."

His friend sympathized with him until he walked in back of the funeral parlor and noticed six stiffs lying there. "Why ya bum!" he shouted. "I thought you said business was lousy. What about those six stiffs back there?"

"Sssssshhh," silenced the undertaker, "five of them are shills!"

It's always foolish to try to put anything over on an undertaker . . . sooner or later, he'll have you dead to rights.

UNEMPLOYMENT (see also Poor)

PROFESSOR: So you think you could end all unemployment, do you? And just how would you accomplish that, may I ask?

COLLEGE VET: It's simple. I'd just put all the men in the world on one island, and all the women on another.

PROFESSOR: How would that solve the unemployment problem?

COLLEGE VET: Why, they'd all be building boats!

UNIVERSITY (see also College, Campus)

A university is an institution which has room for 2,000 in the classroom and over 50,000 in the stadium.

A well-known professor kept warning his college students about the perils of sin. "Would you," he asked his class one afternoon, his voice trembling with excitement, "trade a lifetime of peace of mind and happiness for just one hour of wild, animal pleasure?" A soprano voice attached to a pretty thing was heard from the back of the room, "How do you make it last an hour?"

USED CAR DEALERS

USED CAR DEALER TO CAR OWNER: Let me put it this way . . . if your car were a horse, it would have to be shot. Come to think of it, your car is shot.

USED CAR DEALER MAKING SPIEL: And in this car, you never get car-sickness. We give you a supply of pills to take before each payment is due.

A man just out of the army bought a used car. As the deal was not above board, the dealer refused to give the young man a bill of sale. However, the young man was insistent and finally the dealer said wearily: "Look here, you've got the car, I've got the money, everybody's satisfied—why on earth do you insist upon a bill of sale?"

"Well," explained the young man, "When I die, Saint Peter won't let me into heaven when I tell him what I've paid because he'll think I'm lying . . . and I don't want to look all over Hell for you to prove that I'm not."

A used car dealer who switched to used TV sales, pitched this line to a customer: "This set's hardly been used. It belonged to an old lady in Westchester with weak eyes."

❖❖

V

VACATIONS: (see also Travel, Trips)

BLONDE: You really ought to come to Shrimpton with me next summer. I had a wonderful time there this year. I won a beauty competition.

REDHEAD: No, I think I'd rather go to a more crowded place.

A Scotsman was so tight he wouldn't even tip his hat. After sixty years his wife talked him into taking a vacation, an ocean voyage to America.

He complained on the entire trip about the expense and was still grumbling as he was walking down the gangplank. Suddenly, he noticed a deep-sea diver emerge. "If I had an outfit like that," burned the Scotsman, "I'd have walked over, too."

The boy was on a vacation. The girl was on a vacation, and romance was working overtime.

The fourth drink, and he said, "Y'know, one more drink and I'll feel it."

And she said, "Y'know, one more drink and I'll let you!"

Vacations are easy to plan. The boss tells you when and the wife tells you where.

VAUDEVILLE (see also Comedians)

A vaudeville ventriloquist whose engagements had become fewer and fewer finally dropped off altogether. In desperation the ventriloquist thought of the only possible way he could utilize his talent. He became a spiritualist, using his trick voice, of course, as the ghost's. One night a large bejeweled woman called on the swami. Could he get in touch with her recently departed husband? Could he! In no time at all, the "spirit" was talking quite animatedly with his delighted wife. When the lights came on, the woman thanked the medium, showered him with praise and asked the charge. "That was the $50 seance," he replied, preening like a peacock. Then he added magnanimously, "For $100 madam, your husband will talk to you while drinking a glass of water."

A small-town vaudeville comic was in a plane crash and awoke to find himself in a strange place. "Where am I?" he asked a fellow standing beside him. "You're in Hell," he was informed. "That's my agent for you," sighed the comic, "he's never booked me in a good spot yet."

A TV salesman was trying to convince a vaudevillian to buy a portable model. "Just imagine," he said, "when you're on tour, sitting in a lonely hotel room, all you have to do is press a button and suddenly a gorgeous, scantily dressed girl will be standing in front of you." "The hotels I stop at," said the ham, "I can get the same thing without television."

VIOLIN (see also Music, Instruments)

"He's always up to his chin in music.'"
"Why?"
"He plays violin."

"How much does that violin player get?"
"Eighty dollars a week."
"How much does that guy with the bass fiddle make?"
"Oh you mean the bull fiddle? Sixty dollars per week."
"Well, tell him to stick it under his chin and get the other twenty dollars a week."

"What do you do with that violin?"
"I play numbers."
"You play numbers?"
"That's it. I play any number you want."
"Play number six."

"I hope you'll excuse me; I haven't played this violin since October."
"What year?"

"Don't be too hard on her, she had a great sorrow."
"How was that?"
"She wanted to be a great violinist, but she couldn't tell which chin to put the fiddle under."

"The strings of his fiddle are made of pure catgut."

"From the way it sounds to me I don't think the cat has passed away entirely."

"What do you think of him as a violinist?"
"I think he's grand. He was playing this afternoon and I was accompanying him on the piano."
"What happened?"
"In the middle of it, the piano got up and walked away."

"I used to play the violin, but I gave it up."
"Why?"
"It gave me bumps on the back of the head."
"How so?"
"I sat in front of the trombone player."

VOCABULARY (see also Words)

Pity the minister who bought a used car and then didn't have the vocabulary to run it.

VOCALIST (see also Singer, Warbler)

"Why isn't your mother here tonight?"
"She's home singing a duet."
"With whom?"
"With me."
"But you're here."
"I know, but I finished first."

"If that crooner sings to you again, I'll make him pay the same way he sings."
"How do you mean?"
"Through the nose."

"I have a larger repertoire than Kate Smith."
"You have?"
"Yes."
"Then you should go on a diet."

"I held a note for sixty-five seconds last night."
"That's nothing. My banker has held one of mine for three years."

"Can he sing?"
"He's so flat you can roll him under the door."

"She's going abroad to finish her musical education.
"Where did she get the money?"
"The neighbors all chipped in."

"I just love your songs. When I hear you I go home and sing and cry and sing and cry and sing and cry."
"Why do you cry?"
"Because I can't sing."

"I certainly envy that tenor who is singing now."
"Well, I think his voice is terrible."
"Yes, but think of the nerve he's got."

"Your son has a wonderful voice."
"I suppose you'll have it trained?"
"Yes, sir! I'm going to build the best bathroom money can buy."

"He's got a shortstop voice."
"What do you mean by shortstop voice?"
"It's somewhere between second and third base."

"Can you sing?"
"Sure, anything."
"Do you know 'Old Man River'?"
"Yes, what's he doing now?"

A young woman with aspirations to be a singer went to a vocal teacher for a tryout. The professor sat down and played a selection while the ambitious singer poured out her choicest assortment of notes. When all was over the prof swung around on his stool and said:
"Ach. Never have I heard such a voice. I blay on der vite keys and I blay on der black keys, but you sing in der cracks."

I used to sing soprano and bass in the choir. In fact, my voice changed so often they used to have to swing me on a pendulum from one side of the church to the other.

"I used to sing with a small quartette myself."

"A small quartette?"

"Yes—there were just two of us."

"Are you *really* a singer?"

"Oh, yes, I once sang at the Hollywood Bowl."

"Really—What was the aria?"

"Oh, about 200,000 square feet."

"I'd like to have you sing now. Are you prepared?"

"Oh yes, I practiced all afternoon in my dressing room."

"Oh, is *that* what it was? I thought you were caught in a door."

"Is that a popular song he is singing?"

"It was, before he started singing it."

"There's a soprano across the court from my apartment that's driving me nuts."

"Singing with her windows up?"

"No, undressing with her shades up."

W

WAGES (see also Employment, Salary, Money)

EMPLOYER: Why do you ask me for a raise?

EMPLOYEE: Sir, I wouldn't ask for a raise but somehow my kids found out that other families eat three times a day.

WAITER AND WAITRESS (see also Tipping, Restaurant, Food)

WAITRESS: Would you like to drink Canada Dry, Sir?

WAITER: Yeah, but I'm only here for the week-end.

"What's on the menu today, waiter?"

"Two spots of gravy and a ketchup stain. Just a minute and I'll get a clean one."

"This soup is ice cold, waiter!"

"Why, the very idea. It sure didn't feel like that when my thumb slipped in."

"Waiter, bring me some coffee without cream."

"We haven't any cream sir, but we have milk—you could have some coffee without milk."

"Here is a piece of rubber tire in my hash."
"No doubt. The motor is replacing the horse everywhere."

"What's wrong with these eggs?"
"Don't ask me; I only laid the table."

"Young man, don't you know you'll ruin your stomach by drinking?"
"Oh, thash all right. It won't show with my coat on."

Boss: Who broke this china plate?
Waiter: The cat, sir.
Boss: What cat?
Waiter: What, ain't we got one?

"Just look at the dust on this sideboard, Mary. It's at least six weeks old."
"Then it ain't nothing to do with me, Mum, I've only been here four weeks."

"Do you serve fish here?"
"Sit down, we serve anybody."

Sarcastic Patron: Don't bother to spill that hot coffee on my neck.
Waitress (absentmindedly): No bother at all.

"These are the best oysters we've had for a year."
"Let's see some you've had for a month."

"Waiter, are you sure this ham was cured?"
"Yes, sir."
"Well, it's had a relapse."

A "Honeymoon Salad" is "lettuce alone."

Customer: What does this mean? There's a fly in the bottom of the tea cup!
Waitress: How do I know? I'm a waitress, not a fortune teller.

First Diner: Waitress, bring me a steak.
Second Diner: One for me too— a tender one.
Waitress: (yelling back to cook) Two steaks, one tender.

"Waiter, this fish is awful."
"Why did you insist that I order it?"
"Because otherwise, Monsieur, it would have been served to us in the kitchen."

Diner: I can't eat this food—call the proprietor.
Waiter: It's no use, sir, he won't eat it either.

Sign seen recently in restaurant:

"Our hash is made, not accumulated."

"Will you call me a waiter?"
"Certainly. You're a waiter."

"Waiter, there's a fly in my ice cream."
"Let him freeze, and teach him a lesson."

"Do you serve good meals here?"
"Sure, look at the size of these flies."

JONES (in restaurant with wife): Hey, waiter, where's my honey?
WAITER: Sorry, sir, but she doesn't work here any more.

WAR (see also Army, Air Force)

A Norwegian, during the last war, was talking to the village quisling and asked him what he was going to do when the Allies won the war. The quisling said, "Oh, I'll just put my hat on and leave." The Loyalist said, "Yah, but what are going to put your hat on?"

The Air Force Captain boarded the MATS plane during the Korean War and spotted a seat next to an Army private. He was about to sit down when he noticed a card saying, "Reserved for Proper Load Distribution." So he proceeded to the seat behind it. Several others started toward the seat, read the sign and went on. But when a pretty well-stacked blonde headed for the seat, the Army man promptly removed the sign and placed it in its receptacle on the back of the seat in front of him. The blonde must have had the Proper Load Distribution because she sat next to him for the entire trip.

A personnel clerk at Fort Monmouth received a document in the ordinary course of business, initialed it and passed it on to the officer for whom it was intended. It promptly came back with a note attached: "This document did not concern you. Please erase your initials and initial the erasure."

The paratrooper was on his first jump and as he looked down he froze at the door. The jumpmaster glared at him and snapped, "Yellow." "I am not," retorted the trooper.
JUMPMASTER: Think you're tough?
TROOPER: Pretty tough.
JUMPMASTER: Think you can whip me?
TROOPER: I'd like to try.
JUMPMASTER: Okay, buddy, then just step outside.
And the trooper did.

A sailor brought his girl pearls back from the Pacific War, but she didn't seem too happy so he asked what was wrong.

GIRL: The clasp worries me. The one that comes after.

WARBLER (see also Singer, Vocalist)

"Why did you stop singing in the choir?"

"Because one day I didn't sing and someone asked if the organ had been fixed."

"My voice isn't big enough to fill an auditorium."

"It's bad enough to empty one."

"You ought to be with Caruso."

"But Caruso is dead."

"Take care of yourself!"

"So you want to sing in the choir?"

"Yes."

"What part?"

"Well, I went in as first bass, but they changed it to short stop and then they heard my voice."

"Come up to my house and sing."

"Why; do you like my voice?"

"No, but we want to break our lease."

"I was leading the singing and people were giving, giving, giving."

"I wish you'd come over and sing to my cows sometimes."

"That song haunts me."

"It should. You just murdered it."

"I have a lovely voice, you know, I sang at the Blank Theatre and the audience all ran out in the street."

"What did you do?"

"I went right out in the street and sang and drove them all back in the theatre again."

"Have you had a chance to practice since we've been on the road?"

"Yes, I practised in my hotel room this morning."

"So *that's* what it was—I wish you'd told me sooner, dear."

"Why?"

"I spent fifteen minutes oiling the door."

"I like to sing in the bathtub."

"I'm sorry I can't accommodate you, but no one around here uses one."

WARNING

This is the story about a fellow who shunned American ships to

Europe. Against the pleadings of his friends, he took a Russian boat. When told he would regret it, he sardonically replied, "Do me something—what can you do me?" When he was halfway across the ocean they sent him a radiogram to the Commie ship reading: IF YOU CAN'T KNOCK OFF KHRUSHCHEV, GET GROMYKO!

WEALTH (see also Money, Rich, Snob)

One way to get wealthy is to be able to determine when a piece of junk becomes an antique.

Two movie producers decided to play golf for the first time. On the way to a country club they purchased all the necessary equipment—shoes, sport togs, clubs and so forth—then checked in at the club. "I'm sorry," the starter told them, "but you can't play today." "But why not?" they protested. "Look we're all ready. New clubs, everything." "Sorry," repeated the starter, "but you can't play today. There aren't any caddies." The producers looked at each other. "So who cares?" said one. "For one day we'll take a Buick."

A proud sixteen-year-old turned into the family driveway at the wheel of the family Lincoln.

His father sat beside him. Several younger brothers converged on the scene.

"I passed my driving test," shouted the boy. "You guys can all move up one bike."

Mrs. Rappaport met Mrs. Ginsberg in Miami Beach.

MRS. RAPPAPORT: So where's your son Harold?

MRS. GINSBERG: He's being wheeled around by the valet in his private wheeling chair.

MRS. RAPPAPORT: What's the matter with your son; can't he walk?

MRS. GINSBERG: Sure he can walk but thank goodness he doesn't have to.

WEARING APPAREL (see also Clothing, Business, Retail, Wholesale)

I had a beautiful suit made of awning material. There was only one thing wrong with it. Every time the sun went down, the pants rolled up."

Most girls I know who aren't married are looking for husbands to fill a void in their lives . . . empty clothes closets.

The couple was leaving church.

WIFE: Did you see that floral hat Mrs. Brown was wearing?

HUSBAND: Can't say as I did.
WIFE: And what do you think of Mrs. Green wearing that low cut neck and knee length dress?
HUSBAND: I really didn't notice.
WIFE: Lord . . . a lot of good it does you going to church.

The extravagant new wife went on a shopping spree, and the next day a delivery boy arrived with five new hats.
HUSBAND: For Pete's sake, honey. What do you want with five new hats?
WIFE: Five new dresses.

A friend of mine who despised the bossy-wife type female recently got married and on his honeymoon night got this message across to his new wife. They were undressing for the night and when he took off his pants he tossed them to his bride.
GROOM: Here, put these on.

Not meaning to displease her husband the bride tried them on and they looked ridiculous.
BRIDE: But, honey, they're much too big for me.
GROOM: And don't ever forget that.

The woman had examined every article in the men's shop but nothing suited her.
WOMAN: I'm so sorry, but tomorrow's my husband's birthday and I wanted to surprise him.

CLERK: Then why not hide behind the arm chair and shout Boo!

WEDDINGS (see also Bride, Bridegroom, Marriage)

CORA: It's a dollar-and-sense wedding.
DORA: What do you mean?
CORA: He hasn't a dollar and she hasn't any sense."

A friend of mine was engaged to a movie star. On his wedding day his car stalled, and so he sent her a wire saying: "Delayed for a few hours. Don't marry anyone until I get there."

"On which side of the church should the parents of the bride and bridegroom be seated?"
"On opposite sides and as far apart as possible. A church is no place to start anything."

WEDLOCK (see also Wedding, Marriage, Newlyweds)

An old German and his wife were given to quarreling. One day after a particularly unpleasant scene, the old woman remarked with a sigh, "Vell, I vish I vas in heaven."
"I vish I vas in de beer garten."
"Ach, ja—always you pick out the best for yourself."

"I see that May is going to be married."

"Yes, she's been married so often that the wedding bells sound just like an alarm clock to her."

"I'm running away from my wife. We've been married fifteen years. Do you think she will miss me?"

"If she does—she's a bad shot."

"I don't mind your getting married—I hope you get a wife like I got in your mother."

"She never hits me, mind you, except with the soft end of the mop."

Before marriage he's a suitor; after the ceremony he never does.

"I've been married seven years."

"I'll bet it seems like yesterday."

"No, it seems like seven years."

WIFE: Do you think the mountain air will disagree with me?

HUBBY: I don't think it would dare, my dear.

"Have you been true to me?"

"Let's see.—What day did you leave?"

Many a man sees a wolf at the door because his girl saw a fox in a window.

A young matron had unsuccessfully worked on her husband for an advance on her allowance.

"What's the use," she said drearily after a final refusal "I guess I'll just walk east into the lake. At least I can make the headlines."

"You'd better find out first if Notre Dame is playing," retorted her husband coldly.

"When I married you, I thought you were an angel."

"So that's why you never bought me any clothes!"

"She married a man who is ninety and has a million dollars."

"What's the idea of marrying a man ninety years old?"

"If someone handed you a check for a million dollars would you stop and examine the date?"

The aggressive wife of a meek little man was hauling her husband over the coals for having made a fool of himself at a party. He sat in dejected silence.

"And don't be sitting there," she shouted, "making fists at me in your pockets, either!"

The famous Lou Holtz character gets married on $35 a week. The first week he gives his bride $30 of it—keeping $5 for himself. Next week he reverses that—

keeping $30 and giving his wife $5.

"How do you expect me to get along on this?"

"I dunno. I had a hell of a job myself last week."

"I'm going out after dinner."

"Oh, darling. What will I do without you?"

"The dishes."

Marriage is like a bath. It's not so hot when you get used to it.

Before marriage a man yearns for a woman—after marriage the "Y" is silent.

Marriage is a great thing—no family should be without it.

"I'll love you just like this if I live to be 100."

"And then I suppose you'll start chasing around with women."

"How does it feel to be marrying an heiress?"

"Great—every time I kiss her I feel as if I were clipping a coupon off a government bond."

The trouble with matrimony today is that too many people get married who have never had any experience at it before.

"How come you've been married eight times?"

"Can I help it that I like Niagara Falls?"

"I arranged their marriage."

"You mean you carried the shot gun?"

"I read where your father had a silver weddin' anniversary."

"I didn't know he was that old yet."

"He wasn't, but Ma said she needed the silver."

"You brute, since our marriage you haven't been half as affectionate as you were the night you proposed to me!

"Well, I haven't been half as drunk, either."

A man marries a girl because he likes her limbs and next morning her family tree moves in.

HUSBAND: I feel as though I were going to have appendicitis.

WIFE: Well, I need a new gown, so you'll just have to wait.

"They say that Blinkers went into marriage with his eyes shut."

"No wonder! I'd shut my eyes, too, if I thought a gun was going off."

There are two sides to every question. His side and the wrong side.

Man is but dust and woman settles him.

WIFE: What's the idea of coming home to dinner two hours late?
HUSBAND (in bandages): But, dearest, I've been run over!
WIFE: It doesn't take two hours to be run over.

"Should I marry a chef or a poet?"
"It doesn't make much difference, it's going from batter to verse."

So henpecked he doesn't snore in his sleep—he cackles.

Wifey: (at phone)—How would you like to talk to my mother?
HUBBY: Through a spirit medium.

WIFE: George dear, are there any fashions in that paper?
GEORGE: Yes, but they're out of date—it's the morning paper!

HE: Your meals aren't like my mother used to make.
SHE: Well your salary isn't like my father used to make.

"Do you think it's unlucky to be married on Friday?"
"Well, you can't get a divorce until Monday."

WESTERNS (see also Television, Late Show)

If Horace Greeley were alive in this TV age, he'd probably advise, "Go Western, Young Man . . ."

I saw a Western on TV so modern that the hero chewed filter-tipped tobacco.

This has been a rough year for Western heroes on TV. Not one of them has made it back to his ranch yet without getting ambushed by a commercial.

I saw a Western on TV last night so old that Gabby Hayes had five o'clock shadow.

Nowadays when an American cowboy tells you he's heading for the last roundup, he means his sponsor didn't pick up his option.

A modern cowboy doesn't have to know how to rope a steer as long as he knows how to rope a sponsor.

I saw a Western on TV last night so adult that the gambling house owner didn't lose his life for running a crooked game—he lost his license.

I saw a Western on TV last night so adult that they didn't let

Billy the Kid in the saloon because he was under twenty-one.

I saw a Western on TV last night so modern that the saloon had a press agent.

I saw a Western on TV last night so modern the Indians couldn't burn down the settlement because their lighters weren't working.

WHOLESALE (see also Retail, Business)

The kid was born to one of the biggest wholesalers in the garment business. When he came into the world the first three words out of his mouth were—"Mama, Papa, and linings."

The owner of a wholesale silk business insisted on having all his checks dated ahead. When he died, his tombstone read; "HERE LIES SAM JONES. DIED JUNE 5TH AS OF JULY 2ND."

A wholesaler said to an employee—"Most amazing, you've been with us two weeks and already you're a month behind in your work."

A holdup man entered a wholesale fabric house and ordered the bookkeeper to hand over the payroll.

"I'm very sorry," said the bookkeeper, "but I'm off duty and the union won't let me."

Mankind is divided into two classes, those who earn their living by the sweat of their brows and those who sell them handkerchiefs, cold drinks, and air conditioners.

Two wholesale store owners were discussing an insurance man who just left them.
"That guy tried to sell me earthquake insurance."
"Did you buy?"
"No."
"That's smart. It's very hard to start an earthquake."

WIDOWS

A pretty girl, a young widow and an old maid all lived in the same house, and each agreed to come down in the morning and repeat the word "morning" for each kiss they had received the night before.

The first morning, the pretty girl came down and said: "Good morning! It's a pretty morning this morning."

Then the young widow came down and said: "Good morning! It's a pretty morning this morning. If tomorrow morning is as pretty a morning as this morning, it will be a pretty morning tomorrow morning."

Then the old maid came down and said: "Howdy!"

WIFE (see also Husband, Parents and Children, Marriage, Woman)

1ST MAN: When I complained to my wife about how much she spends on clothes, she said, "Well, I only dress to please you."

2ND MAN: Oh yeah, . . . well, if women dressed to please their husbands, they'd wear last year's clothes.

WIFE: I'm frightfully worried about Judy.

HUSBAND: Why, what's she done now?

WIFE: Well, I gave her a hundred dollars this morning so that she could buy what she needed for her vacation in the mountains. Can you imagine—she spent every last cent of it on clothing!

HUSBAND: Now, now, dear. That's nothing to be so upset about. You must take into consideration that a girl Judy's age is very conscious of her personal appearance. She wants to be attractive to the young men in her life. What did she buy?

WIFE: Oh, that's just it. She spent it all on pink nylon underwear.

WIFE: It's a mistake for a woman to marry in haste.

FRIEND: What do you mean?

WIFE: I made the mistake of marrying my second husband before I got rid of my first.

My wife has been affected by the latest fads. Every time I ask her to do something she says, "Do it yourself!"

WILL

The old man was dictating his will. "To my son," he said, "I leave one hundred thousand. To my daughter—one hundred thousand. To my grandson—ten thousand. To my granddaughter—ten thousand." The lawyer interrupted, "But sir, you only have three thousand dollars." The old man growled, "Let them go out and work for a living like I did."

WISECRACKS (see also Hecklers, Insults)

The cadets called her "Apple," because she is good to the corps.

The last word in cars "I'll walk."

To hell with expense. Give the canary another seed.

Some girls are like bathtubs; they acquire one ring after another.

A bachelor is a guy who didn't have a car when he was young.

They say that bread contains alcohol, so let's drink a little toast.

Her husband sold real estate and she gave lots away.

Flowers are getting cheaper. You can find pansies almost any place.

She was only the optician's daughter—two glasses and she made a spectacle of herself.

A lot of fellows are caught in the act who are not vaudeville performers.

She was only a bottle opener's daughter but nobody could stopper.

We hasten to point out that while every man has his wire, only the iceman has his pick.

They call him cigarette lighter cause he never works.

Have you heard the companionate marriage vow—Love, Honor, and No Baby?

A girl in the bush is worth two in the parlor.

WOLF (see also Flirtation, Bachelor)

The wolf at the bar was trying to make time with a gorgeous creature whose dress was bursting at the seams, which is as good a place as any. "Oh," said the babe, who had been around more than a carousel, "I bet your wife doesn't understand you." "She understands me all right," said the gent, "it's just that she's fat and ugly."

WOMEN (see also Wife, Mother-in-law, Flirtation)

REJECTED SUITOR: I shall go away to some desert island to forget all women . . . I shall go to Honolulu.
FRIEND: But the minute you get to Honolulu you'll find it full of beautiful native girls.
REJECTED SUITOR: Ha, ha. Will I be disappointed!

I can never understand why a woman who can pick up a two-pound bowling ball and pack a bag of golf irons has to sit in the car and wait until the man gets out, walks around and opens the door for her.

1ST MAN: A woman could never be President of the United States.

2ND MAN: Why not?

1ST MAN: To be President you have to be over 35 and a leader of men . . . and how many men would follow a woman over 35?

One characteristic men and women have in common—they both distrust women.

Definition of a married woman: Someone who has absolutely nothing to wear and five closets to keep it in.

Two women were talking. One said to the other, "That Ruth is always knocking her husband. I never saw anything like it in my whole life. She's always complaining about her better half . . . Look at my husband, he's such a louse he should drop dead, but do I ever say anything to anybody?"

SELMA: Where's your husband?

ZELDA: He's diving.

SELMA: I don't see him.

ZELDA: Yeah. He's been under water for twenty minutes.

SELMA: C'mon. Let's go. I wouldn't wait that long for any man.

The two women were watching the funeral procession. After watching the thirty-eighth car go by, Mrs. Alexander turned to Mrs. Davis and asked, "Who died?" . . . "I'm not sure, I think it's the one in the first car."

WORDS (see also Vocabulary)

"That would put me in jeopardy. Don't you know what jeopardy means?"

"Sure—my uncle is one—a jeopardy sheriff."

"Why don't you go straight home?"

"What?"

"I said—go straight home. You know what straight means?"

"Sure—without ginger ale."

"Don't you know what an operetta is?"

"Don't be silly. An operetta is a girl who works for the telephone company."

"We'd better do something to remedy the status quo."

"What's status quo?"

"That is the Latin for the mess we's in."

"Have you ever heard of the Sesquicentennial?"

"No, what's the name of it?"

"What?"

"What did you say?"

"I didn't say anything."

"Oh, I didn't hear you."

"Can you tell me the meaning of the word unaware?"

"Unaware is what you put on first and take off last."

WORK

LENNIE: Why do you work so hard?

RENNIE: I'm too nervous to steal.

FIRST CHARWOMAN: Did your husband love you very much?

SECOND CHARWOMAN: Love me? He wouldn't even leave me to go to work.

"If your wife made you go out and look for a job, what would you look for?" said the impatient social service worker to one of her lazier cases.

"A new wife."

RED GRANGE: I once carried a hundred-pound load on my back for a mile.

FAN: It got heavier with every step, I bet.

RED GRANGE: No—it was ice.

One workingman down on his luck griped to a fellow worker: "It just doesn't figure. Here I am born in America and I can't make a living. Sam has been here only three years and already owes $600,000!"

The personnel director was checking the references of a new secretary. He called her former boss.

"How long did she work for you?" he asked.

"About eight hours," said the boss.

"But she told me she was with you for three years."

The ex-boss replied, "She was! She was!"

A woman was explaining to a friend what kind of work her husband did. "You see, he's an efficiency expert for a large company," she said.

"What's an efficiency expert?" her companion asked.

"Well, put it this way," the spouse explained, "If we women did it, they'd call it nagging."

All work and no play makes a lot of jack.

WORM

"It probably took a thousand silk worms to make that dress."

"Isn't it wonderful what they can train some worms to do?"

"Marilyn Monroe paid a visit to the zoo and all the animals turned and stared as she passed."

"You mean, even the animals turned to watch her?"

"Sure, when Marilyn Monroe walks along, even a worm will turn."

"Is your husband a book-worm?"
"No—just an ordinary one."

"Some day the worm will turn."
"But what's the idea in turning? It's the same on both ends, isn't it?"

WORRY (see also Marriage)

"Cheer up, old man. Why don't you drown your sorrow?" a friend asked Brown, who was having domestic difficulties.
"She's bigger than I am and besides it would be murder," answered Brown.

CLIENT: I'll give you one hundred dollars to do my worrying for me.
LAWYER: Great! Where's the hundred?
CLIENT: That's your first worry.

BRIDE: Dearest, something is troubling you, and I want you to tell me what it is: your worries are not your worries now, they are our worries.
GROOM: Oh, very well. We've just had a letter from a girl in New York and she's suing us for breach of promise.

WRESTLING (see also Sports)

On TV recently, a wrestler was tossed out of the ring and came up in pain. The excited ring announcer actually yelled, "This part is on the level!"

WRITERS

A Broadway columnist was discussing a colleague with a hanger-on at a smart cocktail bar.
"He's achieved quite a lot of success as a ghost writer," said the columnist.
"How do you mean?"
"Well, he is able to hire another ghost writer to write his ghost writing for him."

MARY: Don't you find writing a thankless job?
SALLY: On the contrary, everything I write is returned to me with thanks.

AUTHOR: Well, sir, the upshot of it was that it took me ten years to discover that I had absolutely no talent for writing literature.
FRIEND: And you gave it up?
AUTHOR: Oh, no—by that time I was famous.

ED: I'm going to buy a plot for my brother.
NED: Did he pass away?
ED: Oh, no, he's writing a story.

After some years of marriage, the wife of a successful writer divorced him. Writers were too temperamental and unpredictable, she complained, and she no longer could put up with this one's quirks.

A few short months after shedding one writer husband the little gal was about to take on another famous writer as a husband. The ex-husband read of the wedding and sent his former wife this cable: "Heartiest congratulations and best wishes. (Signed) Frying Pan."

A Washington correspondent, riding a campaign train through a lush valley of California, sat beside a British writer on his first tour of the United States. The Englishman, after silently observing mile after mile of fertile prosperous land, finally spoke up: "Damn George III."

A famous humorist and writer was listening to a lecture about Noah Webster. "Webster," said the lecturer, "had an amazing command of the language. Audiences were spellbound by his mastery of words. His English was just perfect." "Mine would be too," interrupted the humorist, "if I wrote my own dictionary."

I come from a family of writers. My sister wrote books that no one would read. My brother wrote songs that no one would sing. My mother wrote plays that no one would see. And my father wrote checks that no one would cash.

❖❖

X

XMAS (see also Yuletide, Christmas)

A young soldier was depressed. In the spirit of the holidays, I asked him, "Wasn't Santa Claus good to you?" "Good to me?" he said sadly, "Twenty years ago I asked Santa Claus for a soldier suit—and now I get it!"

I love to shop at Gimbel's around Xmas because everybody is so polite and helpful. One woman broke her leg while shopping and they gift-wrapped it.

The Burglars' and Pickpockets' Association of Madison Avenue have asked me to announce that there are just 36 more shoplifting days till Xmas.

You can tell that Xmas is approaching. Macy's has just captured Gimbel's first comparison shopper. And Gimbel's retaliated by capturing a Macy Santa Claus. —A prisoner exchange is being worked out now.

Xmas is the time of the year to get the kids something for the old man to play with.

I'm writing to Santa Claus early this Xmas to tell him what I want.—How do you spell Brigitte Bardot?

I'm getting my girl a fountain pen for Xmas as a surprise, and wotta surprise it's gonna be—she expects a Cadillac.

My uncle did his Xmas shopping early and what do you think he got? Thirty days!

I had a tough time putting my sock over the fireplace last Christmas. I finally had to take it off my foot.

When I was a kid I was so poor, we didn't have any stockings to hang up so instead we hung up empty salami casings.

On Christmas we used to stand my uncle in the window because no tree in the neighborhood was lit up as much as he was.

The department stores are so crowded around Yuletide that one girl I know walked in and they threw a lampshade on her head, a bulb in her mouth, and I bought her for $1.98.

Just as the store was closing for Xmas Eve, a salesman walked over to me and said, "All right, buddy, if you wanna buy something you'd better do it now and take advantage of our special Xmas price, because at 6 PM we close the doors and start marking the stuff down."

X-RAY (see also Doctors)

PATIENT: How much will it cost me for an operation?
DOCTOR: Five hundred dollars.
PATIENT: Listen, for fifty dollars maybe you could touch up my X-rays?

Y

YOKELS (see also Hillbilly)

I know a yokel farmer who married a girl so young he comes in from the fields three or four times a day just to see if his wife came home from school yet.

A yokel was on trial for killing his wife when he caught her with a neighbor, and when he was asked why he shot her instead of her lover, he said, "Aw shucks, Ah'd rather shoot a woman once than a man every week."

The teacher in a small country school was explaining some arithmetic problems when she noticed the class yokel, a tall gangly lad, the dopiest pupil in school, watching rather intently. She was happy to know that at last he was beginning to understand. When she finished, she said to him, "Cicero, you look so interested. I'm sure you want to ask some questions." And Cicero got up and drawled, "Waaal, ma'am, I got one t'ask. Where do them numbers go when yew rub 'm off th' board?"

The yokel found his way to the bar at Reuben's.

"D'you have any ten-cent drinks?" he asked.

"We don't serve ten-cent drinks," the bartender answered haughtily.

"Wal," drawled the yokel, "never mind. Those five-cent drinks don't agree wif me."

The yokel was asked how he liked the sweater girls and he said, "Right fine! They remind me of the hills at home!"

YOUNGMAN, HENNY

The weather is so changeable— I don't know what to hock.

Two convicts were fighting and the warden said, "Whatta ya fighting about?"
One convict said, "Aw, he called me a dirty number."

You know what a harp is— that's a giant egg slicer.

Some people call a harp a nude piano.

Next week my son will be eleven years old—if I let him.

A guy fell off a ten-story building and landed on the sidewalk. A big crowd gathered around him and a cop came over to the guy and said, "What happened?"

Guy said, "I don't know I just got here."

Guy called up the drugstore and said, "Do you have Prince Albert in a can?"

Clerk said, "Yeah."

Guy said, "Well let him out— he's suffocating."

I got a wife and a cigarette lighter and they both work.

Two guys were talking. One said, "Hey, got a match?"

"Other guy said "No, but I got a lighter."

First Guy said, "How can I pick my teeth with a lighter?"

Hear about the nearsighted snake who eloped with a rope?

YOUTH (see also Adolescent, Kids, Children)

The best way for a girl to keep her youth—is not to introduce him to anyone.

I think that every woman should hold on to her youth, but not while he's driving.

You know, a boy is growing up when he stops wanting to go out with girls and wants to stay home with them.

One of the problems with youth today is that there are no more little red schoolhouses but too many little-read schoolboys.

YULETIDE (see also Christmas, Xmas)

"Have you ordered your Christmas tree, sir?"

"Yes, and I'm going to have my broker decorate my tree."

"Why your broker?"

"It's the only thing he hasn't trimmed."

"What does it mean—'Yuletide Greetings'?"

"Lend me $5—you'll tide me over for a few days."

"What did you get in your stocking for Christmas?"

"Nothing but a runner."

"Well, what did you expect— a pole vaulter?"

They wanted to give me some Red Cross Seals for Christmas but I told them I didn't want them— I didn't even know how to feed them.

"I'm going to find out whether there is a Santa Claus."

"How?"

"Christmas eve I'm going to put fish hooks in my chimney."

"My wife hung my socks up, and, boy, did I have a headache!"

"How could hanging up your socks give you a headache?"

"She forgot to take me out of them."

We're having a rubber Christmas this year. I'm going to let my wife and family go in and look at the tree and stretch their imagination.

"Are you sure this is Christmas morning?"

"If it ain't, I washed my socks for nothin'."

"Well, Bobby, did you see Santa Claus this time?"

"No, Auntie. It was too dark to see him, but I heard what he said when he knocked his toe against the bedpost."

❖❖

Z

ZEBRA (see also Animals, Zoo)

A lady in a sleeping car climbed to her upper berth and let out a bloodcurdling screech. "Porter," she cried, "I do declare there's a live zebra here in this upper. Isn't that amazing?"

"Sure is," agreed the porter. "When he got on at Louisville, his ticket called for a drawing room."

A zebra is a sport-model jackass.

A zebra escaped from the circus and ran into a pasture of a nearby farm. He approached a bull and asked, "Are you a strong bull?"

The bull replied, "Take off those silly pajamas and I'll show you!"

ZOO (see also Animals)

A father took his son to the zoo and pointed out the lions to him and said, "Son, there is the most ferocious of all animals. If he should ever get out of that cage, he would tear me to pieces." The kid said, "Papa, if he should, what number bus should I take to get home?"

She's so dumb she went to the zoo to see what a Christmas seal looks like.

She's always attracted to the zoo because she heard that all men are beasts and she just loves animals.

The new lion in the zoo was fed a few bananas, while the old lion in the adjoining cage was fed big chunks of red meat. The new lion finally asked the older lion, "How come I only get bananas while you get steak?" "This zoo," explained the old lion, "works on a low budget and they've got you registered as a monkey."

The beautiful girl was one candidate for the job at the zoo as a lion tamer. The other was an eager young man. The manager said he would give them both a chance, and told the girl to go into the cage. The girl, wearing a big fur coat, did so. The huge lion was let in with her and he immediately started to charge at her. Suddenly she stood upright, opened her fur coat and stood there, completely naked. The lion stopped dead, spun around and went meekly back to the corner. The manager was properly amazed. He turned toward the young man. "Well, pal, do you think you can top that?" "I'd like to try," said the guy, "just get that crazy lion out of there."

The biggest elephant in the Berlin Zoo expired of old age, and his trainer was inconsolable. Finally the zoo superintendent told him, "It's ridiculous to carry on that way about the loss of one elephant. We expect to replace him, you know."
"Easy enough for you to talk," wailed the trainer. "Just remember who has to dig the grave!"

Things were zoo-ming in Bronx Park one day not long ago. In one sector, a lady and her son were inspecting one of the outdoor pens. "Mom," inquired the son, "What's the peculiar object on the ground underneath that funny-looking animal?" She looked intently, then assured him, "There's nothing, son, under the gnu."

Nearby a hatchet-faced lady tapped the keeper of the monkey house indignantly on the shoulder. "Those wretched animals of yours appear to be engaged in shooting dice. I demand that you break up the game at once." "Shucks," shrugged the keeper, "They're keeping strictly within the law, Ma'am. They're only playing for peanuts."

Finally, the headwaiter of a very expensive midtown restaurant and his son were exploring the lion house at feeding time. The keeper casually threw a huge slab of raw meat into the biggest lion's cage and proceeded on his way.

"That wasn't very polite," noted the son. "Why doesn't he serve with style the way you do to your patrons?"

The father made sure the animal was beyond hearing distance, then whispered to his son, "Confidentially, lions are lousy tippers."

ZOOLOGY (see also Animals, Zoo)

An absent-minded professor was conducting a class in zoology and addressing the students. He said, "Now students, this morning we will take this frog apart and see what makes him croak." And he took a paper bag out of his pocket, then emptied the contents on his desk. Out rolled a ham sandwich. He scratched his head and said, "Mmm, now that's funny. I distinctly remember eating my lunch!"

*The
Red
Thread
of
Passion*

The
Red
Thread
of
Passion

*Spirituality
and the
Paradox
of Sex*

DAVID GUY

SHAMBHALA
Boston & London
1999

HOUSTON PUBLIC LIBRARY

R0l151 59152

Shambhala Publications, Inc.
Horticultural Hall
300 Massachusetts Avenue
Boston, MA 02115
http://www.shambhala.com

© 1999 by David Guy

All rights reserved. No part of this book may be reproduced
in any form or by any means, electronic or mechanical,
including photocopying, recording, or by any information
storage and retrieval system, without permission in writing
from the publisher.

9   8   7   6   5   4   3   2   1

First Edition

Printed in the United States of America

⊗ This edition is printed on acid-free paper that meets the
American National Standards Institute Z39.48 Standard.

Distributed in the United States by Random House, Inc.,
and in Canada by Random House of Canada Ltd

Library of Congress Cataloging-in-Publication Data
Guy, David.
    The red thread of passion : spirituality and the
paradox of sex/David Guy.—1st ed.
        p.   cm.
    ISBN 1-57062-359-7
    1. Sex—Religious aspects.   2. Spirituality.   I. Title.
    BL65.S4G88   1999   98-46477
    291.4'2—dc21   CIP

To Alma,

the answer

to my koan

In order to know the Way in perfect clarity, there is one essential point you must penetrate and not avoid: the red thread [of passion] between our legs that cannot be severed. Few face the problem, and it is not at all easy to settle. Attack it directly without hesitation or retreat, for how else can liberation come?

—ZEN KOAN

Why has sex become a problem? Why do we not die to our problems instead of carrying them day after day, year after year?

—J. KRISHNAMURTI

sexual love's attachment pain is deeper than I can know
wind soothes my thoughts this lust my ceaseless koan
impossibly happy

—ZEN MASTER IKKYU,
TRANS. STEPHEN BERG

~ Contents

~ Preface

THIS IS A BOOK about a subject that has always
fascinated me and a period in my life when it came
sharply into focus. In my mid-forties I found that sex
and spirituality—two parts of my life that had always been in
conflict—were becoming one thing. In one way my sex drive
seemed to be waning; in another it was becoming more what
it had always really been. I had also discovered a spiritual
practice that engaged the whole of me. It seemed to be a
part—not recognizably cause or effect—of the sexual change.

I also write this book out of a lifelong frustration with the
sexual teachings of many religious traditions. "Thou shalt not
commit adultery" seems to be the extent of it in mainstream
Christianity, and though Buddhism alters that to "A disciple
of the Buddha does not misuse sexual energy," it comes to
the same thing.

These strictures barely hint at the richness and complex-
ity of sex, and the fact that you are having sex only with your
spouse hardly means that the act is moral. Countless people
are abusive to their spouses, to say nothing of neglectful and

inattentive. It also seems apparent to me that some of the most "sordid" of sexual encounters—gay group sex, for instance—can be profoundly moral and loving.* Some of the best people I've known have been promiscuous. Some of the worst have been monogamous or celibate. And our religious institutions are rife with sexual scandal.

Furthermore, this strictly negative view of sex—here is what you *shouldn't* do—ignores the fact that it is among the most precious gifts of creation and might hold an opportunity for profound realization. Sex is too often seen as a distraction from, not a part of, the path.

The people I examine in this brief study relate as much to the period of my life as to the subject matter. Walt Whitman and D. H. Lawrence are in the long tradition of writer-prophets; they wrote in the hope of changing the world—a profound part of what they thought should change was people's attitudes toward sex—but literary critics dismiss their role as prophets, brush aside their ideas, and discuss them from a strictly aesthetic point of view. I appreciate their artistic greatness, but I also accept them as prophets and find deep truth in what they said.

Alan Watts is generally regarded as a disreputable renegade scholar, a popularizer and a sixties figure who helped bring the East to the West. Often he is rejected by people who get fanatical about spiritual practice because he didn't practice much himself. Actually, Watts was not so much a Buddhist as an independent thinker who was influenced by Eastern thought; he really expresses his own philosophy in his writing and lectures, a kind of sophisticated joie de vivre.

---

*I refer skeptical readers to one of the most fascinating autobiographies I have ever read, *The Motion of Light in Water* by Samuel R. Delany.

He is deeply concerned with the question of how we should live but doesn't get solemn about it. He spent his whole life trying to get people to lighten up and let go, to stop trying to figure things out and just *live*.

For most people—if they have heard it at all—Marco Vassi's name does not belong with these others. He spent his life as a porn writer and a bisexual rebel, and died of AIDS shortly after the epidemic began. He is certainly not a writer on the level of the other literary figures. Yet in another kind of culture, one in which sex were exalted and not feared and repressed, he might have had a rather different career and not been relegated to pulp paperbacks and dirty bookstores.* His sexual theories are as well thought out as anyone's. Like many other seekers, he was out to save the world and himself. And he hoped to do so through sex.

The contemporary figures I've examined are not—with the possible exception of Carol Queen—primarily writers; they address questions of sex and spirituality more directly, through workshops, hands-on bodywork, and performance art. Joseph Kramer is an ex-Jesuit who has set out to rescue gay men from AIDS by teaching them what sex really is, giving them a richer sex life rather than taking away what they already have. Collin Brown started out as a bisexual student of Kramer's, became a teacher, and has since expanded his work to include straight couples. Juliet Carr, a former English teacher and porno star, teaches tactile-hypnotic eroticism. And Carol Queen has worked as a prostitute and stripper, as well as leading workshops, giving lectures, and writing articles and books.

*According to Lin Yutang, for instance—writing in *My Country and My People*—the pornographic novel was a perfectly legitimate genre in pre-Communist China, with classic works and noted practitioners.

From the moment I started telling friends about this book, they have wondered at all I am leaving out. Rumi, Kabir, Saint John of the Cross, Teresa of Ávila, the Kama Sutra, countless Tantric masters and teachers, to say nothing of many contemporary teachers working in this field. I have no excuse for these omissions, and hope to study and learn from the whole tradition, but at this particular moment in my life these people drifted into my attention. They have enriched my understanding of this subject, and I believe them worthy of notice.

My title comes from the Zen tradition, the famous koan that I have quoted as an epigraph at the beginning of this book and that I address directly in my final chapter. It is also expressed in short form: "Why is it that even the most clear-eyed monk cannot sever the red thread of passion between his legs?"* Why, indeed? The question of how to handle sex—which I take this koan to express—is one that has haunted my whole life, and I don't pretend that I have suddenly come up with an answer. I don't claim to be "over" some past behavior; I have not "found" religion; and I do not "know" the truth. I have no special qualifications whatsoever. I am just fascinated by the question.

This koan, like all koans, is not a question that we answer in words but by our lives, by every moment that we live. We don't—as we used to say in the sixties—answer the question; we live it. It is my hope in this book not to answer it but to raise it more profoundly than has previously been done. And to celebrate an aspect of life that I am convinced was meant to be a joy and not a torment.

*For all my information on sex in the Zen tradition, I am greatly indebted to John Stevens's excellent book *Lust for Enlightenment: Buddhism and Sex* (Boston: Shambhala Publications, 1990).

~ Acknowledgments

I would like to offer deep thanks to a number of people who helped me in this project:

Michael Perkins and Don Shewey, two wonderful writers who became my pen pals during the period described in this book, and whose encouragement and wisdom were of great help as I pondered this subject. Michael was of particular help with Marco Vassi, whose work he called to my attention. Don's article in the *Village Voice* introduced me to Joseph Kramer, and Don was extremely generous in allowing me to read and quote from his long unpublished interview with Kramer, one of the most interesting documents about sex I have ever read. For more wisdom on the subject of sex than they will ever find in this book, readers should consult the work of these two men.

Betsy Bickel, my masseuse and friend, who not only taught me a great deal about my body through massage, but who recommended the book *Women of the Light* to me, thereby introducing me to two sexual healers about whom I wrote.

Sy Safransky, who published in his superb magazine *The Sun* the short piece that eventually expanded into this book, and who has endured any number of conversations about sex with me through the years.

Dave O'Neal of Shambhala Publications, who saw me through the editorial process and provided many astute suggestions.

Beth Guy, who allowed me to work in her attic while my house was being renovated, and who put up with my early-morning muttering and grumpiness about my work.

Sally Sexton, who allowed this poverty-stricken author to stay in her San Francisco apartment for free, who showed me the city and listened with a straight face to my rantings about my book, and who later offered her insightful criticism of the manuscript (she must have had an excellent English teacher somewhere along the way). Also to Hal Messison, for showing me an elegant evening on the town.

All of the sexual healers I interviewed, who gave generously of their time.

My son Bill, who has endured twenty-five years as the child of a man who writes about sex all the time, and who has always encouraged my work.

My wife Alma, who—in case you were wondering—finds my sexuality decidedly unspiritual, but who put up with my delusions long enough to let me write this book.

My cat Ambrose (not actually a person, but pretty close), who, by waking me up at 4:30 every morning, gave me an excellent opportunity to look into the emptiness of all existence. I am not actually an insomniac. My cat is an early riser.

Part One

~ 1
The Beautiful Woman
and the Fear of God

hear the cruel no-answer until blood
drips down
beat your head against the wall of it
　　　　　　　—ZEN MASTER IKKYU,
　　　　　　　TRANS. STEPHEN BERG

I WAS RAISED in a middle-class Protestant fifties household and took religion seriously; for a while, at the age
of ten, I wanted to be a minister. But my true spiritual
life went on inside me, and I told no one about it, as if I were
ashamed of it. It was as if I shouldn't be thinking what I was,
I should just accept the answers religion offered. It was as if I
didn't know my place.

I was obsessed in those days with the concepts of infinite
space and eternal time. They seemed to be two sides of the
same coin, because they terrified me in exactly the same way,
and I associated them with the night, partly because that was

when my fears came up, partly because I associated the vastness of infinite space and the blankness of prehistoric night with a dark sky. Nothingness was black.

I pictured myself utterly alone in a blank space scattered with stars, moving, moving, but never getting anywhere. That was infinite space. I similarly tried to conceptualize eternity. I pictured what I thought of as heaven, a vast world floating around in the clouds where everybody was happy all the time, but I couldn't imagine what they did there—what made them so happy—and I couldn't imagine its going on forever. There was something deeply fearful about such a concept. Wouldn't you be afraid it was going to end, no matter what anybody said (even the Big Man himself)? Even if it didn't end, wouldn't something have to *happen?* Didn't there have to be something toward which all this was tending? And what could that be, except an end?

I had similar problems at the other end of eternity. If the universe was created at a particular moment, what was there before that (and before that? and before that)? If God had always existed . . . But I stopped right there. How could something always exist? There was no moment when he first became aware of himself? There *had* to be.

Lots of schoolkids ask this famous conundrum: If God created everything, who created God? I took that question seriously. It worried me to death. It related to the ultimate existential question: Why is there anything? Why, in an infinite universe, is there an infinite universe?

Does God—or whatever we call the ultimate being (if there is an ultimate being)—ask that question? The religion I was raised in said that he knows the answers to all questions, but I didn't—and don't—buy it. How could he know the answer to *that?* How can there *be* an answer to that?

Unless it isn't a question. It is just a fact. We are here, and can never—even an ultimate being—know why. That fact raises anxiety (it certainly raised it in me, when I was ten years old), which I think of, in a play on words, as the fear of God. The ultimate reality in the universe does not know why it is here, and is therefore afraid.

But maybe it is wrong to label that feeling fear. Maybe it is just energy, the energy that creates all there is. It creates because it doesn't know why. There is no why. There is just creating.

I was shielded from that fear throughout my childhood by sexual fantasy. I didn't know it was sexual. I didn't know what sex was. But from as early as I can remember—certainly back to the age of five—I had dreams of embracing, and kissing, a beautiful woman. She was the movie starlet of the early fifties, tall and curvaceous, with large warm lips; she would fold me in her arms and kiss me, in the long, long kiss that was the closest thing movies showed in those days to a sexual act.

The image is comic, a five-year-old being embraced by a movie star, but I saw it from my point of view, as I was enveloped in the embrace. One movie kiss especially thrilled me: the woman had extremely long hair, sat in the man's lap, and tossed it over his head as she kissed him, so they were hidden from view. That was the kiss I wanted. It was the blissful image that carried me off to sleep every night.

It is said that very young boys masturbate, and I may just be repressing the memory, but I don't remember doing that. I didn't connect this image with my penis but with a feeling of warmth throughout my body. One would think that, without some release, the fantasy would have kept me up rather than putting me to sleep, but I would just wear it out. I wasn't concerned with sleeping. I would lie in bed reveling in that image, and at some point—because I didn't care—I would go to sleep.

I established a pattern in those early years that has stayed with me for the rest of my life. I escaped anxiety by dreaming about sex. It was the only image strong enough to pull me away. I would use sex not just for that deep existential anxiety but for all the fears of my life (though they all, in some way, go back to that deepest one). At its heart, it seems to me, that fear is a religious feeling. Thus was sex connected to spirituality: like two cats rolling around in a fight, their claws so deeply sunk into each other that they can't let go.

CLIMBING INTO MY HEAD

I discovered masturbation soon enough, not long after one of my friends, on a day when we were both excused from gym class, told me quickly and rather furtively what sex was ("And that's what people mean when they talk about fucking," he said in conclusion). Masturbation became linked with my fantasies, as if they existed for it, but the fantasies had come first. It is astonishing, as I look back, how much I masturbated, far more than anyone would do for mere pleasure. It is a measure of the anxiety I must have been feeling. I rubbed myself raw.*

---

*In my novel *The Autobiography of My Body* I wrote, through my narrator, about the extent of my compulsive masturbation, and I expected that to be the weird fact that people most often brought up, the one that most surely branded me a pervert. But almost no one mentioned it, and when someone did—at one of the men's gatherings I attended—he always said he had done it at least as much as I. There was apparently a masturbation epidemic in the United States in the early sixties.

I was overweight and self-conscious as an adolescent, tongue-tied around girls, so masturbation was the only sex I would have until I was twenty. My disgust with my body drove me even further into my head, away from my experience. I nevertheless had extreme longings for sex, would have taken any opportunity to have it, and the source of many of my early religious questionings was the church's idiotic attitude toward sex. The answer it offered—wait until you are married and have sex only with that one woman whom you will love all your life—seemed ludicrous. It was as if the church advocated taking a raging bull and keeping it around the house as a parlor pet.

A major factor in my attitude was that I had discovered a lifelong love of literature, and the writers I admired took a dim view of the church and an exalted one of sex. My first great love was Hemingway, whose work I read in its entirety (including the startling early story "Up in Michigan": "The boards were hard. Jim had her dress up and was trying to do something to her. She was frightened but she wanted it. She had to have it but it frightened her. . . . 'Oh, it's so big and it hurts so.'"). I soon read a biography of Theodore Dreiser, who had led a wild and tormented sex life, and that book led me to his freethinking contemporaries, men like Sherwood Anderson and Edgar Lee Masters. But no book I read in my youth had as devastating an impact on my religious convictions as a posthumous collection of Mark Twain's writing, *Letters from the Earth*.

I think of Mark Twain, despite his lofty reputation, as one of the most underestimated of American authors. He is known as the author of one great book, otherwise a puffed-up children's writer, the kind of crusty old humorist with whom you'd like to sit by the fire and swap tall tales. Twain, under the urging of his wife, largely created this image. But—especially if you include his posthumous work—he was one of our most prolific and wide-ranging authors, with a disarmingly natural style that expresses itself effortlessly on every subject. He had a deeper and clearer mind than he is often given credit for.

Letters from the Earth is to some extent just the work of the village atheist: it takes the myths that fundamentalists have accepted as hard reality and blasts them to hell, with the devastating wit and intelligence that Twain was capable of on almost any subject. (One particularly damning fact, I remember, was the number of insects that must have been present on Noah's Ark.) It didn't leave much of my religious heritage standing. But in addition to the fact that—at least to my sixteen-year-old self—Twain seemed more intelligent than anyone in the church, he also seemed to care more. He wrote about those questions with the passion of a true believer.

I became at that age a libertine of the mind who would have been much more adventurous in his life if he hadn't been so timid, but whose ideas were as wild as anyone's. I passed through adolescence at the moment when the laws of censorship were being lifted in this country and had the enormous thrill of reading the great banned works when they were first published, in the mid-sixties. We went from James Gould Cozzens and Grace Metalious to *The Story of O* and the Marquis de Sade in the space of about a year. Of all the writers I read during that impressionable and fertile time, none is more important to me than Henry Miller.*

---

*Miller is a man who wrote equally, and equally well, about sex and spirituality; he is a member in good standing in my pantheon of prophets, and in a different kind of book I would certainly be writing about him. But

In an odd way, I think of Miller and Twain together. They are both essentially humorists with darkly comic visions. They both had wide-ranging, freewheeling styles that express everything from wild humor to deep sadness with equal ease. They were both iconoclasts. They both—while being quintessentially American—felt deep rage against this country. They both expressed the whole of themselves in their work.

I had been longing during my stifled youth for someone to tell me what sex was like, and Miller did. His descriptions weren't realistic, but he gave—with his wild, almost surrealistic descriptions—some idea of how much fun sex was. He inspired in me the certainty that it was best to tell the truth about this subject, to be as bold and explicit as I could. I have never, since reading Henry Miller, thought it would be better if we just didn't talk about it.

Both sex and spirituality, throughout my adolescence, took residence in my head, where they were to reside comfortably for years. I was rescued from my virginity and my lack of sexual experience by the woman who would be my first wife, whom I met when I was in college. Those were wild days, and we couldn't have had much more sex early in our marriage than we did. But that element of fantasy—which was inextricably connected with sex for the rest of my life—still fed on anxiety and was insatiable. It didn't matter how much sex my body had. My mind was always ready for more.

the fact is that, though he knew sex and spirituality to be one, he wrote about them almost entirely separately. There are the famous banned books, which delve into sex with a zest that has seldom been seen in world literature, and there are the books he wrote when he moved back to this country, which hardly contain a dirty word. (*The Rosy Crucifixion* is an exception, but he had planned that trilogy before the *Tropics*.) It is also true that after the Paris years, he was almost entirely a monogamous married man. He fell head over heels in love rather than fooling around.

PAIN IN MY HEART

In my mid-twenties—when I had been married for five years and was the father of a two-year-old, and was an English teacher and chairman of the department at a secondary school—I began to experience a pain beneath my breastbone. It felt like a tightening, a pressure, a slight burning. I had no idea what it was, but in the days after I first noticed it, it seemed to get worse. Finally I went to a doctor, who told me that spot was a referral area for gastric pain.

"I think you've got gastritis," he said (which was probably Latin for "tightening, pressure, slight burning"). He modified my diet, put me on a mild stomach tranquilizer, and told me to buy some antacids. " 'Tis the season for ulcers."

It was the first time in my life I'd had a chronic pain, and it seemed alien and mysterious. I would wake up every morning hoping I wouldn't feel it, but soon—often before I got out of bed—I did, and as the day wore on I felt it more and more. My body tightened around it, as if compensating, and by the end of the day I was stiff and awkward, with a flashing pain burning at my heart. The pills didn't seem to do much good. Neither did the antacids, or my new diet. I was a nervous wreck.

Another aspect of my condition was that I started to wake up early, day after day before 5:00. I would open my eyes wondering if I was going to feel that pain and—wondering—would feel it (am *I* doing this? I would think. Am I making it up?). I would lie there worrying about it, unable to sleep. I stumbled through my days bleary-eyed and on edge.

One spring morning, with breezes and scents of honeysuckle drifting through the window, I lay there in despair, longing to be without pain, to get back to sleep. My wife woke up and I turned to embrace her, hoping to relax in that way that never failed me. I noticed when we touched that I wasn't as excited as usual—the pain seemed to cut me off from my body—but I didn't figure it mattered.

I slipped my half-erect penis into her, expecting the prolonged, relaxed lovemaking we usually had, the spine-snapping orgasm that brought it to an end. Instead, I ejaculated after two or three strokes, with a feeble shudder that felt like an accident. "What was that?" my wife said.

"I don't know," I said, flushing all over, breaking out in a cold sweat. I tried to laugh. "I don't know what happened."

I couldn't work, I was so tense. I couldn't eat what I wanted. I couldn't sleep. Now I couldn't make love.

I had enjoyed teaching since beginning it five years before and thought I was good at it, but my real vocation was as a writer, and in my fourth year of teaching, after years of scribbling away at stories during vacations, I had decided to write a novel. I had the enormous energy of youth and tremendous ambition; I would go to bed early every evening and get up at 5:00 to give myself a couple of hours at my desk. I loved those mornings as I sat there with a strong cup of coffee, watched the sun come up, and did the work that used my best energies.

I had been circulating stories ever since I'd been in college, had never had any accepted, but had always been sure my first novel would be published. The afternoon when I got home from work and saw that the manuscript had been returned was one of the worst shocks of my life. It was a blow to the heart.

Much of my life was a lie at that point. I hadn't told anyone except my wife that I wanted to be a writer. To the rest of the world I presented the bland front of an English teacher perfectly content with what he was doing. I had also—though this wasn't a lie, exactly—started attending church again, partly because everyone in North Carolina seemed to go to church, but primarily because I felt a spiritual need. I genuinely wanted a tradition and felt that the Presbyterian church in which I'd been raised was as good as any. I threw myself into it the same way I did everything else.

When I look back on my life in the church, what I remember more than anything else is tremendous effort. There was something that I had to believe: that's what being a Christian was, believing that thing (though there was some disagreement as to what it was). I read huge tomes of theology, Karl Barth and Paul Tillich, even the Catholic Hans Kung, trying to find a way that I, as a thinking being with my experience of the world, could accept this doctrine. There were moments when I did, when I felt at one with it, but then I would fall away and have to get back. I had to be faithful all the time, I felt. I had to hold steady.

If there was one part of me that didn't fit in with all that, that I kept having to cram into a little box where it didn't belong, it was my sexual self. Christianity as a religion is notoriously antisexual. There have always been people on the inside looking for loopholes (and some notable mavericks— like Paul Tillich himself—who apparently strayed), but the institutional church has treated sex as something that needs to be battened down and repressed, which is why, like a jack-in-the-box, it keeps popping up: ministers having affairs with housewives, priests molesting altar boys, fundamentalist preachers consorting with whores. Spiritual energy is sexy, is the problem. Truly religious people tend to be horny.* And though I was trying to be a Christian, I hadn't given up the convictions of my youth. I still thought Dreiser and Masters and Henry Miller were right.

It was also true that my erotic imagination—that old part of me—had not disappeared when I started attending church. If anything it had flowered. I still had what anyone would have called a fulfilling sex life, but the imagination is as infinite as the anxiety that fuels it and always wants more. I had a fascination for pornography and began to visit massage parlors. Both of these activities expressed fantasies and embodied my lifelong dream of a small room where a woman would do anything I wanted (if I paid enough) and where my acts would have no consequences (as long as nobody saw me sneaking out of the place. Once as I was walking out of a porn shop I ran into the father of one of my seventh graders going in. We both blushed and stammered, stood there dis-

---

*Westerners have tended to divorce the religious and sexual in their minds, as if afraid of tainting their religion. One way they have done that is by convincing themselves that their most cherished religious figures were or are celibate. Most recently, that was done with the great Indian teacher Krishnamurti. Even so fundamentally sexy a man as Alan Watts thought that Krishnamurti didn't "have any genital sex life because he is polymorphously erotic and gets the ecstasy through every nerve-end on his skin" (which he may well have done, though that doesn't seem a reason to leave the genitals out altogether). But Krishnamurti never claimed to be celibate and apparently had one woman friend or another all his life.

Similarly, Jesus has always been regarded as having no sex life at all. He apparently didn't marry, and I don't know what the sexual customs were in his day, but there is no reason to assume they were more refined than now. He definitely spent time with the dregs of society, prostitutes in particular. His conservative followers have always assumed he was trying to save those sinners, but I'm not so sure. He may just have found them to be good company, more open to his message than conventionally religious people. Centuries later, the great Zen master Ikkyu would similarly enjoy the company of whores.

cussing the kid's progress in an impromptu parent-teacher conference. I didn't tell him about the particularly exquisite blow job in booth 12, or whichever it was). I dreamed of a place where I wasn't under the pressure of the outside world, where my stomach didn't hurt, and where I never felt like a failure.

What I needed to do, of course, was pay attention to the feelings I was escaping with my fantasies. It is hard to say just what the pain in my heart was: anxiety, anger, sadness, fear, probably a combination of all those things. Most basically, it was disappointment that the world hadn't turned out the way I wanted, my life as a novelist hadn't materialized. I didn't need to take tranquilizers or chew antacids. I needed to feel my heart's pain.

I did finally stumble into the office of a counselor, through the intervention of my wife. He was a pastoral care counselor, a minister, and I discussed my theological questionings with him. But he also had the good sense to see that I was working as a teacher when I wanted to be a writer. He got this point across when he had me go home and make a list of the five most important things in my life, and teaching—which occupied nine or ten hours of my day—wasn't one of them. It was better to admit to the world what I wanted, even if I fell flat on my face. I was squeezing writing into a small part of my life, when the place it held in my heart was much larger.

The next year, in a new city—my wife had reasons of her own for wanting to make a change—I rode to work every day on a rickety secondhand bicycle that she and I shared. My job at the university library didn't start until noon, but I would go to a carrel in the stacks and write for a few hours before I began. Our small rental house in a working-class neighborhood was too noisy with our son around.

I was composing the book that would become my first published novel. It was lonely at first, not having seventh graders hanging all over me, and our income had taken a severe drop, though my wife was also working part-time. But my wife was happier, I was happier, and the tightness at my chest began to diminish. I was learning the long process of living, and writing, from the heart. I had stopped—for the meantime—going to church at all.

THE FEAR OF CREATION

Writing was my first spiritual discipline. It was a spiritual discipline before I knew what one was. I actually made it into one, as if reinventing the wheel, because that was the way to get the work done. My writing hours have always been as regular as those of a monastery, and I have built my day— writing in the morning, exercise in the afternoon, reading in the evening—around my vocation. It became my religion, and I believed it would lead to my salvation.*

It was also a spiritual discipline because it put me in touch with the energy of creation, made me stare into the void out of which that energy came. I was extremely confident as a rewriter, felt I could always make something good if I just had words on paper to work with, but that initial encounter

---

*I even, at one point—before I knew anything about meditation— instituted a period of quiet sitting before I worked. It was important to see how my body was and what was on my mind. Before you can sit and write, I used to say to myself, you have to be able to sit, and I actually referred to that twenty-minute period as "sitting practice," without ever having heard that term.

with the blank page was terrifying. I created a routine where I would do extremely rapid and often sketchy rough drafts, then spend days and weeks rewriting them. I knew that those drafts were the key to my work, but I hated doing them. In my early years they were so rapid and sketchy that it was as if I were trying not to be aware, just to close my eyes and do it.*

That process—because it was full of anxiety—was always associated with sexual energy, sexual feelings and fantasy. The content of my writing has been sexual not just because I am interested in the subject but because it was often on my mind as I wrote. I didn't look into that fact too carefully, just figured it was how I was ("tangled in red thread from head to foot,"[1] as the Zen master Ikkyu put it). By staring into the void that all writers—all creators—must face, I was creating tremendous anxiety. And I was escaping it in the same old way.

I did notice that my forays into illicit sex bore a relationship to my writing. I felt those urges most strongly on the first day of a project, when I was facing the anxiety of the void, and on the last, when I faced the emptiness of being finished (and when I often gave in to the temptation, as if rewarding myself). The last day of work was often a short one, of typing or revising, and it was as if I had raised that energy and had nothing to do with it. I was all dressed up with no place to go. So I went someplace (and undressed).†

---

*A major part of my learning process as a writer has involved becoming more conscious as I write the first draft, giving myself to it and trusting it more. I rewrite less than I used to, not—I hope—because I am less dedicated, but because I believe in the first draft more.

†The practice of meditation calls up that energy without doing anything with it, just experiences the raw energy itself, and the void from which it emerges. Zen (like other forms of Buddhism) associates itself with various

I believed sex to be a vast and fascinating realm and that to explore it I would have to have a wide variety of experiences. I did just about everything I'd imagined, one way or another. My experiences of paying for sex split along the lines of all sexual encounters; some were deeply satisfying and a lot of fun; others were terrible. I didn't find the women who did sex work to be much different from other working-class women. I liked many of them. They didn't put on airs.

I didn't give up going to massage parlors because of anything about the experiences themselves but because the compulsion became too powerful. A certain situation would arise—I would have some free time and spare money—and the temptation would be irresistible. Sometimes—feeling it—I would lie on my bed for four or five minutes, trembling uncontrollably. I couldn't understand why I was at the mercy of it. The wish often expressed itself in that same ache under my breastbone that I had experienced in my mid-twenties. The only way to soothe it, I had decided, was to hold it against a woman's body.

LOOKING INTO MY HEART

I think of the therapist I began seeing at that point as my first spiritual teacher. He was a tall, well-built, handsome man whose very posture in his chair—utterly open to what I was saying—embodied presence. He was accepting of everything I told him, and his attention was profoundly healing. Much of what he taught was awareness practice. "Just try to stay

artistic enterprises—writing poetry, arranging flowers, making tea—and those are ways to practice Zen (ultimately, anything is a way to practice Zen), but the purest way is just to sit. When I describe meditation to my writing friends, I say, "It's just like writing, only you don't do the writing."

with it," he would say, to whatever feeling I brought up. He led me to other spiritual teachers, was the first person—for instance—to suggest that I read Krishnamurti. He was also skillful in helping me use writing as part of my therapy.

At that point, looking from the outside, you would have said I had no religious life at all. After that change in my late twenties—from teacher to writer—I looked for a church for a while, but the part of me the church wouldn't accept was growing more prominent, not less, especially because I was writing about it. I had become extremely impatient with Protestant religious ritual, all the singing and reading and talking to God. The Quakers captured me for a while because of their silence, but I eventually felt there was a part of me, and of human nature—a violent, aggressive part—that they tried to repress.

Along the way I did meet some authentically religious souls, the kind of person who just has a different feel to him, the air feels different around him. One was named Will Campbell, famous in the South as a renegade iconoclast, a political liberal educated at Yale who had nevertheless ministered to snake handlers and poison drinkers and the Klan (though his stands for racial justice were well known). He ran a small religious organization whose motto was Be Ye Reconciled, and his work was reconciling different groups. He was notorious at religious conferences for chewing tobacco and sneaking off for nips of bourbon, scandalous behavior for a Baptist in the South.

He gave the greatest Christian sermon I ever heard, at the Duke University chapel ("I like it when God tells me to be reconciled to little black girls integrating their schools. I like it when he tells me to be reconciled to snake handlers and poison swallowers. I like it when he tells me to be reconciled to members of the Klan. But how can I be reconciled to this?" He gestured all around him, to the ornate expensive chapel, the decorous congregation in front of him. "But that's what he says."). A few days later, when I sat down with him in the dining hall, I felt that peculiar openness, that lack of a barrier, that I was later to feel with other spiritual teachers.

I also had my first introduction to Buddhist thought, though it wasn't presented that way and I didn't know what it was, while I was working at Duke. I read the student newspaper, and many of the campus controversies were addressed by letters from a professor named Roger Corless, who taught Eastern religions and would later write a book called *The Vision of Buddhism*. His letters captivated me, made a kind of sense I had never heard before; they wouldn't dive into the same old dispute but reframed it in a whole new way. When addressing a controversy about sex, he said something to the effect of, "Anything you do with your deepest energy is a sexual act," and I simultaneously had no idea what he was talking about and was absolutely sure he was right.

My therapist was open to conversation about spiritual matters, though he didn't address them in the abstract, always wanted to stay in the here and now. At that moment in my life I was bristly on the whole subject of religion; I felt a yearning for some spiritual life but couldn't find anything that seemed right. A woman friend mentioned my anger on this subject, and that surprised me; I would have said I was disappointed. But I brought it up with my therapist.

"You are angry," he said.

That was two people who had seen it.

"I don't know why I'd be angry," I said.

He got an odd look on his face, as if trying to decide whether or not to say something. "I know," he said.

He had five clients at that moment who felt the same anger, he said, and all of them had been adolescents when their fathers died.

He had just brought up the tenderest fact of my life. He had also opened up the question about religion in a whole new way.

"What's that got to do with it?" I said.

"That's a time of great religious questioning," he said. "Then this thing happens that turns your whole world upside down and seems so unfair. Instead of acknowledging those feelings and letting you have them, people offer feeble explanations. 'It was all for the best.' 'God has a plan.' "

I heard many such statements after my father died, when I was sixteen.

"Those people mean well," he said. "But they're missing the point. They need to let you roar."

Roaring was something I hadn't done.

Mark Twain had been eleven when his father died. He expressed his rage in biting comedy, often hilarious, but it was the bitter, disappointed anger of a man who deeply wants to believe. I have sensed the same passion in other famous atheists, most notably Jean Paul Sartre and Bertrand Russell, who also lost their fathers when they were young.

People assumed that because I didn't believe what they did, because our religious discussions thrust me into the role of a naysayer, I didn't believe anything, and that wasn't true. I sat down one week and, using my long writing mornings, wrote what I did believe, the tenets of the tiny sect (one member) to which I belonged, not to show anyone, just to have done it.

Not long after that—and why I picked the book up at that particular moment I don't know—I read a book that had belonged to my wife (from whom I was now separated), that everyone had read and been influenced by in the sixties but I had not, buried in literature though I was. The book didn't trace the outlines of my little sect but came closer than anything else I'd read, and I suddenly felt I wasn't entirely alone in the universe. There was a centuries-old spiritual tradition that was much in accord with what I believed. The book was *The Way of Zen*.

In the meantime, I had to roar. That knot beneath my breastbone, which had continued to reappear, now seemed to be unfelt rage, and in order to begin feeling it I did some typically macho things: I bought a heavy punching bag and would go down in the basement to pound on it and scream, sometimes until my knuckles were bloody. On a couple of other occasions, I went to my therapist's building late in the afternoon and beat the hell out of his office with a foam rubber encounter bat, roaring and stomping like a lunatic. It was frightening to see the depth of my rage. But I worked through a lot of the emotion around my father.

Those sessions did untie the knot in my chest, but they were exhausting and would leave me sore for days afterward. I thought at the time that there must be another way. A person shouldn't have to exhaust himself to feel his emotion.

One other kind of therapy that put me in touch with emotion, and brought about an enormous amount of healing, was legitimate massage. The real reason to get a massage is just that it feels good—pleasure is its own excuse—but massage also involved a great deal of learning for me. A woman touching my naked body had always been sexual in the past, but this was not, or at least it wasn't genital. The one place on my body that all such touching had been directed to was not being touched. It brought the rest of me into relief.

A man cut off from his feelings is cut off from his body, because that's where they reside. I had a substantial number of discoveries to make as my masseuse slowly touched me, part by part. I discovered sexual feelings, of course, but also much more tender, vulnerable ones. I found that beneath the anger that I'd held in my chest (and that I'd had to get through before I could feel anything else) was a great sadness. There seemed to be more emotion beneath that.

There was a particularly tender spot far down on my belly that my anger seemed to be trying to protect; when we finally got through to it, I did a great deal of crying and felt a tremendous release of energy. The novel I wrote at the end of my therapy, *The Autobiography of My Body,* explored what I think of now as the small room of my sexuality, the tiny place in my life where I had relegated it. I ended my novel with a feeling that there was more to come. "There is another way to love in me," I said in my last sentence, "lying in my body waiting for me to find it."

I knew there was further to go. Therapy had taken me as far as it could.

BETTER THAN A BROTHEL
The whole subject of religion had come up because, three years after my first wife and I had split up, I fell in love with a woman for whom religion was extremely important. She had been raised a Catholic, had done social justice work with priests and nuns in Nicaragua and El Salvador, and was now planning to go to divinity school in Boston. We had various arguments about religion and spirituality—once again I was

placed in my naysaying role—and Buddhist practice, which interested her also, seemed an uneasy meeting place.

She said that when we moved to Cambridge we should take a course together at the Cambridge Insight Meditation Center. I went along with this suggestion—I had nothing better to do—but would never have made it myself. I had been burned too many times in the past.

But Buddhist practice—at least as it was presented to us—skirted my problems with religion. It didn't posit a set of beliefs that you subscribed to, just said to sit down and see what you saw. It didn't involve talking to God, singing to God, petitioning God, all of which I found ludicrous (since God knows our true thoughts, and what we really need, better than we do). It didn't mention God at all. It seemed to assume that whatever reality there was would present itself if you would just sit and be open to it. That was what I had always believed. Buddhist practice gave specific suggestions about how to be open.

I found the actual experience difficult. Our class met in a dim, cold basement, and there was an ethic of silence around the place (carried over from retreats) that seemed unfriendly. I wasn't good at meditating; I experienced tremendous physical pain, I couldn't stick with the breathing, and my mind was full of cascading thoughts.

Yet something about the practice, even in those early weeks, captured my devotion. I couldn't do it, but it seemed worth doing. The thing I had said about writing—that I had to learn to sit before I could sit and write—seemed true about everything: the practice of awareness was the basis of all activity. I loved the immediacy of it, the down-to-earth quality; people weren't asking what I believed or telling what they did, lambasting my spiritual inadequacies. Week after week, all the teacher said was the instructions, and all we talked about was what happened as we sat.

This was a new way of looking into the self. It was a new way to encounter the body; in fact, it was as if I'd never encountered it before. I was also deeply impressed—though this is a long subject of its own—with the authenticity of our teacher, Larry Rosenberg. He didn't act spiritual. He never even mentioned the word.

My stay in Cambridge—though rich and rewarding—was one of the more difficult transitional periods of my life. I had recently turned forty and had left North Carolina, where I'd lived for more than twenty years. My son had gone off to college. I'd left behind many friends, a men's group, my therapist, my masseuse, and what little reputation I had as a writer.

I'd just published my fourth novel, for which I'd gotten the large advance that enabled me to move at all, but a novel that I'd written in the intervening year had been turned down by my publisher, and I couldn't seem to publish anything in Cambridge. I couldn't even get a book review assignment. My girlfriend (soon to be my second wife) had moved for a purpose and had immediately plugged into intense activity and a whole new group of people, but I had moved just to be with her. I found myself losing confidence, unsure of my identity (not a bad situation to be in when you're taking up spiritual practice).

I was also—and this does not seem unrelated—having trouble with sex. For years I'd had one way to operate, in that small room I was so familiar with. I'd begun to see through that but hadn't found anything to replace it. That feeling of confusion was compounded by the fact that my brother had been diagnosed with prostate cancer and was facing the possibility that he might never have sex again (to say nothing of the fact that he might die). I had a sympathetic reaction to his news. I could hardly function at all.

There is no lack of material on a middle-aged man's problems with sex. Magazine articles abound, as do books with titles like *Sex Over Forty, Sex Over Fifty* (and as the boomers age I'm sure we'll come up with *Sixty, Seventy,* and *Eighty*). The traditional answer has been to find younger and better-looking babes, women that you keep as mistresses (if you're a wealthy businessman) or that you teach (if you're a professor or a wayward Zen master) or that you buy (if you can scrape up the money for a young whore). (The assumption—which neatly puts the blame on the woman—is that middle-aged women aren't attractive, though I have found them attractive all my life.) Articles and books—which can't openly offer that solution—suggest more realistic expectations, more advanced sexual techniques, direct stimulation of the penis, a finer grade of porn flick. . . .

I am convinced that the sexual problems of middle-aged men are the symptoms of a spiritual crisis that has nothing to do with sex. Men are rummaging around in their small rooms looking for younger women, better gadgets, subtler techniques, when the real answer is outside the room altogether. It is a matter of discovering what sexual energy really is, something like what Roger Corless meant when he said that anything you do with your deepest energy is a sexual act. It is a matter not of looking for new places to find sex but of seeing that sex is everywhere.

This is the sex of the Chink in Tom Robbins's *Even Cowgirls Get the Blues,* who could seem to have sex at will; of the Zen master that Alan Watts knew who "on one occasion . . . made it with his lady friend sixteen times in twenty-four hours." It is what Whitman meant when he celebrated the body electric, what D. H. Lawrence meant when he said that sex "consists in infinite different flows between the two beings, different, even apparently contrary. Chastity is part of the flow . . . as is physical passion. And beyond these, an infinite range of subtle communication which we know nothing about."

It is what Marco Vassi understood when he said "the bodhi is the body," what the former porn star Annie Sprinkle refers to when she says, "When you truly let your sexual energy flow freely throughout your entire being, you feel as if you're making love every moment of every day, with everything and with everyone." There is no real prescription for finding it (though some of these workshop leaders do have techniques), and no easy way to describe it. For me, the best way is to tell some stories:

After a year in Cambridge, and many trials, I discovered a wonderful masseuse, one who seemed to have the same magic hands as my friend in North Carolina. At the end of the first massage, I was lying facedown on the table with my eyes closed, practically asleep. I was aware that the masseuse was still in the room but not touching me. I was in such a blissfully relaxed state that I didn't particularly care what she was doing.

At some point, though, I began to feel a tingling glow that began at the base of my spine and spread over my whole body. It was an exquisite sensation, like what I would have imagined a drug rush to be. I almost said something but didn't want it to stop. I wasn't having sexual thoughts at all, but the feeling itself gave me an erection. Eventually the masseuse left the room. When I got downstairs I asked what had been going on at the end. "I was balancing your chakras," she said, "with a crystal. But yours were already balanced." As a result of the massage, no doubt.

• Once when we were visiting my family in Pittsburgh, my second wife and I were staying in a small hotel, and I was meditating early in the morning while she slept. There was nothing special about the sitting, but when I had finished I noticed my wife was awake, and I got into bed with her. I have been known to be too insistent about sex in the morning, before my partner is really awake, so I was being careful not to do that. I actually wasn't thinking about sex at all.

But as I embraced her I had a feeling I'd never had before; it was as if I could feel her energy, through her skin, all over her body. It was racing and seemed to flow into me. It was a marvelous feeling, more intense than what I'd felt from the crystal. I got an erection.* "You want to have sex," my wife said. "How can you tell?" I said. Actually, I didn't care. Sex couldn't have been any more blissful than feeling her energy.

• A number of times while sitting on my cushion I've experienced—for no particular reason—that same feeling of rushing energy. One morning I felt it for almost three hours, sitting and walking, and I remember thinking, quite distinctly, "This is better than sex. This is better than any sex I ever had." Even having that thought didn't stop it. It went on and on.

• My wife and I had returned to North Carolina after she finished her degree, and—following a nine-day meditation retreat—I had visited my old masseuse. I was lying on my back

---

*There is a qualitative difference in the erections that I'm describing in these anecdotes; men will understand what I mean. They are not the kind of erections that someone *gives* you; they are the kind you just get, like a force of nature. They are also not the kind you lose, partly because you never "had" them. They are much harder and more solid than the usual erection, standing there effortlessly as the man gazes at them in wonder. They are the kind of erection cultures build monuments to.

and she had dug her fingers under the base of my skull, an extremely relaxing procedure. Suddenly I had a feeling of falling, as if I'd just stepped into an elevator shaft, but I never landed. The place I'd fallen into was vast and spacious, full of enormous energy. It felt as if the energy were both outside and inside me. I also had an overwhelming feeling of love. The whole experience was somehow larger than any I'd had before. As usual, I got one of those monumental erections.

I later asked my masseuse if she'd felt that energy. I didn't mention the emotional content, which was slightly embarrassing. "No," she said, "I didn't feel any energy. But I felt an enormous feeling of love. Not for you, particularly. It was just love."

• My teacher, Larry Rosenberg, describes this place of peace and energy and love—which people sometimes reach in deep meditation states—as the abode of silence. "You've all entered it many times," he says, "because every night, the experts tell us, we have four or five hours of dreamless sleep. It's the same thing. The ego isn't present."

During that dreamless sleep—another kind of expert tells us—men have an erection. It's as if the body, in its deepest and most natural and energetic state, with the ego not present, is sexual.

Much to my surprise, I have learned more about sex on a meditation cushion than I ever did in a whorehouse. I have learned, for instance, that a great deal of what I thought of as sexual excitement, plain old horniness, was a result of thought, images that come and go, stimulated by certain conditions (often, in my case, a feeling of anxiety). Given enough thought, I can work myself into elaborate states of mind, the conviction, for instance, that if I don't go to a massage parlor I'll go crazy.

But it is all just thought, what D. H. Lawrence calls, with an almost audible contempt, sex in the head. If I actually *went* to the massage parlor, it would still be sex in the head. (A great deal of what passes for physical sex in this world is sex in the head.) It wouldn't belong to that deeper experience of the body that I felt in massage and during that morning with my wife. Often, as I've sat on the cushion, I've noticed that sexual thoughts weren't accompanied by any feeling in the body at all. My body didn't want sex. It was all in my head.

That distinction—between sex in the head and sex in the body—has been vastly important for me. You begin to see when it is really your body that wants sex (though, even then, you don't have to do anything about it. You can just be with it, like any other feeling). That physical reality is more mysterious than the mental activity, not less. Sex in the vast boundless space we call the body is not really something you do. It just happens. Sex Happens, all those bumper stickers should say.

What stimulates sexual thought most readily for me is fear. Beneath the anger I discovered in therapy, the sadness I discovered on the massage table—and interwoven with both of them—is fear, the mind state that I most often encounter on meditation retreats, especially longer ones. ("Anger is here," Zen teacher Ed Brown told us recently during a sesshin, drawing a line just under his ribcage. "Sadness is here, in the stomach. Fear is further down, in the lower abdomen. When you breathe really deeply, you sometimes call up fear.")

All of these emotions can express themselves by that now-familiar knot beneath my breastbone. Last year, on the final full day of a nine-day retreat, I was finally able to do what Larry Rosenberg had been telling me all along, just to be with that feeling, not to try to get rid of it or change it in any way, just to be intimate with that knot in my chest. I was with it for almost the whole day. I was afraid all day, in addition to feeling the knot. But I discovered tremendous energy in that intimacy. We did the usual eight or nine sittings, and I got up from every one as if it had been about thirty seconds. Walking meditation was the same. And after lunch I took my usual three-mile walk—wearing heavy boots, with ten inches of snow on the ground—and it was a breeze. It was like walking across the street.

The fear I am speaking of, I think, is what I referred to earlier as the fear of God, the fear of an aware being in an infinite and mysterious universe, the same fear that has kept me up nights, made me stroke my penis raw, stimulated illicit affairs, chased me into porn parlors, wrapped me in the arms of whores. But it is energy, and by running from it—as I did for most of my life, full tilt—I was running from energy. We can call it creative energy, spiritual energy, sexual energy. Those are just terms that human beings have invented. There is only one energy.

You don't tap into it by running from it. I spent half a lifetime doing that. You tap into it by turning toward it, what the great teacher and writer and mystic Eihei Dogen called "tak[ing] the backward step that turns the light inward to illumine the self." When you do that, they tell me—I have only stuck my toe in that ocean—you discover that everything is the self. The self is everything. The vast empty universe that I am afraid of is me.

NOTE

1. John Stevens, trans., *Wild Ways: Zen Poems of Ikkyu* (Boston: Shambhala Publications, 1991) 70.

~ 2
American Buddha

WALT WHITMAN

When buddhas are truly buddhas they do
not necessarily notice that they are buddhas.
However, they are actualized buddhas, who
go on actualizing buddhas.

—EIHEI DOGEN, *Genjo Koan*

"How did [Walt] make love?" I forced
myself to ask.
"I will show you," he smiled. "Let us go to
bed."

—GAVIN ARTHUR,
on his meeting with Edward Carpenter.

I HAD NOT READ much Walt Whitman, that first year
when I lived in Cambridge and was settling into my spiritual practice. I was not a great reader of poetry in general. But I periodically resolved to read the classics; I loved

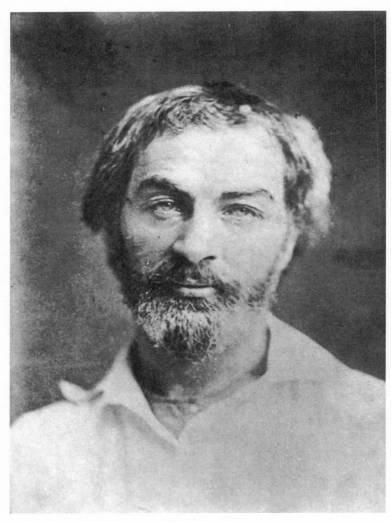

~ WALT WHITMAN, 1854

the Library of America volumes, and when I stumbled across the Whitman volume I resolved to take a month, or whatever it took, and read straight through it. My wife spent most of her time studying, and my evenings were free.*

It was one of the richest reading experiences of my life. I am actually glad I didn't encounter him sooner because—unlike many great poets—he is primarily a poet of middle age, when he began composing poetry seriously and when he is best read.

Never had I read a poet who spoke so personally to the reader, as if you were right there with him, perhaps lolling in a field, as he portrays himself at the beginning of "Song of Myself." Never had I read one who spoke with such spiritual authority, even in the odd, wandering, stream-of-consciousness prose preface of the first edition, in which he suddenly thunders forth like an Old Testament prophet.

> This is what you shall do: Love the earth and sun and the animals, despise riches, give alms to every one that asks, stand up for the stupid and crazy, devote your income and labor to others, hate tyrants, argue not concerning God.[1]

Never had I read a nineteenth-century poet who was so frank about sex; despite his weird diction, there was no question what he was talking about.

> Ebb stung by the flow and flow stung by the ebb, love-flesh swelling and deliciously aching,

---

*One of the major questions with Whitman is deciding which edition of the poetry to read. He called his life's work *Leaves of Grass* but kept revising and adding to it, from the first time he published a volume under that title, in 1855, at the age of thirty-six, until the "Death-Bed" edition of 1892. Some great and essential poems were added along the way, but the first edition had a rough freshness that none of the others could match. The Library of America solved this dilemma by printing both the first and the last editions, one after the other, along with a substantial swatch of prose.

>Limitless limpid jets of love hot and enormous, quivering
>   jelly of love, white-blow and delirious juice,
>Bridegroom night of love working surely and softly into the
>   prostrate dawn[2]

But the most astonishing thing about Whitman was that despite the fact that he could have known little about Buddhism, he seemed to be a Buddhist. He seemed to be the Buddha. In no other classic author had I found so perfect an embodiment of Buddhist teachings. And he wasn't talking about a Bodhi tree in India, or the forests of Thailand. He was talking about the world I walked through every day, the rich American urban landscape.

Whitman let me know that the dharma wasn't something I found just by sitting on a cushion or reading an esoteric Eastern text. This *is* the Buddha dharma, I would think, as I made my way through yet another of his enormous lists, one closely observed American scene after another. "Not till the sun excludes you do I exclude you,"[3] he famously said to a streetwalker, and he passes that attitude on. He let me know that the Buddha was everywhere. He was standing on the next Cambridge street corner, waiting to ask me for a quarter.

Was He or Wasn't He?

The problem really came up at the end of his career, when Whitman was surrounded by slavish admirers who doted on his every word. Until then, people had read his verse and found what they wanted. Some, like Richard Bucke and William O'Connor, found a holy book that changed their lives forever. More than one woman found the same thing, a vital connection to the source of all life, and wrote to Whitman offering deep friendship, her hand in marriage, or (as Groucho Marx would say) her whole body.

Until then his heterosexual poems had been the ones that got him in trouble. The Calamus section (named after a remarkably phallic waterside plant), concerning the dear love of comrades, had been passed over almost without comment, at least by the censors. But in 1890 a British admirer named John Addington Symonds wrote rather timidly to the poet asking his blessing on a certain behavior, about which Symonds, as a married man with three children, was obviously ambivalent.

> In your conception of Comradeship, do you contemplate the possible intrusion of those semi-sexual emotions and actions which no doubt do occur between men? I do not ask, whether you approve of them, or regard them as a necessary part of this relation? But I should like to know whether *you are prepared to leave them to the inclinations and the conscience of the individuals concerned?*[4]

Whitman, who had been the boldest and most outspoken of authors, did not always react well to direct personal questions. At first he planned not to answer the letter, then, when he did, he was reduced to sputtering.

> Ab't the questions on Calamus pieces &c: they quite daze me. L of G. is only to be rightly construed by and within its own atmosphere and essential character—all of its pages & pieces so coming strictly under *that*—that the calamus part has even allow'd the possibility of such construction as mention'd is terrible—I am fain to hope the pages themselves are not to be even mention'd for such gratuitous and quite at the time entirely undream'd & unreck'd possibility of morbid inferences—wh' are disavowed by me and seem damnable. . . .
>
> Tho' always unmarried I have had six children—two are

dead—One living southern grandchild, fine boy, who writes to me occasionally.[5]

David S. Reynolds, in his superbly informative *Walt Whitman's America*, suggests that this was really just a cultural clash. Whitman had come up in the rough-and-ready nineteenth-century American working class, in which men hugged and kissed, even kissed rather passionately (Whitman mentions a half-minute kiss that was a part of his nursing duty during the war, and that he saw it strictly as a gesture of affection and comfort), and often—because of circumstances—slept in the same bed,* while Symonds came from a sophisticated European background in which the idea of homosexuality was just being formulated. He was asking, in effect, Are you one of these homosexuals they just invented? and Whitman answered, Hell, no. I just like to sleep with boys.

A cultural clash may have been part of it. Walt Whitman, the great accepter, the embracer of everyone and everything, didn't want to be crammed into a pigeonhole that had just been created by an effete European intellectual. But there is plenty of evidence that Whitman knew what Symonds was asking and was covering his tracks. The man who spoke so boldly in the great book of his life was not always so bold elsewhere.

Even in his journals, which he knew would be ransacked

---

*Where things occasionally got rather frisky. Reynolds unearthed a correspondence between two of the "great men" of the South, Thomas Withers and James H. Hammond, in which Withers asks Hammond "if he had recently had 'the extravagant delight of poking and punching a writhing Bedfellow with your long fleshen pole—the exquisite touches of which I have often had the honor of feeling?' Withers humorously recalls feeling defenseless before "the crushing force" of Hammond's 'Battering Ram' " (David S. Reynolds, *Walt Whitman's America,* [New York: Vintage Books, 1996], 394).

for information, he referred to Peter Doyle, the great love of his life, as 16.4, and changed the pronouns from *him* to *her* (though the marks of erasure are still evident, along with the dot above the *i*). And toward the end of his life, when he was finally finding some favor, he wasn't so fierce in fighting battles as before.

This is the same dispute that has been raging ever since, the red-faced high school English teacher explaining that customs were different in those days, that the word *love* didn't mean, well, you know, love—"Let's have another look at 'O Captain, My Captain'"—while gay boys in the know are convulsed with laughter, dead certain Walt is one of theirs. The discussion even takes place at a more exalted level, Harold Bloom arguing in a PBS documentary that Whitman wasn't really a sexual being, that he probably almost never had sex, while Allen Ginsberg stated that his relationships with boys were "probably" genital.

We see what we want to. And I, writing a book on sex and spirituality, am hardly exempt. Yet one of my most cherished beliefs is that the great writer cannot help revealing himself.* I don't mean that he can't lie but that he will sooner or later give himself away because he writes from a deep place of truth. Whitman quite consciously did so and knew he did. That was why he didn't sign his name to his book. (He told Horace Traubel, "It would be a sacrilege to put a name there—it would seem just like putting a name on the universe."[6])

But if we sit down and read the poems, it is obvious that

---

*Whitman says as much himself in his prose preface: "The greatest poet . . . is more the channel of thoughts and things without increase or diminution, and is the free channel of himself" (Walt Whitman, *Complete Poetry and Selected Prose* [New York: The Library of America, 1982], 14).

Whitman adored men. The question of his sexual orientation is a howler (and I'm not one of the gay boys in the know).* He also celebrated straight sex, but that sounds more like a paid political announcement. He was an ardent feminist and obviously admired women as much as any other man of his day, but I've never been absolutely convinced he had sex with them.† I believe it was Christopher Isherwood who said that your sexual orientation is reflected not by who you have sex with but by who you fall in love with. Whitman may have had sex with women. But he loved men.

PORTRAIT OF THE ARTIST AS A WORKING-CLASS HACK

The one woman that Whitman did love—and the only experience in his life of fully requited love, according to Justin

---

*Whether or not he expressed that love genitally is—pardon the expression—up for grabs, but I don't really see that it matters. That gets into the whole question of what sex is, which is a real can of worms, but which we will nevertheless be facing throughout this book. Most men believe that sex takes place when a penis becomes erect and emits semen, preferably in the orifice of another person's body. I concede that such an occasion probably is sex. But I once knew a woman—a lesbian—who told me that she often had orgasms when her breasts were kissed. Was that genital sex? I knew a man who had an orgasm when he went down on a woman. Was that genital sex, for him? Did he "have sex"? I don't know! But I don't hesitate to say that Whitman had sex with men.

†Edward Carpenter, who was an outspoken gay apologist and knew Whitman, said that he did. Justin Kaplan offers a contrasting opinion in a footnote: "From an interview with people in Huntington who remembered Whitman from his *Long Islander* days there: 'We inquired whether Walt was a gay lad among the lassies of the village—a beau in the rustic society of his day—and both received the same reply: "Not in the least." "He seemed to hate women," said one of them—a hard, and, I am sure, quite too strong expression'" (Justin Kaplan, *Walt Whitman: A Life* [New York: Simon and Schuster, 1980], 285).

Kaplan—was his mother. Though Whitman's father was a freethinker, a scoffer at religion whose hero was Thomas Paine and who had an obvious intellectual influence on his son, Louisa Whitman's influence is just as important but harder to pin down. She was "strangely knowing,"[7] her son once said, and came from Quaker stock; the whole family, in fact, "tended toward Quakerism,"[8] and even Walt's father admired Elias Hicks, a renegade Quaker and fiery orator who fiercely denied any spiritual authority other than the inner light in all of us.

But the influence of Louisa Whitman was strong. Though Whitman claimed in *Leaves of Grass* to be "one of the roughs," most of his contemporaries found him to be quite feminine, and his love of young men, and especially the nursing he did in military hospitals during the Civil War, often seems motherly. And when Louisa Whitman died at the age of eighty, when Walt himself was fifty-four and already in poor health, his reaction was stronger than to any other sadness in his life.

> He sat up by her coffin all night before the funeral and in the morning he was still sitting there, his head down, both hands clasped on his cane. Over and over again in a keening rhythm he lifted and brought it down on the floor with a thud. Mourners in the next room felt the floor shake.[9]

Walter Whitman Sr. was a carpenter and house builder, and though he was apparently an alcoholic and had an extremely spotty employment record, he did fine work, which his son admired. The elder Whitman didn't fare too well with his children. One daughter married badly and did some time as a prostitute. Three of his sons, according to Justin Kaplan,

were "psychic disasters,"[10] and one was a mental defective.*
One son, of course, was the greatest poet this country has
yet produced.

But the old man could not hold down a job. Whitman
had lived in twelve houses by the time he was eleven years
old, when his formal schooling ended. Like other classic
American writers, he entered the world of letters as a typesetter, apprenticing to a printer at the age of twelve. He had
grown up on Long Island, near the ocean, which was a major
inspiration for his verse. The family moved from town to
town throughout his childhood, and when he was twelve
they settled in Brooklyn, where Walt took a job. When the
family moved that time, he stayed behind.

He was a big boy, six feet and 180 pounds by the age of
sixteen, by which time he was a journeyman printer who had
worked for a number of newspapers. He was an omnivorous
reader of novels and poetry but did not set the world on fire
as an employee. He was actually rather indolent, a big lunk
who liked to sleep late and had trouble showing up on time
(years later, when he was in his fifties and living with his
family again, they would have the same complaint). He
didn't work at all if he could help it and may have started
writing to fill the pages of the papers he worked for.

He also wrote poetry, but his early verse was wooden
and derivative, giving no hint of what was to come. His early
life was unpromising in general.

When he was sixteen and the job market at newspapers
had dried up, he became a schoolmaster for a time. He could
have gone to work on the family farm, but despite his love

---

*Eddy Whitman eventually wound up in an asylum, but until then Walt
often cared for him and sometimes shared his bed. When Whitman stands
up for the stupid and crazy, and for powerful uneducated persons, one can't
help thinking he referred to his brother.

of laborers and of the spectacle of physical labor, "Walt would not farm,"[11] according to his brother. He just enjoyed watching other men sweat. He was apparently a good teacher, liked by his students, but his teaching career ended abruptly, and though that may just be one more instance of his employment problems, David Reynolds believes he may have committed sodomy with one of his students and been tarred and feathered by the townspeople.[12]

It was common for the schoolteacher to board with a local family and share a bed with one of the children, and Whitman supposedly took advantage of the situation. The word *sodomy* is a trifle vague, but people spoke in this case of "bloody bedding." Whitman often spoke to Horace Traubel, his Boswell, of a dark secret from early in his life, and Reynolds believes this may have been it. But the story only surfaced in a pamphlet published in the 1960s, and the usually thorough Justin Kaplan—whose biography of Whitman was published in 1980—does not mention it.

Years later, when Emerson praised the first edition of *Leaves of Grass,* he spoke of the "long foreground" the book must have had, but he could hardly have known how long. Especially for a poet, Whitman had an extraordinarily long apprenticeship, which can be seen in hindsight as a prelude to his great book but looked at the time like the fumblings of a bewildered young man. He had always admired oratory, ever since seeing Elias Hicks at the age of ten, and thought of becoming an itinerant lecturer, rather like Emerson, but nothing came of this plan, perhaps because Whitman was so shy.* He also started his own newspaper, apparently writing most of it himself, but it lasted only a few issues.

---

*In *My Life and Loves,* Frank Harris tells of an evening when he pinch-hit

He moved back to New York in 1841, when he was twenty-two, and all his life would sing the praises of both Brooklyn and Manhattan, the two great urban centers he loved. By that time he was an editor as well as a writer, and by 1845 he had edited at ten different papers. He was constantly trying his hand at various literary genres and wrote a "temperance novel," *Franklin Evans,* in which a young man got in trouble with booze and went down the road to ruin. Whitman later claimed that he had written the book in three days, on port, whiskey, and wine, but it was the most popular of his works in his lifetime, selling a startling twenty thousand copies. He also did a brief stint, in his late twenties, as a short-story writer. Though his stories were, once again, derivative, they made him his first reputation as a writer.

In trying to understand the influences that produced a masterpiece, critics speak of Whitman's cultural heritage, which does seem rich for a nineteenth-century American. *Leaves of Grass* includes much declamatory poetry, and Whitman continued in New York to admire oratory, hearing in 1842 Emerson's talk "The Poet," which virtually predicted Whitman's work. He was an avid theatergoer all his life and especially admired Junius Brutus Booth (father of John Wilkes), the most celebrated Shakespearean actor of his day.

---

for another journalist and went to hear a talk by Whitman on—interestingly—Thomas Paine, his father's old favorite. The talk was sparsely attended—"perhaps thirty persons scattered about in a space that would have accommodated a thousand"—and Whitman was not a captivating speaker, but Harris was impressed by his "perfect simplicity and sincerity of voice and manner." Harris had not at that time been won over to Whitman's poetry—though he would later come around—but he was impressed, when he told Whitman how sorry his friend was not to be there, at the man's reply. " 'I'm sorry too,' said Whitman slowly, 'for your friend Smith must have something large in him to be so interested in Paine and me' " (Frank Harris, *My Life and Loves* [New York: Grove Press, 1963], 190).

In 1845 Whitman became an editor and book reviewer for the Brooklyn *Daily Eagle,* where he stayed for two years and had an extremely fertile period as a reader, reviewing Carlyle, Coleridge, Goethe, George Sand, and Schlegel.[13]

Whitman fell in with a band of New York painters in his early thirties, and their realistic scenes of American streets were important in developing his aesthetic. He was obsessed for a time with an exhibit of Egyptian antiquities that was showing in New York. And he was always, especially in his thirties, a great lover of music, particularly opera, which Justin Kaplan believes freed him from the ballad form of most American poetry and inspired the long lines that were among his most striking innovations.

Whitman was also what would be regarded in our day as a New Age freak. He followed all the latest fads, and they had a profound influence on his work. One of the major movements of his day was hydrotherapy, the water cure, using water for "enemas, wet packs, long soaks, cascades."[14] In an age when most people had to be hog-tied and dragged into the bathtub once a week, Whitman bathed outdoors and daily, even in the coldest weather. That was one of the things he bragged about to Bronson Alcott and Thoreau when they came to visit him after reading his verse. He also boasted of it in the verse itself.

> I keep as delicate around the bowels as around the head and
> heart . . .
> Divine am I inside and out, and I make holy whatever I touch
> or am touch'd from,
> The scent of these arm-pits aroma finer than prayer.[15]

He was a believer in animal magnetism, and some of the stranger images of electricity in his verse—especially in "I Sing the Body Electric"—come from that ideology.

Mine is no callous shell
I have instant conductors all over me whether I pass or stop,
They seize every object and lead it harmlessly through me.[16]

He believed even sexual attraction to be magnetic:

Does the earth gravitate? does not all matter, aching, attract
    all matter?
So the body of me to all I meet or know.[17]

He also put great stock in phrenology, the science of reading the bumps of the skull. He considered putting his phrenological chart in an edition of *Leaves of Grass,* and two of his most characteristic words, *amativeness* (attraction to the opposite sex) and *adhesiveness* (attraction to the same sex) come from that discipline.

Justin Kaplan points out that these fads, however ridiculous they may sound today, gave Whitman the personal mythology that every poet needs, a vocabulary for discussing issues he wanted to raise. Amativeness and adhesiveness were especially helpful as he figured out his sexual makeup. And maybe it was blind luck, but his phrenological chart sounds remarkably accurate.

Leading traits of character appear to be Friendship, Sympathy, Sublimity, and Self-Esteem, and markedly among his combinations the dangerous faults of Indolence, a tendency to the pleasure of Voluptuousness and Alimentiveness, and a certain reckless swing of animal will, too unmindful, probably, of the conviction of others.[18]

Yet nothing explains the great poet. David Reynolds wrote 632 pages about the cultural influences on Whitman, and though he has produced a fascinating book that gives a richer explanation of these influences than anything else I have read, in another way he misses the point altogether. It is like telling us what a Zen master wore and who he talked to in the days preceding his awakening. Those details may be interesting, but they have nothing to do with the essential experience.

A SUMMER MORNING

Even during Whitman's life there were people who felt he had had some profound experience that in a single thunder-stroke had made him a great poet. An English biographer named Henry Bryan Binns believed, apparently on the basis of a single poem, that it was a trip Whitman had made to New Orleans, where he had had an affair with a mysterious Creole woman. This rumor even survived the discovery by a later biographer that the poem had originally been written about a man.

Henry Miller, who disliked the conventional image of Whitman ("I have never understood why he should be called 'the good gray poet.' The color of his language, his tempera-ment, his whole being is electric blue"[19]) had no doubt that there had been such an experience: "From the moment of his awakening—for it was truly an awakening and not a mere development of creative talent—he marches on, calm, steady, sure of himself, certain of ultimate victory."[20]

Academic critics put such a notion on roughly the level of Whitman's interest in phrenology. Yet they have no better explanation for how this itinerant typesetter, reporter, editor, hack novelist and short-story writer, derivative apprentice poet, apparent dilettante, sucker for the latest quack theory, who had written countless pages but nothing of any lasting interest, suddenly, at the age of thirty-six, became a world-class poet. David Reynolds believes he had been composing scraps of poetry for years. Justin Kaplan thinks he wrote it all rather quickly, in that final year before the first edition.

In any case, he assembled and printed the first edition of *Leaves of Grass*—typesetting some of it himself—in considerable haste. And toward the beginning is an image that is one of the greatest in all his poetry, that obviously describes a profound transformative experience, and that—significantly, for our concerns, and for all of Whitman's work—is sexual. It is this image, in fact, that Allen Ginsberg cites as proof that Whitman was gay, though the partner's gender is not specified. The poet seems to be addressing his soul.

> I mind how once we lay such a transparent summer morning,
> How you settled your head athwart my hips and gently turn'd over upon me,
> And parted the shirt from my bosom-bone, and plunged your tongue to my bare-stript heart,
> And reach'd till you felt my beard, and reach'd till you held my feet.
>
> Swiftly arose and spread around me the peace and knowledge that pass all the argument of the earth,
> And I know that the hand of God is the promise of my own,
> And I know that the spirit of God is the brother of my own,
> And that all the men ever born are also my brothers, and the women my sisters and lovers,
> And that a kelson of the creation is love,
> And limitless are leaves stiff or drooping in the fields,
> And brown ants in the little wells beneath them,
> And mossy scabs of the worm fence, heap'd stones, elder, mullein and poke-weed.[21]

There are many great poems in the final edition of *Leaves of Grass*, but "Song of Myself" is perhaps the greatest, the poem out of which all the others grew, and this image seems to be the one out of which the poem grew; this is the moment when Whitman became Whitman. It is a strikingly sexual image, even for the modern reader, and does seem homoerotic; it suggests fellatio, then a much deeper communion, which penetrates straight to the heart.

The speaker is in a passive position, and Whitman is the great poet of passivity, of letting the world come to him. Though the image is blatantly sexual, it is not genital; the feeling settles over his whole body. He discovers in this feeling a knowledge that is not of the intellect: it passes all argument (hence his command in the prose preface about arguments concerning God).

In a single moment this lifelong freethinker discovers his relationship to the Creator and to all created beings and feels love at the heart of everything. And in a brilliant shift in focus, and a prefiguring of the immense lists that are to come, he sees that even the smallest things are part of that love: leaves, and ants crawling under the leaves, mullein and pokeweed, even stones.

Thus may we understand Whitman's haste in assembling his book. He had discovered the one essential thing and wanted to communicate it to people not by the various means he had considered throughout his life—oratory, drama, the novel, short stories, journalism—but in the only genre that could really do it justice: a King James Bible–like poetry that burst the bounds of conventional verse. It was not really that he had become a poet. He had become a prophet.

His reception around home wasn't exactly spectacular: "I saw the book," his brother George said, "—didn't read it at all—didn't think it worth reading—fingered it a little";[22] but he did strike gold with a promotional copy he sent out to the one American writer who was considered an equal of the great Europeans he had studied.

Concord Massachusetts 21 July 1855

> Dear Sir,
> I am not blind to the worth of the wonderful gift of "Leaves of Grass." I find it the most extraordinary piece of wit and wisdom but America has yet contributed. I am very happy in reading it, as great power makes us happy. . . .
> I give you joy of your free & brave thought. I have great joy in it. I find incomparable things said incomparably well. . . .
> I greet you at the beginning of a great career. . . .
>
> R. W. Emerson[23]

Much has been made of the way Whitman bungled this communication. This ink-stained hack, a Brooklyn boy, receiving a letter from one of the great New England Brahmins, not only allowed it to be printed in a newspaper but published it, along with his own reply, in a second edition of *Leaves of Grass*, implying Emerson's endorsement of a number of poems he had not seen. Emerson was understandably disgusted with this oafish behavior, eventually grew disenchanted with Whitman, and, years later, didn't include him in an anthology of notable American verse (though he did feature such luminaries as E. C. Stedman and Forceythe Willson).

But he had been as startled as the rest of us by his first glimpse into *Leaves of Grass*, referring to Whitman in conversation as "an American Buddha."[24] And Justin Kaplan has pointed out that though Whitman was a shameless self-promoter all his life—writing a number of reviews of his own book, sometimes sending them to disciples for them to sign—he was not really promoting himself. He never asked much for himself (and received less). He was promoting his book and the dramatic understanding he had come to one transparent summer morning when he saw into the nature of all things.

CONTEMPLATIVE BY NATURE

It is probably senseless to speak of someone as a Buddhist who had barely heard of the Buddha, who had never been instructed in Buddhist practice. Yet the word *buddha* simply means "awakened one," and the Zen tradition tells us there are ten thousand ways to enlightenment. The reputation that Whitman had for indolence all his life, as a man who liked to drift aimlessly out-of-doors, observing the passing show, is that of a natural contemplative. And the state in which he said he wrote is an almost perfect description of a meditative state.

> . . . a trance, yet with all the senses alert—only a state of high exalted musing—the tangible and material with all its shows, the objective world suspended or surmounted for a while, & the powers in exaltation, freedom, vision—yet the *senses* nor lost or counteracted.[25]

He said, according to Kaplan, that he had "the capacity to 'stop thinking' at will, to go 'negative' and suspend all conscious striving."[26] His object of contemplation—also the primary symbol of his book—was the grass, and so simple an object, when really noticed, becomes mesmerizing.

> I loafe and invite my soul
> I lean and loafe at my ease observing a spear of summer
> grass.[27]

The contemplative process he describes is the meditative technique of choiceless awareness, in which the meditator simply allows himself to be present in the moment, noticing physical sensations, passing thoughts, the world around him: perceiving inside and out, until it all becomes one thing.

> The smoke of my own breath,
> Echoes, ripples, buzz'd whispers, love-root, silk-thread,
>   crotch and vine,
> My respiration and inspiration, the beating of my heart, the
>   passing of blood and air through my lungs,
> The sniff of green leaves and dry leaves, and of the shore and
>   dark-color'd sea-rocks, and of hay in the barn . . .[28]

Much later, in the prose work *Democratic Vistas,* Whitman would state a larger theory behind such behavior. He understood the joy of pure awareness.

> A fitly born and bred race, growing up in right conditions of out-door as much as in-door harmony, activity and development, would probably, from and in those conditions, find it enough merely *to live*—and would, in their relations to the sky, air, water, trees, &c., and to the countless common shows, and in the fact of life itself, discover and achieve happiness—with Being suffused night and day by wholesome extasy, surpassing all the pleasures that wealth, amusement, and even gratified intellect, erudition, or the sense of art, can give.[29]

For him, as for anyone, all kinds of things came up in the act of contemplation, and he was as capable as anyone else of doubting himself. But he understands that beneath the discursive part of the mind is a deeper part; beneath the self that questions, a deeper self. He called it his soul. But his description is quite true to the Original Mind that Buddhist masters describe.

Trippers and askers surround me,
People I meet, the effect upon me of my early life or the
    ward and city I live in, or the nation,
The latest dates, discoveries, inventions, societies, authors old
    and new,
My dinner, dress, associates, looks, compliments, dues,
The real or fancied indifference of some man or woman I
    love,
The sickness of one of my folks or of myself, or ill-doing or
    loss or lack of money, or depressions or exaltations,
Battles, the horrors of fratricidal war, the fever of doubtful
    news, the fitful events;
These come to me days and nights and go from me again,
But they are not the Me myself.
Apart from the pulling and hauling stands what I am,
Stands amused, complacent, compassionating, idle, unitary,
Looks down, is erect, or bends an arm on an impalpable cer-
    tain rest,
Looking with side-curved head curious what will come next,
Both in and out of the game and watching and wondering
    at it.[30]

ACTUALIZED BY ALL THINGS

The great Zen teacher and writer Eihei Dogen described this process of coming to know the self, then passing through it as if through a door that opens onto the universe: "To study the buddha way is to study the self. To study the self is to forget the self. To forget the self is to be actualized by myriad things."

And ringing down through the centuries since the time of the third Zen patriarch are the opening lines of the first Zen poem; they state the whole message of Buddhism in a few words, easy to say but extremely difficult to practice.

The great way is not difficult
For those who make no distinctions.
When like and dislike disappear
The true nature of things becomes clear and undisguised.

Whitman is the great world poet of nondiscrimination. In his enormous lists—the first of which appear in "Song of Myself"—he not only proclaims his own feelings of nondiscrimination but (as Lewis Hyde points out in his superb book *The Gift*[31]) produces the same feeling in the reader. These closely observed passages are mesmerizing in the opposite way from Whitman's blades of grass. We strain to take the scenes in, see some logical connection, until finally, suddenly, they become one thing, even the most disparate elements.

> The President holding a cabinet council is surrounded by the
>   great Secretaries,
> On the piazza walk three matrons stately and friendly with
>   twined arms,
> The crew of the fish-smack pack repeated layers of halibut in
>   the hold.[32]

Whitman states the basis of his nondiscrimination in a slightly knotty passage about a visitor who stays with him and leaves behind what seem to be baskets of rising dough. In later editions he refers to the visitor just as a bedfellow, but in the first edition he is God.

> As God comes a loving bedfellow and sleeps at my side all
>   night and close on the peep of the day,
> And leaves for me baskets covered with white towels bulging
>   the house with their plenty,
> Shall I postpone my acceptation and realization and scream
>   at my eyes,
> That they turn from gazing after and down the road,
> And forthwith cipher and show me to a cent,

> Exactly the contents of one, and exactly the contents of two,
> and which is ahead?[33]

His reckoning mind might want to make distinctions about what he has found, but with such abundance, what is the point? He has everything he needs, and it is all a gift.

Line after line in *Leaves of Grass* echoes Buddha dharma, to the point that it is astonishing to realize that it was written by a nineteenth-century American unschooled in the teachings of the East. In his prose preface, for instance, he seems to state the law of karma.

> All that a male or female does that is vigorous and benevolent and clean is so much sure profit to him or her in the unshakable order of the universe and through the whole scope of it forever.[34]

He understands that form and emptiness are one thing.

> I will make the poems of materials, for I think they are to be
> the most spiritual poems,
> And I will make the poems of my body and of mortality,
> For I think I shall then supply myself with the poems of my
> soul and of immortality.[35]

He sees that all of history is in the present moment.

> All forces have been steadily employ'd to complete and de-
> light me,
> Now on this spot I stand with my robust soul.[36]

He believes, in fact, that he was present at the creation.

> Afar down I see the huge first Nothing, I know I was even
> there,
> I waited unseen and always, and slept through the lethargic
> mist,
> And took my time, and took no hurt from the fetid carbon.[37]

He also agrees with the Buddha in the nontheistic nature of his teaching. He is a deeply spiritual poet but not in the least theological.

And I say to mankind, Be not curious about God,
For I who am curious about each am not curious about God,
(No array of terms can say how much I am at peace about
    God and about death.)
I hear and behold God in every object, yet understand God
    not in the least,
Nor do I understand who there can be more wonderful than
    myself.[38]

Ultimately, of course, Whitman's enlightened view of things is not in particular lines of *Leaves of Grass* but in the scope of the work as a whole. His understanding of the nature of things may have arrived on a single summer morning (or may not; he may have been dramatizing a realization that took place over a longer period). But he spent forty years writing it down.

WITHOUT SEX, NOTHING

By 1860 Whitman had published two editions of *Leaves of Grass* himself and had heard from a Boston publisher—Thayer and Eldridge—who was interested in publishing a third. He traveled to Boston and while there received a cordial visit from Emerson, who called on him in his rented rooms. Emerson's essay calling for a new American poet had virtually predicted Whitman, and his early letter had recognized the man's greatness. But he had something he wanted to discuss, and the two men went for a long walk out on the Boston Commons. He wanted to suggest that Whitman remove the poems about sex.

Emerson was a sophisticated man and knew some of the liveliest spirits of his day. He was not particularly a prude and did not deny the worth of the sexual poems. ("I did not say as good a book," he said about an expurgated edition. "I said a good book."[39]) He just believed the book would be better received if they were removed. He was probably right.

Whitman, the great nondiscriminator, did not discriminate in this case. "Each point of E.'s statement was unanswerable, no judge's charge ever more complete or convincing, I could never hear the points better put—and then I felt down in my soul the clear and unmistakable conviction to disobey all, and pursue my own way."[40] "If I had cut sex out," he said years later, "I might just as well have cut everything out."[41]

Whitman's task in *Leaves of Grass* was a spiritual one. He wanted nothing less than to enlighten the reader, to "wipe the gum" from his eyes so he could "habit [him]self to the dazzle of the light and of every moment of [his] life."[42] But Whitman knew that sex and spirit were intimately connected. "I think Swedenborg was right," he once remarked to a friend, "when he said there was a close connection—a very close connection—between the state we call religious ecstasy and the desire to copulate. . . . It is a peculiar discovery."[43] He knew that the basic energy of the world is erotic, and our sexual feelings an expression of it.

> Urge and urge and urge,
> Always the procreant urge of the world.[44]

Whitman presents himself in *Leaves of Grass* as a tough, sensual man.

> Walt Whitman, a kosmos, of Manhattan the son,
> Turbulent, fleshy, sensual, eating, drinking and breeding . . .[45]

In the first edition he famously included a daguerreotype of himself in this pose, dressed in workingman's clothes (he did sometimes work as a carpenter, like his father), his pelvis thrust forward suggestively and provocatively. The persona he adopted in his poetry was an ideal American type for him. It was also his erotic ideal.

He lets us know only a few lines later that in contrast to this image of a bold and hearty breeder, he was extraordinarily sensitive to touch.

> I merely stir, press, feel with my fingers, and am happy,
> To touch my person to some one else's is about as much as I
>   can stand.[46]

We might have known that already, from his sensitiveness to nature. When he does allow himself to be fully sexual, the feeling takes him over.

> Is this then a touch? quivering me to a new identity,
> Flames and ether making a rush for my veins,
> Treacherous tip of me reaching and crowding to help them,
> My flesh and blood playing out lightning to strike what is
>   hardly different from myself . . .[47]

Critics who discuss Whitman's sexuality sometimes speak of this as an inferior sexual makeup. Harold Bloom, in the television documentary already mentioned, implied that Whitman had been so hurt by a difficult childhood that he positively cringed from touch, could hardly be sexual at all. Almost the opposite seems true to me. Whitman is describing the polymorphous whole-body sexuality of someone in touch with sex all the time, who finds just the presence of people, or the touch of a passing breeze, erotic.*

*In their adamant belief that sex is a genital event, men seem determined

Whatever his sexual makeup, Whitman insisted on celebrating sexuality in his poems, whatever the cost.

> From what I am determin'd to make illustrious, even if I
>   stand sole among men,
> From my own voice resonant, singing the phallus,
> Singing the song of procreation . . .[48]

He wasn't always so solemn, though; he could make sly, joking references as well, which seem almost more surprising in a nineteenth-century author. He could also get slightly raunchy.

> The real poems, (what we call poems being merely pictures,)
> The poems of the privacy of the night, and of men like me,
> This poem drooping shy and unseen that I always carry, and
>   that all men carry,
> (Know once for all, avow'd on purpose, wherever are men
>   like me, are our lusty lurking masculine poems,)
> Love-thoughts, love-juice, love-odor, love-yielding, love-
>   climbers, and the climbing sap,
> Arms and hands of love, lips of love, phallic thumb of love,
>   breasts of love, bellies press'd and glued together with
>   love . . .[49]

He believes the entire body is sacred; before beginning a catalog of body parts, which resembles the kind of body scan a meditation teacher leads (but which includes, as the teacher often does not, "man balls, man root . . . the bowels sweet and clean"), he proclaims it loudly.

to confine it to the genitals, but Wilhelm Reich clearly states in *The Function of the Orgasm* that orgasm is a function of the whole body and that sexual and emotional health involve having this kind of whole-body orgasm. One of the interesting by-products of my meditation practice—the Buddha didn't mention this—is that I am much more sensitive to my body, and my orgasms are more a full-body event. "More like a woman," as one of my friends said.

If anything is sacred the human body is sacred,
And the glory and sweet of a man is the token of manhood
untainted,
And in man or woman a clean, strong, firm-fibred body, is
more beautiful than the most beautiful face.[50]

Just as sacred as the man's body is the woman's, and the
sexual act itself.

A woman waits for me, she contains all, nothing is lacking,
Yet all were lacking if sex were lacking, or if the moisture of
the right man were lacking . . .

Without shame the man I like knows and avows the deli-
ciousness of his sex,
Without shame the woman I like knows and avows hers.[51]

He was bold in describing the sexual act they would have.

I am stern, acrid, large, undissuadable, but I love you,
I do not hurt you any more than is necessary for you,
I pour the stuff to start sons and daughters fit for these States,
I press with slow rude muscle,
I brace myself effectually, I listen to no entreaties,
I dare not withdraw till I deposit what has so long accumu-
lated within me.[52]

And though there are places in *Leaves of Grass* in which—
reflecting the beliefs of his day—he mentions the "sick-gray
faces of onanists," in "Spontaneous Me" he speaks openly of
masturbation.

The young man that wakes deep at night, the hot hand seeking to repress what would master him,
The mystic amorous night, the strange half-welcome pangs,
visions, sweats,
The pulse pounding through palms and trembling encircling
fingers, the young man all color'd, red, ashamed,
angry . . .[53]

THE TENDEREST LOVER

In Whitman's day it was the bold heterosexual imagery that people objected to; more recently it has been the gay poetry. Gay men in Whitman's day certainly understood what he meant; they just didn't call attention to it, until old John Addington Symonds came blundering in. It was as if Whitman were using the heterosexual poems as a blind for what he really wanted to say about sex and love.

He treaded a fine line, pretending to write about male friendship when he was really dealing with something much deeper. His description of his enlightenment experience, his early reference to God as his bedfellow, were hints of his essentially homoerotic view of the world. But however much he disguises it as innocent friendship, he knows that he is writing about something forbidden by his culture and states so clearly in the first lines of the Calamus section.

> In paths untrodden,
> In the growth by margins of pond-waters,
> Escaped from the life that exhibits itself,
> From all the standards hitherto publish'd, from the pleasures,
>   profits, conformities,
> Which too long I was offering to feed my soul . . .
>
> Afternoon this delicious Ninth-month in my forty-first year,
> I proceed for all who are or have been young men,
> To tell the secret of my nights and days,
> To celebrate the need of comrades.[54]

His brash masculine pose has also been a blind, and the clue has been that he doth protest too much, sometimes in the bizarre diction that only Walt Whitman used in all the world. "No dainty dolce affettuoso I."[55] Rather than the lusty sower of his seed that he pretended to be, he was more like

a caring mother. That feminine side, combined with his un-
kempt beard and his rough masculine clothing, created a pe-
culiarly androgynous figure, a rosy-cheeked, sweet-smelling,
cuddly old man.

The rough he pretended to be was the man he was
drawn to.

> I am for those who believe in loose delights, I share the mid-
> night orgies of young men,
> I dance with the dancers and drink with the drinkers,
> The echoes ring with our indecent calls, I pick out some low
> person for my dearest friend,
> He shall be lawless, rude, illiterate, he shall be one con-
> demn'd by others for deeds done,
> I will play a part no longer, why should I exile myself from
> my companions?[56]

He loved to go where men were working and had particular
affection for the Manhattan omnibus drivers and the ferry-
boat pilots who took him back and forth to Brooklyn. He
often rode on the upper decks just for the sake of riding,
sometimes—out of sheer exuberance—declaming Shakespeare or singing opera.

With the peculiar intimacy that he establishes with the
reader ("Camerado, this is no book, / Who touches this
touches a man"[57]), he makes the reader into something between a lover and a disciple and lets him know that the affair
will not be easy.

> Whoever you are holding me now in hand . . .
> I give you fair warning before you attempt me further,
> I am not what you supposed, but far different. . . .
>
> The way is suspicious, the result uncertain, perhaps destruc-
> tive,

You would have to give up all else, I alone would expect to
be your sole and exclusive standard.[58]

Whitman was not just talking about the difficulty of his
message. There was something difficult about him as a person as well, which those around him often noticed. It was
the same thing, in a way, that was difficult about both the
man and the message. They were both right there, in home-
spun cloth. But they proved hard to grasp.

"I am by no means the benevolent, equable, happy creature you portray," he told an early biographer, "but let that
pass—I have left it as you wrote."[59] And even in his old age,
Edward Carpenter wrote, a certain "reserve and sadness"
were in evidence, "a sense of remoteness and inaccessibility.
He celebrates in his poems the fluid, all-solvent disposition,
but he was often himself less the river than the rock."[60]

The problem was not that he was erotically demanding.
His real satisfaction was just being in the presence of his
lover.

> A glimpse through an interstice caught,
> Of a crowd of workmen and drivers in a bar-room around
>   the stove late of a winter night, and I unremark'd seated
>   in a corner,
> Of a youth who loves me and whom I love, silently ap-
>   proaching and seating himself near, that he may hold
>   me by the hand,
> A long while amid the noises of coming and going, of drink-
>   ing and oath and smutty jest,
> There we two, content, happy in being together, speaking
>   little, perhaps not a word.[61]

Unfortunately, there often wasn't a lover around. The
real problem of Whitman's life was not that he was gay—he
celebrated that—but that he yearned for a long-term faithful

relationship but had a thing for straight men.* One after another would be his dear friend for a while, then move on to a more conventional life. This difficult emotional situation created the great sadness of Whitman's life but may also have contributed to his spiritual depth.

His major love affairs, at least the ones we know about, happened later in life, but he predicted his fate in the beautiful lyric in which he tells how he would like to be remembered.†

> Recorder ages hence,
> Come, I will take you down underneath this impassive exterior, I will tell you what to say of me,
> Publish my name and hang up my picture as that of the tenderest lover,
> The friend the lover's portrait, of whom his friend his lover was fondest,
> Who was not proud of his songs, but of the measureless ocean of love within him, and freely pour'd it forth,
> Who often walk'd lonesome walks thinking of his dear friends, his lovers,
> Who pensive away from one he lov'd often lay sleepless and dissatisfied at night,
> Who knew too well the sick, sick dread lest the one he lov'd might secretly be indifferent to him.[62]

Yet it is Whitman's erotic makeup that makes him an especially prophetic voice for men today, both gay and

---

*In our own day, Allen Ginsberg felt that the same erotic preference had been fortunate for him. "I've had a couple of tests for myself for AIDS, and apparently have come out negative. *Maybe* been saved by my preference for straight kids" (*Whole Earth Review* 56 [Fall 1987]). He seemed to handle a long-term relationship with a man—Peter Orlovsky—who was not strictly gay, and he apparently seduced countless straight boys with his fame and charm. Whitman may have been a shyer man, or just lived in a more repressed time.

†Just as prophetic are two other poems, "I Saw in Louisiana a Live-Oak Growing" and the magnificent "Out of the Cradle Endlessly Rocking."

straight. Allen Ginsberg remarked on that fact in a remarkably prescient interview in the magazine *Gay Sunshine
Journal.*

> I know lots of men who are thinking along those lines.
> They may not want to sleep naked together but there's a
> love thrill in the breast they have for each other, and yet are
> completely heterosexual. And I wouldn't be surprised if that
> *is,* among the mass of men, a universal experience, com-
> pletely accepted, completely common, completely shared.
>
> The idea of a buddy is just the thin . . . vulgarization of
> it. The tradition of comradeship, of companionship, spoken
> of in the Bible . . . between David and Jonathan . . . all the
> way up to the body relationships as we know them . . . all
> these probably are intense love relationships which the gay
> lib group, in its political phase, has not yet accepted and inte-
> grated as delightful manifestation of human communication,
> satisfactory to everybody. In other words, there's a lot of
> political and communal development open to the gay lib
> movement as it includes more and more varieties of love,
> besides genital, and it may be that the bridge between gay
> liberation and men's liberation may be in the mutual recogni-
> tion of the masculine tenderness that was denied by both
> groups for so long. . . .
>
> Walt Whitman is very important on male tenderness.
> He's never been brought forth as a totem or as a prophet by
> either gay lib or by the radical left for some very precise
> statements he made on the subject of men's lib.[63]

It has seemed to me as I have grown older that a major
limiting factor in straight men's lives is not that they don't
act out sexually with other men but that their fear of being
gay cuts them off from tender feelings for one another. These
feelings are natural and show up in boyhood, but in manhood they are seldom expressed or even felt. The typical pattern for straight men in my generation has been to have a

competitive relationship with other men—at work, or on the basketball court—and sexual and emotional relationships with women. We don't see either gender as whole people and can't be whole ourselves.

We can't be erotic with men and can't be anything else with women, even in situations—like the workplace—where it is inappropriate. The problem is not really what men feel for women but what they don't feel for men. They have to dump all their emotional needs on women—typically, on the one woman in their lives—because they have nowhere else to go with them.*

Men don't have to have sex with men to become less tight-assed, but that tight-assed tension is, among other things, a fear of being queer and creates a general physical tension that keeps men hard with each other (their bodies, not their cocks) rather than soft.† When men allow these tender feelings to flow, they discover emotional resources among themselves that they didn't know to exist. They don't need to go to women with all their emotional needs. That also reduces some of the sexual pressure on women, because many supposed sexual needs are really emotional.

Whitman's vision was not really of sex among men but of hearty, affectionate love. That is the part of his vision that

---

*One of the great discoveries of the men's movement has been the simple pleasure of being among a group of men who are not being competitive, or doing business, but just being friends, being supportive and loving. I vividly remember the first time I encountered that feeling—it was almost palpable, in the air—at a Robert Bly day for men in 1988. I joined a men's group that formed out of that event and have been a part of it ever since, and I believe that the legions of people—men and women—who make nervous jokes about such groups are actually just uncomfortable at the thought of tenderness among men. Their homophobia is showing.

†Alan Watts believed that such physical tension is an important factor in creating the illusion of the ego, of separation from the rest of humanity.

makes the academic establishment cringe. They can accept the occasional furtive blow job in a toilet stall, but the thought that they might actually love—and show affection for—their colleagues down the hall is beyond the pale. That is the love that dare not speak its name.

Whitman's political vision, often mocked, was not really a pie-in-the-sky notion that democracy would work out for the best. It was a utopian spiritual vision. He believed that democracy was the logical political embodiment of his spiritual vision, and he imagined a world not of cutthroat capitalists who were looking out for number one but of men who didn't feel that greed because they were emotionally satisfied in their love for each other.

> It is to the development, identification, and general prevalence of that fervid comradeship . . . that I look for the counterbalance and offset of our materialistic and vulgar American democracy, and for the spiritualization thereof. Many will say it is a dream, and will not follow my inferences, but I confidently expect a time when there will be seen, running like a half-hid warp through all the myriad audible and visible worldly interests of America, threads of manly friendship, fond and loving, pure and sweet, strong and life-long, carried to degrees hitherto unknown—not only giving tone to individual character, and making it unprecedently emotional, muscular, heroic, and refined, but having the deepest relations to general politics. I say democracy infers such loving comradeship, as its most inevitable twin or counterpart, without which it will be incomplete, in vain, and incapable of perpetuating itself.[64]

Whitman was not a gay poet in a narrow sense; that label diminishes him. He is the great poet of love among men. He envisioned that love having consequences that were much more than sexual.

HEALING THE WOUNDED

Whitman would say later in life that the Civil War had made him who he was, would even say that *Leaves of Grass* would have been impossible without it, and from an aesthetic or even spiritual standpoint, that statement is puzzling. His awakening had happened years before the war, as had his extreme haste to put together the book's first edition. And in some ways all of Whitman's works seem to be footnotes to "Song of Myself," some of them great and unforgettable, without which his status would be much diminished. But all of his work seems to be present in that first long poem.

Yet it is also true that his work during the war was the logical fulfillment of who he was. After the first edition of *Leaves of Grass*—actually, while he was working on the first three editions—he went through a difficult period. He did have that flash of acceptance from Emerson, and a few other luminaries took note. (Thoreau and Bronson Alcott came calling in Brooklyn, and Thoreau—wearing his nonconformity like a badge—helped himself without asking to a cake that Louisa Whitman had baked for the family.) But it was not what he had hoped.

In the five years between the first edition and the war, he went back to journalism to earn a living. He continued to compose poetry at a furious rate, including fourteen of the poems of the Calamus section, which in their original order told the story of an unhappy love affair. Eventually, for personal or aesthetic reasons, he would publish them in a different order. He also composed "Out of the Cradle Endlessly Rocking," a great long poem on the same theme.

He became a regular at a bohemian Manhattan saloon called Pfaff's, riding over on the ferry from Brooklyn almost every evening. He went through a depression around the age of forty, what he called a slough, which may have had something to do with the shape the country was in. He saw Lincoln pass through New York on his way to take office in Washington, the man he would later call "the sweetest, wisest soul of all my days and lands."[65]

When the war began, Whitman felt he was too old—at forty-one—to fight (he actually looked much older) but decided to change his life.

> I have this hour, this day, resolved to inaugurate for myself a pure, perfect, sweet, cleanblooded robust body by ignoring all drinks but water and pure milk—and all fat meats, late suppers—a great body—a purged, cleansed, spiritualized, invigorated body.[66]

His brother George did enlist in the Union forces, and when word came that he had been wounded, Walt made his way to Virginia, arriving penniless because his wallet had been stolen on the way. He eventually found George (who had an extremely eventful career as a soldier and survived the war), but to do so he had to pass through several military hospitals, where he saw tremendous suffering. The cure for all ills in the Civil War seemed to be amputation, and one of the first sights he encountered outside a hospital was a pile of amputated limbs.

Whitman became a nurse to the wounded during the war, what he called a wound dresser.

> Arous'd and angry, I'd thought to beat the alarum, and urge
>   relentless war,
> But soon my fingers fail'd me, my face droop'd and I resign'd
>   myself,
> To sit by the wounded and soothe them, or silently watch
>   the dead.[67]

This was not an official position, certainly not a paid one, and he had to make his living in other ways; he spent months seeking a government clerkship and eventually found one, but during much of that time he lived in poverty. "I can be satisfied and happy henceforward if I can get one meal a day, and know that mother and all are in good health."[68]

At the end of each workday, wherever he had been, he would prepare himself almost ritually by bathing and dressing, then go and visit the men—often just boys—at the hospital. He took treats with him—"fruit, preserves, pickles, ice cream, candy, cookies, wine and brandy, chewing and smoking tobacco, handkerchiefs, shirts, socks, and underwear, reading and writing materials, postage stamps, and small change"[69]—which he bought with donations from benefactors. He would sit with the men, talk with them, hold their hands, write letters to their families. He stayed with a number of them as they suffered and died.

This was a perfect vocation for Whitman. It allowed him to show his motherly side, to express his deep compassion. He could be physically affectionate with men, embrace and kiss them. He could forget the part of himself that was lonely and demanding and just give, with his enormous generosity.

Yet the work must have been almost unbearably difficult. It would have been so even for someone able to harden and distance himself, but Whitman loved these men and was constantly watching them suffer. His health was never the same after the war, and though David Reynolds argues that Whitman's lifelong hypertension was the cause of his later strokes, his war work certainly aggravated his condition, whether or not he was harmed from the "effluvia of gangrene" as the doctors warned.

A cynic might argue that this work was selfish—he hung

around with the boys because he was hot for them—but it included a major selfless component as well. Really it was neither selfish nor selfless, just a perfect match of the man and the vocation.

It was after the war that he met the great love of his life, a streetcar conductor twenty-eight years his junior named Peter Doyle. "We felt to each other at once," Doyle said, about their first meeting, on the streetcar. "Walt had his blanket—it was thrown around his shoulders—he seemed like an old sea-captain. He was the only passenger, it was a lonely night, so I thought I would go talk to him. Something in me made me do it and something in him drew me that way. . . . We were familiar at once—I put my hand on his knee—we understood."[70]

For a while they were constant companions, and Whitman spoke of him almost as a son. "That is my rebel friend, you know . . . a great big hearty full-blooded everyday divinely generous working man: a hail fellow well met—a little too fond of his beer, now and then, and of the women."[71] They would be friends for years afterward, but the kind of deep and long-lasting relationship that Whitman wanted was probably doomed from the start. The passages in his journal in which he swore off the relationship are terribly painful, from this great poet of expansive love. (He changed the pronouns to put future researchers off the track.)

> Remember where I am most weak, & most lacking. Yet always preserve a kind spirit and demeanor to 16. But pursue her no more.
>
> July 15—1870—
> To give up absolutely & for good, from this present hour, this feverish, fluctuating, useless undignified pursuit of 16.4— too long (much too long) persevered in—so humiliating—It

must come at last & had better come now—(It cannot possibly be a success). Let there from this hour be no faltering, no getting [word erased] at all henceforth, (not once, under any circumstances)—avoid seeing her, or meeting her, or any talk or explanations—or any meeting, whatsoever, from this hour forth, for life[72]

Whitman would have other one-sided affairs in his old age, most notably with a young man whose family he lived with named Harry Stafford. "When he traveled with Harry he introduced him as 'my (adopted) son,' 'my nephew,' 'my young man,' and explained that they were in the habit of sharing a room and a bed."[73] Ironically, at roughly the same time, he was the object of a fierce unrequited love on the part of a woman named Anne Gilchrist, who had moved to this country from England with three children in the hope of marrying Whitman. "I saw that Anne Gilchrist was suffering," Edward Carpenter said. "I saw that Whitman was all *kindness*—kindness itself toward her; but at the same time that his relation to her did not go farther than that word would indicate."[74]

Whitman was surrounded by admirers and disciples as he grew older. The prophetic writer seems to attract that kind of devotion. They were of great help to him as his health began to fail—he had a series of strokes—and he needed assistance. But finally in his old age and semi-invalidism, this great celebrator of sex discovered a new kind of eroticism, a physical relationship with nature itself. "I never really saw the skies before,"[75] he said, a startling statement for one who had described nature so exquisitely. This aging health faddist, now partly paralyzed, was not able to do much but took great joy in what he could.

For several summers he performed a solitary "Adamic" ritual in his garden. Off to one side of the creek was an aban-

doned marlpit with a little spring running through the middle
of it under some willows. He stripped himself naked, dug his
feet into the black mud and rolled in it, rinsed away the mud,
rasped his body with a stiff brush until his skin turned scarlet,
rinsed again in the spring. After his mud and water bath he
bathed in the sun and air, making slow promenades on the
turf and declaiming and singing—"vocalism"—at the top of
his voice. "I make the echoes ring, I tell you!" He toned his
muscles, borrowed "elastic fiber and clear sap," wrestling
with oak and hickory saplings, just as he wrestled with Harry
Stafford and drew strength from him. As he hauled and
pushed he took great draughts of fragrant air into his lungs.
"After I wrestle with the tree awhile, I can feel its young sap
and virtue welling up out of the ground and tingling through
me from crown to toe, like health's wine. . . .

"Somehow I seem'd to get identity with each and every
thing around me, in its condition," he said at Timber Creek.
"Nature was naked, and I was also."[76]

He recorded countless scenes of just sitting and contem-
plating nature in the late prose work *Specimen Days*. It was as
if he had grown into the persona of his poetry and was able
to live with the serenity with which he once had only written. "Almost alone among the major American writers," Justin Kaplan says, "he achieved in his last years radiance,
serenity, and generosity of spirit."[77]

Whitman may never—other than fleetingly—have found
the sexual happiness he hoped for, but he wrote about it
beautifully, uniting sex with spirit and expanding our vision
of what sex is. Like many prophets, he was more important
in paving the way than in finding happiness for himself. Allen
Ginsberg in our own day seemed to be a reincarnation of
Whitman, with the same kind of bountiful love and generosity and acceptance that his great predecessor had shown. In
his own day, Whitman was an inspiration to the British poet

and social critic Edward Carpenter, a man not nearly as well known, or as talented, but who lived out the life Whitman had envisioned.

Carpenter lived in the country that prosecuted Oscar Wilde, where many gay men would remain closeted for generations afterward, but he was entirely open about the way he lived, even wrote about it. He was a part of the great laying on of hands (and not just hands) that Ginsberg was so proud of: Whitman had sex with Carpenter, who had sex with Gavin Arthur, who had sex with Neal Cassady, who had sex with Ginsberg (who managed to pass the succession on to a great many others).

Ginsberg asked Gavin Arthur in his old age to write out his reminiscences of his encounter with Carpenter, and though petty moralists will find any number of reasons to be put off, the scene has an undeniable sweetness. It embodies everything that Whitman envisioned.

> I was 23 and came up the garden path with the letter of introduction awkwardly in my hand. He seemed to know I was coming for he opened the door and held out his arms. "Welcome my son" he growled affectionately as if he had known me for ever. He did not read the letter but drew me into the cozy study by the fire and introduced me to his comrade George and George's comrade Ted. George was about 60 and was pouring tea. Ted was about 40 and was sticking flowers in a vase. Both were warm in their welcome. I was about 20 and Carpenter about 80.
>
> They all talked to me as if we were old friends. That is what Mother used to call "Le don fatale de la familiarite" which only a few people like Havelock Ellis, Kinsey and F.D.R. possess. We talked about Walt and E.C. gave me the young picture which is the frontispiece of his book about WW. He said Walt would have loved me and the others agreed and my heart beat hard. . . .

[Later] We had some matte someone had sent him from Brazil (his mail snowed in from all over the world). Carpenter asked me if I would do him a favor and sleep with him. "George and Ted need a rest," he grinned. He had a growly way of talking like an old dog that growls his affection. The other two went up to bed, and the old man and I sat by the fire. I wish I had had a camera. The firelight on that wonderfully human face with its sensitive bones and rough silver beard, the skin so coppery from the sun, the eyes so blue. . . . I asked him if he had ever been to bed with a woman and he said no—that he liked and admired women but that he had never felt any need to copulate with them. "But that wasn't true of Walt, was it?" I asked.

"No. Walt was ambigenic," he said. "His contact with women was far less than his contact with men. But he did engender several children and his greatest female contact was the Creole in New Orleans. I don't think he ever loved any of them as much as he loved Peter Doyle."

"I suppose you slept with him?" I blurted out half scared to ask.

"Oh yes—once in a while—he regarded it as the best way to get together with another man. He thought that people should 'know' each other on the physical and emotional plane as well as the mental. And that the best part of comrade love was that there was no limit to the number of comrades one could have—whereas the very fact of engendering children made the man-woman relationship more singular. . . .

"How did he make love?" I forced myself to ask.

"I will show you," he smiled. "Let us go to bed."

It was a warm night and we had just a light eiderdown over us. We were both naked and we lay side by side on our backs holding hands. Then he was holding my head in his two hands and making little growly noises, staring at me in the moonlight. "This is the laying on of hands," I thought reverently. "Walt. Then him. Then me." I had recently seen some neophytes made priests in Maynooth and their faces had shown the same emotions as I now felt.

He snuggled up to me and kissed my ear. His beard tickled my neck. He smelled like the leaves and ferns and soil of autumn woods. . . . [He] was stroking my body with the most expert touch. It was as exquisite as the little bubbles that come up from the decaying vegetation in a mud bath, caressing the flesh with a feather lightness.

I just lay there in the moonlight that poured in at the window and gave myself up to the loving old man's marvelous petting. Every now and then he would bury his face in the hair of my chest, agitate a nipple with the end of his tongue, or breathe in deeply from my armpit. I had of course a throbbing erection but he ignored it for a long time. Very gradually, however, he got nearer and nearer, first with his hand and later with his tongue which was now flickering all over me like summer lightning. I stroked whatever part of him came within reach of my hand but I felt instinctively that this was a one-sided affair, he being so old and I so young, and that he enjoyed petting me as much as I delighted in being petted. There are so many possible relationships, and one misses so much if one limits oneself to one sex or age or color.

At last his hand was moving between my legs and his tongue was in my belly-button. And then when he was tickling my fundament just behind the balls and I could not hold it any longer, his mouth closed just over the head of my penis and I could feel my young vitality flowing into his old age. He did not suck me at all. It was really *karezza*, which I knew he recommended in his books. I had not learned the control necessary to *karezza* and he did not want to waste that life-giving fluid. As he said afterward, "It isn't the chemical ingredients which are so full of vitality—it's the electrical content, like you get in milk if you get it direct from the cow—so different from cold milk!" He was in no sense a succubus like so many old men, draining the young men of all the vitality they can get, like a vampire. The emphasis was on the caressing and loving. I fell asleep like a child safe in father-mother arms, the arms of God. And dreamed of autumn woods with their seminal milk.[78]

NOTES

1. Walt Whitman, *Complete Poetry and Selected Prose* (The Library of America, 1982), 11.
2. Ibid., 253.
3. Ibid., 512.
4. Justin Kaplan, *Walt Whitman: A Life* (New York: Simon and Schuster, 1980), 46.
5. Ibid., 47.
6. David S. Reynolds, *Walt Whitman's America* (New York: Vintage Books, 1996), 324.
7. Kaplan, *Walt Whitman: A Life*, 63.
8. Ibid., 70.
9. Ibid., 347.
10. Ibid., 56.
11. Ibid., 82.
12. Reynolds, *Walt Whitman's America*, 70–73.
13. Kaplan, *Walt Whitman: A Life*, 128.
14. Ibid., 146.
15. Ibid., 151.
16. Ibid., 150.
17. Ibid., 151.
18. Ibid., 152.
19. Henry Miller, *Stand Still Like the Hummingbird* (New York: New Directions), 108.
20. Ibid.
21. Whitman, *Complete Poetry and Selected Prose*, 192.
22. Kaplan, *Walt Whitman: A Life*, 184.
23. Ibid., 202–3.
24. Ibid., 202.
25. Ibid., 189.
26. Ibid.
27. Whitman, *Complete Poetry and Selected Prose*, 188.
28. Ibid., 189.
29. Ibid., 983–84.

30. Ibid., 191.
31. Lewis Hyde, *The Gift: Imagination and the Erotic Life of Property* (New York: Vintage Books, 1983).
32. Whitman, *Complete Poetry and Selected Prose*, 202.
33. Ibid., 29.
34. Ibid., 22.
35. Ibid., 178–79.
36. Ibid., 239.
37. Ibid.
38. Ibid., 244–45.
39. Kaplan, *Walt Whitman: A Life*, 249.
40. Whitman, *Complete Poetry and Selected Prose*, 915.
41. Ibid., 249.
42. Ibid., 242.
43. Kaplan, *Walt Whitman: A Life*, 192–93.
44. Whitman, *Complete Poetry and Selected Prose*, 28.
45. Ibid., 210.
46. Ibid., 55.
47. Ibid., 215.
48. Ibid., 248.
49. Ibid., 260–61.
50. Ibid., 256.
51. Ibid., 258–59.
52. Ibid., 259.
53. Ibid., 261–62.
54. Ibid., 268.
55. Ibid., 186.
56. Ibid., 265.
57. Ibid., 611.
58. Ibid., 270.
59. Kaplan, *Walt Whitman: A Life*, 17.
60. Ibid., 17–18.
61. Whitman, *Complete Poetry and Selected Prose*, 283.
62. Ibid., 275–76.
63. Winston Leyland, ed. *Gay Sunshine Interviews* (San Francisco: Gay Sunshine Press, 1984), 102, 104.
64. Whitman, *Complete Poetry and Selected Prose*, 981–82.
65. Ibid., 467.
66. Kaplan, *Walt Whitman: A Life*, 262.
67. Whitman, *Complete Poetry and Selected Prose*, 442–43.

68. Kaplan, *Walt Whitman: A Life,* 269.
69. Ibid., 276.
70. Ibid., 311–12.
71. Ibid., 313.
72. Ibid., 316.
73. Ibid., 359.
74. Ibid., 366.
75. Ibid., 367.
76. Ibid., 369–70.
77. Ibid., 372.
78. Leyland, *Gay Sunshine Interviews,* 126–28.

~ D.H. AND FRIEDA LAWRENCE IN CHALAPA,
MEXICO, 1923

~ 3
The Sacred Bond

D. H. LAWRENCE

*Your most vital necessity in this life is that
you shall love your wife completely and
implicitly and in entire nakedness of body
and spirit.*

—D. H. LAWRENCE

*for us no difference between reading eating
singing
making love not one thing or the other*

—ZEN MASTER IKKYU,
trans. Stephen Berg

IN THE SUMMER of 1992, in the midst of my midlife confusion about sexuality, my wife and I traveled to Mexico and spent a week in Oaxaca. It was our second visit, but she had spent a great deal of time in the country before we met and had amassed a substantial collection of

primitive religious art, including—her favorite—multiple images of the Virgin of Guadalupe.

One morning we were shopping at the booths outside
one of Oaxaca's most beautiful cathedrals, the Virgin of Solitude, when she noticed that mass was about to begin and
decided to go. She is a lifelong Catholic, disaffected from the
church in this country but drawn to the devotion she finds in
Latin America. I'm a non-Catholic and speak only a few hundred words of Spanish. I decided to come back when mass
was over.

I wandered toward the center of town and came to a
bookstore. It seemed stupid to go in there with my limited
Spanish, but I rarely pass a bookstore without stopping. The
proprietor soon assessed the situation. "Tengo un libro en
inglés," he said, and handed me a beautifully bound volume
entitled *Lawrence in Oaxaca,* by Ross Parmenter. I opened to
the photographs and saw one of Lawrence standing in front
of the cathedral I'd just left.

Ross Parmenter had written a book that explores in intimate detail the three months Lawrence spent in Oaxaca in
1924 and 1925. Making reference to the whole of Lawrence's
work, Parmenter saw the whole man in that brief stay, primarily because those months marked a turning point in Lawrence's life.

It was while he was in Oaxaca that Lawrence wrote the
final version of *The Plumed Serpent,* a flawed and difficult book
but one that presents his fullest view of spirituality. At the
end of his stay—and of an intense period of work—he fell ill
with a relapse of malaria that, on top of his chronic tuberculosis, nearly killed him. That brush with death brought about
a major change in his outlook, best expressed in the touching
late story "The Man Who Died." He returned to Europe and

spent his last years composing his final paean to life, *Lady Chatterley's Lover.*

I read *Lawrence in Oaxaca* during the remainder of my stay, and it taught me much about Mexico—and about Lawrence—that I could never have learned otherwise. It also led me back to his work, to his great books about relationship, *The Rainbow* and *Women in Love;* to the quirky and often startling essays in the *Phoenix* volumes; and to *Lady Chatterley,* the most touching erotic novel that I know of in English. Especially in the essays and in *Lady Chatterley,* Lawrence spoke directly to my questionings about sex.

As his friend Aldous Huxley pointed out, Lawrence was a mystical materialist.[1] He associated with no spiritual tradition, had no spiritual practice, and vehemently rejected the religions of his day. But he seemed to understand Eastern teachings instinctively.* He especially saw the close connection between sex and spirituality.

This mystical understanding put him out of touch with the writers of his day and with the tradition of Western literature in general. The critics who praise the power of his novels often find his sexual theories laughable. But Lawrence wrote from the heart and—as he often said—the solar plexus. He wrote the deepest truths he knew. Like Whitman, he was a prophet first and an artist second.

Lawrence lived just forty-four years, most of them in poor health, with significant stretches of severe illness. He restlessly traveled the globe, all over Europe and to Ceylon, Australia, the United States, and Mexico. But his shelf of

---

*Lawrence's father was an amateur botanist and taught his son a great deal of what he knew. Lawrence's work is jammed with references to the natural world. It may be that, as with Whitman, his close attention to nature became a kind of meditation.

work is enormous, like that of a man who lived into his eighties and stayed in one place. Though all his work has flaws—his aesthetic was entirely spontaneous—he wrote everything with the whole of his attention. He can seem wrongheaded and stubborn, but he is never less than fully engaged.

He rewrote a great deal but not in the patchwork way that most writers do; he just set the book aside and wrote it again. The number of times he started over—tossing away millions of words—on the huge manuscript that became *The Rainbow* and *Women in Love* is almost maddening, and there are three distinct versions of *Lady Chatterley*.

His pace is nevertheless astonishing. It is stunning to read *The Plumed Serpent* and know that this rich work—495 dense pages in my paperback edition—was composed in six weeks of apparently casual mornings.* John Middleton Murry lived with Lawrence while he composed *Women in Love* and had no idea he was even writing, much less that in his spare time he was reading the books he would later feature in *Studies in Classic American Literature*.

Lawrence just lived at a different level of intensity from the rest of us. To take a walk with him, Cynthia Asquith once said, "made you feel that hitherto you had walked the earth with your eyes blindfolded and your ears plugged."[2] And Aldous Huxley reports that Lawrence—here he sounds like a true Zen man—"could never be bored and so could never be boring. He was able to absorb himself completely in what he was doing at the moment; and he regarded no task as too

---

*In his 106 days in Oaxaca, according to Parmenter, Lawrence rewrote *The Plumed Serpent* and also wrote nine essays, the beginning of a poetic drama, the start of a novel he never finished, and sixty letters.

humble for him to undertake, nor so trivial that it was not worth his while to do it well."[3]

For Lawrence, sex and relationship are one sacred thing. He is vaguely associated with sexual permissiveness but saw promiscuity as wicked and misguided. He had—by a recent biographer's count—perhaps five female lovers and one male, and probably didn't even have much sex with his wife after their initial coming together; she complained—loudly and in the presence of others—of his clumsiness in bed and was unfaithful with any number of other men, behavior that he can't have liked but that he seemed, in his great love and need for her, to have overlooked.

Yet no writer ever had a more exalted view of relationship.

> It is in relationship to one another that [men and women] have their true individuality and their distinct being. . . .
>
> Man or woman, each is a flow, a flowing life. And without one another, we can't flow, just as a river cannot flow without banks. A woman is one bank of the river of my life, and the world is the other. Without the two shores, my life would be a marsh. It is the relationship to woman, and to my fellowmen, which makes me myself a river of life.[4]

This understanding enabled him to take a broad view of sex, seeing it as far more than just an act. He saw it as a constantly varying energy between two people.

> Chastity is part of the flow between man and woman, as [is] physical passion. And beyond these, an infinite range of subtle communication which we know nothing about. . . . The long course of marriage is a long event of perpetual change, in which a man and woman mutually build up their souls and make themselves whole. It is like rivers flowing on, through new country, always unknown.[5]

From the standpoint of the nineties, Lawrence is homophobic. He did think the relationship of man to man was vital—and much neglected in our day—but he didn't speak much of its sexual possibilities, though his work alludes to them and he apparently had sex with at least one man himself.

He has also been attacked by feminists—most famously Kate Millett—for being sexist and misogynistic, and there are definitely passages in his work that support such charges. Brenda Maddox, in her recent biography, explores some notable examples. Lawrence was stubbornly outspoken, and if an idea or image came to him he would stand behind it.

But to dismiss all of his work for these lapses seems misguided. What he has to say is so important and unique that it is worth overlooking a few flaws. Lawrence obviously loved women and was much influenced by them, beginning with his mother and moving eventually on to a notably strong and passionate wife. Many of the correspondents with whom he had deep and important exchanges were women. And the overall thrust of his work, with its emphasis on relationship, is strongly pro-woman.

THE WOMAN FOR HIM

The most daunting aspect of writing about Lawrence is that he wrote so well—and so extensively—about himself. *Sons and Lovers* is so full a portrait of his childhood and youth that it leaves nothing to say. He grew up a miner's son, the last person in the world one would expect to wind up as a man of letters. He maintained throughout his life the status of an outsider.

His mother was a cultivated woman who felt she had

married beneath herself. She claimed rather bitterly that her husband misrepresented his prospects before their marriage. Arthur Lawrence led the manly life of a laborer while she railed against his drinking and insensitivity and smothered her children with love. She was closest to David Herbert, particularly after his older brother died of tuberculosis.

Through the haze of the mother's disapproval, the father in *Sons and Lovers* seems a likable working-class type, something of a model for Mellors in *Lady Chatterley,* fond of his children but alienated from them by his wife. As Lawrence got older—and especially after his mother died—he liked and appreciated his father more. But the effect of his upbringing was to make him very much a woman's man: his closest confidants were women; he created some of the great female characters in British literature; he was—after he married— virtually lost when Frieda wasn't around; and he often regretted that he didn't have closer relationships with men.

In a bizarre work entitled *Fantasia of the Unconscious* (an expansion of the earlier *Psychoanalysis and the Unconscious*), Lawrence invented a psychology and physiology out of whole cloth. Like much of his work, it can seem extraordinarily perceptive on one page and strangely demented on the next; he develops an elaborate theory of centers of consciousness and how they develop. Along the way he has some interesting things to say about his own background.

> Now we come to the greater peril of our particular form of idealism. It is the idealism of love and of the spirit: the idealism of yearning, outgoing love, of pure sympathetic communion and "understanding." And this idealism recognizes as the highest earthly love, the love of mother and child.
>
> . . . It means, for every delicately brought up child, in-

deed for all the children who matter, a steady and persistent pressure upon the upper sympathetic centres, and a steady and persistent starving of the lower centres. . . . The warm, swift, sensual self is steadily and persistently denied, damped, weakened, throughout all the periods of childhood.[6]

Lawrence spent his whole life ridding himself of that idealism, believing that we must all live from the lower "centres." He also remarked on an incidental result of such an upbringing.

The true polarity of the sympathetic-voluntary system within the child is so disturbed as to be almost deranged. Then we have an exaggerated sensitiveness alternating with a sort of helpless fury.[7]

Lawrence was nothing if not sensitive, and he was famous all his life for his rages; they seemed to get worse—and more physical—as he got older. That temperament is also associated with tuberculosis, and he was consumptive from the time of his youth.

He went through the same painful and protracted virginity in Great Britain that Alan Watts would experience thirty years later, complicated in Lawrence's case by his attachment to his mother. His love for her was enormous, and he was aware even as a youth how difficult it would be for another woman to live up to that ideal. At the same time, he felt a yearning for sex and resented the repression of his culture.

He eventually lost his virginity to a young woman named Jessie Chambers, with whom he had a long relationship and to whom he was engaged for a while. Upon his mother's death he proposed to another woman, Louise Burrows, said to be "conventional, highly religious, and easily shocked."[8]

Lawrence had been a schoolmaster in his early twenties,

writing fiction and poetry on the side and sharing it with his friends. With his mother's unhappiness as an example, he wanted to be well established when he married and kept waiting until he had enough money. But after an early flare-up of tuberculosis he broke off with Louise Burrows, saying the doctor had told him he shouldn't marry. Probably that was just an excuse. At some deep place he knew she wasn't right for him.

It was at this point that Lawrence met the woman— married to one of his former professors and the mother of three children—with whom he would have a deep and tem-pestuous relationship for the rest of his life, who probably had a greater influence on him than even his mother, and who may have made him a great writer (various commenta-tors—herself included—thought so). What Frieda Weekly gave Lawrence, after his tentative and tepid relationships with other women, was wholehearted acceptance of his physical, spontaneous, sexual self. It was as if he met his sex-ual healer, then ran off and married her.

The story goes that Frieda seduced Lawrence within twenty minutes of their meeting. She was a German woman who, along with her sisters, had adopted a bold philosophy.

> She believed in Eros—the liberating power of sexual love—a doctrine taught her by a lover, the Austrian psycho-analyst Otto Gross. . . . She also believed that women should use their strength to nurture male genius and that in giving her body she was also giving her mind.[9]

Frieda was bored in her relationship with Weekly, and in the young Lawrence she believed she had found her genius. Within days they had run off together and become partners for life.

Frieda knew she was taking a chance in leaving her husband but had no idea she was abandoning her children forever. Divorce was much less common at that time, and
female sexual freedom was not regarded with much favor.
Weekly, bitter about what his wife had done, resolved to
keep her from ever seeing her children again and largely succeeded.

Frieda's life with Lawrence sounds in one way selfless
and almost submissive; she had no other work, as long as
they were together, than nurturing him. On the other hand,
she had almost nothing to do. Lawrence not only made all
the money—through his voluminous writing—but did the
household chores as well. "He could cook," Huxley tells us,
"he could sew, he could darn a stocking and milk a cow, he
was an efficient wood-cutter and a good hand at embroidery,
fires always burned when he had laid them and a floor, after
Lawrence had scrubbed it, was thoroughly clean."[10] Despite
his lifelong illness, he had enormous energy and loved to stay
busy. Frieda's major pastime seemed to be chasing men.

In all his writing Lawrence expressed a fervent belief in
monogamy, an abhorrence of casual promiscuity, an almost
mystical belief in the couple. But he lived at a time and
among various groups—the Bloomsburys, for one—where
casual sex was common, and though he can't have liked it,
he seemed to accept that Frieda participated. In some way
that transcended their problems, he knew she was the
woman for him. He was the sexual theorist, she the practitioner. Even in their photos, she is the robust woman ruddy
with good health, he the emaciated, consumptive intellectual.

Their fights were monumental, bitter verbally, and—as
they got older—physical as well. "He beat her," an apparently startled Katherine Mansfield said about one encounter,
"he beat her to death—her head and face and breast and

pulled out her hair." The next morning, she was just as startled to see Lawrence "taking Frieda breakfast in bed and
making her a hat while she wove flowers into her hair."[11]

Brenda Maddox believes that their fights had two sources:
her sexual voraciousness and the fact that she had been
forced to give up her children. Lawrence believed that fights
were natural, that in addition to being drawn to one another,
men and women were natural antagonists.

(Maddox has a theory—which she seems rather too sure
of—that the Lawrences dealt with their aggressions and sexual difficulties by means of anal intercourse. Frieda supposedly enjoyed submitting, and Lawrence thereby avoided the
devouring vagina. Even allowing for the proprieties of the
day, some of Maddox's literary evidence seems flimsy:

> Ah no, I cannot tell you what it is, the new world.
> I cannot tell you the mad, astounded rapture of its dis-
>   covery.[12]

But once you have the idea in your mind, you stumble across
various suggestive passages, including one toward the end of
Lady Chatterley.

> It was a night of sensual passion, in which she was a little
> startled and almost unwilling: yet pierced again with piercing
> thrills of sensuality, different, sharper, more terrible than the
> thrills of tenderness, but, at the moment, more desirable.
> Though a little frightened, she let him have his way. . . .
> Burning out the shames, the deepest, oldest shames, in
> the most secret places. It cost her an effort to let him have
> his way and his will of her. She had to be a passive, consent-
> ing thing, like a slave.[13])

There were many strains on their marriage that were not
their fault. They lived through the First World War: Lawrence opposed it and was excused because of his lungs; Frieda
was German, so they were under constant surveillance by

British authorities. Lawrence's great novel *The Rainbow* was banned for indecency at about this time, and he wrote *Women in Love* with no hope of publishing it. That was probably the worst period of poverty they endured, though there were others. They also spent years wandering the globe, looking for a healthy place for Lawrence to live but never finding it.

Through it all he worked furiously. He rewrote *Sons and Lovers* soon after meeting Frieda, that brilliant novel about a young man's attachment to his mother. *The Rainbow* and *Women in Love,* perhaps his most aesthetically successful novels, were originally intended to be one novel, with characters based on Frieda and her sister. Lawrence was one of the best travel writers who ever lived; he left behind a huge volume of poetry and multiple books of stories; and he did a great deal of incidental journalism (he felt he could always do journalism to make money). And Cambridge has published seven volumes of his letters.

But he was more than just an artist. He believed the world was headed in the wrong direction and that people needed to change their lives. Not only was he forever seeking the perfect place to live; he hoped to form a utopian society—which he would call Rananim, with the phoenix as its symbol—and was always asking friends to join him, though he never got past the planning stage. Lawrence may have produced his best work in the middle of his career, but as a prophet and thinker he continued to evolve all his life. He composed what is to me his most interesting work—novels, journalism, travel books, stories, essays—toward the end.

DARK KNOWLEDGE

Lawrence had theories all his life that there were people who lived from their deeper centers, as he wanted to. At one point he believed the North American Indians were such a people, and he traveled to New Mexico and Mexico in hopes of en-countering them.* Later he believed—apparently on the basis of a few cave paintings—the same thing about the Etruscans, that they had developed an ideal society crushed by the mor-alistic, lawgiving Romans. Really, of course, he was writing about the spontaneous person he wanted to be. Probably the best example he could have found was the woman he was married to.

His obsession with indigenous people is most boldly ex-pressed in *The Plumed Serpent,* his novel about Mexico. It con-cerns a religious revolution, and Lawrence has been misunderstood as having thought there once really was such a religion in Mexico. But he was just borrowing locations and symbols. The religion was pure D. H. Lawrence and can be pieced together partly from the novel and partly from other writings.

Lawrence rejected all existing religions because they didn't speak to him, but he did not reject what was behind them. He saw them all as flawed approximations of the un-fathomable and unnamable. It is natural for them to vary in different places, and to change over time.

> Gods die with men who have conceived them. But the god-stuff roars eternally, like the sea, with too vast a sound to be heard.[14]

Indigenous people are—theoretically at least—closer to the life of the earth, therefore to the god-stuff.

---

*He apparently appreciated them more in the abstract than in the partic-ular. Mabel Dodge Sterne, who invited him to New Mexico, had a romance with a Native American while he was there and eventually married the man, becoming Mabel Dodge Luhan. Lawrence seemed as shocked as if she were consorting with a servant. He wasn't sure they should all eat together.

> We have lost almost entirely the great and intricately
> developed sensual awareness, or sense-awareness, and sense-
> knowledge, of the ancients. It was a great depth of knowledge
> arrived at direct, by instinct and intuition, as we say, not by
> reason.[15]

There was a time, in fact, when they were so close to the
earth that they hadn't formulated the idea of God.

> The very ancient world was entirely religious and god-
> less. While men still lived in close physical unison, like flocks
> of birds on the wing, in a close physical oneness, an ancient
> tribal unison in which the individual was hardly separated
> out, then the tribe lived breast to breast, as it were, with the
> cosmos, in naked contact with the cosmos, the whole cosmos
> was alive and in contact with the flesh of man, there was no
> room for the intrusion of the god idea.[16]

He therefore felt that Christianity was not an appropriate
religion for a place with such a rich indigenous culture as
Mexico. In its stead he proposed a religion based on the
plumed serpent, Quetzalcoatl, and envisioned a god figure.

> It was a naked man, carved archaic and rather flat, hold-
> ing his right arm over his head, and on the right arm balanced
> a carved wooden eagle with outspread wings whose upper
> surface gleamed with gold, near the light, whose under sur-
> face was black shadow. Round the heavy left leg of the man-
> image was carved a serpent, also glimmering gold, and its
> golden head rested in the hand of the figure, near the thigh.
> The face of the figure was dark.[17]

The eagle represents the powers of the air, the serpent
the deep powers of the earth. They come together, and are
united, in the god figure. They also represent an ancient consciousness and a modern one.

> . . . the fusion of the old blood-and-vertebrate conscious-
> ness with the white man's present mental-spiritual conscious-
> ness. The sinking of both beings, into a new being.[18]

The other necessary coming together, and a key for the
religion he was creating, was between man and woman.

> The clue to all living and to all moving-on into new living
> lay in the vivid blood-relation between man and women. A
> man and a woman in this togetherness were the clue to all
> present living and future possibility.[19]

When Lawrence spoke mystically of the blood, of phallic-
ism, of phallic power—as he does throughout his work, as if
we should know what he means—he is speaking of this mystical union of man and woman.

> Sex is our deepest form of consciousness. It is utterly
> non-ideal, non-mental. It is pure blood-consciousness. It is . . .
> the nearest thing in us to pure material consciousness. It is
> the consciousness of the night, when the soul is *almost*
> asleep.[20]

Blood enters the erect penis and the engorged vagina, and in
the act of intercourse two blood sources merge and react
together, a part of the endless coming together (and splitting
apart) of yin and yang in the universe. That was why Lawrence took intercourse so seriously. He saw it as a mystical
union.

Sex is a doorway to the dark sensual consciousness of the
ancients, which put them in touch with the divine. And a key
ritual of Lawrence's religion is a primitive dance that brings
the dancers' consciousness down into their bodies and sym-
bolizes the coming together of male and female.

> Men and women alike danced with faces lowered and
> expressionless, abstract, gone in the deep absorption of men

into the greater manhood, women into the greater womanhood. It was sex, but the greater, not the lesser sex. The waters over the earth wheeling upon the waters under the earth, like an eagle silently wheeling above its own shadow.[21]

THE MAN WHO NEARLY DIED

The Plumed Serpent is a mess as a novel but fascinating as a book; it expresses Lawrence's deepest hopes for humanity, his religious view of the world. His wish to start a utopian community—though he couldn't seem to get along with anyone for more than a few days—and his restless search for an ideal place to live were really just external manifestations of a deeper search.

Inasmuch as he was searching for the perfect place, his trips to Mexico were fiascoes; his stay in Oaxaca lasted just three months. Toward the end he went through a horrible illness that nearly killed him and that deepened his vision still further. As he thought he was dying, the author of some of the great books of world literature made a startling statement to Frieda. "But if I die, nothing has mattered but you, nothing at all."[22]

That didn't seem just the emotion of the moment. It seemed—from the evidence of what followed—a new realization, beyond what he had written in *The Plumed Serpent*.

Out of this brush with death came "The Man Who Died," among the most painful of Lawrence's stories to read—knowing what was behind it—but one in which he expresses a new religious vision. On the surface it is a retelling of the Christ story: Christ rises from the grave because he had been taken down from the cross too soon and hadn't really died; he finds healing at the farm of a peasant couple, then makes his way to Egypt, where he meets a priestess from the Isis cult and cohabits with her. At that level the story conveys a similar message to *The Plumed Serpent:* abandon Christianity and embrace the pagan gods.

Actually, like all Lawrence's work, it is largely about Lawrence himself. It begins with his protagonist's coming to life and his feelings about that. This man of bright bold consciousness had apparently found something attractive about his nearness to death.

> He resented already the fact of the strange, incalculable moving that had already taken place in him; the moving back into consciousness. He had not wished it. He had wanted to stay outside, in the place where even memory is stone dead.[23]

He sees life around him but no longer feels the desire that was once a part of it.

> He opened his eyes, and saw the world again bright as glass. It was life, in which he had no share any more. But it shone outside him, blue sky, and a bare fig tree with little jets of green leaf. Bright as glass, and he was not of it, for desire had failed.[24]

Precisely because he is empty of desire, however, he sees the true beauty of the world and decides that his role as a prophet was deluded. This is Jesus abandoning his teaching but also Lawrence giving up his obsessive preaching and system making. The Man Who Died abandons his life as a teacher for simple existence in the phenomenal world.

> I will wander the earth, and say nothing. For nothing is so marvelous as to be alone in the phenomenal world, which is raging, and yet apart.[25]

We don't see Jesus' journey to Egypt, just his arrival there, as he meets a woman who serves the goddess Isis. The

goddess herself—in myth—is searching for the god, and her
task is to make him whole with her sexual embrace.

> She was looking for the fragments of the dead Osiris,
> dead and scattered asunder, dead, torn apart, and thrown in
> fragments over the wide world. . . . She must gather him
> together and fold her arms round the re-assembled body till
> it became warm again, and roused to life, and could embrace
> her, and could fecundate her womb.[26]

He sees the healing in her—"How could I be blind to the
healing and the bliss in the . . . body of a tender woman!"—
and accepts the possibility that he is the god.

> "And art thou not Osiris?" she asked.
> He flushed suddenly.
> "Yes, if thou wilt heal me!" he said. "For the death aloof-
> ness is still upon me, and I cannot escape it."[27]

He therefore realizes the healing power of sex, the force
that—in effect—creates a god.

> He untied the string on the linen tunic and slipped the
> garment down, till he saw the white glow of her white-gold
> breasts. . . .
> "This is the great atonement, the being in touch. The
> grey sea and the rain, the wet narcissus and the woman I wait
> for, the invisible Isis and the unseen sun are all in touch, and
> at one."[28]

He had discovered the tender touch of a man for a
woman, which is in itself divine. There was no need to create
a religion around it—as he had tried to do in *The Plumed
Serpent*—but just to live it.

Tenderness at the End

Lawrence was ready to compose his final hymn to life, the
lyric, pastoral *Lady Chatterley's Lover*. It is not the Lawrence

novel that is most studied or most praised by critics, but it is probably the most read. It may not be his fullest or most aesthetically pleasing work, and as a narrative it is curiously inert: little happens except that a woman takes a lover and leaves her husband. It has often been excoriated as vile, obscene, and pornographic.

Yet there is something basically gentle about the book, serene and tender (Lawrence had wanted to call it *Tenderness*). It is really just the story of these two people, and has the feeling of a writer's final statement. Though Lawrence knew the seriousness of his condition in those final years— earlier he had denied it—he took the time to write three different versions. He was never interested in aesthetic perfection. He was clarifying what he had to say.

The book has its historical ironies. This most famous of erotic novels was written by a man who was probably— weakened by his illness—impotent. It is the ultimate tribute to relationship, but as he wrote it Frieda had taken a new lover, whom she was to marry after Lawrence died.

Brenda Maddox believes Lawrence saw himself as Chatterley—paralyzed from the waist down—and that his narrative was about Frieda and her new lover, but that seems to me a perverse misreading. Connie Chatterley does sound like Frieda.

> Constance, his wife, was a ruddy, country-looking girl with soft brown hair and sturdy body, and slow movements, full of unusual energy.[29]

But Mellors just as surely sounds like Lawrence, not the wasted man who would weigh eighty-five pounds when he died, but the vital spirit who had produced a huge shelf of books over the course of a tumultuous life. Mellors is both bold and gentle, a working-class man—a gamekeeper—

educated beyond his background. When Connie first sees him—spying on him as he washes up—he exhibits the peculiar beauty of man in his solitude.

> She saw the clumsy breeches slipping down over the pure, delicate, white loins, the bones showing a little, and the sense of aloneness, of a creature purely alone, overwhelmed her. Perfect, white, solitary nudity of a creature that lives alone, and inwardly alone.[30]*

Mellors has been wounded by life, particularly by women, and is not seeking them out. But Connie arouses him—"For suddenly he was aware of the old flame shooting and leaping up in his loins, that he had hoped was quiescent for ever"[31]—and he gives in: "And there his hand softly, softly, stroked the curve of her flank, in the blind instinctive caress."[32] He understands that—whatever pain it brings—he must open up to that feeling.

> "It's life," he said. "There's no keeping clear. And if you do keep clear you might almost as well die. So if I've got to be broken open again, I have."[33]

Sex is sacred specifically because it opens us to the energy behind all life. For Lawrence, people misuse sex when they just seek sensual gratification. That attitude is symbolized in *Lady Chatterley* by women who don't really give themselves.

> For she only had to hold herself back in sexual intercourse, and let him finish and expend himself without herself

---

*Lawrence had elaborated on male solitude in *Fantasia of the Unconscious*. "The central fulfillment, for a man, is that he possesses his own soul in strength within him, deep and alone." The soul for him is not an individual entity but the stuff out of which everything comes, what a Buddhist would call the unconditioned. "The individual soul originated everything, and has itself no origin." (*Fantasia of the Unconscious and Psychoanalysis and the Unconscious* [New York: Penguin Books, 1960], 123).

coming to the crisis: and then she could prolong the connection and achieve her orgasm and her crisis while he was merely her tool.[34]

Mellors's wife had been like that, and at first Connie is also. Finally she surrenders, not some regressive surrendering to a man, but a giving in to the energy itself. The mutual surrender of male and female yields simultaneous orgasm, symbolic for Lawrence of true union.

> Then he began to move, in the sudden helpless orgasm, there awoke in her new strange thrills rippling inside her. Rippling, rippling, rippling, like a flapping overlapping of soft flames, soft as feathers, running to points of brilliance, exquisite, exquisite and melting her all molten inside.[35]

The real evil, for Lawrence, is what he calls sex in the head; with a man like Chatterley, who believes in the supremacy of the mind, Mellors—and Lawrence—emphatically disagree.

> Give me the body. I believe the life of the body is a greater reality than the life of the mind: when the body is really wakened to life.[36]

Mellors's great virtue is that he has the courage of bodily feeling—"the courage of your own tenderness,"[37] as Connie tells him—and Mellors sees awareness of the body as the key.

> It's a question of awareness, as the Buddha said. But even he fought shy of the bodily awareness, and that natural physical tenderness, which is the best, even between men; in a proper manly way. . . . Sex is really only touch, the closest of all touch. And it's touch we're afraid of.[38]

Sex for Mellors is not just the act but the whole ebb and flow of the energy, even when he and Connie are apart, as he states in the book's final soliloquy.

So I love chastity now, because it is the peace that comes of fucking. I love being chaste now. I love it as snowdrops love the snow. I love this chastity, which is the pause of peace of our fucking, between us now like a snowdrop of forked white fire. And when the real spring comes, when the drawing together comes, then we can fuck the little flame brilliant and yellow, brilliant. But not now, not yet! Now is the time to be chaste, it is so good to be chaste, like a river of cool water in my soul.[39]

This devotion to the body ultimately expands beyond sex, teaching us not just how to make love but how to live.

If they could dance and hop and skip, and sing and swagger and be handsome, they could do with very little cash. And amuse the women themselves, and be amused by the women. They ought to learn to be naked and handsome, and to sing in a mass and dance the old group dances, and carve the stools they sit on, and embroider their own emblems. Then they wouldn't need money. And that's the only way to solve the industrial problem: train the people to be able to live and live in handsomeness, without needing to spend.[40]

That was Lawrence's final answer to life, just to live it in the simple way he always had, utterly absorbed in its details.

Lady Chatterley was banned in Lawrence's day, and he died soon after its publication; he did not live to see its exoneration or the huge sales it has enjoyed. It has never really been seen for what it is; it is still known as his dirty novel, an aberration in his career rather than its capstone. But Lawrence was an artist, not a pornographer, and before he was an artist he was a mystic who saw into the heart of sex as few people have. *Lady Chatterley*—though still somewhat preachy—is not a falling off from his best work. It is a lyric final novel that takes the subject of sex and relationship—the one he wrote about best—to its ultimate conclusions.

NOTES

1. D. H. Lawrence, *Selected Letters* (New York: Penguin Books, 1950), 16.
2. Brenda Maddox, *D. H. Lawrence: The Story of a Marriage* (New York: Simon and Schuster, 1994), 174.
3. Lawrence, *Selected Letters*, 27.
4. D. H. Lawrence, *Phoenix: The Posthumous Papers of D. H. Lawrence* (1936; reprint New York: Viking Press, 1968), 191–92.
5. Ibid., 193.
6. D. H. Lawrence, *Fantasia of the Unconscious and Psychoanalysis and the Unconscious* (New York: Penguin Books, 1960), 17.
7. Ibid., 118.
8. Maddox, *D. H. Lawrence*, 67.
9. Ibid., 96.
10. Lawrence, *Selected Letteres*, 27–28.
11. Maddox, *D. H. Lawrence*, 226.
12. Ibid., 146.
13. D. H. Lawrence, *Lady Chatterley's Lover* (New York: Bantam Books, 1983), 267.
14. D. H. Lawrence, *The Plumed Serpent* (New York: Vintage Books, 1992), 54.
15. D. H. Lawrence, *Apocalypse* (New York: Penguin Books, 1976), 48.
16. Ibid., 101.
17. Lawrence, *The Plumed Serpent*, 337.
18. Ibid., 415.
19. Ibid., 398.
20. Lawrence, *Fantasia*, 173.
21. Lawrence, *The Plumed Serpent*, 128.
22. Maddox, *D. H. Lawrence*, 369.
23. D. H. Lawrence, *Love among the Haystacks and Other Stories* (New York: Penguin Books, 1960), 127.
24. Ibid., 132.
25. Ibid., 143.
26. Ibid., 149.
27. Ibid., 159.
28. Ibid., 170.
29. Lawrence, *Lady Chatterley's Lover*, 2.
30. Ibid., 68.
31. Ibid., 122.

32. Ibid., 123.
33. Ibid., 125.
34. Ibid., 4.
35. Ibid., 141–2.
36. Ibid., 254.
37. Ibid., 300.
38. Ibid., 301.
39. Ibid., 328.
40. Ibid., 326.

4

The Twain Shall Meet

ALAN WATTS

A Zen master was asked, "I have heard that there is one thing which cannot be named. It has not been born; it will not die when the body dies. When the universe burns up it will not be affected. What is that one thing?" The master answered, "A sesame bun."

—ALAN WATTS, *Nature, Man, and Woman*

SERIOUS PRACTITIONERS OF Zen often scorn Alan Watts, though he was one of the people most responsible for bringing the practice to the West. He was for many practitioners one of the first Buddhist writers they came across, and they associate him with their early elementary understanding. Watts himself didn't practice much—he at least didn't do much sitting—and he was a wild man in other ways, taking LSD, drinking to the point of alco-

~ ALAN WATTS

holism, and running around on all his wives. He seems not so much a Buddhist (and he fiercely resisted the label) as a scholar of Buddhism, someone who had read about it a lot. A serious practitioner wants his teacher to have known the aching knees of long sesshins.

But I will always be grateful to Alan Watts for the first glimpse of Buddhism that he gave me, when I was entering middle age and terribly frustrated by the fact that I had no religious tradition. Religion had been a terrific intellectual struggle for me—as I tried to hack Christianity into something I could swallow—and a tremendous moral and physical one, as I tried to keep my body and mind from straying. Watts, with his vision of a Buddhism that celebrated impermanence and change, that saw body and mind as basically one thing, that saw the whole secret of life in discovering and following one's true nature, released me from all that. For *The Way of Zen* alone I am deeply grateful.

But I also believe that Watts's understanding was deeper than people give him credit for. It is true that he didn't do much sitting, but he did practice more active forms of Zen, especially walking meditation, and also "archery, *t'ai-chi* exercises, mantra-chanting, . . . Chinese calligraphy, tea ceremony, swimming, and cooking."[1] He had a wild side and a real weakness for booze, but he was also quite disciplined, never missing a speaking engagement and getting up every morning when he was at home—often quite early—to write.* His writing was a spiritual discipline worthy of a master. And his explanations of Zen—despite their apparent glib-

---

*Watts's son Mark—who helped me with an earlier piece—told me a fascinating detail about his father's rhythms: he preferred to sleep for three five-hour periods in a given forty-eight hours. He therefore might keep quite irregular hours but averaged seven and one-half hours of sleep per night.

ness and ease—seem to me to be of the very highest quality.*
He didn't learn the truths of Buddhism sitting on a cushion,
but he learned them somewhere. And if he was condescend-
ing to people who spend hours sitting, we will just have to
forgive him.

As various people have noticed, Watts was more a Taoist
than a Buddhist, and he was more an independent thinker
than anything else. He described his "tastes" in religion—and
it was characteristic of him to make them sound frivolous;
he insisted on a light touch—as lying "between Mahayana
Buddhism and Taoism, with a certain leaning towards Ved-
anta and Catholicism, or rather the Orthodox Church of
Eastern Europe."[2] He was a genuine mystic who had a marvelous logical mind; he was a lucid and fluent writer who
often achieved a kind of poetry; he was a superb public
speaker; and he wrote a number of excellent books, including
the best book I have read on the subject of sex and spirituality. It is no wonder I feel indebted to him. He has immeasur-
ably enriched my life.

No Shit

The second floor of his childhood home was not a happy
place for Alan Watts. That was where his bedroom was,

*Listen, for instance, to this offhanded explanation of sitting meditation,
taken from his autobiography: "Zen meditation is a trickily simple affair, for
it consists only in watching everything that is happening, including your own
thoughts and your breathing, without comment. After a while thinking, or
talking to yourself, drops away and you find that there is no 'yourself' other
than everything which is going on, both inside and outside the skin. Your
consciousness, your breathing, and your feelings are all the same process as
the wind, the trees growing, the insects buzzing, the water flowing, and the
distant prattle of the city. All this is a single many-featured 'happening,' a
perpetual now without either past or future, and you are aware of it with the

which he always felt—as the only child of older parents—as a place of exile.* It was also where the bathroom was, a place he detested so much that he included a detailed line drawing, and an explanation of its shortcomings, in his autobiography. That was the room, for some reason, where his mother chose to spank him, actually sitting on the throne and pulling him over her knee. It was also where his bowels were required to move every day, and where—if they didn't—he was dosed with a powerful laxative.

The bowel movement became a potent symbol for the adult Alan Watts. In the midst of a fascinating lecture on sex entitled "The Spectrum of Love," he must have startled his audience by pausing at a key moment, then letting them know that they had to trust themselves to have bowel movements. The function of the bowels is a perfectly adequate focus for all that he wanted to teach. Everything on earth is a part of the Tao, and the Tao must be allowed to flow freely.

In all matters of human functioning, his advice was basically the same: let the thing happen as it wants to. Don't force it. The rhythm of the body isn't necessarily the rhythm of the clock, and the fact that you haven't shit today doesn't mean the world is coming to an end. As Watts's favorite psychologist, Georg Groddeck, said, "There is a hole at the bottom and it has to come out eventually."[3]

Watts's mother was the bad guy throughout his life.

rapt fascination of a child dropping pebbles into a stream. The trick—which cannot be forced—is to be in this state of consciousness all the time, even when you are filling out tax forms or being angry" (Alan Watts, *In My Own Way: An Autobiography, 1915–1965* [New York: Pantheon Books, 1972], 367).

*Despite his love of sex, Watts never liked bedrooms. He much preferred the Japanese custom of bringing out mats and sleeping in the regular living space. He saw no reason to devote the whole room of a house to nothing but sleep.

From his father—this is an unusual fact for anyone and almost certainly influenced Watts's spiritual beliefs—he always felt unconditional love. They were easy companions when Alan was a teenager, touring country pubs to sample the bread and cheese and ale; Laurence Watts actually joined the Buddhist Lodge at the same time as his son, even though he had shown no interest in Buddhism before that; and the old boy even wrote the forward to his son's autobiography. But young Alan didn't like his mother's looks* and never felt close to her. She wasn't physically affectionate. Watts felt she didn't like her own body—a grave flaw in the Watts universe—and that she had been overly influenced by the dour fundamentalist Protestantism in which she had been raised.

Emily Mary Watts did give her son his love of oriental art, which she loved herself. His attraction to the East was at least as aesthetic as it was spiritual, and he adored the style of Eastern art, its empty spaces and isolated objects. But probably the worst thing his parents did—and both must share the blame for this error—was to send their son to boarding school at the tender age of seven. Watts complained of British life in general, but he hated its educational system, despite the fact that, to some extent, his great virtues as a writer must be partly a product of it.†

He hated the uniform he had to wear and the food he

---

*To my eyes, she is a dead ringer for the adult Alan Watts.

†Watts speaks in his preface to *The Way of Zen* of how he was a particularly good person to bring Zen to the West because he was deeply interested in the subject but not really immersed in that world. But the real reason he was so good a messenger was that he had a superb version of the linear thinking mind that he so often criticized. He had a remarkable capacity to read and absorb huge amounts of information and an uncanny knack for expressing it briefly and clearly. He had the impeccably clear mind of a British schoolmaster and the mystical nature of an oriental sage.

had to eat. He disliked the fact that he was separated from girls, who had always been important companions for him. He hated the whole system of rote learning, which didn't produce first-rate minds. He speaks of his first night at boarding school with real bitterness. "My first lesson, given at night in a six-bed dormitory by the other occupants, was in the vocabulary of scatology and sexual anatomy, with a brief introduction to buttock fetishism."⁴ And he profoundly disliked the system of discipline, especially the practice of flogging, which he objected to for its "sexual complications."⁵ He raised this objection to authorities while he was still in school.

He therefore became the kind of intelligent and sensitive young man who grows alienated from his surroundings and finds subtle ways to rebel. He was also alienated because he was a scholarship boy and—especially as the Depression came on—his father was often unemployed. He wasn't just the kind of alienated schoolboy who takes up Buddhism to be a pain in the ass to the authorities. But there was something of that boy in him.

Yet he was not in general negative or critical. He was actually an enthusiast—he went quite overboard in his enthusiasms—and a great lover of life. Even when he was in school he knew the kind of mentor he was looking for and the person he wanted to be (and did become, in spades). It was the kind of person who, instead of the dull sober clothing of the British establishment, wore whatever he wanted, with an accent on comfort.* It was someone who indulged in the multifarious delights of international cuisine. It was definitely

---

*Watts actually wore a kimono in Japan, much to the amusement of the Japanese in their Western business suits.

someone who enjoyed living in a body, who took great delight in earthiness and sensuality. It was someone who confronted the great questions of existence with a certain lightness and playfulness, a *gaieté d'esprit*. One can see why Watts appreciated the playful eccentric Zen masters more than the harsh stern ones.

Charles Johnson, the brother of an early headmaster, was such a mentor.

> Charles could give me more education in five minutes than his brothers in five years—simply by his attitude and his pleasure in his work. . . . But Charles wasn't trying to *teach;* he was simply following his own weird and allowing me to watch.[6]

An even more significant mentor was Francis Croshaw, the father of a schoolboy friend.

> The first thing that Francis Croshaw did for me was to release me from the boiled-beef culture of England and let me realize that I was at least a European. In 1929 he took me with his family to France, via Jersey, sat me down in a cafe in Saint-Malo, and bought me my first drink [Watts was fourteen]. . . .
>
> Within an hour we were eating melons, artichokes, *pate maison,* and *coq au vin* at the Hotel Chateaubriand, and it suddenly dawned upon me that eating could be an art.[7]

But the most exemplary of all Watts's mentors was the head of London's Buddhist Lodge—the man Watts wrote to at the age of fifteen with all the bravado of an adolescent rebel and who wrote back thinking Watts was a teacher at the school rather than a student—who, Watts said, "gave me an education which no money could buy" and "put me on my whole way of life"[8] and who had the odd name, especially for a Buddhist, of Christmas Humphreys.

> He and [his wife] . . . maintained an establishment that was full of mystery. It wasn't just the oriental art and the smell of pine or sandalwood incense. It was also that, on and off, they were visited by enigmatic and astonishing people such as Tai-hus (patriarch of Chinese Buddhism), Nicolas Roerich (Russian artist and Buddhist), G. P. Malalasekera (Buddhist scholar and diplomat of Ceylon, who is probably the most reasonable man in the world), Alice Bailey (an up-dated Blavatsky), and, above all, Daisetsu Teitaro Suzuki, un-official lay master of Zen Buddhism, humorous offbeat scholar, and about the most gentle and enlightened person I have ever known, for he combined the most complex learn-ing with utter simplicity. He was versed in Japanese, English, Chinese, Sanskrit, Tibetan, French, Pali, and German, but while attending a meeting of the Buddhist Lodge he would play with a kitten, looking right into its Buddha-nature.[9]

Watts was extraordinarily precocious as a Buddhist scholar. He read widely in esoterica as a teenager, the first of his massive programs of self-education, "Suzuki, Keyserling, Nietzsche, Vivkananda, Lao-tzu, the *Upanishads,* Feucht-wanger, Bergson, Blavatsky, the *Bhagavad-Gita,* Lafcadio Hearn, Anatole France, Havelock Ellis, Bernard Shaw, the *Diamond Sutra,* Dwight Goddard . . . Robert Graves, and Carl Jung."[10] He would write his first book on Buddhism—later admired by so discerning a reader as Henry Miller—at the age of nineteen. The only experiences of kensho that he de-scribed in his autobiography happened early in his life. And it was through Buddhism that he met his first wife, a woman who not only led him into a larger world of Buddhism but also took him to the country where he would have his great success as a writer and lecturer.

He's Gotta Have It

Watts seemed to have a clear-eyed and sensible view of sex all his life.

> Over the years it has become my firm opinion that sexual activity (even if only through masturbation) is "requisite and necessary, as well for the body as for the soul"; for men and women alike. It stimulates your glands, exercises your pelvis, thrills your nerves, brings mind and body together as one, and culminates in an ecstasy in which there is neither past nor future nor separation between self and other. We need that as we need vitamins, proteins, water, and air.[11]

He actually saw sex as an aid to understanding.

> I have the strong impression that religious celibates who actually refrain entirely from sex (as do some of the swamis and yogis of modern India) become sentimental, sour, and greedy for power. The married Tibetan lamas and Zen priests I have known seem to have a far greater "spiritual presence," including a *roshi* or Zen master who, on one occasion, made it with his lady friend sixteen times in twenty-four hours.[12]

And he was eloquent in stating the sexual dilemma of a young man of his generation.

> I had not realized to what a degree sex is used as a bait and a prize in amazingly complex social games. Furthermore, girls of my own age and set seemed to be content and satisfactorily excited by purely titillatory sex, and could keep one dangling in foreplay for so many months that the relationship soured.[13]

He would eventually become a representative man of the sixties. But he turned twenty in 1935.

It does seem that despite his sensible views, Watts married the first girl who would let him in her pants. Eleanor Everett's mother was Ruth Fuller Everett, later Ruth Fuller Sasaki, who in some ways was as important a figure in American Zen as Watts. She had already been to Japan and studied with a Zen master—the first Western woman to do so—when Watts met her, and she would eventually become an important benefactor of the First Zen Institute of America, marry its founder—Sokei-an Sasaki—and travel to Japan after his death to see to the English translation of the *Rinzai-roku*.

Watts's biographer Monica Furlong speculates that he may at first have been more attracted to Mrs. Everett than to her daughter. But in 1937 Ruth Fuller Everett was still married to a wealthy American businessman and on her way back to the states. She was a sophisticated woman and must have known what she was doing when she left her teenage daughter behind, in the hands of one of the horniest men in the British Isles. The eighteen-year-old Eleanor was two months pregnant when she and Watts were married, in April of 1938.

Watts had not gone to university. He had flunked the scholarship exam, supposedly because he had answered questions "in the style of Nietzsche."[14] That seems yet another example of the rebellion of the overly bright alienated youth, resentful of his lifelong scholarship status.

His first book, *The Spirit of Zen*, was really just a condensation of the ideas of D. T. Suzuki, the first example of a task Watts always did extremely well: absorbing a huge amount of material and summarizing it in a small space. Once he had married Eleanor, and with the possible object of avoiding military service, he moved to the United States, where he lived on her family's wealth.

Watts in America pursued the life of an independent scholar, reading widely, continuing to write, and conducting occasional seminars. He had his first close encounter with a Zen master, the unjustly neglected Sokei-an Sasaki,* whom he had a chance to study with, but he found Sasaki's regimented way of moving through koans to be stifling. Watts seemed to resist regimented systems and official teachers all his life, though he had great affection and respect for the master himself.

> Sokei-an would say that Zen is to realize that life is simply nonsense, without meaning other than itself or future purpose beyond itself. The trick was to dig the nonsense, for—as Tibetans say—you can tell the true yogi by his laugh. . . .
>
> He never fidgeted nor showed the nervous politeness of ordinary Japanese, but moved slowly and easily, with relaxed but complete attention to whatever was going on.[15]

It was while he was in the United States, and married to Eleanor, that Watts made the bizarre decision to become an Episcopal priest. This was really just a brief blip in his life; within six years of his ordination he left the church. People still think of him as a clergyman with an interest in Buddhism, when actually his interest in Buddhism came much earlier.

One factor in his decision to enter the ministry was Eleanor, who had grown depressed in her role as a young mother, had started gaining weight, and had—one day when

---

*Sokei-an's eccentric and fascinating collection of talks, *The Zen Eye*, is available from Weatherhill (New York: 1993).

she stepped into a cathedral to take a rest—had a vision of Christ. Watts was also, in his wide reading, discovering ways in which the Western tradition seemed to accord with the Eastern, so he could in all conscience embrace it. He was an extremely talented young man who was looking for a vocation and wouldn't have minded having a job. And despite the obvious problems (he was still a Taoist/Buddhist who loved the good life—and whose friends couldn't believe what he was doing) he thought this might be the one.

There was the minor problem, of course, that he had no university degree, but when he found a sympathetic bishop to sponsor him and submitted a list of his reading ("four pages in single-spaced typewriting"[16]) to Seabury-Weston Theological Seminary in Evanston, Illinois, he was admitted immediately. He soon found that he could do all the required work in one evening per week and spent the rest of his time in his voluminous reading.

When he took a position afterward as chaplain at the Evanston campus of Northwestern University, he by all accounts did a superb job. He changed the worship service to make it more accessible and to indulge his lifelong love of ritual.

> We trained a small ensemble of men and women students to sing Gregorian chant and Renaissance polyphony, and a group of acolytes to assist at the Mass according to a stately Anglican version of the Western rite. . . . We banned all corny hymns, and I never let a sermon run for longer than fifteen minutes. . . . I tried to exorcise their idea of God as a Victorian paterfamilias, saying instead that Creator and creation were an outpouring of reckless and ecstatic love.[17]

He made himself available to students in formal and informal settings. He also wrote a book, *Behold the Spirit*, which was extraordinarily well received by reviewers, one of them calling it "one of the half dozen most significant books on religion published in the twentieth century."[18]

But Eleanor, sitting at home with two small children, felt more out of it than ever. She was still depressed, and according to Furlong was physically abusive to her younger daughter. One student, speaking cruelly in the way that only students can, said that she seemed entirely out of place in Watts's life, "fat, dumpy, and stupid."[19] And Watts began to get into trouble in the way that talented dynamic young men—especially clergymen—often seem to.

EVERYONE NEEDS A HOBBY

Both Watts's biographers agree that it was while he was at Evanston—if not before—that he began having affairs outside his marriage, a pastime that he would continue for the rest of his life. Neither Furlong nor Stuart particularly documents this assertion, and they don't say how they know (though Furlong does name a couple of later lovers). But Watts himself, in his autobiography, cheerfully admits, "My life would be much, much poorer were it not for certain particular women with whom I have most happily and congenially committed adultery."[20] And it seems to be the first thing that everyone says about him.

The story that Furlong tells of the end of his first marriage is much more lurid, bizarre, and—ultimately—interesting than any account of affairs could have been. She quotes extensively from letters that Eleanor wrote to Watts's bishop, so in this instance at least she doesn't seem to be dealing in hearsay.

According to Eleanor, she discovered long after they

were married that Watts was obsessed with sex, masturbated daily, and stimulated himself with fantasies of flagellation. He said he had contracted this pathology at school, where flagellation was carried out extensively, often with sexual associations. He confessed these details in an all-night session with Eleanor during which, at one point, he asked if she wanted to beat him. Watts, of course, was hardly the first Englishman to make such a confession to a startled bride. British public schools were rife with flagellation, and most of the great S/M pornography is British.*

One reason that people associate spanking with sexual excitement (other than the fact that the bottom is a key part of our sexual equipment) is early imprinting, and Watts certainly experienced that, from his earliest days at boarding school if not back in the bathroom at Chislehurst. It must have been one of the few ways his mother was physical with him. Scenes of punishment look and sound sexy—bare skin, loud smacks, groans, cries—and stimulation of the buttocks often stimulates the genitals. The traditional Freudian explanation is that the S/M devotee associates sex with pain and guilt and can only receive pleasure from it if he is punished.

But Freud's wayward disciple Wilhelm Reich—who followed Freud's theories to their logical conclusions and really

---

*Mark Watts does not believe that any of this ever happened and was furious when I mentioned this incident in an earlier piece. When Furlong's biography came out, Mark asked his mother—Watts's second wife—if she had seen any indication of such inclinations, and she said she hadn't, that their sex life had been perfectly normal, even ordinary. But neither Furlong nor I suggested that he practiced erotic flagellation, just that he told Eleanor he'd had fantasies. I feel confident about this assertion because Eleanor wrote of it to Watts's bishop, and I can't imagine why she would make up such a thing. Watts also—as we shall see—spoke quite knowingly of the association of pain and sex in his writing. He seemed to have more than a passing interest in the subject.

understood the subject better than the master—believed that we are all encased in body armor, which we have created through years of tensing up and shrinking so as not to feel things, especially those that are painful. This tensing itself is a kind of pain, and we long to be released from it. The S/M devotee does so by being beaten, releasing waves of energy that loosen the body armor and resemble the full-body orgasm that Reich saw as necessary for health.

Watts himself wrote quite knowingly of this byway of sex in *Nature, Man, and Woman*. He was actually dealing not with sex but with our need to feel the pain of our lives rather than avoiding all pain and seeking out only pleasure. He spoke with the relaxed common sense characteristic of his best writing.

> The masochist finds in pain of certain types a positive stimulant to sexual orgasm, and as the intensity of his feeling increases he is able to delight in harsher and harsher degrees of pain. . . . To this it should be added that the masochist's desire to be subjugated or humiliated is allied to the fact that all sexual ecstasy, male or female, has a quality of self-abandonment, of surrender to a force greater than the ego.[21]

Sexual submission ultimately expresses a wish to surrender in general, not just to a master, but to our lives as they are, that whole world of pleasure and pain. Watts would eventually learn—and show the rest of us—how to do exactly that. In the meantime, he dreamed of this more limited surrender.

What really seems to have been the case in this unhappy moment of Watts's first marriage is that he was what was to be a sixties sensibility trapped in the late 1940s. He was a sexy man—the daily masturbation is no surprise—married to an overweight, depressed, unhappy woman. He had hoped to practice his vocation as a spiritual teacher but in doing so had put on the odd straitjacket known as a clerical collar. He was trapped and constricted in every direction.

A bizarre sexual soap opera ensued, in which Eleanor struck up a liason with a student ten years younger than she and admitted the fact to her husband—probably to make him jealous—and he, to her surprise, suggested the young man move in. He may have been as free of sexual jealousy as he later claimed ("I can see no good reason for regarding anyone as my exclusive sexual property"[22]), or he may have wanted an excuse for his own wandering. Eleanor actually had a child with this young man, whose parents were horrified to discover that their son was cavorting with the chaplain's wife.

Eleanor eventually traveled to Las Vegas and, instead of seeking a divorce, had the marriage annulled, on the grounds (according to Watts) that he "believed in free love"[23] or (according to Furlong) that he was a "sexual pervert."[24]* He had paired up with (and was later to marry) a graduate student named Dorothy DeWitt who had been his children's babysitter—a suggestive detail if I ever heard one—and left the chaplaincy in disgrace. He wrote a series of letters—reprinted in his autobiography—in which he defended his decision from a theological position, but they sound fairly lame. He should probably never have entered the clergy in the first place.

INSECURITY INDEED

Watts's position at this point seemed desperate. He had lost the only job opportunity that had been open to him and

*Watts skims over the end of his first marriage in his autobiography and goes into none of the sordid details. He is generous to both of his former wives in that book, and Furlong says that the passages about Eleanor finally

would never be able to work in the church again. He had largely been living off Eleanor's wealth and had now given up all claim to it. He had, of course, published some books, but they hadn't made the kind of money that could support him. And he had custody of his two daughters, who—despite his lifelong claim that he was a lousy father—had chosen to live with him rather than their unhappy mother.

But Watts—at least as he presented himself in his autobiography—seemed all his life to be extremely lucky, a man of great gifts who stumbled into one situation after another that used them. At this juncture he met Joseph Campbell, who would remain a friend for the rest of his life. Campbell suggested that he apply to the Bollingen Foundation to fund his next book, entitled—appropriately—*The Wisdom of Insecurity*. He got the grant and spent six months in isolation writing it. It was in some ways his first work as a true freelancer, which was always his most creative mode. He was very good at living by his wits.

The Wisdom of Insecurity is not quite vintage Watts; his prose had not taken on the free-flowing ease that it would eventually settle into. But the book does express a key Watts idea: that the existential anxiety we are all heir to simply by being human is not something we should avoid—as conventional Christianity does—by creating a system of belief that protects us from it. We should instead encounter that anxiety in all its raw power. Any other attitude involves a form of avoidance that can only lead to suffering.

He draws the interesting distinction between belief (in

---

reconciled her to Watts, many years after their divorce. Actually, Watts is generous in that book to almost everyone who passed through his life; it is one of the least malicious literary memoirs I have ever read. It says a lot for his gentleness of spirit.

which you hold on to a metaphysical system for dear life) and faith (in which you let go of all systems and encounter life as it is). And he lets us know that the religious life is not the perpetual calm that we keep expecting it to be.

> We, too, would like to be [a person wholly free from fear and attachment], but as we start to meditate and look into ourselves we find mostly a quaking and palpitating mess of anxiety which lusts and loathes, needs love and attention, and lives in terror of death putting an end to its misery. So we despise that mess, and put "how the true mystic feels" in its place, not realizing that this ambition is simply one of the lusts of the quaking mess, and that this, in turn, is a natural form of the universe like rain and frost, slugs and snails.[25]

His second stroke of luck came when he ran into a friend from his Buddhist Lodge days, Frederic Spiegelberg, who had decided to start the American Academy of Asian Studies in San Francisco. Watts was obviously a perfect person to assist in this project, and it moved him to California, where he would make his home for the rest of his life, and which was extremely important in shaping him.

Though it was probably doomed from the start financially, and though the idea of Watts's using his considerable talents as a fourteen-hour-day administrator is painful, the academy played an important part in his development. Virtually everyone interested in the East seemed to pass through the place at one time or another, including many people who would be important in the sixties: Michael Murphy and Richard Price, who would found the Esalen Institute; Richard Hittleman, who later became famous as a yoga teacher; and the poet Gary Snyder were all students at one time or another.

Watts had managed all his life to find small pockets of people who shared his interests, first at the Buddhist Lodge, later among the students surrounding Sokei-an Sasaki, but now he was surrounded by such people. He must have been a wonderful—if undisciplined—teacher, though it was hard to say just what he was teaching.

> I think it will now be clear that my own approach to Asian philosophy was part of an individual philosophical quest. I am not interested in Buddhism or Taoism as particular entities or subjects to be studied and defined in such a way that one must avoid "mixing up" one's thinking about Buddhism with interests in quantum theory, phychoanalysis, Gestalt psychology, semantics, and aesthetics, or in Eckhart, Goethe, Whitehead, Jung, or Krishnamurti. I feel about academic "subjects" just as the Balinese feel about "Art" when they say, "We have no Art: we just do everything as well as possible.[26]

He also finally had the opportunity to "spend days on end exploring Chinese dictionaries, working through ancient Taoist and Buddhist texts, and practicing calligraphy with the brush."[27]

Among the lesser-knowns who passed through the academy, one who seemed especially important to Watts was Japanese artist Sabro Hasegawa, mentioned twice in *The Way of Zen* and with great affection in Watts's autobiography. Hasegawa used to come into Watts's office at stressful moments and conduct impromptu tea ceremonies, which were "worth fifteen visits to a psychiatrist."[28] He also taught Watts an oriental concept that would be extremely important to his work: *li,* which is a free-flowing pattern that arises in nature, like the pattern of the grain in wood, of a waterfall, or of smoke trailing through the sky. Such patterns form the basis of oriental art, which is created spontaneously, by means of a "controlled accident," the same way that all of creation emerges from the Tao.

That kind of pattern is also evident in the individual life, expressing itself in the moment-by-moment flow of feeling and experience; and by following this flow instead of fighting it, a person can live his life both naturally and artfully. When Hasegawa's students expressed puzzlement as to how that might be done, he would thunder at them, "Can't you *feel?*"

Spiegelberg had given up on the academy as a financial venture in 1952, and Watts tried to keep it afloat himself, finally giving up in 1957. It was in that year that he published *The Way of Zen,* his most famous book and the one that was so important in bringing Zen to the West. In terms of his own career it is an interim book and marks a turning point: though it expresses something of himself (like everyone who wrote or talked about it, Watts gives his own flavor to Zen), it is largely a work of scholarship, the fruit of years of interest and a far cry from *The Spirit of Zen,* which he had written when he was just out of school.

Watts puts Zen into its cultural context and emphasizes—by showing how oriental it is—its differences from other kinds of Buddhism, its deep roots in Taoism, and its opposition to the Western view of things. He speaks, for instance, of the way that Western language itself expresses a worldview, one in which subjects perform actions, while the Chinese language sees things more as processes, both because its written characters are pictures—often representing processes—and because many of them can be used as both nouns and verbs.

He also points out that in China, Confucionism is the system of law, the means by which people are acculturated, and Taoism is an opposing spirit of mystery, dark and elusive. One speaks of the relation of men to men, the other of men to the metaphysical. Christianity unites these two strains—

God gives the law—disastrously, in Watts's opinion, because it makes the law into an absolute and sets man against his own nature. Taoism is specifically a practice of being at one with that nature, and even Confucionism regards human-heartedness as the highest virtue, supplanting every law.

Watts discusses terms that will be important in all his writing. The Tao is the dark, mysterious, spontaneous principle behind everything, constantly unfolding with no particular plan. *Wu wei* is the principle of following the Tao, the doerless doing with which Sabro Hasegawa created a work of art and out of which the great spiritual masters live their lives. And *te* is virtue, not in the sense of following some set of rules but of being in accord with the Tao.

Watts definitely deemphasizes sitting meditation in this and all of his books, as did—coincidentally, it seems—other writers important in bringing Zen to the West. He cites both R. H. Blythe and D. T. Suzuki as agreeing with him, along with such great and eccentric Zen masters as Bankei. Part of the truth seemed to be just that Watts didn't like to sit, except occasionally. He was like Krishnamurti in emphasizing awareness in all activities, and he therefore believed that Zen could be practiced by doing anything—including his favorite activity, the one he would feature in his next book.

WATTS NEW

The Way of Zen made Watts famous; he refers to it in his autobiography as a minor best-seller, and it introduced Zen to countless Westerners, including a number of sixties hippies who were looking for an alternative to the traditional Western viewpoint. As we look back on it now, it seems restrained and scholarly. Watts hadn't quite broken through to the free-wheeling style of his later work.

It does stand, however, at the beginning of an extremely important four-year period in his life, when he broke into the career of a freelance writer and lecturer, when he left his second marriage, when he began leading a much more bohemian life, and when he wrote his two greatest books. Watts was a superb interpreter of the East to the West, but he was at his best when expounding his own views, fertilized by his interests. He would continue to do wonderful writing for the rest of his life, but he did his most original work, and discovered the richest vein of his thought, between 1957 and 1961.

The point that Watts was always trying to get across was a simple one, what he called his "most basic intuition: that here and now, without any artificial striving and straining, the flow of life in man is inseparably one with the Tao, the flow of the universe—call it God, Brahman, the Divine Ground, or what you will."[29] He hadn't worked to achieve that notion—claimed, in fact, to have always known it. But it had ramifications for every aspect of life, and he spent the rest of his career spelling them out.

The people who led him to his most important concepts did not necessarily think of themselves as spiritual teachers. Some were women; unlike many men of his generation, Watts was open all his life to their teaching and influence. One was the woman to whom he dedicated his autobiography, Elsa Gidlow, about whom he went on at considerable length in the text.

> From the first meeting Elsa enchanted me, in the strict sense of that word, which is that of a witch casting a spell. But I could not quite make out at first at which band on the spectrum of love I should meet her. . . . I soon saw that we were to meet on the green and not the red band . . . where intense friendship lies between vermillion lust and violet

agape, and that she was to fulfill exactly the role in my life that would have been taken by a very companionable older sister.[30]

It was Elsa whose cottage Watts moved to when his second marriage ended and some of his more conventional friends abandoned him.

Watts was also much influenced at this moment by Charlotte Selver, the primary teacher in this country of the odd nonsystem known as Sensory Awareness. It was created by a German woman named Elsa Gindler who, when diagnosed with tuberculosis, went off to a forest hermitage and cured herself simply by becoming acutely aware of her bodily processes, discovering that "what came by itself can go by itself."[31]

Though not really a spiritual discipline, Sensory Awareness does resemble meditation practice, especially Zen, which emphasizes awareness of the body. "The principle is to find out what one is actually feeling all over and everywhere, without naming it, and then to respond to it in such a way that the act of responding is no longer separated from the act of feeling."[32] As Watts said about Charlotte Selver, "She puts you in love with the simple fact of physical existence."[33]

Watts taught workshops with Selver, actually met the woman who would be his third wife at one of them, and stated in his autobiography that Selver was a particular influence on his next book, which he published just a year after *The Way of Zen* and which he regarded as his best, *Nature, Man, and Woman.*

I also regard this as Watt's best book and as the best book I have read on the subject of sex and spirituality. Watts had not plumbed the esoteric texts for this book, as he had for *The Way of Zen;* he had read them—in the effortless way he had of absorbing huge amounts of material—but made the material his own. *Nature* is not a how-to book, except for a few pages at the end. It is actually a book of philosophy and presents Watts's overall view of things as well as anything he ever wrote.

He begins by raising a central difference between the Eastern and Western viewpoints.* In the West, spirit and nature are separate, and to some extent in opposition; God created the universe and broods over it as a separate being. In the same way, a human being's "spirit" is often at war with his unruly "nature." In the East, spirit and nature are one thing. The Tao did not, at some specific moment, create the natural world; rather, nature is a perpetual unfolding of the Tao, which is, in effect, within it. In the West God is the architect of the universe and has a plan, but in the East the universe is a spontanous process of growth.

There is, therefore, in the East no conflict between our "spiritual" side and our "natural" side. There is also no conflict between man (whom the West identified with spirit) and woman (whom the West identified with nature and regarded as part of the "problem"). The East identifies these gender characteristics as yang and yin but sees them as part of a larger, unifying whole.

Watts regards Christianity as a particularly urban religion, always somewhat at war—and trying to unify itself—with the pagan religions of the countryside. Christianity is largely a religion of ideas, while the essence of Eastern religion is an experience, of oneness with everything. There is often a conflict between the ideas of Christianity and the reality of

*To some extent, as Watts acknowledged, these represent not geographical terms but states of mind.

experience. Christianity posits, for instance, an opposition between good and evil, and in theory one should be able to be good all the time. But the reality is quite otherwise.

In a similar way, Western science (the new religion) creates a vast system of things that can be measured, classified, and quantified. Standing out against this system is man, who is supposed—God knows how—to control it. The last two centuries of science are thought to be in opposition to religion, but in some ways they represent a similar view. Both systems see a human being who stands out separate from nature.

But for Watts—and for Eastern thought in general—the separate self is an illusion created by thought and memory and to some extent by a bodily tension that keeps us from feeling. If we drop this illusion, what is left is just a stream of experiencing, which is natural, like the grain in wood or the streaming of a waterfall. The key to living is to tune in to this flow. We tend to use more energy than we need to, straining against things as they are, especially straining the mind. If instead we give in to our feelings and go with the stream of experiencing, things work themselves out in a natural way.

Western man often feels his body as a difficulty, sometimes an embarrassment; he could lead a spiritual life if it weren't for his clunky body with its unfortunate needs for food, shelter, and sex. We have a soft body in an often hard world, which raises the whole question of pain, a tremendous conundrum for the Western thinker (why did God allow pain and suffering into the world?).

For Watts, pain is just the flip side of its opposite; there would be no pleasure without it. The problem (and this is a major part of our straining) is that we try to create a world where there is only pleasure. But shrinking from pain—

tensing up and pulling back—is itself a form of pain, while giving in to it opens us up to ecstasy, which for Watts is a feeling of connection with things as they are.

Thus the art of living is to live a perfectly ordinary life. "The birds and beasts indeed pursue their business of eating and breeding with the utmost devotion. But they do not justify it; they do not pretend that it serves higher ends, or that it makes a significant contribution to the progress of the world."[44] The world as it exists is not at variance with spirit but is contained within it, as the eighth-century Zen master Hui-neng said.

> The emptiness of universal space can contain the myriad things of every shape and form—the sun, moon, and stars, the mountains and rivers, the great earth with its springs, streams, and waterfalls, grass, trees, and dense forests, its sinners and saints, and the ways of good and evil. . . . All these are in the void, and the ordinary person's nature is void in just this way.[35]

Watts does not get to sex, appropriately, until two-thirds of the way through the book, when he has set it in context. The mentality that sees sex as separate from spirit is the same one that sees nature as separate from spirit (and identifies woman with nature). It sets the ego up against an uncontrollable human nature, the thinking mind against the outside world. But these are false dichotomies, and if the true religious attitude—as Watts believes—is to see man at one with all of nature, sex is obviously a part of that oneness.

The problem is that when man does not feel the ecstasy of being at one with things, sex seems to be his only means to ecstasy, and it is used as an escape.

> Both sexuality and sensuality may become *maya* in its proper sense . . . when the mind seeks more from nature than

she can offer, when isolated aspects of nature are pursued in the attempt to force from them a life of joy without sorrow, or pleasure without pain. Thus the desire for sexual experience is *maya* when it is "on the brain," when it is a purely willful and imaginative craving to which the organism responds reluctantly, or not at all.[36]

This problem cannot be approached in isolation.

Sexuality will remain a problem so long as it continues to be the isolated area in which the individual transcends himself and experiences spontaneity. . . . Only as the senses in general can learn to accept without grasping, or to be conscious without straining, can the special sensations of sex be free from the grasping of abstract lust.[37]

The real wonder of sex is apparent once it assumes its proper place.

It is the most common and dramatic instance of union between oneself and the other. But to serve as a means of initiation to the "one body" of the universe, it requires what we have called a contemplative approach. This is not love "without desire" in the sense of love without delight, but love which is not contrived or willfully provoked as an escape from the habitual empty feeling of an isolated ego.[38]

Watts describes at the end of his book an ideal kind of lovemaking in which no particular response is expected, but neither is anything resisted (the Tantric yogi who resolves not to ejaculate is in a way no different from the person who hankers after that moment as the only one that is worthwhile; neither is accepting the experience as it—so to speak—comes). In contrast to modern books on spiritual sex, Watts offers little in the way of prescriptions, because there is no one way to do what he is suggesting. He is offering a contemplative view of sex and of life itself.

NATURE, MAN, AND THE OTHER WOMAN

The irony of Watts's publishing his great book in 1958 was that he was no longer finding this kind of sexual bliss with his wife but with other women. Furlong believes that he had married Dorothy in the first place because she was an extremely practical woman and had helped him pick up the pieces at the end of his first marriage. Dorothy must have felt that they were settling into a conventional life in Watts's early years at the academy; they lived a life that to some people would sound idyllic, but for Watts it was constricting.

> We had then a rather pleasant house in Mill Valley, which had formerly been a garden nursery, with an expansive lawn, four great pine trees, twenty-seven fruit trees, four children . . . a colossal family enterprise in which I should never have allowed myself to be involved.[39]

It was still the late fifties, but—as we know in retrospect—Watts was on the cusp of a countercultural wave that would break over the country in the sixties, hitting first in California. His work and his whole life were pushing him in a new direction, and it hardly seems surprising that he met the woman he would now decide to marry—Mary Jane Yates—at one of his workshops with Charlotte Selver.

> She was as relentlessly drawn into Chinese nature-mysticism and Charlotte's Western-grown Taoism as I was fascinated by her voice, her gestures, the humor in her eyes, her knowledge of painting, of music, of colors and textures, her skill in the art of the love-letter, and her general embodiment of something I had been looking for all down my ages to be chief traveling companion.[40]

Watts was thrown into a whole new bohemian world, which he describes with great exhuberance in his autobiography, living part of the time in a small cabin in the woods and part on a houseboat in Sausalito, from which he sometimes conducted seminars. This was probably—as he came to believe—the life he was meant to lead all along, though he had chosen those other wives and there was no way they could have known such great changes were coming.

This was the Alan Watts who became famous, not the freethinking clergyman of the forties or the hardworking scholar of the fifties, but the bearded teacher/rascal of the sixties, sporting the Eastern garb that he loved and smiling with a wicked gleam in his eye. He began leading a wilder life (Mark Watts believes his father hadn't really been an alcoholic until his third marriage) and met much wilder friends.

Watts published his third great book, *Psychotherapy East and West,* in 1961. Though he had done much throughout his career to discover the affinities between Eastern and Western religions, particularly in their mystical traditions, the real comparison is between Eastern religion and psychotherapy, because they are both—as Watts pointed out—ways of liberation. He believed that both psychotherapy and Eastern spiritual practice have a similar technique, which he calls the counter-game: they paint the practitioner into a corner with an impossible conundrum until he finally gives up and sees—in effect—that there is no problem, that life is not a mystery to be solved but one to be celebrated.

As interesting as this whole book is, it is in the final chapter that Watts transcends the ostensible subject and links the book with the whole of his work. He believes that the ego may be a necessary creation of socialization, as we are taught how the world expects us to be, much in the way that Confucionism gave Chinese culture rules to live by. But real maturity for Watts is seeing that this ego has no reality, and he expresses dismay that no psychologist (even Jung, who was much influenced by the East) understood that necessity. That is where Eastern thought moves beyond psychotherapy. It is why therapy can only take us so far.

He thus wishes that Freud and his successors had seen their system through to its logical end and advised us to live without repression. He was referring not to a life of sheer indulgence but to one in which our desires are allowed to arise and express themselves, giving us a choice as to how we act. The suppression of Eros cannot be a good thing.

> For when we have Eros dominated by reason instead of Eros expressing itself with reason, we create a culture that is simply against life, in which the human organism has to submit more and more to the needs of mechanical organization, to postpone enjoyment in the name of an ever more futile utility.[41]

Liberation for Watts does not deny the body, as some traditions would have it.

> Liberation is not the release of the soul from the body; it is recovery from the tactical split between the soul and the body which seems to be necessary for the social discipline of the young. It therefore sets reason and culture not against Eros but at the disposal of Eros, of the "polymorphous perverse" body which always retains the potentiality of a fully erotic relationship with the world—not just through the genital system but through the whole sensory capacity.[42]

The way of liberation is thus to do everything in the way of Zen, to have an erotic relationship with all activity.

> He is the artist in whatever he does, not just in the sense of doing it beautifully, but in the sense of *playing* it. In the expressive lingo of the jazz world, whatever the scene, he

makes it. Whatever he does, he *dances* it—like a Negro boot-black shining shoes. He swings.[43]

Watts was to live another ten years after publishing this book; they were the years of his great fame, when he continued writing—nine more books—and traveled all over the country giving lectures and seminars. Watts is almost unparalleled in his combined talents as a speaker and writer. He apparently didn't prepare his talks at all, and though as a group they include a certain amount of repetition—he kept explaining his basic ideas to one group after another—they are uniformly witty, instructive, and entertaining.*

Watts had been an incessant smoker for most of his life and became an increasingly heavy drinker. Furlong recounts an occasion when one of his daughters was driving him to a lecture and found him already drunk.

> They drove a few blocks, and Watts insisted that they stop at a liquor store, where he bought a bottle of vodka. He put it on the back seat, and they drove off with Watts sitting between them in the front, but soon he had to turn round and take a swig out of the bottle. Joan was amused at the sight of the famous Alan Watts with his bottom in the air drinking neat vodka; she was also fully aware of the tragic implications. When they arrived at the lecture hall Watts walked onto the podium and gave his usual admirable lecture.[44]

He apparently often gave talks drunk, and he sometimes sounds rather boozy on the tapes, though he is never less than coherent. Some stories about his last days make him sound like a depressed alcoholic who just doesn't care any-

---

*Mark Watts has collected a large number in his Electronic University, listed in the Resources section at the end of this book.

more. Others make him sound like the proverbial Zen master who delights in life but doesn't cling to it. Mark Watts told me a poignant story about how he and his father were on a walk one day and he asked the man to take better care of himself; Watts began laughing so hard that he had to sit down. He finally said he only hoped that Mark enjoyed his own life as much as he had enjoyed his.

One can't help feeling, though, that—at fifty-eight—he died prematurely. He had come home exhausted from a long lecture tour, and when his wife tried to awaken him the next morning she found him " 'strangely unmoveable.' With deep shock she realized he was dead."[45] There were various stories about people feeling his presence after his death. And Furlong tells a hilarious story about how he claimed he was going to come back as the child of his daughter, Joan, who did conceive a child not long after his death.

> Once, when Laura was a tiny girl, she and Joan visited a friend's house, and Laura went to the cupboard where the liquor was kept, pushed a number of bottles out of the way, reached in, and removed a bottle of vodka from the back of the cupboard.[46]

Like a number of other teachers in recent years, Watts presents us with the delicate task of separating the teacher from the teaching. But he never posed as a teacher and never claimed to be anything he wasn't. He just enjoyed speculating on the nature of things and believed that what he saw would lead people to happier lives.

He presents the odd paradox that we find with some other teachers, the man with a superb mind who keeps insisting that the answer isn't to be found through thinking. There is no problem with thinking, of course; it can be as much a part of practice as anything else. The problem is in identifying with thought. At the end of his late tribute to D. T. Suzuki, Watts quotes Suzuki on this subject. The man might have been talking about himself, or about Alan Watts.

> Man is a thinking reed but his great works are done when he is not calculating and thinking. "Childlikeness" has to be restored with long years of training in the art of self-forgetfulness. When this is attained, man thinks yet he does not think. He thinks like showers coming down from the sky; he thinks like the waves rolling on the ocean; he thinks like the stars illuminating the nightly heavens; he thinks like the green foliage shooting forth in the relaxing spring breeze. Indeed, he is the showers, the ocean, the stars, the foliage.[47]

NOTES

1. Alan Watts, *In My Own Way: An Autobiography, 1915–1965* (New York: Pantheon Books, 1972), 122.
2. Ibid., 64.
3. Ibid., 35.
4. Ibid., 89.
5. Ibid., 90.
6. Ibid., 68.
7. Ibid., 70–71.
8. Ibid., 77.
9. Ibid., 78.
10. Ibid., 104–5.
11. Ibid., 129.
12. Ibid., 129–30.
13. Ibid., 129.
14. Ibid., 102.
15. Ibid., 144–45.
16. Ibid., 174.
17. Ibid., 188.
18. Monica Furlong, *Zen Effects: The Life of Alan Watts* (Boston: Houghton Mifflin, 1986), 105.

19. David Stuart, *Alan Watts* (Radnor, Pa.: Chilton Book Co., 1976), 112.
20. Watts, *In My Own Way*, 201.
21. Alan Watts, *Nature, Man, and Woman* (New York: Vintage Books, 1970), 106–7.
22. Watts, *In My Own Way*, 200.
23. Ibid., 203.
24. Furlong, *Zen Effects*, 118.
25. Ibid., 128–29.
26. Ibid., 273.
27. Watts, *In My Own Way*, 297.
28. Ibid., 270.
29. Ibid., 166.
30. Ibid., 281–82.
31. Ibid., 293.
32. Ibid., 294.
33. Ibid., 296.
34. Watts, *Nature, Man, and Woman*, 123.
35. Ibid., 134.
36. Ibid., 153.
37. Ibid., 157.
38. Ibid., 189.
39. Watts, *In My Own Way*, 276.
40. Ibid., 306.
41. Alan Watts, *Psychotherapy East and West* (New York: Vintage Books, 1975), 173–74.
42. Ibid.
43. Ibid., 183.
44. Furlong, *Zen Effects*, 200.
45. Ibid., 213.
46. Ibid., 216.
47. Alan Watts, *Does It Matter?* (New York: Vintage Books, 1971), 125.

~ MARCO VASSI. Reproduced courtesy The Permanent Press/Second Chance Press.

5

The Big Bang Theory

MARCO VASSI

*a woman is enlightenment when you're with
   her and the red thread
of both your passions flares inside you and
   you see*

—ZEN MASTER IKKYU,
trans. Stephen Berg

MARCO VASSI IS hardly a literary figure in the same sense as Whitman, Lawrence, or even Alan Watts; he was a pornographer who wrote for small presses and men's magazines, and a spiritual seeker who most often expressed himself in mimeographed newsletters to friends. When we move from those ancestor figures to a contemporary writer like Vassi, we are moving from people who saw sex as vitally important, intricately connected to the source of all being, to a man who took it on as a kind of priestly vocation.

When Vassi speaks of a minimum of two hours of hard

intercourse per day, the same way a marathon runner tries to get in his fifteen miles, we have come a long way from Whitman holding hands with his beloved in a saloon, or even Alan Watts's extensive philandering. Sex assumes a different status in the life of a man like Vassi. It almost *is* his life.

Watts clearly stated the danger of this attitude: "Sexuality . . . may become *maya* in its proper sense . . . when the mind seeks more from nature than she can offer."[1] Marco Vassi was especially prone to that error and could find himself— despite what sounds like an extraordinary sex life—mightily disappointed.

I should make my own attitude clear from the outset. I believe sex to be absolutely sacred—any acts you want to describe, any words you care to use. Hard-core S/M, complete with whips and chains, is deeply sacred (and as ritualistic as any ceremony an archbishop performs). But so is taking out the garbage. Fixing lunch. Talking with your wife over coffee. All of life is sacred. And I have no interest in taking sex on as a spiritual vocation. Sitting meditation is a lively enough practice for me.

Yet there is an old Zen saying: To know one thing well is to know everything. When the Zen master Tesshu took on the Red Thread koan, he vowed to make love to every courtesan in Japan.[2] And when I raise a difficult question, I look for an expert in the field, someone who has explored every corner. Even if that exploring has involved some stumbling and mistakes. We learn by hard experience.

I regard Marco Vassi as a contemporary because he could easily be alive today. He would have been only sixty in the year I'm writing this book and—despite a lifetime of excesses—would doubtless have been a fiery sixty. But we live in a time when many of our most vitally sexual people have died young, and we have lost much that they might have told us. Except for the few talented writers whose work has survived.

THE ROAD TO MADNESS

The first thing people mention about Marco Vassi is his intensity. Michael Perkins, in a moving obituary of his friend, says, "Many who encountered Marco Vassi thought him slightly mad. His dark eyes could be threateningly intense," and psychiatrist Martin Shepard remarked on "a sense of great anguish pouring from dark, deep-set eyes."[3]

A reader hardly needs to be told. Vassi's intensity leaps off the page, especially in his novels. He was a great erotic writer not just because he wrote better than other people but because the act he was describing was at a different level, an odd mixture of yoga routine, aerobic workout, and knife fight to the death. He wrote better about sex because he did it better. I could—quite literally—quote from dozens of passages illustrating this point, and go on for pages, but a short selection from *The Saline Solution,* one of his best-written novels, will give some idea.

> I rode her for almost an hour, going through dozens of changes, sometimes smashing brutally into her, and then just letting the tip of my cock gently nudge the edges of her inner lips; or swinging from side to side in erratic patterns, and then lying quietly, feeling my organ throb in her depths like a submarine in a grotto listening for echoes. I pumped into her with even strokes, like a carpenter sawing wood, and exploded into her like an epileptic having a fit; I rose up and hit into her at a sharp downward angle, and then sank down to slip my cock in from underneath and erupt to the roof of her cunt.[4]

This virtuoso of the erotic was a virgin until he was nineteen and lost his innocence in a Brooklyn bordello with an ejaculation so premature that he didn't achieve penetration. He then proceeded to make up for lost time. Stationed in Japan in the service, he fucked himself silly in Japanese brothels, and then wrote fondly of that experience in *The Saline Solution*.

He had been born Ferdinand William Vasquez-D'Acugno in 1937 to a Puerto Rican mother and an Italian father.* He always remembered the moment when he realized his outlaw nature, when he was eight years old and had been entrusted with the care of a two-year-old neighbor. As soon as the grown-ups left, he took down her diaper, took out his penis, and began rubbing against her. It wasn't long before his mother returned.

> That what I was doing . . . would be judged a crime by the world I lived in . . . is a wedge of knowledge that must have entered me through a thousand informal channels during my childhood. Without an explicit word ever having been spoken to me, I had introjected the judgment of civilization on the body.[5]

Vassi was the kind of wild sixties character who married on impulse (three times), changed his name repeatedly†— often legally—and frequently picked up and moved, sometimes from coast to coast. He recorded his journey through

---

*Though I have been dealing up to this point in this book with authoritative sources, the information on Vassi is sketchy and uncertain, and I write it with much less confidence. There has been—so far—no authorized biography.

†In addition to the name we know him by, he also assumed such names as Sa'shi, Madhava, Maddao, Freddie Vasquez, Fred Vassi, Mamou, Frater Cesare, Daksuri, Yen, Margo, Godfrey, Narci, Freda, Mark Elliot, Tocco, and Gigo Maitreya.

the sixties in *The Stoned Apocalypse,* possibly his best-written book and the one he seemed to have been proudest of. The story goes that he began writing because he saw a classified ad seeking porn writers, but he had a rapid, witty mind and a natural verbal gift and wrote at a professional level almost from the start.*

"Are you . . . searching?" a woman asks him in the first line, and it is a perfect question for that book and for the goofy, agonizing, and fantastic decade it describes. It is also a question that nails Vassi to the wall (and his statement at the end of the book that he has stopped searching is about on a par with his repeated assertions that he has grown tired of sex; his spirits tended to revive rather rapidly). He tries everything in that book, Gurdjieff, the Communist Party, Gestalt therapy, Scientology, psychedelics, swinging, speed, gay life, and—finally—a stretch in a madhouse.

He is adept at all of it. Despite the harangues of his Gurdjieff instructor ("I think you are such an utter fool that if you have acquired, by the age of forty, the courage to kill yourself, it will be the one significant act of which you are capable"[6]), he is an immediate success at awareness practice: "It was one of the most astounding experiences of my life. I wasn't feeling my body; my body was aware of itself, and the 'I' which I usually identified with became a kind of shadowy presence."[7]

At San Francisco State he teaches a class called "Relax-

---

*He could also, even after writing for years, sound like a rank amateur; he is one of the most uneven writers I have ever come across, both in the conception of his books and in the line-by-line prose. *In Touch* contains an idiotic plot worked out in awkward pulpy prose, while *The Saline Solution* comes across as the work of a serious accomplished artist. One does have the feeling that Vassi didn't always respect his porn. He had turned himself into a literary whore, and he sometimes turned his tricks halfheartedly.

ation, Awareness, and Breathing" and two hundred people sign up instead of the twelve he was expecting. His stony (and often stoned) affect is taken to reflect some form of deep wisdom. He begins to dress weirdly—"I . . . had begun going barefoot, wearing a leopard-skin cloak, carrying a wooden staff, and playing a harmonica instead of talking"[8]—and to seduce almost every woman he comes across. One class ends in a wild orgy.

He also has moments of plain sanity. It wasn't until he had switched to Gestalt therapy that he could look back and see the truth concealed in Gurdjieff: "There was for me the suspicion that the only thing Gurdjieff was saying was to wake up and enjoy life, its total joy and terror, its mystery and its revelations."[9] Like many spiritual seekers, he has his deepest realization when he quits trying.

> Almost two years later, on a chill night in the desert outside of Tucson, with some fine Southwest grass coursing through my brain, I woke up simply to the fact of existence. . . . I was returned to myself, and I knew that, paradoxically, I had found the place Gurdjieff talks about, without being a Gurdjieffite. Of course, I fall in and out of enlightenment, as I fall in and out of all the states which compose the human condition. [10]

He has limited tolerance for the New Age disciplines he is working through (which doesn't stop him from hungering after them like a kid in a candy shop). He doesn't avoid hard questions and detests easy answers, like glib talk about reincarnation.

> My feeling is that life is once around for each of us, and there is something amounting to a sacred trust for each of us to live it most intelligently, most lovingly, most honestly. I am given the creeps by people who think, somehow, that death isn't real. It indicates that they think life isn't real.[11]

He looks quite squarely at the question that tormented me in my youth:

> There is no one, there never has been anyone, nor can there ever be anyone, including the total Overmind of all Being, who has the foggiest notion why anything exists at all, and all speculation in that direction is as futile as it seems to be ineluctable.[12]

The Stoned Apocalypse can seem just a wild, hilarious, and often pointless romp through the sixties except in the ninth chapter, where it takes on, quite brilliantly, the subject of madness, one that Vassi faced throughout his work and throughout his life. His theories relate to his social critique; he clearly believes that it is society that is mad, and the people who can't fit into it often sane. The schizophrenic is often a spiritual visionary. And just as he dropped in and out of enlightenment, he had dropped in and out of madness.

> "I've been crazy a few times," I said. "I mean, I've been in a place where I was trapped in what felt like eternal suffering, where no other person could ever reach me, and which I couldn't communicate to anyone. And when I took acid, I realized that it was possible for me to go over that edge and never come back."[13]

Toward the end of the book Vassi takes a job at a psychiatric institution that sees madness as just such a spiritual condition, a sense of extreme isolation where one feels disconnected from everything. The idea was to create a therapeutic situation in which the patients were not differentiated from the staff, where everybody was in the soup together. But—as often seems to happen—money came along and changed things. The staff, in particular, began to worry about their careers more than their devotion to the experiment.

The key question was whether the patients would be able to leave the institution at will, and when it was decided—in order to keep a grant—that they wouldn't, the whole atmosphere changed.

Vassi—characteristically—remained the one true man, still dedicated to the original purpose. Because of an administrative snafu that had kept his money from coming in, he had to work as a volunteer, wasn't given a set of keys, and—since he was low on money—ran out of clothes and had to wear hospital issue. He began to adopt the patients' point of view, to see that—with their narrow careerist concerns—it was the doctors who often seemed to be crazy.

The predictable moment arrives. He loses his temper about something that staff does, expresses himself impulsively and rather crazily, breaks through to a place of deep sanity, then feels afraid. "For the moment, I was sheer essence, inchoate and raw. The fear began to choke me. I felt an animal need to escape, to get out."[14] But when he asks to leave, the staff person won't let him.

"I was penniless, dressed in patient's clothing. And the ward psychiatrist wouldn't let me out. By any standard, the door had closed behind me. I was mad."[15]

That moment is a perfect metaphor for Vassi's life. Was he a healing person helping sick people or a madman himself? A cheap porn writer or a serious thinker and artist? A spiritual seeker or a New Age flake? A slimy pervert or a man who made sex into spiritual practice? He deliberately blurs these lines and leaves the decision to us, thereby showing—as less vulnerable writers rarely do—that there are no final answers to any of these questions. We confront this or that fact in a person's life, this or that piece of writing. And we decide what we think.

The Stoned Apocalypse ends with its narrator happy to get back to, of all places, New York City. "The one comforting thing about New York is its utter imperviousness to individual madness."[16] He visits a friend who has had a psychotic experience of his own, and the two men ponder their lives.

> "After that night," Aaron was saying, "I realized that I am dead, and that everyone around me is dead, and that every breath I take is pure miracle, and I should never expect another. But it makes it so hard to live in the world, because so few others understand that, that we are all dead already."
>
> At that point some essential tension which I had carried with me since the moment the cold steel of the forceps clasped my skull and pulled me from my mother's womb, relaxed, and I was set free.[17]

He was ready to become a writer.

PORN AGAIN

Vassi wrote his nine porn novels between 1970 and 1976.* In *What Wild Ecstasy,* his book about the sexual revolution, John Heidenry cites publisher Maurice Girodias's prediction of a new kind of porn in the late sixties, "more autobiographical and with greater erotic content. . . . From the hippie-yippie business and drugs and the fusion of yoga and Zen and Oriental eroticism will come the basis of tomorrow's style and research."[18]

Vassi was the man Girodias had envisaged. The porn that preceded him—and that stoked the erotic fires of my youth—

---

*Michael Perkins deals with a cluster of these books in a chapter on Vassi in *The Secret Record,* his fascinating examination of pornographic literature. I have read a sampling of four, including one—*Contours of Darkness*—that Perkins personally recommended.

was set in Victorian boarding schools or in the mansions of wealthy Edwardian businessmen who were taking charge of an orphaned niece. Vassi's novels took place—as we used to say—in the Now and concerned issues that mainstream novels dealt with. They just happened to include an enormous amount of sex, described in mind- (and penis-) numbing detail.

These are genre novels and they sometimes exhibit the failings of other genres: predictable plots, stock characters, wooden dialogue, scenes that do not proceed naturally out of the action but are included to produce a specific effect.

Vassi doesn't transcend the form but gives us some fascinating insights within it and lets us know that we have lost something by relegating such work to cheap editions, pulpy paper, and bookstores that smell of disinfectant. Toward the end of his life, many of his titles were picked up by a mainstream house, Second Chance Press. They have also been widely translated—and are quite popular—overseas.

In the three major novels that I read, the issue was always one of relationship. The characters—both men and women—are sexually adventurous and erotically accomplished.* The problems arise when they try to do something other than sex. The whole plot of *The Gentle Degenerates,* for instance, revolves around our hero's agonizing decision about whether or not to follow his girlfriend to California. He states his lifetime dilemma around sex and relationship quite succinctly.

---

*In one scene, for instance, our narrator drops in on a woman who is "into snakes" (actually, it's the other way around), and she proceeds to insert a two-foot baby boa constrictor into her vagina. "For almost a half hour she seemed to be going mad. She bit the pillow and screamed, she called out to God, she rolled all over the bed" (Marco Vassi, *The Gentle Degenerates* [Sag Harbor, N.Y.: Second Chance Press, 1993], 114). An early precursor to the electric vibrator.

Why is it that the minute I begin having sex with someone, the quality of our relationship so radically changes as to
make it a different kind of organism? Why, with sex, do freedom and respect and friendship so often go out the window?
Why can I be happy for any woman's sexual freedom, and
have that same joy turn into jealousy the minute she becomes "my" woman.[19]

Vassi sees the sexual act itself as a way to wholeness,
quite apart from who his partner is. "The reason sex gets
boring in marriage is that both partners forget how to be
impersonal with one another,"[20] he tells us in one novel, and
in another he states that in the middle of a sexual act, "I don't
really care what the other person's name is. I don't even care
what my own name is. Ecstasy has no name."[21]

Moments of realization seem to arise not because of any
emotional connection but out of the sheer erotic energy generated. In *Contours Of Darkness*, for instance, there is a spectacular final scene—"She ground her teeth together and bit
into his face, severing the flesh and causing a shower of blood
to burst into her mouth"—that results in a kind of satori.

He had gone past all convention and she had soared beyond all inhibition. He saw that every idea he had ever held
was as ephemeral as the clouds; there was nothing real but
the raw insatiable drive of life itself. He had reached the point
where he had nothing more to lose, and could literally de-
stroy the foundations of his slavery by demolishing the physical structure in which it had found expression. Their attacks
on one another's body were only the symbols for the deeper
desire to abolish the conditioning inherent in their bones and
muscles and nerve endings.[22]

This is not your average stroke book.

But the attitude toward sex in these novels, while it can

express itself as a hope for realization, is just a shade away from the old male wish to have satisfaction without getting involved. Sometimes Vassi sounds like a Zen practitioner trying to get beyond the self, sometimes like Joe Six-Pack trying to get his rocks off. In *The Saline Solution*, the narrator suspects that his wish for impersonality is behind all his problems with women.

> With me, after the initial period of infatuation, a good fuck with the woman I'm living with becomes just that. It's no different, in its way, from a fine meal or a stunning sunset. But with her, whoever she happens to be, fucking gets all entangled with emotions. And, of course, the practical result of fucking: children.[23]

The highs of sex invariably lead to lows. One arrives after our narrator has been unfaithful.

> Nightmares visited me and my dreams were filled with terror. A dozen times figures climbed in through windows to slit my throat and suffocate me with my pillow. Several times I awoke gasping for air, a cold sweat on my forehead.[24]

Another narrator associates this anxiety with his tendency toward withdrawal.

> We drifted off into the state between wakefulness and sleep, into the area of thought dreams. I felt some slimy force rousing itself in me, and the sickeningly familiar symptoms of withdrawal flared up in my belly. A terrible mixture of anxiety and revulsion. I looked at the existential monster sliding up from its foul corner of the soul and caught its full ugliness in my gaze. For a long time we stood locked in deadly energy combat or struggle.[25]

It is this kind of honesty that raises Vassi above the traditional porn novel. He doesn't give us sex the way we want it to be. He gives it the way it is.

If the problem is that men want impersonal sex, while the essence of sex for women is personal, there is an easy solution, and it is one that Vassi often took. If he did not actually have more sex with men than with women, he at least had more contacts. Impersonality to the point of anonymity was the essence of gay sex to him. He speaks in *The Stoned Apocalypse* of an ideal occasion of group sex.

> The next fifteen minutes had no description, simply because there were no discrete units of activity. It was all touch, all liquid, all sound, all excitement, all images. . . . It provided me with the single most glorious moment of total anonymity I had ever experienced in my life, and when I finally crawled out, I felt as though I had gone through a baptism of orgasm.[26]

But when a friend approaches him he is not able to respond.

> He looked at me. "Let's go to my room," he said. My stomach dropped, and I lowered my eyes. I was still at the stage of pre-coming out where I was too embarrassed to make it with someone I knew. I could only do it with strangers.[27]

He did eventually overcome that barrier, with that same friend. And some time later, when he worked in a gay steam bath, he entered into gay life more personally and began to think of himself as a gay man. Vassi was throughout his life a kind of chameleon—an ideal quality for a writer—who immediately began to take on the characteristics of those around him.

But he found that however much he romanticized it, gay life was just life.

> [Gay men] have the same range of problems, from impotence to promiscuity, struggles with fidelity, guilt. They have

the same joys, the same fears. And they completely share the general sexual sickness of the nation.[28]

He loved the passive role in gay sex but wondered sometimes where it led.

> Fear always followed, especially when, after a while, I noticed that I was not getting erections any longer, nor missing them.[29]

He was also acutely aware of all he would be giving up.

> I saw three young girls passing on the street, and my heart filled with dread at the idea that I would never have a woman again. To make a choice which sexually rules out half the human race seemed idiotic.[30]

Vassi seemed to be a true bi- (or perhaps poly-) sexual and regarded this as an advanced state. "I quoted Jesus to myself, 'In paradise there is neither male or female.' "[31] It was in anonymous gay sex that he took on a passivity, and an impersonality, that led to an experience of no self. The long gay orgy scene in *The Gentle Degenerates* is almost terrifying in that regard, as the narrator allows himself to be used and is treated rather brutally. Whatever it is in his past that impels him to seek out such a scene, it has its reward.

> I looked up and saw the four gleaming bodies like giants over me. I became very small; very helpless. . . .
>
> I went totally under and let myself drown, seeing my life flash before me, understanding everything in a glance, getting a preview of final meaning. . . .
>
> But more than anything else I felt peace, a great pervading calm that reached to the outermost edges of the universe. Whatever demons had been haunting me were now either driven off or appeased.[32]

Vassi turned degradation and sleaze into virtues, went down so far it looked like up. And in so doing, he saw that down and up are one thing.

BODHI IS THE BODY

All of Vassi's life was one great effort of understanding. Though he did skitter through various New Age paths in the sixties and seemed the kind of person who couldn't settle on anything, he spoke later in life of routinely practicing yoga and sitting in meditation, and though he spent an enormous amount of energy on sex and relationship, he also spent plenty of time by himself, reading, writing, and just musing on things.

He did strictly spiritual writing under the name Sa'shi—mimeographing pieces and sending them to his friends—in which he gave an overview of the teachers who had been important to him. And in the seventies he wrote some essays and erotic fables that, more than anything else he had done, combined his interests in the sexual and the spiritual. They were first collected in a volume entitled *Metasex, Mirth, and Madness,* later reprinted by Permanent Press as *The Erotic Comedies.*

For a brainy, didactic, and essentially autobiographical writer like Vassi, the essay is probably the ideal form. The most interesting passages in his novels are those in which he breaks through and speaks to the reader; the sexual descriptions—though extraordinary—grow tiresome. If he hadn't continued to grind out formula erotica to make a living, he might have gone on to do a different kind of writing altogether. *The Erotic Comedies* give some idea of what that writing might have been.

Vassi brings up in his opening essay* a fact that the Tantric teachers, and even Alan Watts, fail to mention: that in the East as well as the West, whatever the more enlightened and modern teachers might say, there has always been a prejudice against women and against sex. Sex was regarded as a hindrance and enlightenment as the preserve of men. Vassi himself had had a lifetime of problems with women, beginning with his mother, and had always—sometimes unconsciously—been looking for a male teacher who would show him the way.

But on a particular occasion of lovemaking with a woman, he realizes that the truths he has been seeking are inside him—the man he has been looking for is himself—and that his real teachers have been women, because they have brought him into his body. "To know oneself as a body is more important, at this moment in history, than to read the words of all the wise men who have ever lived."[33] Men are identified not so much with spirit, as Watts had said, as with thought—they are always trying to think their way into truth—while women *embody* truth. And Vassi makes a resounding statement about sex that goes beyond anything even Watts said and stands as a coda for his entire book.

> The orgasm is *the* life-enhancing process. From its physiological function of discharging tension and toning the organism, to its biological function of improving the quality of children that are born, to its spiritual function of putting one in touch with higher forms of energy, it contains all the keys anyone might want. Sex is a complete activity, bringing all the fragments into a whole, operating as the most subtle and

---

*I begin my discussion with the essays, the second half of the book, "A Collection of Bones." Vassi himself chose to open with his erotic fables, many of which make the same points as the essays.

immediate communication between human being and human being. It acts resoundingly to affirm the pulse of life; in its contractions and expansions, it *is* the pulse of life itself. How on earth, I wondered, could anyone view it as anything but a central factor in a person's attempts to live most fully?[34]

He asks the questions that no one else does ("And what of Jesus? What mammoth insensitivity is involved in presuming that he had nothing to learn in the arms of Mary Magdalen? Did Meher Baba fuck? Does Krishnamurti fuck?"[35]) and addresses the fact that it is our silence about these things, about speaking of sex and spirituality together, that is the problem. "These questions seem blasphemous. Yet why should that be if we were not so conditioned to believe that holiness and wisdom are incompatible with sexuality, that an enlightened man will no longer have intimate contact with a woman's body?"[36]

The next couple of essays deal specifically with gay life, though they transcend any narrow concern with sexual orientation. Vassi believed that gays as a group were doing a better job than other men of getting in touch with their feelings and their bodies. The gay world had achieved a kind of camaraderie that the world of men as a whole badly needed and needs. It expressed itself most clearly in large group sexual encounters, particularly in some parked trucks near the Hudson River in Greenwich Village.* Gay men therefore had a kind of sexual freedom that other men did not.

> Sexual freedom is not a political movement, not an idea, not a new life style, not an organization. It is the moment-to-moment sensitivity to the fluctuations of the sexual state.

*Samuel R. Delany writes rather more archetypally of this same scene in *The Motion of Light in Water.*

And anyone human enough to brave the imprinted taboos, the repressive influences of all society including one's friends, and the very real police danger, ought to understand that the desperation which surrounds sex is due to the times we live in, and does not inhere in the act itself.[37]

Vassi's piece "Bisexuality, Therapy, and Revolution" is difficult to read today, knowing that he died of AIDS; it is an account of a four-hour session at the St. Marks Baths, during which he was repeatedly receptive to anal intercourse, to the point that he was bleeding. Yet it is one of his most remarkable stream-of-consciousness pieces—a great example of finding the sacred in the profane—as he reflects on the act of surrender that he is undergoing; the way that, in such an intense situation, pain and pleasure become one thing; the feminine nature inside him; the universal feces phobia that is a primary cause of neurosis; and the deep sorrow beneath all the pain he puts himself through.

But his ultimate goal—as he makes clear in his next piece—is to move beyond false dichotomies like bisexuality. He discusses a threesome with a man and woman in which he realized he had moved beyond gender altogether. "With a buzzing connection, the male and female inside me began to undulate in a series of sine waves. I lost my sexual *identity* and became a sexual *entity*."[38] His obsession with impersonal sex has done much to help him reach this place. And in a startling statement—especially for a man in his mid-thirties—he proclaims himself to be in command of it.

At the far edge of bisexuality I realized that all that had gone before was but the task of perfecting the instrument, the mindbody that is myself. My adventures had served a single purpose: to exhaust all the subjective aspects of the sexual act. The many modes, which had been challenges, areas of exploration, were now my tools—homosexuality, heterosexuality, bisexuality, abstruse psychosexual states and practices, the so-called perversions, the many masks of libidinal displacement . . . these were now at my command, to be used the way a director uses a cast of characters to realize a vision.[39]

All of this is preparatory to Vassi's describing his theory of metasexuality, the idea that he is best known for and that may be his greatest contribution to the larger sexual dialogue. He states, quite rightly, that a great deal of our confusion about sex has to do with the fact that we don't understand its purpose in our lives. If we assume—as many people do—that the only purpose of sex is procreation, then it is natural to see all kinds of behaviors as wrong: premarital sex, extramarital, oral, anal, manual, homosexual . . . The list goes on and on.

But it is apparent to a man like Vassi—and to Wilhelm Reich, the Tantric masters, Taoist teachers—that sexual behavior has far more purposes than just procreation. Vassi therefore defines *sex* as the act of intercourse that a man and woman perform in order to have a child. *Metasex* is any other form of sexual behavior, for any other purpose. And he states that these two categories—which he gathers into a larger one, the eroticum—should never be discussed together. They just aren't comparable.

The repercussions of this simple act of classification are endless. In sex, for instance, two is the only number of participants; any other number is a gross perversion. But all numbers are valid in metasex, and Vassi goes on to discuss the virtues of three, four, five. . . . He also validates, once and for all, the number one, giving thirteen-year-olds and lonely old solitaries a sexual dignity they never before had.

> To masturbate to full orgasm . . . is a sublime and solitary
> act, requiring capacity for fear and awe. To bring about one's
> own orgasm, without the company of others, without fanta-
> sies to mask the facticity of the deed, requires great inner
> resources.[40]

He expands on these theories in "The Metasexual Mani-
festo," in which he threatens to become the Aristotle of eroticism. While sex "involves the continuation of the species,"
metasex is "for pleasure, for exchanging energy, for money,
for communication and exploration, for meditation."[41] Sex
should be characterized by reverence and responsibility, metasex by compassion, which he defines as "no exploitation, no
lying, and no damage."[42]

He offers six sexual/metasexual modes, though it would
seem (and he admits) that the list could be expanded endlessly: procreative, theatrical, therapeutic, romantic, masturbatory, and Zen. Most interesting to me are the last two.
He sees the masturbatory mode, surprisingly, as perhaps the
highest state.

> Much has been made of this form of gratification's being
> a substitute for "the real thing," but again, this is a sexual
> judgment upon a metasexual matter. Metasexually, someone
> choosing masturbation as a sometime or often or even total
> means of expression is no more or less valid than any other
> way. . . .
>
> Behaviorally, the masturbatory mode favors the ten-
> dency to celibacy, which is the final step in auto-eroticism.
> Not by repression, but by progression, one learns to cycle the
> erotic energy totally within one's body, and thus becomes
> self-contained. This homeostasis is considered by some to be
> the highest form of erotic evolution.[43]

The Zen mode, like Zen itself, is the most mysterious.

The Zen Mode: is produced through transmodality. An act may begin in the theatrical mode and shift to the therapeutic. Or different participants may play different modes at the same time, something like a piece of music played by instruments in different keys. . . . The concept of mode is itself shaken, and finally bursts open, until the conceptual curtain lifts and all imagery dissolves. As with the Zen experience proper, there is little to say about this mode. It carries a unique sense of the moment's utter reality, and within that there lie all the joy and terror of coming face to face with the Nakedness.[44]

Just as interesting a part of the book are the sexual fables of the first half, in which Vassi shows a humorous side not much in evidence in the rest of his writing.* Fables either do or don't work, for different people, but particularly memorable for me were the dying gynecologist who, on his deathbed, envisions a gigantic cunt; the doctor who, deciding that all neurosis is a fear of shitting, offers enema therapy; and the woman who becomes such a virtuoso in the art of masturbation that when God appears and asks to have sex with her—with immortality as a perk—she has to think about it. And "Land of the Sperm King" has a stunning ending: as an entire culture has decided to commit suicide.

"Before we all return to the flow, can you tell us what the secret question is?"

The guide turned around and looked into the child's open face. "There is only one question," he said slowly, "and that is this:

"Why are there no questions at all?"

The boy's lips began to move and he started to speak.

*Michael Perkins, however, mentions it as a strong part of his character, and *A Driving Passion,* a collection of talks that he gave at a human potential center in 1975, shows the verbal humor that was an obvious part of his charm.

But then as though a light had gone on within the light of the sun, his entire expression changed and became one of perfect understanding. His face relaxed and his eyes grew soft. He looked back at the guide, and said nothing.

The guide smiled.

"Yes," he said to the boy and to the whole people, "the answer is not to say the answer, but to be the answer." And then to the child alone, "You might have been guide after me."[45]

DYING TIME

One difficulty with a renegade and underappreciated writer like Vassi is that his work is in disarray, and it is difficult to know when he wrote what he did or how his thoughts progressed. Most of his published writing comes from the early seventies, but Vassi didn't die until 1989. He had a creative intensity that would hardly have rested idle.

John Heidenry writes of a Vassi who, in the eighties—his own forties—was increasingly depressed.

> Marco found that he was growing "a trifle impotent," an inconvenience he attributed to sexual excess, drugs, and the strenuousness of many of his encounters. Yet he also knew he was aging, and he began to refer to himself as "a metaphysical eunuch." Increasingly, too, he was plagued by anxiety attacks. Dread gnawed at his mind, and at times he felt as though he were "fifteen billion years old."[46]

He would be diagnosed with HIV in 1986 but may have contracted the virus—and therefore have been feeling poorly—much earlier. He had certainly led a difficult life. But one can't help wondering if there was something about his sexual quest itself that had left him depressed.

Vassi seemed honestly to believe that sex—especially a

certain kind of impersonal sex—led to ecstasy, to an encounter with the divine, and he pursued that ecstasy without limit all his life. But he seemed too often to be straining after it, trying too hard, and also seemed to miss something that was right before him: that simple human intimacy is also an encounter with the divine.

A novel like *The Gentle Degenerates,* for instance—which Vassi called 90 percent autobiographical—is almost maddening in the way that its narrator compulsively pursues sexual adventure and ignores the relationship that he committed to when the novel opened. One can't help wondering if he was afraid of that intimacy, not the intense intimacy of some wild sexual act, but the simple intimacy of life as it is.* For the intense man everything needs to be intense, and he thereby reaches amazing heights, but he misses out on a whole side of existence. Walt Whitman, with his simple wish to sit and hold his beloved's hand, can sound like a laughable old fairy. But in that act he experienced precisely everything.

In the early eighties Vassi met porn star and performance artist Annie Sprinkle, the one woman who might have matched him as a sexual adventurer. That night, naturally, they had sex, which Annie inaugurated with the bizarre act of peeing in his ear. He moved in with her in 1983, mostly as a matter of convenience, though their lives as lovers did intensify for a while.

From the moment he heard the first rumors of AIDS, he ceased all risky sexual activity; he even pulled back from a French kiss Annie gave him at a party in 1986, and she realized that he was afraid of catching the virus from her. But

---

*In the narrator's defense, his woman friend seems just as scared. And she expresses her fear in the same way, by bringing home one man after another, activating the narrator's jealousy and increasing his fear.

when they finally worked up the courage to be tested, it was he who was positive, while Annie was negative.

The cliché about Vassi's illness—repeated in various places—was that he grew depressed after his diagnosis and died rather quickly. Actually, he lived more than two years, and Annie remained loyal to the end. They decided that no sexual act was entirely safe, so they were intimate simply by lying together.

> We'd do breathing and eye gazing; we'd set the timer for a half-hour and just sit and look into each other's eyes. And we were being *lovers,* we were turned on to each other, and it became so erotic that we didn't even have to fuck—when that timer went off we felt like we'd been fucking for half an hour.[47]

Sex, they realized, was a subtle exchange of energy, a fact that Vassi had written about some fifteen years before but that he was seeing as if for the first time. He was discovering an intimacy that didn't depend on a sexual act.

Vassi's end was definitely a sad one; he tried to live by himself but finally had to move to an AIDS facility when he was so broke that his utilities had been shut off. Some people would see that as a commentary on the life he had led, but it speaks just as much to how we treat our artists and thinkers (though many cultures, at many times, have let their artists languish in poverty). He died on January 16, 1989.

Norman Mailer was one of the mainstream writers who praised Vassi's work. He thought that the man's core belief was that metasex brought health and that when Vassi fell ill he took it as a repudiation of his ideas and died a discouraged man. One can't know what a man was thinking when he died, but AIDS is certainly not a repudiation of metasex (which, to repeat, includes masturbation and celibacy as perfectly viable options). The virus is transmitted by certain behaviors but is no more a repudiation of those behaviors than the flu is a repudiation of shaking hands and touching doorknobs. If we are going to judge a person's life—if we ever have any right to do that—we need to do it by something other than the disease that killed him.

More than any other writer I have encountered, Vassi represents the male libido writ large. He wanted the same things that many men do, the only difference being that he had the nerve to act on his desires. I'm not at all sure that was the right course of action, but he acted honorably and honestly and wrote about it in a prose that was as intense, intelligent, and exciting as he must have been in person. He went to the furthest edges of one kind of human experience, and came back—too briefly—to tell the tale. If the rest of us don't lead such intense lives, we can certainly learn from his. And we should remember that, however he stumbled to get there, his ultimate perspective on sex was a large one.

> The erotic ambiance, the erotic communication, the erotic mood is the source of beauty and art. Our painting, our poetry, our filmmaking—and in my head, even our state of consciousness—are all variations of that feeling. And that feeling is nothing more than the healthy body in its full sensitivity, vibrating to the fact of being alive.[48]

N O T E S

1. Alan Watts, *Nature, Man, and Woman* (New York: Vintage Books, 1970), p. 153.
2. John Stevens, *Lust for Enlightenment* (Boston: Shambhala Publications, 1990) 121.

3. Martin Shepard, introduction to *The Erotic Comedies,* by Marco Vassi (Sag Harbor, N.Y.: Permanent Press, 1981).

4. Marco Vassi, *The Saline Solution* (Sag Harbor, N.Y.: Second Chance Press, 1993), 7.

5. Vassi, *The Erotic Comedies,* 221.

6. Marco Vassi, *The Stoned Apocalypse* (Sag Harbor, N.Y.: Second Chance Press, 1993), 21.

7. Ibid., 22.

8. Ibid., 63.

9. Ibid., 34.

10. Ibid., 34.

11. Ibid., 123.

12. Ibid., 125.

13. Ibid., 198.

14. Ibid., 230.

15. Ibid., 231.

16. Ibid., 236.

17. Ibid., 249.

18. John Heidenry, *What Wild Ecstasy: The Rise and Fall of the Sexual Revolution.* (New York: Simon and Schuster, 1997), 135.

19. Marco Vassi, *The Gentle Degenerates* (Sag Harbor, N.Y.: Second Chance Press, 1993), 216–17.

20. Ibid., 140.

21. Vassi, *The Saline Solution,* 30.

22. Marco Vassi, *Contours of Darkness* (Sag Harbor, N.Y.: Second Chance Press, 1993), 269.

23. Vassi, *The Saline Solution,* 45.

24. Vassi, *The Gentle Degenerates,* 38.

25. Vassi, *The Saline Solution,* 132.

26. Vassi, *The Stoned Apocalypse,* 139.

27. Ibid.

28. Ibid., 193.

29. Vassi, *The Gentle Degenerates,* 109.

30. Vassi, *The Stoned Apocalypse,* 195.

31. Vassi, *The Gentle Degenerates,* 109.

32. Ibid., 104.

33. Vassi, *The Erotic Comedies,* 137.

34. Ibid., 134.

35. Ibid., 139.

36. Ibid.

37. Ibid., 150.
38. Ibid., 178.
39. Ibid., 180.
40. Ibid., 181.
41. Ibid., 188.
42. Ibid., 189.
43. Ibid., 199.
44. Ibid., 199–200.
45. Ibid., 45.
46. Heidenry, *What Wild Ecstasy*, 235.
47. Andrea Juno and V. Vale, eds., Angry *Women* (San Francisco: Re/ Search Publications, 1991), 31.
48. Marco Vassi, *A Driving Passion* (Sag Harbor, N.Y.: Permanent Press, 1992), 149.

Part Two

~ *Prologue*
Eliminating Boundaries

I HAVE JUST ARRIVED in San Francisco, a long way
from North Carolina and a long way, in spirit, from any-
place I've ever been. I left home at 7:00 AM and have
been traveling for eight hours, but here—this in itself is
weird—it's just after noon. I've had two meals and it isn't
even time for lunch.

I have come to San Francisco to talk to the whores.

"You can relax now, you're among family," our limo
driver tells us, a middle-aged black man named Reggie.
"You're in one of the great cities of the world, it's a beautiful
day"—sunny and bright, billowy clouds blowing around—
"and life is a bowl of cherries. I've got the cherries to prove
it." He had a bag of them beside him on the seat and snacked
as he drove.

Reggie kept us laughing, a van full of strangers in a new
city, slightly weary, slightly anxious, perhaps a little jet-

lagged. It was possible, of course, for my East Coast self to see him differently. His uniform jacket was faded and rumpled, his shirt collar ragged, and his eyes—when he first addressed me—didn't meet mine. His patter seemed to have a slight intention to keep us off balance, give him the advantage. But it was better to talk than sit quietly in the van, nursing our anxieties.

"You're a student?" Reggie said to a woman in the backseat, who had identified her destination as a college campus.

"I'm a teacher," she said. "I'm going to a conference of teachers."

Reggie paused, driving down the freeway, then looked back in the mirror.

"We teach best what we love to learn," he said.

There was a moment of silence. We all pondered this remark.

"I don't know where these things come from," Reggie said. "They just pop out on me."

"I'm going to remember that one," I said.

I don't suppose I have ever taught sex, unless writing is a form of teaching. But I have always loved to learn about it, ever since I was a horny fifteen-year-old ransacking the local bookstores, ever since I worked summers dusting books in a medical library and discovered a huge cache—three jammed shelves—of classic texts on sex. There is no other subject that so reliably enlivens my spirit. It must be—as Buddhists say—my karma.

It isn't quite fair to say that I've come out here to talk to whores. I've come to interview sexual healers, people whom I've read about in books, whose names have been passed on to me, all of whom—uncannily—live in the Bay Area. One gay man I'm visiting has produced videos like *Fire on the*

Mountain: An Intimate Guide to Male Genital Massage, has taught classes and led workshops in Taoist erotic massage all over the country and around the world, does massage (erotic and otherwise), and coaches men in masturbation.

Another couple—a bisexual man and woman with a two-year-old child—do similar workshops with straight couples. A former porno star—whose movies I not only saw but still remember—does a form of erotic massage. Another woman is a writer, teacher, and performance artist but has also worked as a prostitute and peep show stripper. All of these people, in one way or another, have been erotic for pay. Hence the word whores.

There is a centuries-old tradition, in various pagan religions, of sacred prostitutes. Probably these were people with an erotic gift, in touch with that energy in a particularly vital way. Some prostitutes had the gift but didn't identify as sacred. The Korean Zen master Seung Sahn tells of such a woman in ancient times.

> When the Buddha was alive, there was a prostitute called Pass-a-million. Every day she sold her body many times. . . . But any man who had sex with her would become enlightened. So she was only using sex to teach Buddhism. When a man came to her, he had many desires. But after being with her, he had no desires, he understood his true self, and he went away with a clear mind.[1]

Most healers would acknowledge that it is not they who do the healing; it is God, or nature, the energy itself. The medicine—another way to put it—is concealed in the illness. Healers are just people who have a special connection to the energy, a particular attraction to it. Perhaps because they need to be healed themselves.

We teach best what we love to learn.

San Francisco is renowned for its Chinatown, its Japan-
town, its Hispanic Mission district, its gay Castro Street, but
everywhere you go you see Asians, Hispanics, and gays. An
elderly and elegantly dressed lesbian couple walks down the
street arm in arm. Burly muscular men in tank tops and jeans
kiss on the mouth as they part. In a spacious, brightly lit sex
shop run entirely by women—already we know we're not in
Kansas anymore—the dildos are actually out on display, and
I examine one for a moment, put it back. It is then picked up
by the person beside me, a tall, muscular, heavily tattooed
bald woman. There is no hostility in this gesture (Whatsa
matter, bub, that one too big fer ya?). We're just a couple of
patrons checking out the merchandise.

I will no doubt exaggerate San Francisco's virtues and
romanticize the week I spent there.* I am sure that the city
has its class, ethnic, gender, and sexual-orientation problems
just like any other. But I spent five days in San Francisco
having some of the most intense and interesting conversations of my life, and so help me (though I hadn't anticipated
such a thing), it was healing—there was something about just
taking up the subject, seeing how large it was, how many
manifestations it took, and being with people who embraced
them all, no matter how weird they might have sounded.

"My tribe is the people who honor that vibration,"
Joseph Kramer told me, explaining that he didn't identify just
as a gay man or as a bodyworker. As California as that
statement sounds, I agreed with it immediately. My tribe is—
always has been—the people who honor that vibration—
though I'm not at war with other tribes. We can all get along.

"There is something in me that doesn't like a wall,"

*So sue me. I'm a writer.

Kramer said, quoting Robert Frost. "You're walling some-thing in. But you're also walling something out." And though he understands why some people who work with sex—in the fields of addiction, for instance, or sexual abuse—feel a need to set boundaries, he doesn't like them. They wall us off from other people, from other worlds, from transcendent states. His work is liberation. In one way or another, every healer I spoke to said the same thing. Their work is liberation—for others, and for themselves.

"It's amazing how deeply wounded, fearful, and confused people are about sex," Annie Sprinkle once said. "I know for a fact that even the world's greatest sex experts are wounded, fearful, and confused."[2] It is rather like the psychiatric institu-tion in Marco Vassi's *The Stoned Apocalypse*. It isn't a group of healers working with the sick. It is everybody in the soup together, all of us wounded, fearful, and confused, but talk-ing, touching, eliminating boundaries, letting ourselves feel the energy. That is the healing act. Anything that lets the energy flow. Anything that honors the vibration.

You can relax now, as Reggie said in the van. You're among family.

You can let go of your suspicious East Coast self.

NOTES

1. Stephen Mitchell, *Dropping Ashes on the Buddha: The Teaching of Zen Master Seung Sahn* (New York: Grove Press, 1976), 65.
2. David Jay Brown and Rebecca McClen Novick, *Voices from the Edge* (Freedom, Calif.: Crossing Press, 1995), 29.

~ CAROL QUEEN. Photo by Lynne Winklebleck.

~ 6
The Bashful Stripper

CAROL QUEEN

IF YOU'RE A LESBIAN, WHO'S THE GUY
IN THE BEDROOM?

I was to get together with Carol Queen at Good Vibrations, the sex shop in the heart of San Francisco where she works part-time as a clerk. From the outside it looked like a sex shop anywhere, a large storefront with whitewashed windows, a sign on the door warning underage kids away. The inside, however, was not populated by a crowd of haunted men who looked as if they had the word *masturbator* stamped on their foreheads.* There were probably more women than men, and there were even couples, both same-gender and mixed.

All of the merchandise—books, videos, vibrators, dildos, restraints, paddles—was out on display, not locked in a glass case guarded by a small-time Mafia hood. There was hard-

---

*Or more specific designations: Lonely Pervert; Can't Get a Date; Wife Won't Put Out.

core porn, but also works of art, and everything sat side by side on the shelves. The most startling thing was that the clerks were women. And they were extremely attentive. They would come right up and tell you what vibrator they thought you would like.

But which one was Carol Queen? She was expecting me. We were making a date to meet again later in the week.

I knew her primarily from her writing, especially her recent book of essays, *Real Live Nude Girl*. She had come out as a lesbian in the mid-seventies, when the lesbian image was androgynous and when coming out was as much a political statement as a sexual one. Though she was as much an activist as anyone, she began at some point to realize that—though there wasn't supposed to be such a thing anymore—she liked butch women. She even liked to be slightly femme herself, wearing lipstick and perhaps—God help us all—a skirt.

She also liked to sleep with the occasional man. Not that she wasn't still a lesbian. She didn't know why she wanted to do it. To complicate matters, she was attracted to gay men. At the Gay Pride march, she was secretly turned on by the macho leather guys with rings through their nipples.

This multifaceted libido proved to be too much for the Oregon communities where she had spent most of her life, so she moved to San Francisco, where she really ran amuck. She discovered a submissive streak, that she liked to be thrown over a partner's knee and spanked, or tied to the bed and tormented. She then became a prostitute, not in order to do some kind of anthropological study, but because she needed the money. She actually enjoyed the work.

She also began to indulge a newfound exhibitionistic streak. It was one thing to engage in a sacred sex ritual, masturbating in front of four hundred people with sex goddess Annie Sprinkle and assorted other women. But she also worked in a peep show parlor, the kind of place where a man enters a booth, deposits a token, and sees a real live nude girl on the other side of a thick pane of glass.* He is free to indulge himself, within the limits of what he can do on his side of the glass. It is a kind of poor man's whorehouse. A voyeur's paradise.

Of all the people I talked to, Carol had run the fullest gamut in her erotic life. She'd been everything from a politically correct lesbian to a whore. I planned to feature her as a lesbian in my book, if I could gloss over the fact that she lived with a man. And she practiced in the wiccan spiritual tradition, the one that most noticeably connects the sexual and the spiritual.

But which of these Good Vibrations clerks was she? I knew she wasn't black. I didn't think she was bald. She couldn't be . . . Wait a minute. Could Carol Queen be *mousy?*

Indeed. Not since my high school librarian had I encountered a woman who seemed so initially flustered by my presence, fussing around with her date book and averting her eyes. It almost seemed an act. Any minute now she would dash into a phone booth and come out wearing hot pants, eye shadow, and stiletto heels.

When we met in her apartment a couple of days later, my impression was rather different. She was the only healer I talked to who actually lived in San Francisco, in a funky second-floor apartment in the middle of the city. We were on her turf—the very apartment, I assumed, where she used

---

*It probably isn't literally bulletproof, but that isn't the kind of shots that are fired against it.

to meet clients as a prostitute—and she was still quiet and polite but rather more sure of herself. Her partner, Robert Morgan, was in the front bedroom, answering the phone and waiting to do some work with her. She took me to a small study that included a studio couch, a smattering of erotic art on the walls, and the finest collection of books on sex that I had ever seen in a private residence.

Carol is probably the most intellectual of all the people I talked to. She has not only done more things than other healers, she has thought—and written—about them more. She considers her work to be "education about sexuality" but has little respect for "the kind of teaching that purports to be about scientific facts and that doesn't own the biases and passions of the person teaching. The way I teach is to speak about my experience."

She is also the most—perhaps the only—truly political person among the healers. She cut her teeth on the lesbian/feminist politics of the late seventies and still engages in that discourse, though with a dissenting voice. She is the best writer in the group and very much lives as one, with regular gigs as a journalist and several books in the works, including her first novel. And she gave the most thought-out answers to my questions, as if they had all occurred to her before. You couldn't get ahead of this woman.

Carol Queen has taken half a lifetime to discover all the ways she is sexual (and—one has the feeling—she ain't through yet). There is something sexy about the sheer force of her intelligence, as she gives elaborate answers to even the most trivial of questions.

More than anything else, though, she struck me as courageous. "My sexual wounds were shyness, isolation, and secrecy," she said, and she has overcome them in a rather spectacular fashion, thereby developing great compassion for the wounds of others. Few writers have spoken out so forcefully for the rights of sex workers, and especially the rights of their clients, as Carol Queen.

"I believe that sex is sacred and healing. This idea pervades my work as a prostitute, and this vantage point often startles people accustomed to negative ideas about sex workers' lives. They press me to delve into the negative side, and it often seems that what they're really looking for is evidence that men who patronize prostitutes are contemptible. I don't believe this; I believe that every client, every *person*, has the right to seek out sexual pleasure and comfort. I've been treated with a good deal more respect by ninety-nine percent of my clients than by the average guy on the street."[1]

THE JEWEL WITH MANY FACES

Carol grew up in small towns in Oregon, the child of a schoolteacher father and a mother who was an alcoholic and who worked part-time as a bookkeeper. A major part of Carol's early secrecy was the natural reaction of the child of an alcoholic. She also feels she absorbed her parents' wounds. It wasn't until Carol was eighteen that her mother told her she had been married before, and it was years after that that she was able to admit she had been sexually abused. Her parents, Carol believes, were shut down and unhappy sexually, and it is in a conscious effort to avoid their unhappiness that she has opened up so much.

"Queen the Queer" was one of the names her school friends gave her (little did they know she would one day be a prominent lesbian activist), and one can imagine that to those loggers' and ranchers' children she did seem queer, if only because she was so sensitive and intelligent. She grew up in a breathtakingly beautiful place and spent much of her early life communing with nature. "I was a little animist as a child, with nature spirits that I talked to. That spectacular environment was a solace to me as I became a teenager and began to have a sense of how weird I was going to be."

She was twelve, and under the influence of the sixties hippie culture, when she and a friend sent away for a book entitled *Potions and Spells of Witchcraft*. "There was not a word in it of philosophy, or spirituality, or religious understanding, not a discussion of the goddess or the god. It was just how you can affect your environment by your will." That was her introduction to the wiccan religion that is the basis of her spiritual practice today. A major part of what eventually drew her to it was its positive view of the erotic.

"I began to explore my sexuality in confluence with the natural world. My boyfriends and I didn't have any other place, so we'd drive up a logging road and do it on the ground. One of my earliest sexual memories is looking up at the pine trees." She was sexually active early, partly because she had nothing to lose. "It was clear to me I wasn't a nice girl, so there was no point in restricting my curiosity." One relationship was particularly definitive. She was fifteen years old when she had an affair with a twenty-eight-year-old married man.

Thus began her career as a sexual outlaw. What they were doing was literally illegal and would have caused a scandal in the small community where they lived. She didn't feel she was victimized; she engaged in the affair willingly. "After the first time, when he got scared, I leaned on him to continue. I knew I couldn't get what I needed in terms of growing up from my peers." But she was also reenacting the secrecy and isolation of her childhood. "I had to keep my emotional responses quiet, and I couldn't conceptualize myself as being in a relationship, which are both things that teenagers very much want.

"When I look at men I meet in the sex industry, one of my places of compassion is that they are almost all straight guys with secrets. So many people are walking around with some kind of sexual secret. But that experience gave me an emotional drive not to have secrets in my life."

She fled that relationship a year later by traveling to Europe, and it was there that she discovered her attraction to women. "By the time I left Germany I had fallen for a wild, cat-eyed young woman who looked like she never slept at home, a baby-dyke who tutored me in French, my boyfriend's sister, a woman I saw on the bus every day, and a schoolteacher from England who befriended me."[2]

Her pattern of secrecy, however, was coming to an end. In 1974 she cofounded one of the nation's first gay and lesbian youth groups, and not long after that she sued the school district for the right to place an ad in the South Eugene High School newspaper. She would continue to be a renegade, but now she would do so publicly.

Carol came out at a time when that was largely a political act, and there is a political tinge to all her work. The rallying cry of the day was that the personal is the political, and she obviously still believes that, but what she means now is that the political world has to accept her as a person, with all her little quirks. The longer she lives, the more quirks she finds.

Why bother to identify? was the question I asked, reflecting the most succinct statement of the Buddha's teaching: Under no circumstances identify with anything as being me or mine. The problem with identifying is that it inevitably leads to suffering. No sooner do you assume the image of an androgynous lesbian, for instance, than you find yourself being attracted by women a little more butch than that, or maybe a lot more: "Worn Levi's and rolled T-shirt sleeves, a stance like James Dean hustling on Forty-Second Street."[3] Suddenly you've got a problem.

My question was uncomfortably close to one she gets all the time: So what? So what if you want to wear lipstick, or masturbate to gay male porn, or work in a peep show? Why do you have to keep talking about it? But the answer to both questions is the same: for whatever reason, Carol is a person who goes outward in order to go inward.

"I really see this community affiliation and disaffiliation as helping me know myself better and understand what's really there. Not letting a piece of myself be cut off." And in speaking for herself, she is speaking for everyone. "Many people want to own more pieces of themselves. They feel they've fallen through the cracks."

Her modus operandi is to join groups and identify with the prevailing majority, then add one more thing, the thing they won't accept. But she insists. And no sooner does she speak up than other voices are raised. It turns out there is a sizable minority of lesbian-identified women who occasionally sleep with men. Or feminist women who, in the right circumstances, like to be dominated. They might have been shutting down that part of themselves because it didn't seem acceptable. Once Carol spoke up, they could too.

"My task in life has been to be integral with myself, to follow what my fascinations and passions are. I consistently place myself a little tweaked from whatever community I'm affiliated with. And it's a project to live in that community that way, and to bridge into another one.

"For many of us, an either/or doesn't fit, and the way to get beyond that is to embody both, get into what's real, stop thinking in terms of a linear continuum. We could instead see sexuality as a multifaceted jewel. It might make us think of ourselves and our behaviors in different ways."

Despite her multiple identities, she has found a way to embody them all, and thrive. She has a queer-identified part-ner* who not only loves her and lives with her but has sup-ported her work in the sex industry, and who leads classes and workshops with her. She is a trainer for San Francisco Sex Information, writes columns for two Bay Area publica-tions, works at Good Vibrations, hosts a public-access televi-sion show, and lectures at local universities.

Maybe it's a good idea to insist on all you want.

"I feel connected and centered in my sexuality in a way that is extremely rich and safe and full of possibility," she says. "That's the effect of taking sex and sexual exploration seriously."

THE CHARGE OF THE GODDESS

Though sex is central to the lives of all the healers I spoke to, for Carol Queen it permeates everything, all the work she does, the space on her walls, the shelves in her bookcase. It is the way she opens to life.

"Sex is my spiritual path," she says. "It's a path that a lot of religious systems haven't respected. Or maybe they've respected it too much. They've feared it, or considered it a rival."

The interest in witchcraft that Carol discovered as a

---

*Calling him gay, she says, doesn't quite cover it.

twelve-year-old has deepened into something much larger as she has gotten older. It has become an important part of her work and of her vision as a whole.

Wicca is an ancient pagan spiritual tradition that celebrates seasonal change and is theoretically based on the harvest cycle. Covens that began to organize in this country in the fifties—under the influence of earlier practitioners like Aleister Crowley—saw it as a heterosexual eroticized spiritual practice, at the heart of which was a ritual called the Great Rite, by which the priest and priestess formed energy for the whole group. "They did that by having intercourse, either with the coven in the next room aware that they were doing it or with the coven arranged around them in a circle."

Wiccans today are not likely to practice that rite, Queen hastens to add, partly because wicca's existence as a heterosexual system has largely broken down. A major Dianic branch has evolved, in which men aren't present at all. But even in that wing, sex is honored, if it isn't practiced.

"I think that the reason wicca has resurged today is the notion, whether or not it's expressed by the Great Rite, of how meaningful sex is, how potentially transformative."

Carol first discovered group sex outside a spiritual context, at San Francisco's inaugural Jack and Jill Off party in 1987. Early in the AIDS epidemic, gay men had started to get together for safe-sex parties. In San Francisco—and only there can one imagine such a thing coming up—women wanted to attend too. About that first party, Queen writes, "It wasn't going to be a jack-off party—women would be there. Not a swing party—gay men would be very much in evidence."[4] People could express themselves sexually, but only in safe ways. And intercourse wasn't allowed.

For a multifaceted person like Carol, the occasion was

transformative. "Any phenomenon that resulted in my becoming . . . multiply orgasmic—much less getting sexual attention from gay men, something I'd always wanted—certainly deserved further attention."[5] She met her partner Robert at a subsequent party. They have since founded their own series of parties, called Queen of Heaven, in order to introduce a sacred element.

"We open with a wiccan ritual in which the directions are called, and the god and goddess are evoked. We create a safe sexual environment, a shared understanding that we're not here for people to paw at each other without permission. It's not as organized as a religious rite. But people find in it a space that is somehow sweeter than at another kind of sex party.

"We're setting up a space in which people can come in and be as erotic as they want"—it is perfectly all right, for instance, just to watch—"without considering sexual orientation or gender. We're trying to create that click experience that says, I don't have to differentiate. I'm sexual with these people right now, even though the person two feet over from me is doing something I don't want to do at all."

In other words, Queen of Heaven parties are a tangible manifestation of an attitude: However people are in their sexuality is all right.

"The sexual space that acknowledges everyone is what I try to live in," Carol says. "It is what gives me hope, and is the basis of my spiritual understanding.

"I don't want a place where people just come in and honor the seasons. I want a place where they get larger sexually."

But sex parties are not—needless to say—for everyone, and Carol has also taught in classes and workshops, through her writing, and as a sex worker, both as a prostitute and as a peep show stripper. She doesn't look down on her clients or on the work she has done with them. She considers it as sacred as anything else.

She has read the literature likening modern-day prostitutes to ancient sacred prostitutes and doesn't think its importance lies in its historical accuracy. "What matters is that men and women today are using that image to make a space where they can feel better about what they are doing and to begin to grow a philosophy that takes it seriously, which the rest of the culture does not."

Men patronize sex workers for a variety of reasons, she believes, but most of what they want is to be affirmed in their sexuality. Peep show patrons, for instance, are not doing anything they can't do by themselves, with videos or magazines.

"I had the feeling I was often there to give permission. To be a compassionate female figure who wanted to watch men play with themselves. A noticeable subset of those guys wanted to call me Mommy."

She was giving permission not just about masturbation but about various sex acts that men brought to her as a prostitute. "There was always this thing hanging in the air of 'I can't do this with my wife.' Those men didn't have the experience of their female partner digging their sexuality. Or at least respecting it."

She feels that some women become sex workers for the same reason that men patronize them. "In the good girl–bad girl split, if you're looking for a chance to be a bad girl and get support, the sex industry can be a great place."

In some ways, that was why she—as a lifelong bad girl— went into that line of work. ("I was a dyke long before I

became a whore," she writes, "but first I was a slut."[6]) Her
career as a prostitute was unique, because she didn't enter
the profession until she was past thirty. She had spent ten
years as a feminist lesbian—not necessarily favorably dis-
posed, all that time, to men and their sexual needs—and had
only recently come out as bisexual.

"Here were all these men to experiment with. I liked the
variety, the frisson of anonymity and adventuring. Answering
the door to a stranger was exciting to me. I had found
through my experiments with group sex that as my sexuality
opened up, I was more versatile about what was erotic. I
could have good sexual experiences with most of my clients.
And in the rare case that I felt no chemistry at all, I still had
a sense of respect that the person was there to get his erotic
needs met. That was completely positive as far as I was concerned.

"It was one aspect of what I was doing to learn about my
sexuality and to open out sexually. Even when it wasn't literally a sacred space, it was figuratively one."

At the heart of all these questions about sexuality, Queen
acknowledges, is the fact of relationship. Men were often
coming to her—whether they knew it or not—for sexual
healing, but the question was why they had to leave the relationship for healing, and whether they would be able to take
the healing back into it.

"There are people who explore sex best outside of relationship, and people who explore it best within. I don't think
that's strictly a gender difference, although, for whatever reason, women seem to have a tougher time splitting sex and
relationship apart.

"The big question is: how do I get my partner to see that
there is a fantasy or a behavior that I want to explore without

coloring the relationship?" That is, without raising the partner's disapproval. "There are deep levels of judgment that live within relationship. There are also deep levels of potential when we can get over the self-censoring that tends to happen when we don't want to rock the boat."

It is that second potential, one suspects, that needs to be explored. Though her customers often said they couldn't explore a particular behavior with their wives, she wasn't always sure how hard they had tried. They hadn't been willing to fight for the freedom of expression in the same way that gay activists—for instance—have fought for it out in society.

Carol Queen has never been afraid to fight. She has never been afraid to rock the boat and ask for what she needs and wants. From a childhood of shyness, isolation, and secrecy, she has grown into a remarkably public and fruitful career and into a full expression of her sexuality. Her work enables others to grow in the same way, to be who they are as sexual beings and, ultimately, as people. The two things are intimately related.

And ultimately she—and the tradition she has embraced—sees that as a spiritual task. Though it would not be welcome in many spiritual traditions, the Charge of the Goddess is one of the most powerful aspects of her tradition: "Make music and love, all in My presence. . . . Behold, all acts of love and pleasure are my rituals."[7]

NOTES

1. Carol Queen, *Real Live Nude Girl: Chronicles of Sex-Positive Culture* (Pittsburgh: Cleis Press, 1997), 202–3.
2. Ibid., 10–11.
3. Ibid., 153.

4. Ibid., 68.
5. Ibid., 69.
6. Ibid., 177.
7. Ibid., 94.

~ JULIET CARR. Photo by Paul Johnson.

~ 7
The Energetic Invalid

JULIET CARR

BETTER LET YOUR AUNT PEG HANDLE THAT

"Oh, Aunt Peg, it's so big."

With those words, a star was born.

The scripting of late-seventies adult films, as it turns out (and we're not surprised) was casual: the "players" sometimes just got together and imagined situations that might lead to sex. As anyone knows who has seen one of those films, it could be almost anything. On one occasion a forty-year-old actress named—sometimes—Juliet Anderson* suggested she might be a film producer showing her friends around the set. When the director asked what her name should be, she suggested Peggy. She thought she looked like a Peggy.

Her costars were younger, Sharon Kane and the world-renowned John Holmes, who gave new meaning to the

---

*Juliet Anderson/Aunt Peg was her film and stage name.

phrase Big John. Sharon soon found herself kneeling in front of Holmes, and as she exclaimed at what she saw, the Aunt in front of Peg just popped out of her. "Oh, Aunt Peg, it's so big." You've said a mouthful, young lady.

Aunt Peg was a perfect film persona for Juliet Carr. She was older than other porno stars—fifteen or twenty years older than many of the women—but still looked fabulous: tall, blond, leggy, and curvaceous. She exuded energy and had an offbeat sense of humor. She was the wonderful aunt you always wanted to have, who would teach you the ways of the world and wink at your indiscretions, the kind of woman who was known to have a notorious past but whom the whole family adored. She entered the sleazy world of adult films—crummy theaters, peep show houses with slippery spots on the floor—and made it clean. She made it fun.

Juliet Carr today—twenty years later—is the same person, living in Berkeley and working as a sex educator. Despite a lifelong history of chronic illness, she exudes energy and health. You might take her for a fitness instructor or a beauty consultant who follows an elaborate regimen: "regular exercise, good nutrition, yoga, laughter, intellectual pursuits, meditation, lots of quiet time alone, especially in the wilderness, and regular, passionate sex with both women and men."

She has a fascinating mind, is extremely articulate, and is obviously—as a born performer—comfortable in the limelight. The cottage where she lives and works is beautifully decorated and immaculately kept. The books on the shelves bespeak a discerning reader. And she doesn't own a television.

So when she launches into her reasons for staying away from younger men, you might think it would be because they couldn't satisfy her mind, or because their life experiences don't intersect with hers. You wouldn't guess it is because she doesn't want them to be disappointed with future lovers. You also might not predict the language she uses.

"How do I politely explain that I have the most talented tongue and hands west of the Mississippi?"

You could take the advice I always give writers: show, don't tell.

"I'm not bragging," she said, on more than one occasion in our interview, and I had the feeling she really wasn't, though she was obviously at ease talking about herself. She has multiple gifts and isn't shy about mentioning them, but not with the sense that they are *hers,* just that they *are.* She talks just as freely about her shortcomings. ("I'm a difficult person to be around. I *know.* I'm around myself all the time.") But it takes a woman as brash and self-confident as Juliet Anderson to live the life she's lived. She's been swimming against the current the whole time. And if there was ever a model of a strong, independent, sexy woman, she is it.

She was born in southern California in 1938, the child of the lead trumpet player in the Pinky Tomlin band and an aspiring actress. She speaks with great fondness of her parents, who she says had a wonderful marriage and enjoyed fabulous sex.

Surrounded by showbiz types, Juliet wanted that life for herself, especially as a singer and dancer. "I wanted to share my love and enthusiasm for life with people." Her parents, perhaps because they had seen a seamier side of the business, didn't want that for her. When Juliet became an invalid, her sickbed became her stage, but it wasn't the kind of attention she craved. She had to wait until adulthood to find healthy outlets for her unusual artistic temperament.

When the subject of her lifelong illnesses comes up, we

enter a shadowy world that is very much a part of her personality but that seems bizarre for a person of such vitality. She now knows that she has suffered all her life from two incurable but treatable conditions, Crohn's disease and manic depression. She is the kind of woman who would once have been called a hypochondriac but has more recently been recognized—at least by some people—as a highly sensitive person, someone who feels things and responds to them more than most people.

"My father was the same way. I honestly think he died of it. He finally just could not live in this world." And indeed, while I was with her, she was soaking a problematic toe, told me she might be suffering from chronic fatigue syndrome (though she seemed to have more energy than I), and called a neighbor on the phone who was playing music too loud. ("This is your Aunt Peg," I half expected her to say.)

Her condition has its upside: she feels pleasure as intensely as pain. And after long periods of pain, when she is finally able to relax, "I'm in euphoria. I have the most wonderful creative ideas."

She has nevertheless spent much of her life in pain and was a virtual invalid for ten years of her childhood and youth. There was a time, she says, when she was not expected to live. There was a time when she was not expected to walk. When she got wind of these prognostications, she took her healing into her own hands and controlled her illnesses— once she was old enough to leave home—through "yoga, macrobiotics, acupuncture, herbs, and meditation."[1] An important part of the healing process was sex.

Like the headstrong, opinionated person she has always been, Juliet engineered her own sexual initiation. She decided when she wanted to lose her virginity and had herself fitted with a diaphragm (though such behavior must have been scandalous in the late fifties). She assured her summer lover that their romance would end happily but said she wanted to spend plenty of time kissing and exploring each other's bodies first. When the big moment finally arrived, she was stunned at the results.

"For the first time in my life, I felt shivers of pleasure coursing through my whole body. . . . Later I learned that endorphins, natural pain inhibitors, are released during good sex. At that moment, however, all I cared about was that I floated free of pain. I was astonished, ecstatic, and an immediate convert to the healing aspects of guilt-free sex."[2]

She has made sex a regular part of her life ever since, has had "numerous" lovers, but has never taken sex lightly, even in a fling.

"We're playing with the gods and goddesses," she says. "You don't fool around with that stuff. I know I have tremendous influence on people, and I want it to be positive.

"From the start I engaged in sex for pleasure and for relief from pain, and at the same time it was putting me in touch with a universal spirit. I didn't have a container for that, because I didn't belong to any religion. I didn't have a guide. I traveled the path alone."

Juliet has never felt comfortable in any religious tradition, because they have all struck her as antisex. Nowadays she observes seasonal changes with Native American groups and does goddess rituals with women's groups. She has also, since 1985, practiced vipassana meditation, though that tradition too has struggled to integrate sex and spirituality.

"I take what works for me and leave the rest," she says. "I'm able to do that now."

Ever since the age of three, she has felt marked out for

an unusual existence. She used to pray to understand why she had to suffer so much and what her life was supposed to be. The only answer she ever got—she still gets it today— was a voice that said, Patience. Patience. "It has never worked for me to rush things."

She has changed professions every six to eight years, either by design or by circumstance. She spent the early sixties in Japan, immersing herself in the culture and becoming fluent in the language. After moving to Miami for a while and working as a secretary and fashion model, she landed in Mexico City, where she taught English. She spent some time in Greece, then moved on to Finland, where she was a radio program producer for the Finnish Broadcasting Company. In the late seventies she moved to the Bay Area, hoping to get a start as a documentary filmmaker.

Her early days in San Francisco were miserable. She suffered from "culture shock, depression, lack of money and a job, poor health, and horniness."[3] She hadn't realized that San Francisco had become an enclave for gay men. "I couldn't get laid no matter how hard I tried."[4]

It was at about that time that she saw an ad that read, "Attractive women over 18 wanted for soft-core sex show. Lots of fun, short hours, good pay." She was nervous about answering it—but also rather desperate—and was immediately hired not just for the soft-core show but for a hard-core movie as well. Just don't tell the boss your age, she was advised. "You're considered too old for this kind of work."

Porno movies have never been the art form they could be—the subject matter is riveting and inherently beautiful— but at least in the seventies they had some humor and a little flare. Juliet livened up a number of lame scripts with her own brand of humor and her personal magnetism and embodied an age-old male fantasy: the older, intelligent, sophisticated woman who is not only lustier than the girls but knows more about what she's doing.

The pay for actresses was poor, so she did other jobs as well: "production manager, scriptwriter, still photographer, casting consultant, location finder, makeup artist, set decorator, and props and construction coordinator." Eventually she developed an erotic stage show in which she portrayed roles other than Aunt Peg: Helen the Housewife, Cassie the Cook, Elaine the Executive, "women who beneath their facades of respectability were wanton and proud of it."[5] She had a fan club and enjoyed a period of real renown.

After seven years, however, it was time to quit. She had founded her own company, Afterglow Productions, with the idea of making high-class erotica but was able to make only one video before she ran into a crooked distributor. "It broke me, both emotionally and financially." She had always been a person with a great need for privacy, and she wasn't getting much of that in her newfound celebrity.

For five years in the early eighties she lived in a small town in the Sierras. She managed a bed and breakfast, cleaned houses, cared for children, and studied the healing arts. She abstained from sex, she says, in order to "replenish my sexual fires," and opened a therapeutic massage business. The idea of erotic massage—which naturally comes up in that line of work—intrigued her, though her training was in conventional bodywork. For a while she traveled to the Bay Area one week per month to do erotic massage. Finally she decided to move back there. A new period of her life had begun.

AUNT PEG IS STUNNED AT THE MAGNIFICENT TORSO SHE BEHOLDS

Juliet sees a number of married men but doesn't feel that she detracts from their primary relationships. She has women come to her for sessions after their partners have shown a sudden improvement in their lovemaking skills and confessed where they had been. She also regularly sees couples together.

She would like, especially as she gets older, to have more women clients, but she finds them difficult to attract because they are not accustomed to paying for sexual services. Her work with women is more overtly instructional, though she teaches largely by means of touch.

"Most women don't know their bodies," she says. "They don't know what they like and aren't able to express it if they do. It hasn't been okay for women to say what they want sexually in this culture. I try to get them to a point where they can do that with a partner."

She sees herself as a cross between a teacher and an artist. "Life is an art to me, and I teach people to live their lives more fully," she says. "My specialty is healing the split between body and mind, sexuality and spirituality."

She teaches through the body itself, by means of an experience.

"My nature as a highly sensitive person makes me extremely intuitive. I pick up things when I'm around people, especially if I can put my body next to them, especially skin on skin. I call the method I use Tender Loving Touch. It's a gift I was born with, an exquisite way of touching.

"I'm getting clients to shed their armor. I do it with the sound of my voice, with laughter, with humor, with light touch using my entire body. The music I choose is very important. I use all these things to strip away barriers and access the soul. Then we can address what's really going on. There's so much denial around sexuality, distortion around spirituality. Once that's out of the way we can see things straight on."

What she is really teaching clients is the practice of awareness, to leave old scenarios behind and have this present experience. She is teaching erotic meditation.

"I use the sexual feelings that come up, and the denial around them, as a focus," she says. "I tell my clients to turn off their minds, to let their bodies inform their minds, rather than their minds censoring their bodies. That's a pretty radical thing for most people. Then the two of us connect, but not through words. We connect through the language of touch."

Juliet's work as a healer is much like what she did in her film career. She goes into a world that many think of as dirty—erotic massage, which they expect to see in neon on some lurid street—and opens it up for them, shows them there is a larger truth. If she doesn't quite—like Pass-a-million—enlighten them, she at least makes a start.

"There are many kinds of healing touch. What makes mine different is that my client and I are both nude. We have an erotic skin dance. I try to touch every part of their body with every part of mine. I'm passing knowledge along cell to cell. They've never had an experience like that."

One can imagine the experience: making an appointment but not quite sure what to expect; arriving in that small but extremely tasteful cottage, a meditation shrine right there in the living room; encountering this tall, vivacious, extremely sexy woman—a former porno star—whose energy fills the place; hearing her describe what she does.

But the description wouldn't last long. Words can't con-

vey the message. She even grew impatient trying to explain
it to me.

"Take off your shirt and I'll show you," she said.

The woman has a commanding way about her. You
wouldn't think to say no.

She invited me to the sofa, where she had been sitting for
our interview. She asked me to sit with my back to her and
lean forward on the arm of the sofa so she could do my back.
"Now," she said. It was just her fingertips touching me, the
lightest possible touch; they did a fluttering little dance up
and down my back, along my neck, over my shoulders, down
my sides. She turned her hands to use her fingernails, lightly.
Thrills ran up and down my body. I could feel my energy
start to move.

"You have to imagine that I'm using not just my hands
but also my hair, and my face, and my breasts, my whole
naked body. We might start here on the sofa and roll our
way onto the floor, finally make it into the bedroom. By that
time you'd have your pants off, and I wouldn't have anything
on either, and there we'd be, with a whole hour in front of
us. Nothing for you to do but lie back with no expectations
and be pampered. Feel what pleasure can do. Can you see
that that might be healing?"

It was healing just to hear about it.

NOTES

1. Kenneth Ray Stubbs, PhD., ed. *Women of the Light: The New Sacred
   Prostitute* (Larkspur, Calif.: Secret Garden, 1994), 36.
2. Ibid., 37.
3. Ibid., 29.
4. Ibid., 30.
5. Ibid., 31.

8

Whitman's Child

JOSEPH KRAMER

JOSEPH KRAMER IS warm, friendly, affectionate, expansive, and just slightly—shall we say—hyper. He had recently turned fifty when I visited him at his home in Oakland, but there is something boyish about him, like a boy genius who can't keep the words from flowing. He kept reaching out to grab me as we walked along the sidewalk to lunch, as if to make sure we were still in touch; he constantly—as a practitioner of rebirthing—took in large gusts of air and let them out with an audible sigh; he frequently burst into shouts of barrel-chested laughter; and as we sat together at a sushi bar he let out audible murmurs of pleasure at the tastes. He took delight in everything, even—it seemed—our footsteps as we strolled along the sidewalk.

There was nothing phony about this. It was too spontaneous and irrepressible. Kramer is a genuinely generous per-

~ JOSEPH KRAMER. Photo by Mark Thompson.

son, with his time, his energy, with everything he has.* He is especially generous with his ideas, and if there is a problem, it is that they pour out of him at such a terrific clip. He is the perpetually exuberant young man with too much to say.

Kramer is not only Jesuit trained; he was a Jesuit, spent

*Before I arrived in San Francisco, he had sent me six audio- and three videotapes free of charge, since I'd told him I was on a tight budget. "Just pass them along when you're through," he said. He came from Oakland to San Francisco to pick me up in his car, had left the whole day unscheduled, ten years in the order, and dropped out one year short of the priesthood. He has the theoretical and encyclopedic brilliance of the Jesuits, their interest in ordering information and developing pedagogic techniques. Of all the healers I visited, he is probably the leading theoretician, the person you would go to when you want to locate your practice in a tradition.

He begins his series of six tapes, for instance *(Ecstatic Sex, Healthy Sex)* with an effortless exposition of three views on sex, Taoist, Tantric, and Reichian, an obvious comparison that I had never heard anyone make. And he contrasted those traditions with the way most men have sex, which he calls— like the high school biology teacher trying to give us something we'll remember—balloon sex. Kramer's talks are loaded with such tags.

In balloon sex, you tighten at the quadriceps, tighten at the belly and in the chest, isolate all the feeling in your genitals, then blow up and blow up until you pop. Picture a twelve-year-old alone in bed at night, masturbating so his brothers won't hear. It is an act that takes place quickly, is entirely genital, and—because it involves limited satisfaction— needs to be repeated. And repeated. Picture the same boy all grown up now, haunting bath houses or massage parlors.

In contrast to that, Kramer offers—here comes another tag—the Pan dick state. The Greek god Pan—though the Disney version doesn't include this detail—had a perpetual flaming erection, and the suggestion was not so much that he was always ready for sex as that he represents man in a

bought me lunch, gave me—when I expressed interest in it—yet another video, and on my way out spontaneously made me a gift of a crystal phallus that was sitting in a large collection on a shelf. It was for sale—his home is also his business—but he ripped the price tag off.

vibrant, energetic state. When the energy is flowing, we're hard.* A corollary of that is that the state of sexual excitement is not one of tension and discomfort. "We're such an antipleasure culture that we don't even know when we're feeling pleasure," Kramer says.

It is in support of this view that Kramer goes to the ancient Eastern traditions, Taoism in particular, which has been a major influence on his life. Taoism dates from centuries before Christ; has been variously described as a religion, a philosophy, and a way of life; and speaks to sex because it speaks to every aspect of our lives, also because it sees sex as a central focus.

Taoism regards everything in life as energy, in constant change; the energy of the life force is *chi,* and energy flowing from the genitals—what we think of as erotic energy—is *ching chi. Chi* takes on two major forms, *yang* and *yin*—which correspond roughly to male and female—and the key to skillful living is to keep these forces in balance. *Chi* is both a force for healing and a pathway to transcendence.

Tantra is a specifically spiritual path that arose out of the Hindu and Buddhist traditions. While many traditions avoid or deny erotic energy, Tantra embraces it as a pathway to the divine. A Tantric cultivates erotic energy—or erotic *prana*—and lives in a perpetually erotic state. The sexual partner is a vehicle for divine energy.

In both Taoism and Tantra, the way to keep erotic energy flowing between heterosexual partners is to stimulate female

*There have been Zen teachers who say the same thing about meditation, that when you're sitting in intimate touch with the energy—as Lawrence Shainberg's hilarious teacher Kyudo Roshi put it—"Your sausage stands up." Nobody says what you're supposed to do when it's time for walking practice.

orgasm—which raises the energy higher and higher—but avoid male ejaculation, which stops the flow. Both of these disciplines see sex not as a linear event, moving toward a goal, but as one in which the energy keeps circulating, getting more and more intense, opening into ecstasy.

In contrast to these ancient and venerable systems, Wilhelm Reich was a maverick twentieth-century psychologist, a disciple of Freud who took the master's theories to their logical conclusions. He concentrated on the body more than the mind and is the father of all the modern body therapies, rolfing, bioenergetics, primal scream, rebirthing. He believed that all neurosis is repressed sexuality and that if we could be fully and freely sexual our problems would clear up.

Reich called the healing energy orgone and believed—like the Eastern traditions—that it was important to keep it moving through the body. He felt that most people are not truly orgasmic because their orgasms are confined to the genitals. He did not have a theory about retention of sperm; he believed in discharge. He felt that the function of the orgasm was to release accumulated tension in our bodies.

All of these systems have elaborate theories about the flow of energy. Reich referred to body armoring: tensions in our bodies occur because we draw back from experience, and they become a part of our musculature, blocking the flow. He referred to seven segments of armoring—starting with the eyes and moving down to the hips—and believed that the orgone moves downward, so that bodywork begins at the higher centers.

Taoism referred to channels of energy on both sides of the body, one running from the base of the genitals to the tongue, the other from the tailbone through the skull to the roof of the mouth (hence the meditation instruction, in many

Eastern traditions, to touch the tongue to the roof of the mouth, connecting the two channels and allowing the energy to flow).

Tantra—from the somewhat better-known Indian system—speaks of seven energy centers, known as the chakras, beginning with the base chakra, at the perineum, and moving up to the crown chakra at the top of the skull. It associates different energy centers with different human capacities and sees the purpose of sex as moving the energy through all the chakras, making the sexual spiritual and creating a state of wholeness. You consciously connect your chakras with those of your partner, embracing at all levels and circulating energy through your bodies.

All of this is a far cry from balloon sex, which localizes feeling in the genitals and doesn't move it anywhere. It doesn't—to name one obvious center—connect sex with the heart. Balloon sex actually shuts off other energy centers, because it tightens the body. It doesn't allow energy to flow, and it isn't healing.

As Joseph Kramer would say, it is compulsive, addictive, and paltry. Worst of all, paltry.

JERK-OFF VIRTUOSO
Kramer grew up in a Catholic family in St. Louis that was not—to say the least—without boundaries. This was the Catholicism of the fifties: compulsory mass on Sunday, tuna casserole on Fridays, and a strict moral code. "We weren't even supposed to play with Protestant kids," he says, and he doesn't mean sex play, just cops and robbers. But he isn't overly critical of his background, or of the Jesuit order he eventually entered; when I asked him about his spirituality

today, the first influence he mentioned was Catholicism, and when we spoke of his vocation, he turned back, rather touchingly, to the lessons of his boyhood.

"I felt from early on that my life's work was to be of service," he says. "I still do." In his family, that meant service in both a religious and social sense; they were influenced by the traditional church and by the radical Catholic worker movement. For Kramer today it has meant serving the gay and straight men whom he sees as his tribe, rescuing them not just from the compulsive sex that was taking their lives but from the paltry sex that was sapping their spirits.

In that extremely restricted world of fifties Catholic morality, the one place he found freedom and ecstasy was in masturbation. That is still a key act in Kramer's teachings about sex, and he started off with a bang.

"The Catholic church helped me because it was a mortal sin to masturbate. I figured, if it's a mortal sin, maybe even after coming I would just keep stroking, so it would only be one mortal sin. So I learned multiple orgasms.

"The other thing that the repressiveness of Catholicism did was to bring God and sex together in my mind. God cared every time I had sex. Later on, once I got rid of the guilt, I realized that the God space, the religious space, was intimately tied up with sex. This was a part of what spirituality meant to me."

He decided in his youth that he had a vocation for the priesthood. He had plenty of help making the decision. "I think that's a coded message in the Catholic community, people telling you that you have a vocation. I must have heard that two hundred times when I was young. What they often mean is that they think you're not marrying material."

He entered the Jesuit order in 1965, at the age of eighteen.

"It was homosexual heaven," he says, meaning just that he found himself in a group of like-minded men. "The Jesuits were masters of male bonding."

Kramer at that point had had almost no partner sex at all. There had been some fooling around when he was a child and one "hitchhiking experience" when he was a teenager. During his ten years with the Jesuits, he had several slipups with other men, all of which resembled the first occurrence.

"It was an occasion of boyish wrestling that turned into mutual masturbation," he says. "It caused a lot of guilt and travail." This extremely sensual and sexual man had been bottling himself up for years, and though he felt bad about breaking his vows, there were other feelings as well. "My heart opened up. I laughed. There was a level of freedom emerging, a new understanding of myself. I knew who I was"—that he was gay, he means—"and that all was right with the world, that if I chose to stay with the Jesuits it wasn't my path to have sex, but sex wasn't a mortal sin."

In 1972 he went to Berkeley to study at the Graduate Theological Union. He took courses at the University of California at Berkeley and was much inspired by the milieu of Sproul Plaza, where the free speech movement had started in the sixties.

"You'd see professors walk by and students and wheelchair people and street people and entertainers and preachers and political people and the Hare Krishnas, the Moonies. There was a celebration of diversity. I realized I was not celebrating my diversity. I was fitting into a Jesuit mold, the Catholic mold, and I'd never been who I was.

"So 1972 was my coming out in Sproul Plaza. I was a gay man, and I wanted to say it. That didn't fit in with the Jesuit thing, because if you're celibate you don't have to say it.

They have power over you if you're guilty. And many Jesuits are guilty."

He eventually decided that he didn't want just to identify as a gay man, he wanted to live as one. He left the order in 1976 and moved from Berkeley to New York.

Some people look back on gay life in the seventies with horror, seeing it as a time of moral license and degeneracy that sowed the seeds of the AIDS epidemic. Kramer—who went from being celibate to having sex for hours every day—takes a different view. He believes that he was doing a form of Reichian therapy, shaking off his body armor and ridding himself of years of repression.

"I was vibrating out all the dead spots in myself. It wasn't compulsive, addictive acting out. It was openhearted, fun, innocent. It was enlightening. Everybody realized we were doing something that hadn't been done before. I felt that consciousness all around me."

People wonder how he survived. "There are three tribes in the gay world," he says. "The anal tribe, the oral tribe, and the hand tribe." Kramer, as a future masseur, was in the hand tribe. He actually enjoys all kinds of sex and has learned from all of it, but he doesn't give any primacy to intercourse. It is all sex to him. Foreplay. Afterplay. Even massage.

"Penetration has always been very special for me, reserved for a lover, not for a casual contact," he says. "That's probably why I'm alive today."

Even in those days, Kramer's life was not about scoring, about—as he puts it—"getting hard and squirting." He had not yet studied Taoism, but what he enjoyed was getting in an erotic vibration and staying there. Kramer is an intuitive person, kinesthetic, a kind of sexual mystic. What attracts him is not a certain look but a feeling.

"There is almost no correlation between how a person looks and how you will get along with him," he says. "But there is a strong correlation between your first feeling and how you will get along. What I learned in New York was to go for the vibrancy and aliveness."

Especially important to him was a man he met in a bathhouse after he moved back to the Bay Area in the late seventies. "I had some experiences of conscious sex that just blew me away. One was with a very old man, in a bathhouse called the Steam Works.

"He said, 'Take some deep breaths.' He knelt down and started sucking me. Then he started doing things with his hands. He was holding accupressure points, at first on my shoulders, neck, and chest. Eventually he worked his way all the way down to my feet, and up on to my head. This went on for about an hour. I wasn't sure what was happening, but I knew I was in the hands of a master. Finally I said, 'What is this?' He said, 'I was just doing accupressure, pulling the erotic energy around through your body.'

"I soon began to study accupressure myself. Now it's a major part of all my trainings."

Get Your Damn Hands on Me

After leaving the Jesuits, Kramer had made his living as a teacher at a Catholic girls school in Manhattan. He was fired for being openly gay and eventually moved back to California, where he worked as a counselor to young gay men while finishing his degree in theology. He concentrated on the link between sexuality and spirituality and began to study the Eastern traditions. He thought all along that he would continue as a counselor.

But despite his intellectual accomplishments, Kramer has always believed more in the wisdom of the body than of the mind. "I think that maybe a third of the people who go to psychotherapists just need to learn to masturbate better," he says. He had been studying massage, had been much impressed by a statement of Joseph Campbell's: "People don't need to know the meaning of life. They need to have the experience of it." He decided he wanted to take some of the young men he'd been counseling and do a massage weekend with them. "Absolutely not," his department head said. "This is a counseling program." That was when he decided to become a bodyworker.

"I wanted to find wonderful ways to touch men. I didn't look at my massage table as a place of therapy but as one of celebration, almost like an altar. A man is on the table, and I anoint him with oil and make him shudder with delight at his own being."

At around the same time, in 1981, Kramer began to study rebirthing, a system of conscious breathing that circulates energy in the body. It doesn't have a specifically sexual component, but he found that when he did conscious breathing he had "wonderful full-body orgasms," not ejaculating but experiencing the wave of energy that Reich had spoken of. With his knowledge of Taoism and Tantra, it seemed natural to hook conscious breathing up with sex.

"You can have an orgasm from breath energy and an orgasm from erotic energy"—from stimulating the genitals—"and when the two come together, there's a synergy that causes a leap in consciousness. The ego dissolves. That's the core of Tantric teaching and Taoist sexual theories. The synergy of yin and yang come together, and something extraordinary happens."

Breathing and sexuality also combine rather naturally with massage, and Kramer began—in addition to conventional bodywork—to do erotic massage. Normally that means a regular massage followed by a hand job, but Kramer wasn't interested in the standard procedure. Massage opened the channels of energy and got it flowing, as did the breathing techniques of rebirthing. Genital touching got the specifically erotic energy involved. But the point wasn't genital release. It was to put the client into an erotic vibration and leave him there.

All of Kramer's interests—including his spiritual studies—were coming together. But he was making these discoveries in the early eighties, when AIDS was beginning to surface. And the sex that he saw as deeper and more satisfying was also safe, mostly because it was manual but also because it didn't involve ejaculation. There was no exchange of body fluids.

In addition to his bodywork, Kramer was lecturing on what he had studied, sometimes informally at his house, other times in more formal settings. One day at the Gay People's Alliance at the University of California, one of his students said, "This is a great class. When is the lab period?" Never one to refuse a challenge, Kramer said, "If any of you men is interested in a lab period, come up afterward and give me your name and address."

Twelve men signed up. "I was really nervous—what to do? And I thought, 'Oh Joe, you had five hours of sex a day for four years in New York City. What do you mean, what are you going to do?' "

That was the beginning of what—three years later— would become the Body Electric School of erotic massage.

THE DEAR LOVE OF COMRADES

When you speak to Joseph Kramer about his spirituality—he prefers the term spiritualities, to emphasize multiple influences on his life—he does speak, not surprisingly, of Taoism, which is the oldest system that describes the circulation of energy. But he also speaks in all seriousness of Catholicism, both in its ideal of service and in the Jesuit practice of discernment, going deeply into yourself to see what your gifts are and what the world needs from them. We are all, as Saint Paul said, a part of the body of Christ. Some are the hands, some the eyes, some the feet. Which of us, Kramer wondered, are the genitals?

It didn't take much discernment in 1983 to see that the world needed a safe alternative to the ecstatic sex that gay men had experienced in the seventies. Kramer actually believed his brand of sex was superior. He would have offered it if AIDS had never happened.

The moment utilized some of his strongest gifts. "One of my shamanistic, tribal names is Sacred Weaver. I have this ability to weave people and things together in rituals. I also have the gift of foresight. I can see things ten years in the future, where things are going, where things need to go.

"The very first time I read about gay cancer, I stopped having unsafe sex. I started developing alternatives that were no risk. I didn't even like the idea of low risk.

"What had happened in the seventies was that gay men had become my people. All of a sudden I'd found a community. As I'd committed myself to the Jesuits, I committed my life to this. This is my path. This is my purpose. I want to celebrate—this is where Whitman comes in—the dear love of comrades."

Whitman was also a major spiritual influence, though Kramer had never studied him formally.

"I remember in college in St. Louis reading *Leaves of Grass*. I started reading it aloud, and I got high. I'd never smoked marijuana, and later when I did I remembered I'd had that feeling reading *Leaves of Grass*. I didn't even know Whitman was gay. I just got into this state.

"Then years later, when I was starting my school, I thought of naming it after the fifty-sixth hexagram of the I Ching, Fire on the Mountain. But something happened in 1983 in Berkeley that made Body Electric come to me. I felt that Walt Whitman's energy was there. He loved men, and I had the exact same feelings he did. I feel there is a part of him alive in me."

Kramer through the years has taught by various means. He has given countless lectures expounding his evolving theories; they are perhaps best summed up in the six tapes *Ecstatic Sex, Healthy Sex*. For years he did workshops teaching his brand of Taoist erotic massage, including "conscious breathing . . . continuous eye contact, simultaneous heart and genital connection, and building ecstatic energy without ejaculating."[1] The Body Electric School, under its present owner Collin Brown, continues to offer these workshops.

Kramer also teaches men to enter high ecstatic states by masturbation, or—the term he prefers—soloing. He sees it as a liberation practice, a central human ritual that connects us not only with ourselves but with the whole cosmos. It is a standard cliché that we cannot love others until we love ourselves. Kramer takes that statement quite literally, in a physical sense.

"Reich believed that masturbation was a perversion because there was no love object. I thought, no *love* object?

Wait a minute." Masturbation involves the most important love object of all.

Kramer doesn't hesitate to adopt the terms of pop psychology when they are useful to him. He refers to a person being in a head space when his consciousness is up in his head, a physical space when it is down in the body. The erotic space is a subset of the physical. Being in an erotic space doesn't mean you're *thinking* about sex but that your consciousness is focused in the specifically erotic energy of the body. There has been a fear of that space in the eighties and nineties because of AIDS. That fear has driven people into a head space, the locale of phone sex, cyber sex, erotic videos and pictures.

Kramer refers to that kind of sex as hot-wiring. People have a fantasy up in their heads and use it to become aroused. They might continue with the fantasy all the way to orgasm. They are, in effect, having sex in a head space. For many people—even those with partners—that is the only sex they ever have. That makes sex extremely narrow, because most people only have one or two fantasies that work.

The Taoist and Tantric traditions avoid fantasy. They have sex in a physical space and focus on the feelings of the body in the present moment.

The other distinction that these traditions make is to separate the concept of orgasm from that of ejaculation. Most men—and women—think of male orgasm as the emission of semen from the penis, no matter what the accompanying feeling.* But even Reich—who was all in favor of ejacu-

---

*Premature ejaculation, as any man can tell you who has experienced it, is not really orgasmic. The erotic energy doesn't build up enough to give a satisfying, full-bodied feeling. It is therefore extremely frustrating. It is as if you can't have an orgasm.

lation—taught that orgasm was a full-bodied event, an S-shaped whiplash of energy that moves through the whole body. That sensation can take place without an accompanying ejaculation. The Tantric male is not a wildly frustrated person, bursting with pent-up sexual energy. He probably has more orgasms than most men. He just doesn't ejaculate.

Kramer also makes a distinction between a Pan dick erection, the result of energy moving through the body, and a hot-wiring erection, which is created by an image in the mind and can actually be disturbed by what happens in the body. The energy of the Pan dick state is healing. Men can engage in masturbation or partner sex for one hour, two hours, and charge their bodies with more and more energy. They can notice—when they are not tensing at the belly and thighs—that this state is pleasurable. Men tend to think of sexual arousal as a tense uncomfortable state, but it doesn't have to be. It can be exhilarating, man in his power.

Kramer teaches six steps to get into the high ecstatic state, in which orgasm can be a prolonged event rather than a brief spasm.

1. Learn to be in a physical space. This is a long-term discipline, practiced over the course of a lifetime. It is fundamental to many meditative traditions, as well as to yoga, the martial arts, and other physical disciplines. Kramer recommends any form of full-body exercise, like running, swimming, aerobic dance. He advocates an hour of intense physical activity each day to charge the body.

2. Learn to relax during sex. Balloon sex is an act of tensing and tensing until you pop. But a tense body cannot feel, so many men don't know what full-bodied sexual pleasure is like. We reach ecstatic states through a relaxed mode, in which the energy has a chance to flow.

Humans have both a sympathetic and a parasympathetic nervous system. The sympathetic system involves the fight or flight response and operates when men are aggressive in sex. The parasympathetic system is involuntary and operates when we are relaxed. Some men can get an erection only when they are aggressive. One way to expand the capacity for erection is through erotic situations—like massage—in which you are entirely passive.

3. Breathe consciously. An important part of Kramer's teaching comes from the breathing techniques that he learned in rebirthing. We are a nation of subventilators and often diminish breathing in order not to feel things.

Conscious breathing has many virtues. It helps you feel. It keeps you in the present moment. It circulates energy. It also sometimes produces the kind of full-bodied orgasm that Kramer experienced when he was studying rebirthing.

4. Focus on the sensations of the body. This seems an obvious instruction, but most of us hot-wire straight into fantasy. That is an old habit and can be frustratingly difficult to break, but the technique is the same as that of meditation: when you find yourself wandering away into fantasy, gently come back to the sensations of the body. They are infinitely subtle and fascinating. Annie Sprinkle calls this process— when practiced during masturbation—medibation.

5. Take time to build the charge. Most of us think of sex as an event that is over in minutes, but high ecstatic states take time to build, forty-five minutes to an hour. Kramer and his associates practice for hours at a time.

6. Include movement and sound. Many of us learned sex in situations where we had to be still so we wouldn't be detected. There is also a prejudice against movement on the part of men, especially around the hips, perhaps because it is

perceived as effeminate, or gay. But ecstatic energy circulates through movement, and it is helpful to stand and move, even dance, with your sexual feelings. It also helps to vocalize the feelings, raising the energy into the throat chakra and circulating it even further.

SEX PRIEST

Kramer often sees the world through the lens of archetypes, like the shamanic "weaver of dreams," which explains his skill in creating the Body Electric workshops. Another such archetype is one he borrowed from Karen Finley, consciousness scout, or—in his case—erotic consciousness scout, the person who goes to the far edges of erotic experience and comes back to tell the rest of us about it.

Marco Vassi was such a person; we still, eight years after his death, haven't caught up with all he taught us. His lover Annie Sprinkle was, and continues to be, one, instructing by means of performance and other erotic art. Betty Dodson, author of the groundbreaking book for women *Liberating Masturbation*,* is such a person. And so is Joseph Kramer, the kind of visionary who sees the form of something long before it takes shape. By the time it does, he is ready to move on.

He built his informal classes and workshops on sex into the Body Electric School and for years taught workshops entitled "Celebrating the Body Erotic" all over this country and in Europe. Demand for his classes was such that he took on more people to help teach and gradually became a trainer of teachers. He began to realize that he was encountering

---

*Dodson published a revised and updated version in 1996, *Sex for One: The Joy of Selfloving* (Crown Trade Paperbacks).

people who were erotically gifted, even though—in our homophobic and antisex culture—they had often been marginalized. Kramer coined the term *Sacred Intimate* and conducted his first workshop for them at the Wildwood Conference Center in 1991.

Now the system of training Sacred Intimates has become self-perpetuating, and Kramer—as he enters his fifties—is pulling back. He sold the Body Electric School to Collin Brown in 1992. He felt he was a good teacher, and a good trainer of teachers, but didn't want to spend his time as an administrator. He thought he could teach just as effectively by means of the Internet and videos. He sells videos through his Erospirit Research Institute, a business that he runs out of his home. Otherwise he spends his time doing bodywork and expanding his practice as a masturbation coach.

It is ironic that after all these years, and all the experience he's had, he has come back to the simple act with which he—and most of us—began. He arrived at this place through the process of discernment; he saw the need for such work and didn't know of anyone else who was offering it. He asks a basic question to advertise his service: Are you still masturbating the way you did ten years ago? Not a question you want to ask at the local pool hall, but a good one nevertheless.

He invites clients to the room where he does bodywork. He teaches them techniques he has developed through the years: conscious breathing, eye gazing (in a mirror), various inventive ways to stroke the penis, preparing for sex by stretching and movement.* But basically he just invites men to masturbate and serves as a witness, like a young boy who

*He reviews these steps in the video *Evolutionary Masturbation*.

wants to see how it is done, or like a man watching his buddy do it. He shares his learning with his clients and tells them what he sees.

The subject that comes up most often these days is shame, an emotion discussed in some depth by Robert Bly and addressed by the men's movement. Kramer admires much that the men's movement has done but feels that it stalled when it came to physical intimacy. Iron John had no genitals. Bly teaches from his gifts and has a great deal to contribute, but he isn't especially comfortable in the area of sexuality.

Shame for Kramer is the great interrupter; it rises up in men and keeps them from reaching ecstatic states, from achieving wholeness. It often steps in before that, of course, and keeps us from taking joy in our daily lives. Men feel shame about all kinds of things connected with sex: feeling lust, desiring specific sexual acts, being naked, having less than a perfect body, having an aging body, having an erection, not having an erection, not performing well, not satisfying their partner. . . . The list goes on and on.

There is an enormous amount of shame around masturbation itself. Kramer's way of dealing with it is really just the technique of awareness practice: see that it is present and allow yourself to experience it. Don't repress it, and don't get lost in it. See how much a part of your life it is. And begin to see that erotic energy itself can vibrate it away.

Kramer is not as strict now as he was when he was formulating his theories. In the early years he and some of the men he worked with were fanatical about not ejaculating, and there was one year at least when no one ejaculated during erotic massage on his table. "I was a rabid authoritarian Taoist," he says with a grin.

But he doesn't believe that even the Taoists were totally against ejaculation. "That was coded," he says. Having sex without ejaculating is really just a technique for learning. You learn how to charge your body erotically, learn that excitement can be a pleasurable and ecstatic state, learn to have orgasms without ejaculating, learn that sex doesn't need to have a goal. Once you have learned these things you can ejaculate or not. Freedom is all about choice.

There is nothing wrong with getting off quickly, for instance, if you're looking for a sedative. "It's better than a sleeping pill, or a Scotch." And if you take the time to charge your body erotically—fifteen minutes or more—you don't lose energy by ejaculating. The charge stays in your body.

About fantasy he is still adamant. He believes that our tendency to hot-wire keeps us not only from intimacy with our partner but from the reality of our experience. That is why conscious breathing is important; it keeps us in contact with the body. If clients are really devoted to fantasy— pictures, videos, or just their own imaginings—Kramer suggests that they use it to raise the erotic charge but that once the energy is flowing they drop it and stay with their present experience.

He has made it a general rule not to get sexually involved with clients or with students from his workshops. He enjoys living alone and does not have one steady sexual partner, but he has five intimate friends with whom he is erotic on a regular basis. One of them—startlingly—is Annie Sprinkle, the woman who seems to keep turning up in the erotic history of our time.

Kramer has worked with Sprinkle in various situations, teaching workshops to men and women, and they are obviously kindred spirits. He really meant it when he said it is the erotic vibration that attracts him and not anything superficial (like gender!) about his partner. Though he is a lifelong gay man, sex with this woman has seemed perfectly natural; they started at a place that was beyond gender. "We'd have sex for an hour, two hours," Kramer said. "I never had any trouble staying hard." They actually contemplated getting married for a while, and having children. But they decided that their work wasn't compatible with that kind of life.

Or, as Sprinkle suddenly said one day: "We can't get married. We're sacred prostitutes."

"I think you're a priest," I said to Kramer at the end of our long day together. "You trained as a priest, and you are one." In addition to helping men with their sex lives, he volunteers at an AIDS hospice, doing massage; and as he has gotten older he spends more and more time working with older men, who are often looked down on by other bodyworkers. A third of his clients are over sixty.

"I actually feel that I've kept my Jesuit vows," he said. "This isn't really poverty, of course," he said, gesturing to his surroundings. He lives well, but not extravagantly, in the same rental house he has occupied for eleven years. "But I try to practice poverty by not being attached to things. I practice obedience by being true to my vision. And I practice chastity when I honor the erotic vibration. What brings up shame for me is when I use sex in a paltry or compulsive way. I feel I'm being chaste when I honor it."

Poverty, maybe. Obedience, for sure. But chastity? Joseph Kramer? I'll have to think about that.

NOTE

1. Don Shewey. "Joe Kramer Sings the Body Electric." *The Village Voice* 37:16; 21 April 1992, pp. 37–38.

9

Exploring the Infinite Body

COLLIN BROWN AND SELAH MARTHA

BOVE ALL IN MY search for sexual healers I had
hoped to avoid the airbrushed celebrities who teach
Tantric techniques to bored suburbanites, charging
huge fees and massaging enormous egos. Bookstores are
loaded with titles by such people, beaming at you glamor-
ously from dust jackets. I talked the question over with an
old friend, a magazine editor in North Carolina.

"There are undoubtedly authentic teachers," he said.
"But they're probably not the people you hear about.
They're not on the best-seller list."

One of my most valuable tips came from a writer friend,
Don Shewey, who had written about Joseph Kramer in the
Village Voice and trained as a Sacred Intimate.

"You should see Collin Brown when you're in San Francisco," he said. "He did the Body Electric work with Joseph
Kramer and actually bought the school. But he's bisexual and
has a woman partner named Selah Martha. They teach workshops to straight couples."

~ SELAH MARTHA AND COLLIN BROWN.
Photo by Steve Savage.

As I walked the streets of Oakland looking for the Body Electric School, I had a feeling I'd come to the right place. Oakland is San Francisco's working-class cousin, modest houses and small, well-kept yards. The school was on a slightly more commercial street, in the second floor of what could have been a duplex. There was a large room for classes and bodywork, two much smaller—and rather cramped—rooms for administrative offices.

Collin Brown, when he arrived, looked like any other guy just getting to work, loaded down with materials and still not quite awake. He wanted to talk about ecstatic sex, sure, but first he wanted an eye-opener at a local juice bar. He proposed we talk at a nearby park, where kids were playing and a family was having a picnic. He was quiet, modest, and thoughtful, not pushy about promoting his work but endlessly energetic in talking about it. He was nothing like the Tantric teachers I'd been worried about, whom he referred to as the Marin Tantric goddesses, who speak in perpetually breathy voices, as if constantly on the verge of orgasm.

Brown and Martha work together at the Body Electric School, which still caters largely to gay men but also has classes for women and for straight couples. They share care of their two-year-old daughter, Molly, and juggle their lives in the way that many two-career families do. It isn't easy, especially when they do their four-day intensives and have to take her along, with a baby-sitter. But their lives have led them to this work, and they deeply believe in doing it.

THE ORPHAN BOY AND THE ALL-AMERICAN GIRL
It wasn't the story I expected to hear when I asked why he associated sex and spirituality. But as Collin Brown himself says, we all have rich internal lives once we've taken off our social masks. His was very much the kind of story that might have been told at a Body Electric workshop. It probably has been.

His parents lived in southern California, got married when they were seventeen, and split up when they were twenty-four. In that brief time they had six children. Collin was the fourth, and the first boy. His mother was still young when she left her husband, hadn't really had an adolescence. She began dating bikers and neglecting the children, who started to get into trouble, setting fires, wandering off and getting lost. It was finally decided, when Collin was six, that they should be put into an orphanage run by Irish nuns. The women weren't Irish American. They were actually from Ireland.

Collin was their angel, a bright energetic student who would eventually make his way to the Ivy League. He sang in the school choir, acted in dramatic productions, and loved God and Jesus. He experienced spiritual ecstasy in the rituals of the church.

And at night, back in the dorm, he had wild sex with the boys.

Wild sex at the age of six was mostly just a matter of touching, having erections, getting into bed with friends. As Collin got older it became more than that. But the dormitory space belonged to the boys; the nuns didn't violate it. There was a spiritual paradise out in the chapel, a sexual paradise back in the dorms. It all became one thing.

"It was a mystical erotic experience," Brown says. "I'm enough of a rebel that I didn't buy the hell and damnation part of Catholicism. I did go to confession, but that was all coded. You didn't spell out what you were actually doing."

Brown got out of the orphanage at the age of ten, living after that with his mother, but his early experience was formative. Like Joseph Kramer, he was much impressed with the Catholic ideal of service, the belief that life is precious and we should try to make a difference in the world. He continued to be an all-star at high school, a student-body president who started programs for students to work with the blind and the retarded. He was also active in church, especially with a group that established an alliance with evangelical Christians.

It was the sixties, and life in California was wild. Brown had his wild side, riding a motorcycle everywhere from the time he was fifteen, throwing himself into social justice work. But most of his rebelliousness was in his sex life.

"I used to have sex with my best friend," he says. "We

couldn't figure out how to persuade girls to do it, so we'd have double dates together, go off somewhere and make out with the girls, then drop them off, come back home, and have sex with each other."

Brown thought throughout his youth that he would stop with the boys once he began having sex with girls. At the age of eighteen, as he'd expected, he fell in love and had an idyllic heterosexual initiation with a girl he really cared for. But it didn't make him want to stop with the boys. He was having too much fun.

He was the only person from his graduating class to leave the state for college. He went about as far east as he could go, to Harvard, and it was there—bizarrely, after all the pitfalls he'd avoided—that he began to have trouble.

"I was miserable on the East Coast," he says. "I lost my way." He had left high school thinking he might go into politics, but at Harvard he ran into the real insiders and found them pushy and aggressive. It was his first experience of humility, when he wasn't able to accomplish just what he wanted.

Harvard was extremely closeted for gay men. It was a university that people attended because they wanted success, and coming out could only interfere. Even Brown didn't make a point of coming out; he didn't consider himself gay and was only gradually deciding he was bisexual. He continued to see both men and women, but most of his gay life was away from Harvard, in Boston.

He took a first job teaching at a prep school, then lucked into a dream job as the head of a summer publishing institute at a major university. He was in charge of admitting students and locating visiting lecturers, and met many of the bright lights in publishing. He took the job when he was twenty-seven, left when he was thirty-four, and greatly expanded the program while he was there.

But something had gone out of his life. When I asked what his sex life was like in those days, he said, "Masturbating to porn magazines." Actually, he was still having relations with both men and women but not finding them satisfying. He wasn't connecting emotionally. His sexual initiation had gone beautifully. It was as he approached midlife that he had problems.

"I didn't know how to integrate who I was into that world," he says. "I had a prestigious job and was so visible. I didn't know how to be gay. I was also shut down emotionally. I didn't know how to have a relationship."

People thought he was crazy, at the age of thirty-four, to give up a job that other men would have killed to have. He felt he could go on doing it well but that he would wind up outwardly successful and inwardly impoverished. He decided to return to California and enroll in a master's program in psychology. He wasn't sure what he wanted but felt he had some healing to do.

As Selah Martha would put it years later—when asked what kind of person took the workshops she and Collin taught—he had a "felt sense that his body had more to offer him." In the group of men who took—and eventually taught—Joseph Kramer's workshop in Taoist erotic massage, he found once again that feeling of being freely and fully sexual, in a world where that impulse was honored. It was like being back in the sexual paradise of his childhood.

Selah Martha had come home much sooner. Home in her case was Anchorage, Alaska, but she had also gone east to college, to Yale, where she had finished as a film major. Her life up to then had been much different from Brown's. She had grown up in an all-American family, one of two daughters of an attorney who worked in public office as a liaison between government and the oil companies. Her mother was a teacher.

"My family was very alive in certain ways," she says, "and I still carry those gifts. They were involved in the community, intellectually vibrant, very active physically. I knew they loved me, but there was a real emotional hole, a lack of information and development. I often experienced emotional confusion."

Martha frequently speaks in terms of light and dark, in the sense of standing in the light—the truth—or staying in the shadows. She speaks of parts of herself, at various moments in her life, as having been in eclipse, and sees eclipse as a coping strategy, a way of getting on in the world, but one that doesn't give us what we need.

She is also—like Joseph Kramer—a kinesthetic person who learns by doing, learns and teaches through the body. It is not surprising that one of the most important revelations of her life came through a physical experience.

She was twenty-six years old and married, living in Anchorage, leading very much the life she had grown up in, when she gave birth to her first daughter, who is now fifteen. Something about the physical experience, the opening of the muscles in her pelvis, brought up memories from years before. She realized she had been sexually abused and hadn't had anywhere to go with it.

"Sexual abuse is terrible," she says. "But doubly terrible is that no one will talk about it."

Her entire life changed.

"I realized that my history was not what I'd thought it

was. There was a dark side that I'd been blocking out. I also became aware that I was drinking alcoholically. I knew I couldn't stay in that life."

That revelation was a stunning one for Martha, but not entirely surprising in terms of a discipline she would study years later, a therapeutic process known as transformational movement. The premise—as with Taoism—is that everything in life is motion. There is movement going on constantly in our bodies and in the world around us, at levels we can perceive and at some we can't. Life begins to shut down, or break down, when we do something to stop the movement.

A child expresses everything, with no feeling that one form of expression is good and another bad. But socialization teaches us to curtail certain expressions by contracting our muscles and restricting our breathing. We also, characteristically, run a particular thought loop through our minds, which we think of as reality.

Transformational movement locates the constellation of tension—what Reich would have called body armoring—and goes into it further, creating more tension and embodying the fear and pain that produced it. Often associations come up and you see, or remember, why you contracted in the first place. You are also able to see that there could be more breathing in that place, more movement. And you see that the thought loop you've been circulating might not be reality. There is a deeper reality.

The process might take place naturally. A woman gives birth. The muscles in her pelvis open up. And a reality emerges that she had not, up to that time, been aware of.

Martha did not disappear sexually after her early abuse. She has always been a sensual and sexual person. But she

began having what she describes as disconnected sex, which didn't engage the whole of her.

"I was always in relationship," she says. "I was married to men a couple of times, had a couple of women lovers. But it always felt like work to get my heart and genitals together. There was a lot of confusion. I kept choosing the wrong partner. We'd have great sex, but the person would be emotionally treacherous for me."

Transformational movement was an important part of her recovery, as had been, earlier, the 12-step movement, re-evaluation co-counseling, and feminist Gestalt therapy. The therapies she used became progressively less mental and more physical. But none was so deeply physical as the work she began doing with the Body Electric School in 1994.

"Sexual energy is the root energy in human creativity and in enjoying life," she says. "When we're fully alive in our bodies, we understand not only what it is to be in a body, and to share that contact with someone else, but also what a tremendous resource sexual energy is, both individually and in partnership."

Martha's spiritual life has been less institutional than Brown's and is rather more difficult to talk about. For a brief time, as an adolescent, she tried the Episcopal Church. Much later, yoga was important to her, hatha yoga while she was in college and kundalini yoga after she had moved back to Anchorage.

But her real spiritual life takes place outside of any structure. "I just have experiences of God," she says. "I've had them constantly. I had one running down a hill with a pack of kids in fifth grade." When she speaks of her vocation in a larger sense, she doesn't point to a tradition of service, just a lifelong feeling.

"My heart's work is to allow myself to know my hunger for God," she says. "And to learn how to love people."

Her spiritual practice is just that of presence. "How do we fully embody the hugeness of who we are now, this moment, in all our cells? What is that?"

Collin Brown, despite his long background with the institutional church, espouses the same method. "You can throw out two thousand years of theology," he says. "You just let your body take you on the journey to find God."

FREEDOM IN THE CIRCLE

It is unusual for sexual healers to be partnered at all, much less with each other. Of all the healers I spoke to in the Bay Area, only one other—Carol Queen—had a partner, and most of them had been lone wolves for much of their lives. Many people, of course, would not want to be paired with someone in that field. They don't want their lover interacting sexually with other people.

Brown and Martha had discussed the parameters of their relationship, particularly the question of monogamy, from the moment they got together. But when Martha found out she was pregnant, the issue became more visceral for her.

"I couldn't contemplate anything but monogamy when I was pregnant with Molly," Martha says. "Collin hadn't generally been monogamous."

The whole question is highly charged for Brown, because it is in the freedom of tribal gay sex that he has largely experienced his ecstatic body. That was the part of himself that he neglected on the East Coast, when he felt emotionally dead. He and Martha have continued to be monogamous in the two years since Molly was born. But neither expects they will continue that way. "She knows who I am and what I ultimately need," he says.

Brown believes that the most important thing about sex in relationship is that we allow ourselves to be fluid and to communicate.

"Sex is often a subterranean conversation in a relationship," he says. "Where people are in their erotic honesty says a lot about where they are in relationship. Are we satisfied? Can I know who I am and share that with you? If you can be fluid erotically, you can be fluid on all levels."

Their work is a saving grace for them because they allow each other freedom in ritual space. They have that opportunity to experience real erotic freedom in their bodies.

Ritual space, or what Martha describes as the circle, is something most couples don't experience at all, at least not in an erotic context, but both Brown and Martha describe it as an extremely powerful tool that largely allows their work to happen.

The tradition comes out of the tribal gay culture of the seventies, though it is rather trickier to handle when the genders are mixed. There is a great deal of talking in their Body Electric workshops, along with icebreaking activities like eye gazing and ritual breathing. Each gender group spends a fair amount of time off by themselves. There is instruction in sensual massage, and much sharing of feelings.

Other Tantric teachers lead workshops in which couples receive instruction in the group but go off in private before they do anything sexual. But the Body Electric workshops involve sexual touching in the group context and thereby create, according to Brown, a "hyper-state of awareness" akin to what people experience through drugs or spiritual practice.

Martha is particularly eloquent on the subject of the circle, which has been a part of other work she has done, often just with women. The erotic energy that flows so powerfully in an individual can be even more powerful in a group, where it is generated collectively. It can also be blocked by people who withhold it.

"I'm completely fascinated by the dynamics of the circle," she says. "There is an epiphany in every one I work with. The circle clears, it gathers, sometimes just for a few seconds. Everything is different after that. It's as if we, as a group, moved our group shadow. We reach a new level of freedom."

These are not just feel-good workshops in which people learn to have better orgasms. They are about sexuality and deal with techniques—inventive methods for stroking the genitals, for one—but techniques are not the focus.

"The most consistent revelation about our work is how little it has to do with the erotic," Brown says. "Sex quickly loses its charge in the group atmosphere, after people have admitted their fears and hopes, the desires that they have been holding back, after they've gotten—literally and figuratively—naked.

"Once you can see we're all sexual beings, we all have permission to be erotic, it opens the flow for everything else. When people take off the social masks they wear out in the world, they have rich internal selves. They've been keeping the erotic in a tiny space. They haven't allowed it to inform their lives.

"But when it expands beyond that space, people feel alive in their bodies, on fire with their energy; they feel the full richness of being human, and they begin to see things with a greater perspective. They see the way everything is connected. We tend to keep parts of our lives in little boxes, but this group energy blows those boxes apart and shows us that everything is one. You can't isolate the spiritual from the erotic or the erotic from the spiritual. And you can't remove either one from your body."

For women, Martha says, the problem is often that they have taken their cues from others. "I'm not a sexual being because a man finds me attractive, or a woman finds me attractive," she says. "I'm a sexual being, period. That is the place where sexuality and spirituality meet. It is also a radical political act, to live completely in your body, to claim your sexuality as your own."

Their real work, then, is personal liberation, releasing people from places where they are stuck. Erotic energy is a potent force for making that change, and Body Electric workshops are a powerful place to generate it. But the atmosphere is highly charged because men and women go about things so differently.

"Men have a different socialization process around this subject," Martha says. "They're free about saying, Yes, I want sex. Women have trouble with that." It is therefore harder for them to participate in the workshops, and they enroll in smaller numbers.

"We've gone over all the ways we've oppressed and been oppressed by each other," Martha says. "I like to see where we come together. Where we can learn from each other. There's an interdependence and balance that is also a fact."

Martha leads groups just with women as well as the mixed-gender groups and finds the tasks much different. In mixed groups the work is about softening to each other, balancing the energy. With women alone it is about the raw energy itself and how they want to use it. They often fear they can't, that it's not safe.

"What they're saying is that they can't be in their full sexual energy," Martha says. "The workshops are about stepping into what they want, saying what it is, asking for it. Letting the hunger come through their bodies."

For men, who have learned to say what they want—sometimes too forcefully—the workshops are more about receiving. There is a technique at the end of Taoist erotic massage called the Big Draw. The recipient has had a full-body massage, has done a great deal of conscious breathing, has raised erotic energy through genital stroking, and finally holds his breath, tenses all his muscles, then—abruptly—relaxes and lets go. The effects are often powerful. What Martha often sees in men is grief at the fact that they've never been vulnerable.

"The level of their grieving." She shakes her head. "It's heartbreaking."

So women need to feel their erotic power, men their vulnerability. Men need to know their power isn't a problem; their erection isn't—as it has sometimes been portrayed—a weapon.

Brown sees massive wounding around phallic energy, a lot of shame and guilt. "Where is the softness and playfulness around having a cock, like the teenager who jerks off three times a day?" he wonders. "People say men are obsessed with their cocks. I don't think so. They're obsessed with sublimating it. Making money, being successful."

Ultimately the wound is just being male. "You're not supposed to be wounded. You're supposed to be powerful." Hence the deep grief men feel when they let themselves be vulnerable.

The real goal is for men and women to embody the qualities of both genders. Brown and Martha are a good example.

He is quiet and thoughtful, slightly reserved, she rather more forceful, with a powerful voice developed through years of vocal training.

"I love to do drag," Brown says. "I transform into a beautiful woman. Straight women freak because they're drawn to me as a woman. Lesbians are too, but they know I'm a man. Gay men are attracted, so are straights. It pushes everyone's buttons."

It also gives them a chance to lighten up on gender. It allows them to be—as he would say—more fluid.

THE INFINITE BODY

For both Brown and Martha, the body is the site of all their teaching and learning. It is a vast unexplored realm for many people who spend their time off in their heads. Erotic energy is the key.

"If you can get to the root," Brown says, "everything else relaxes. Sex is the root. Ever since we were little kids, we were told to stay away from that place. If we can actually remember how against our nature that felt, to be shut down there, it's very powerful. We took that energy and went underground with it, where it took all kinds of weird manifestations."

Martha believes that workshop participants have felt a characteristic physical yearning. "Our work is for people who want it, not for people who need it. Lots of people need it. But there has to be a body-felt desire to go deeper, to tap into the deeper resources that the body has to offer about what life really is."

The workshops aren't a quick fix. They help people see that their sexuality is much larger than what they'd thought. They see what it has really been all along.

"It's when you surrender to it that it opens up," Brown says, "a massive expansiveness. But it's necessary that we not need to know how to get there, that we can give up that control. It's a letting go into the unknown. We also need to be able to handle a big charge of energy. That's something we emphasize in the workshops. That energy, which can feel as if it's going to blow you apart, is really not dangerous. Feeling it is the goal. That's what expands you."

It is much more to the point, Martha says, than complicated instructions in technique.

"It's a way of coming back wholeheartedly to the place where we're learning together, where we can say, We don't know how to do this. What should we try? If you're present in compassion, vulnerability, exploration, and desire, you'll find out everything you need to know about giving and receiving pleasure. You'll discover it, or you'll make it up."

~ 10
Even Educated Fleas

you stand inside me naked infinite love
the dawn bell rips my dreaming heart
> —ZEN MASTER IKKYU,
> trans. *Stephen Berg*

HUMAN BEINGS ARE sexual. That is a fact, not a problem. It becomes a problem when we deny it, imagining we can eliminate that vital part of ourselves, or when—on the other hand—we too much affirm it, believing it is all that matters, that we can section it off in our lives and devote ourselves to nothing else. We try to make personal and private the primal energy of the universe. We try to make it our own.

That has been my own mistake for much of my life. I pursued sex with an ardor that women found exciting at first but eventually found tiresome, if not infuriating. I could not let sex be. I was always trying to force it. I embraced it so desperately that I squeezed the life out of it.

Then at midlife I began to have experiences that brought

into question the way I'd been, and the months during which I've written this book—reading extensively, talking to friends, pondering the subject, interviewing sexual healers—have intensified the process. I began with some notion of what sex is and what—theoretically—a good sex life might be. I no longer have any idea. I've gone so far into the subject that I've turned it—or it's turned me—inside out. I don't know what sex is. But I see it everywhere.

Sex is the boy I was when I was five years old—I can remember it that far back—lying in bed at night dreaming of kissing movie stars. It is the boy I was at seven, kissing a neighbor girl in imitation of those movie kisses. It is a much heavier and shyer boy at the age of twelve, sneaking off to masturbate any chance he got, finding in those brief frantic spasms some comfort for his life. It is that numb frightened boy in his teens, finding the opportunity very occasionally to kiss a girl on her doorstep or in the front seat of a car, longing to do more but having no idea how. It is that young man at the age of twenty, finally having a lover and discovering in his brief first act of intercourse the intense full-bodied ecstasy he had been looking for all along. It is that same man later in his twenties and into his thirties, enraptured with that ecstasy, stumbling through porn palaces and massage parlors and occasional affairs in search of more intense and varied forms of it.

But it is much more than that. It is the young women who walk boldly hand in hand down a street of shops in our city, deliberately kissing in public to claim their passion. It is women who feel brash and sexy when they dress as men, men who get a melting feeling in their bellies as they pull on women's lingerie. It is men who pay women to tie them up and beat them, humiliate them with words. It is the gruff character who sat wearing sunglasses every day in a toilet stall at the public library, asking whoever entered if they had the time, pulling open the door to reveal his erection. It is the old man who sits in the porn theater on weekday afternoons, stroking his flaccid penis by the hour. It is the aging couple that doesn't make love anymore but lies at night in each other's arms, finding comfort in touch. It is the young Jesuits who have taken a vow of celibacy but masturbate fiercely and talk about it with their friends. It is the nun who is celibate to the extent that she doesn't stimulate her genitals at all, but who feels waves of sexual energy throughout her body in everything she does.

It is the male fetus in the womb—modern technology has shown us this image—floating in the amniotic fluid with an erection.

And it is far more than these things, more than we can ever name, more than we can know. It is with us all the time, in everything we do. We can no more separate ourselves from sex than we can separate ourselves from the spirit.

Many people—perhaps most—are infuriated by the suggestion that the spiritual has anything to do with the sexual, but the connection is right under their noses. Even in the most decorous middle-class congregations, fervent women wear a sexual glow during the sermon and fall all over the minister afterward, thanking him; at black churches and among white Pentecostals the rites are positively orgiastic. It is no exaggeration to call the relationship between a minister and his devoted parishioners erotic, and on occasion—as novelists have been telling us for centuries—it becomes physical. Priests notoriously make moves on altar boys; a noted televangelist consorted with a prostitute in a sleazy motel; and our most revered African American minister, a tireless proponent of integration, apparently had a thing for white women. It has been rumored for years that the finest collection of pornography in the world is housed in the Vatican, and a Catholic friend of mine, with a knowing air, said, "We can't imagine the sex that goes on in that place." Really? I said. The Vatican? "You better believe it," he said.

American practitioners of Eastern religions turn away from such Western hypocrisy to a tradition that they believe expresses greater wholeness, but they have turned up enough sexual scandals to make Christians look positively righteous. A noted Korean teacher, Zen masters both Japanese and American, and Tibetan teachers from more than one lineage have gotten involved in affairs that—at the very least— disappointed their followers and in some cases tore whole sanghas apart. We're one big happy American dharma family: that's the good news. The bad news is that we're often dys- functional and sexually abusive.

All of these incidents were deeply disturbing when they happened, some actually tragic, but I can't help—as I look back on the aggregate—finding them funny. Are we starting to see a pattern here? An age-old human pattern? Human beings want to be good, to be pure, to be truly spiritual, they want to have authentic teachers, and no sooner do they find one than *boing!*—as we said in junior high school—up pops a penis. Even babies in the womb are getting hard-ons these days.

We try to see these isolated incidents as aberrations, but when the aberrations pile up to this extent they start to look like the norm. There is something so close about what we call our sexual and spiritual energies that they keep merging, in characteristic ways. They are, as the old expression goes, strange bedfellows.

Some of these teachers claimed that these affairs were a part of their teaching, that the women in some way needed them; sex helped them on their path to realization. I don't believe it for a minute. No doubt the women did need it and learned from the experience; for all I know they were helped on the path. But that isn't why the men did it. They wanted to get laid. They wanted to get their rocks off. Who can blame them? Everybody wants it.

Human beings fuck. And they fuck up. No two facts about us are more dependable. So we can be disturbed by sexual scandals, we can be deeply disappointed, but we should never be surprised. No sexual behavior should surprise us. One thing is no more wacky than another.

We should also ask if we would have it any other way. In his fascinating book on sex and Buddhism, *Lust for Enlightenment,* John Stevens tells of a man in Japan who was looking for a community priest.

> I recommended a monk who was known for his strong aversion to women and his strict vegetarian, teetotalling diet. To my surprise, the parishioners were not at all pleased with my choice. "A young monk who detests women and good food and drink? There must be something wrong with him!"[1]

He also recounts an ancient story that tells of an aging monk and his patron.

> An old woman built a hermitage for a monk and supported him for twenty years. One day, to test the extent of his enlightenment, the old woman sent a young girl to the hut with orders to seduce him. When the girl embraced the monk and asked, "How is this?" the monk replied stiffly,* "A withered tree among the frozen rocks; not a trace of warmth

*Not the best choice of words, perhaps.

for three winters." Hearing the monk's response, the old woman chased him out and put the hermitage to the torch.[2]

A certain kind of benign goodness—paradoxically—is not so good; it argues a lack of balance and wholeness. In his superb memoir *Ambivalent Zen*, Lawrence Shainberg talks to his teacher Kyudo Roshi about a fellow student who is "devoted to his teacher, attending sesshin regularly, very kind and considerate in his dealings with other people . . . I've heard more than one person say that no American student has a better chance of becoming a Zen master than he does." Kyudo Roshi disagrees.

> "Soon," he replies, correctly as it turns out, "he finish with Zen."
> "What?"
> "One year, two years at most. After that, no sitting at all."
> "How come?"
> "Too nice! Like drunk on religion. Zen monk must corrupt, Larry-san! Guerrilla! Vietcong monk! Better drink saki every night than too much sit on cushion!"[3]

I do think there is a place for celibacy in the world (and that celibacy is a form of sexual behavior, not the absence of it), for periods of our lives and perhaps for some people's entire lives. It is an advanced state, suitable for someone well along the path of either spiritual or sexual practice. Our sexual energy exists in us all the time, but when we bring it to a sexual act we drag in fears, fantasies, psychic defenses, weird distortions. To some extent—in the case of an aware person perhaps a small extent—a sexual act is a warding-off of that energy, dissipating it through orgasm. That is why Joseph Kramer and his Sacred Intimates masturbate for hours at a time without fantasizing and without ejaculating. They are staying in touch with the energy.

But a greater intimacy might be to feel that energy in a pure form, without genital stimulation. That is what happens in deep states of meditation, when the mind grows quiet and the body feels its connection with something deeply primal. Sexual activity would only disturb that connection, and it may be that one can only reach it so deeply by avoiding sex, not because there is anything wrong with it, but because it is so powerfully distracting.

That connection with deep energy is extremely pleasurable; it is positively—though I have never heard anyone say so—sexy. Annie Sprinkle says that her extensive practice of sex has enabled her to feel sexual energy in everything she does. A celibate—coming from the opposite direction—might feel the same way. A true celibate might be the sexiest person of all.

That is why—in the ancient story—the old woman throws out the monk and torches the hermitage. He had handled sexual energy by repressing it, deadening it within him, but that energy is not just sexual. His spiritual practice couldn't be authentic without it.

Alan Watts was therefore wary of the celibate life, seeing its practitioners becoming "sentimental, sour, and greedy for power."[4] It may be easy to become attached to sex—that is the danger—but we cannot entirely avoid it. According to John Stevens, Zen monks are celibate in their early training, but it is assumed that they jump the wall from time to time for trips to the red-light district. It is one of those rules that must be broken in order to be maintained.

The most famous incident of jumping the wall was accomplished by a man later named Bobo-roshi. "Roshi" is the honored title for a Zen priest, and *bobo* is a vulgar Japanese word for intercourse, so this name has been inventively translated Friar Fuck. The story has been told in various places, but my favorite is the long account in Janwillem van de Wetering's *The Empty Mirror*, his book about his eighteen months in a Japanese monastery. A fellow monk tells him the story.

> Bobo-roshi is a Zen master, but different. . . . They say he has spent years in a Zen monastery, in the southern part of Kyoto. It's a severe monastery, the rules are applied very strictly, more strictly than here. For instance, I believe they get up at 2 a.m. every day. He is supposed to have been a very diligent monk, rather overdoing things even, making extra rules for himself and all that. But he didn't understand his *koan* and the master was hard on him; whenever he wanted to say something the master would pick up his bell and ring him out of the room. He was treated that way for years on end. He was doing extra meditation, sleeping in the lotus position, trying everything he could think of, but the *koan* remained as mysterious as ever. I don't know how long this situation lasted, six years, ten years maybe, but then he had enough. I don't think he even said goodbye, he just left, in ordinary clothes, with a little money he had saved, or which had been sent to him from home.
>
> Now you must realize that he had been a monk a long time and didn't know anything about civilian life. He had never climbed the wall at night. He was a real monk, sober, quiet, always in command of himself. And there he was, in a sunny street, in a busy city, thousands of people about, all doing something, all going somewhere. He wandered about the city and found himself in the willow quarter, perhaps within an hour of leaving the monastery gate. In the willow quarter there are always women standing in their doors, or pretending to be busy in their gardens. One of the women called him, but he was so innocent that he didn't know what

she wanted. He went to her and asked politely what he could do for her. She took him by the hand and led him into her little house. They say she was beautiful; who knows? Some of these women aren't beautiful at all but they are attractive in a way, or they wouldn't have any earnings.

She helped him undress—he must have understood then what was going on. She must have asked him for money and he must have given it to her. Then she took him to her bath, that's the custom here. Your shoulders are massaged and you are dried with a clean towel and they talk to you. Slowly you become very excited and when she feels you are ready she takes you to the bedroom. He must have been quite excited after so many years of abstaining. At the moment he went into her he solved his *koan*.* He had an enormous *satori*, one of those very rare *satoris* which are described in our books, not a little understanding which can be deepened later but the lot at once, an explosion which tears you to pieces and you think the world has come to an end, that you can fill the emptiness of the universe in every possible sphere. When he left the woman he was a master. He never took the trouble to have his insight tested by other masters, but kept away from the Zen sect for many years. He wandered the country and had many different jobs. . . . They say he never forgot the link between his *satori* and sex.[5]

A koan in Zen is a question that makes no rational sense and that takes you out of your thinking mind into a deeper place. As weird as many koans sound, they reflect human experience and genuine human dilemmas, but we don't solve them by thinking or by trying to solve them. Only when Bobo-roshi gave up—rather spectacularly—did he discover the answer to his koan. He found it in an area of human behavior that is profoundly irrational and impossible to control.

*In some versions of the story, satori happens at the moment of orgasm.

Sex therefore has great potential for realization, but not if you are trying for it. For that reason I am skeptical of all the courses and books on sacred sex, shelf after shelf of advice on how to make sex sacred and use it to achieve enlightenment. Their intention is good—to remove sex from the gutter where too many spiritual people put it—and they often include valuable knowledge and helpful techniques.

But sex simply *is* sacred; we don't make it that way. The penis—here I speak only for my own precious and representative organ—does not follow instructions, or undertake elaborate programs. And sex does not easily remove from the gutter; we need to include the gutter if we want to encompass all of it.

The realizations available from sex occur not through step-by-step programs but when you abandon programs altogether and give yourself to the experience, to the energy itself, when you have no idea what is supposed to happen or what will. Realizations come not when you have learned to control sex but when you've seen there is no controlling it. There are no masters of sex. Sex is not mastered.

Thus we arrive at the koan that gave me my title. It was formulated by a Chinese monk named Sung-yuan, who gave its long form one day when he was addressing an assembly.

> In order to know the Way in perfect clarity, there is one essential point you must penetrate and not avoid: the red thread [of passion] between our legs that cannot be severed.*
> Few face the problem, and it is not at all easy to settle. Attack it directly without hesitation or retreat, for how else can liberation come?[6]

It also has a short form, supposedly Sung-yuan's dying words.

---

*I do wish that Sung-yuan had not mentioned severing in connection with this particular thread.

Why is it that even the most clear-eyed monk cannot
sever the red thread of passion between his legs?[7]

This is a great religious question because, finally, it addresses sex in a religious context. It brings up the matter
boldly, without qualifications. Koans are the questions of life,
and we cannot avoid this one, because it is our lives that ask
it. They ask it in every moment.

There is no answer. Only a fool would offer one (which
hasn't stopped any number of distinguished people from
stepping forward). Celibacy is not an answer, nor is monogamy, nor promiscuity. These strategies change the parameters in which the question is addressed. They don't answer it.
It continues to sit there like an angry Zen master, waiting for
your best reply before it rings you out of the room. A follower of the Buddha vows not to misuse sexual energy, but
what, in light of all we've examined, is misuse of sexual energy? What is correct use? What is right sex?

The vows of Buddhism are impossible. They are that way
intentionally, so that we never imagine we can quit working
with them. Whatever enlightenment is, it doesn't bypass this
moment-by-moment encounter with impossible vows. Our
task with sexuality is the same as with any other energy that
arises: not to deny it, not to attach to it, but to perceive it
with as much clarity as we can bring, to make ourselves one
with it. When we are able to do that, the energy itself tells
us how to act. It isn't that we find the answer to the koan.
It's that there is no koan. There never was one.

NOTES

1. John Stevens, *Lust for Enlightenment: Buddhism and Sex* (Boston:
Shambhala Publications, 1990), 124.

2. Ibid., 124–25.
3. Lawrence Shainberg, *Ambivalent Zen: A Memoir* (New York: Pantheon Books, 1995), 135.
4. Alan Watts, *In My Own Way: An Autobiography, 1915–1965* (New York: Pantheon Books, 1972), 130.
5. Janwillem van de Wetering, *The Empty Mirror: Experiences in a Japanese Zen Monastery* (New York: Ballantine Books, 1973), 100–102.
6. Stevens, *Lust for Enlightenment,* 91.
7. Ibid.

~ Epilogue

EVERYTHING I EVER WANTED

passion's red thread is infinite
like the earth always under me
> —ZEN MASTER IKKYU,
> *trans. Stephen Berg*

WHEN I WAS YOUNG I dreamed of meeting a woman in a small secluded room that was cut off from the rest of the world, where my acts had no consequences. I didn't necessarily know the woman who entered that room with me. Our lives didn't touch. She had a certain look—auburn hair, perhaps, that just touched her shoulders, and deep brown eyes, small firm breasts with perfect pink nipples—and she performed particular acts that I had always dreamed of, sliding down my torso to take me in her mouth as she eyed me coyly, slinging her legs over my shoulders as I entered her. She loved whatever I wanted and was deeply satisfied by what we did, satisfied as she had never been. She thought I was the greatest lover in the world.

As the years passed I began to suspect that this room didn't exist. There is no such thing as an act without consequences, and the room where a woman makes love—at least the women I know—is at the heart of the vast mansion that is her life, where all the rooms connect.

Yet men are persistent, and their dreams are precious. I continued to build that room. Sex was an act there, an act that took place. It was primarily, though not solely, genital: if the genitals weren't involved it didn't happen (We "didn't" have sex. We "couldn't" have sex), so that at some level, one that wasn't often mentioned, everything in the room existed to give me an erection, and if the erection didn't happen the party was over. Sex in that room was a drama, a performance, and could be measured against past performances or imagined future ones. The erection should be *this* hard; it should last *this* long; the act itself should last *this* long; the orgasm should be *this* strong.

As I got older those things began to change. This is not a subject that often gets raised down at the pool hall, but one hears whispers in sex manuals and magazine articles about lost erections (I'm sure it's around here somewhere), diminished erections, longer periods between erections, orgasms that diminish in force. The already small room began to shrink. It took on the appearance of a mausoleum. It could sometimes be revitalized by a new partner, but then that partner had to be replaced, and that partner . . .

In psychological terms, this is the room of the ego. Buddhists call it the place of monkey mind. Its walls, apparently constructed of reinforced concrete, are actually made of tissue paper. A man can step through them any time. If he just looks at them hard enough they disappear. When they do, he finds himself in a vast empty space. It is frightening but also liberating. A younger man is not likely to have the courage to open to that space. But an older man who finds his already small room shrinking even more just might.

The best way to step into that space, I found, was the way women had been urging me all along, through my emotions. The realm of feeling was a vast and varied landscape that I had barely explored. When I was young my libido, my dream of the small room, my strictly sexual energy, were strong enough to overcome any emotion; I used sex to avoid emotion or repress emotion (though now and then I was so angry or sad that I couldn't do it and was crushed), but as I got older my moods interfered more and more with my erections. That could seem a sad thing—my body was failing me—but it was also an opportunity to explore a rich world that I had been neglecting. My energy was tied up in my emotions, and my energy *was* my sexuality. I needed to focus on my emotions to contact it. That didn't mean I had to have some tender feeling in order to make love but that I had to know what I was feeling and act out of that. The diminishment of sexual feeling was not a shrinking room. It was an invitation to step out of that room into a much larger place, the vast empty spaces of the heart.

In these vast spaces, sex is not an act that takes place. It is a power, a force, that is with us all the time. It is not strictly genital but involves the whole body, mind and heart and spirit. It does not have much to do with how a woman looks and does not involve specific (what I used to think of as sexual) acts. It involves a much more subtle connection that does seem to be physical but beneath the level of words. It might involve physical contact, and a certain mingling of energies, but is not necessarily harmonious. Male and female energies often meet with a loud crack. It might emerge during deep conversations, even arguments, when the couple is passionately involved in what they are saying. It is present when they take a walk together, or watch the clouds in the winter sky, or listen to music, or have a drink in the evening.

It also—lest it sound too tame—takes the form of hard hugs and playful ones, long embraces where bare bodies luxuriate in touch, the caresses of fingertips on skin, of palms that press harder and hands that knead the flesh; it involves mild affectionate kisses and wet fierce ones and can proceed from there into a whole host of delightful and inventive maneuvers, including the well-known act of sexual intercourse. It can be tender or violent, with assorted scratches, slaps, and bites. It often, in contrast to a well-known saying, involves uproarious laughter. It might lead to orgasm on the part of one or both partners, or it might not. It might be accomplished in a matter of moments or go on for hours. Most profoundly, it is an act of opening up to one another. It is a sharing of energies. It doesn't ask you to be a certain way. It shows you how you are.

My dreams often come in clusters, as if my mind—or whatever part of me it is that dreams—were working over some question, or as if my dream self had a life of its own, quite apart from whatever else I'm doing. Recently, in the space of a single week, I had three dreams about sex, and I realized that they summed up much that I'd understood about the subject in the past few years.

In the third dream, which took place at the end of the week, I was in a bordello. The place was hardly opulent, more like a bathhouse operated by female attendants, but sex was taking place all around me. I was aware of the threat to my health and wasn't participating. I comforted myself about being there with the thought that I was just watching. Yet there was an ambiguity to that feeling: I knew I was tempted and might give in. It was the ambiguity that made the place exciting.

Into that establishment—much to my surprise and somewhat to my embarrassment—walked my men's group. They had come to rescue me because they didn't want me to get AIDS. I wasn't in any danger, I protested as they dragged me out. You can't catch anything from watching. One of them stopped and turned and spoke distinctly: "We want you to be above even the suspicion of catching AIDS."

That was a dream about illicit sex and the attraction it has always had for me. Some version of that bordello has been appearing in my dreams for years. I have gradually become aware that such sex has little to do with physical needs but is overwhelmingly emotional (much of what I used to think of as physical I now think of as emotional; horniness, I'm convinced, is 99 percent loneliness). It is a wild need, to break down barriers, explore taboos, a need that your wife, or legitimate lover, can do nothing to satisfy, as men have been trying to explain for years ("This has nothing to do with you"). Interestingly, though, I have found that it can be satisfied by emotional connection with men; the affirmations that a wife can't give you, just because she is your wife, can be given by other men. That has been the great discovery of the men's movement.

I have no doubt that my men's group would rescue me from a bordello if it were ever necessary. But that dream was about the way that male friendship can save a man from damaging relationships.

In the second dream—pardon my embarrassment—I was masturbating. I had rather liberally oiled myself, and my penis, as if in a cartoon, kept changing sizes; it would grow long and lean, like a famous porn star's, then shrink back to short and thick; it would become not especially hard, stretching like elastic. Still I kept stroking away, thoroughly enjoying myself.

That dream seemed to be about the physical changes I've already mentioned, the middle-aged penis that becomes suddenly, comically, unpredictable. It is like a cartoon penis, though its owner isn't laughing. However your penis is, this dream seemed to say, is all right. You can still enjoy yourself. Behind that simple meaning was a larger one, which I felt strongly when I woke up: You can take care of yourself. The dream you've always had in the past, that you will find someone who will give you an ideal sex life, is one you can give up now. That's a young man's dream. The key to your sexual happiness lies in yourself.

But it was the first dream, the one that inaugurated the series, that was really spectacular. I was the age I am now, in my late forties, and in bed with two women, also my age, whom I hadn't seen in thirty years. One was the girl who, when we were young, was the most universally admired and sought after in our social set. The other, whom I personally had always found just as pretty, was perhaps the most aristocratic one in the group. In my dream they were both now beautiful mature women, quite ravishing.

The universally admired one was lying beneath me, naked, in my arms. We weren't making love, but it was obvious we were going to. The aristocratic one was kneeling behind me, and was kissing—like a true aristocrat—my ass. When her friend left she made it clear, not by words but by bold gestures, that we were going to make love too. The statement of this dream was blaringly obvious: You have everything you ever wanted. All that you ever longed for, through a painful lonely adolescence, you now have.

I was immediately convinced when I woke up that this dream was about my meditation practice. It is through sitting on a cushion for hours at a time that I have come to see that all wishes are alike. The wish to make love to the woman of your dreams is the same as the wish to get off this fucking cushion and go have some fun is the same as the wish to write a great novel and become rich and famous is the same as the wish to scratch your nose. Any of those wishes can become a deep painful yearning. Sometimes you think that if you can't scratch your nose you'll die. Yet if you satisfy one of those wishes (go ahead, scratch your nose), another appears in its place (your ear itches).

As you sit on the cushion and stare at your yearning, you have put yourself in a position where there is nothing you can do to satisfy it. You realize that, in a deeper sense, there never is. You begin to experience the yearning itself. You feel its energy, the very energy that powers the universe. You feel it as pleasurable. Energy is—as William Blake said in a great statement—eternal delight.

Once you have learned to enjoy it for itself, you can share it with someone—that's what sex really is, sharing that energy—but you won't have to. You won't *need* that person. Most of us have touched that energy only in sexual connection, so we think that's the only place it's available, but it isn't. It is endlessly available, wherever you are. You don't have to seek it out. You don't need another person. You have everything you need. You have everything you ever wanted.

~ Resources

Carol Queen
2215-R Market #455
San Francisco, California 94114
Web page: *www.carolqueen.com*
E-mail: *CarolQueen@aol.com*

Juliet Carr
2124 Kittredge St. #103
Berkeley, California 94704
(510) 848-1218.
E-mail: *jcarr@auntpeg.com*

Joseph Kramer
Erospirit Research Institute
P.O. Box 3893
Oakland, CA 94609
Web page: *www.erospirit.org*
E-mail: *kramer@erospirit.org.*

Collin Brown and Selah Martha
The Body Electric School
6527A Telegraph Ave.
Oakland, CA 94609
(510) 653-1594
Web page: *www.bodyelectric.org.*
E-mail: *bodyelec@aol.com.*

The Electronic University (Alan Watts tapes)
P.O. Box 2309
San Anselmo, CA 94979
800-969-2887

The Permanent Press/Second Chance Press
4170 Noyac Road
Sag Harbor, NY 11963
Publishers of the works of Marco Vassi:
A Driving Passion
The Erotic Comedies
The Other Hand Clapping
The Stoned Apocalypse
Mind Blower
The Gentle Degenerates
The Saline Solution
Contours of Darkness
Tackling the Team
In Touch
The Devil's Sperm Is Cold
The Sensual Mirror
Slave Lover

~ Credits

Excerpts from *The Empty Mirror* by Janwillem van de Wetering by arrangement with the author. All rights reserved.

Permission granted for excerpt from interview of Allen Ginsberg by Allen Young, as published in *Gay Sunshine Interviews*, vol. 1, edited by Winston Leyland.

The account of Gavin Arthur's encounter with Edward Carpenter © Allen Ginsberg Trust.

Quotations from Marco Vassi reprinted by permission of the Permanent Press/Second Chance Press, 4170 Noyac Road, Sag Harbor, NY 11963.

Selections from *Crow with No Mouth*, versions by Stephen Berg © 1995 by Stephen Berg, reprinted by permission of Copper Canyon Press, Post Office Box 271, Port Townsend, WA 98368.

Selections from *Nature, Man, and Woman*, and *In My Own Way: An Autobiography* by Alan Watts, reprinted by the permission of Russell & Volkening as agents for the author.